Wings Above the Planet

The History of Antonov Airlines

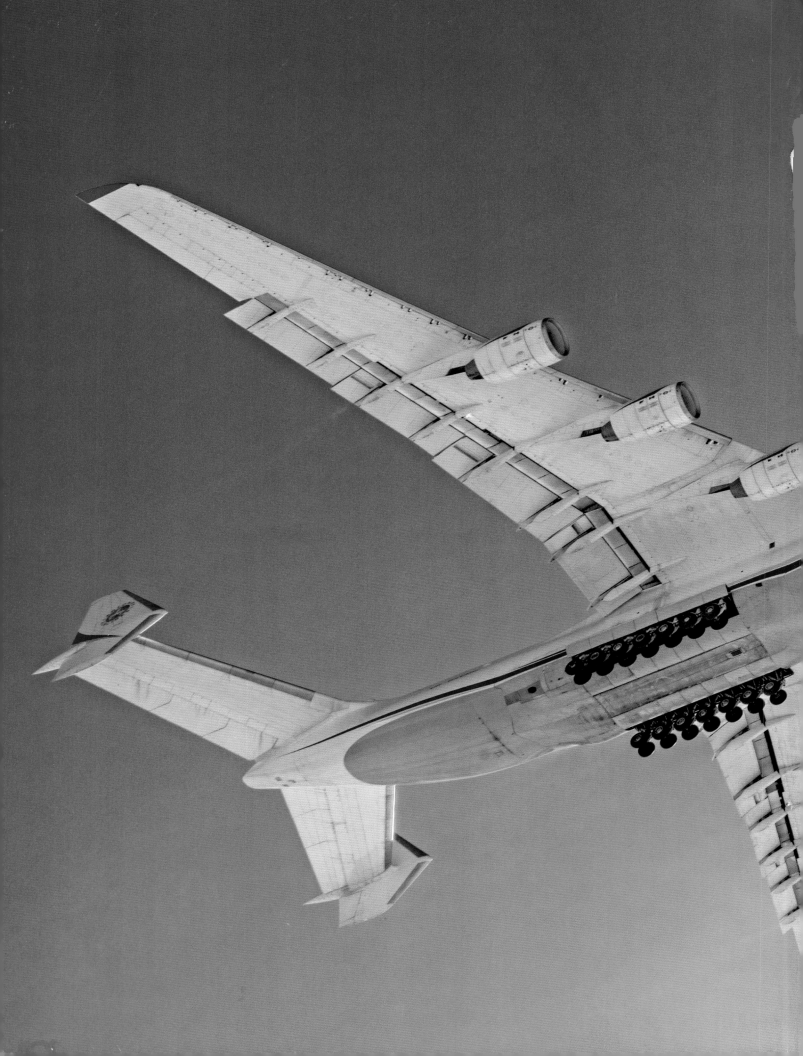

Wings Above the Planet

The History of Antonov Airlines

Andrii Sovenko

CFP

CHRISTOPHER FOYLE PUBLISHING

First published in 2019 by Christopher Foyle Publishing

113–119 Charing Cross Road
London WC2H 0EB

© Andrii Sovenko, 2019

ISBN: 978-0-9548896-3-0

Printed in China

Design: Oleksander Ostapets

Translation into English: Natalia Antonyuk, Olga Chaban, Irina Liashuga, Vladyslav Maksymenko, Oleksandra Vasyl, Sergii Zavalniuk

English editors: Nick Grant, Simon Forty

Index and Glossary composer: Roman Vasyl

Photo credits: I. D. Babenko, A. V. Blahovisnii, Yu. V. Brodovskii, Ye. A. Golovnov, A. V. Denyskin, A. I. Zasieda, A. V. Klimov, Yu. Korolov, N. I. Lyzohubenko, V. Neseniuk, G. G. Nesterenko, A. V. Postornak, A. Yu. Sovenko, Ye. Soroka, M. A. Toporikov, S. V. Yurikov. Also, there are pictures from the personal archives of V. S. Andrushchakevych, I. D. Babenko, Yu. V. Baitsur, A. A. Bohatov, W.R.C Foyle, D. K. Gedz, A. N. Naumenko, V. I. Terskii, V. A. Tkachenko, V. M. Tkachuk, M. H. Kharchenko, Graham Pearce and the collections of Antonov Airlines, Volga-Dnepr Airlines, Air Foyle, the photo lab and museum of Antonov StC and the Ukrainian aviation magazine *Aviation and Time*.

Cover photo credits: A. V. Blahovisnii, A. V. Denyskin, Ye. A. Golovnov, A. Yu. Sovenko

Half title page and title page photo credits:
A. V. Denyskin

Sales and distribution by:
Crécy Publishing
1a Ringway Trading Estate
Shadowmoss Road
Manchester M22 5LH

Tel: +44 161 499 0024
Web: www.crecy.co.uk

Glossary

ACMI	Aircraft, Crew, Maintenance, Insurance
ADB	Antonov Design Bureau
AWACS	Airborne Warning and Control System
BBC	British Broadcasting Corporation
CC CPSU	Central Committee of the Communist Party of the Soviet Union
CC CPU	The Central Committee of the Communist Party of Ukraine
CIS	Commonwealth of Independent States
CMEA	Council for Mutual Economic Assistance
CPSU	Communist Party of the Soviet Union
EADS	European Aeronautic Defence and Space Company
ECAP	European Capability Airlift Programme
EU	European Union
FAA	Federal Aviation Administration
FADEC	Full Authority Digital Engine Control
FBW	fly-by-wire
FT&DB	Flight Test and Development Base
FTS	Flight Test Station
GMT	Greenwich Mean Time
GPS	Global Positioning System
GPWS	Ground Proximity Warning System
IAC	Interstate Aviation Committee
IBM	Intercontinental ballistic missiles
ICAO	International Civil Aviation Organization)
ITP	Integrated Target Program
KiAPO	Kyiv Aviation Production Association
KMP	Kyiv Mechanical Plant
MAI	Ministry of the Aviation Industry
MCA	Ministry of Civil Aviation
MTA	Military Transport Aviation
NAMSA	NATO Maintenance and Supply Agency
NII VVS	Air Force Scientific Research Institute
NIIERAT	Air Force Scientific Research Institute for Aircraft Maintenance and Repair
NPO	Molniya (Scientific Production Association Molniya)
OCHE	onboard cargo handling equipment
RI	Ruslan International
RS	Ruslan SALIS
SALIS	Strategic Airlift Interim Solution
SPFU	State Property Fund of Ukraine
StC	State Company
TAPOiCH	Chkalov Tashkent Aviation Production Association
TCAS	Traffic Collision Avoidance System
TsAGI	Central Aerohydrodynamic Institute
UAPK	Ulyanovsk Aviation Production Complex
UIA	Ukraine International Airlines
UN	United Nations)
UNESCO	United Nations Educational, Scientific and Cultural Organization
VDA	Volga Dnepr Airlines
ZMKB Progress	Zaporizhia Machine-Building Design Bureau Progress

Table of contents

Andrii Sovenko

Preface

Every book usually opens or closes with a short chapter, in which the author expresses gratitude to everyone who has helped collect the facts and materials, offered a piece of advice, shared their reminiscences or simply encouraged them to persevere in the hard work of a writer. And a book that is entirely based on the accounts of the parties involved, original documents and original photo content cannot go without enlisting the names of those who have preserved all that and gave it to the author. I, too, am not going to diverge from this tradition. All the more so as for this book to see the light of day required not only hard work of the people mentioned here, but also their exceptional commitment to see the project through and the strong belief that all of the obstacles were going to be overcome.

The many issues that Ukraine has faced and faces today have made the book's journey to its reader quite difficult and long. It's hard to believe now, but the book was conceived almost 20 years ago, when the airline company had successfully passed through the first decade of its operation on the world stage, and there appeared an idea to somehow document the company's accomplishments in breaking this truly new ground. In the spring of 2001, the Managing Director of Antonov Airlines, K. F. Lushakov, approached me with an offer I could not reject. Judge for yourself: *"The task is not to rewrite the history,"* said Konstantin Fedorovych, *"but merely to write it down and tell everything as it was. But we have to do it in a way that would be interesting for everyone: the top echelon of the industry, the ordinary employees, and the incidental reader."* You can imagine that setting such an objective is the dream of any journalist.

The initiative was supported by Antonov's chief of that day, the late General Aircraft Designer P. V. Balabuev. This remarkable person, who contributed greatly to the airline company's establishment, managed to provide such a writing atmosphere that by October 2001 a significant part of the book was almost completed. However, later the process slowed down, and soon after the tragic retirement of Piotr Vasylovych in 2005 it stalled completely.

Nevertheless, everyone involved in its making set their heart on completing what they have started. In March 2009, in the days when the airline company celebrated its 20th anniversary, the book was finished and fully prepared for print in Russian. However, a number of reasons did not allow it to emerge either then, or during the next nine long years. And only thanks to the goodwill of Christopher Foyle, has the book finally seen the light of day. This is its first edition, and, hopefully, not the last one. For the chronicles of Antonov Airlines should most certainly find a fine audience not only in the English-speaking world, but also in Ukraine and Russia, and therefore, the Russian edition also should have a good chance to get to the printing-press.

With deepest appreciation, I would like to acknowledge that in the making of this book I used the reminiscences and materials of the present and the former employees of the Antonov Company: Ye. I. Abramov, A. S. Albats, V. H. Anisenko, V. N. Artamonov, O. K. Bogdanov, A. H. Bulanenko, V. V. Burlaienko, L. F. Vyshnevskii, A. H. Vovnianko, V. M. Vorotnikov, Ya. D. Goloborodko, V. P. Golovanov, V. I. Goncharenko, A. D. Grydasov, B. V. Husiev, I. H. Yermokhin, V. F. Yeroshyn, V. A. Kariaka, D. S. Kiva, Yu. M. Kirzhner, L. B. Kovalchuk, A. V. Koreniak, A. V. Kotlobovskii, A. N. Krasnoshchokov, P. A. Levochkin, A. P. Leonenko, H. A. Lugovii, A. S. Makiian, A. N. Naumenko, V. I. Novikov, Yu. V. Pakhomov, N. V. Ra-khimberdina, I. I. Serdiuk, M. H. Kharchenko, Ye. A. Shakhatuni, O. Ya. Shmatko, A. V. Shcherbukha, N. S. Yaresko. Many interesting details came from test pilots V. A. Bezmaternych, A. V. Halunenko, A. N. Kulykov, Yu. V. Kurlin, A. Z. Moiseiev, V. I. Terskii, V. A. Tkachenko. The text of the book employs the reminiscences of the late test pilot H. I. Lysenko and the late lead designer B. N. Shchelkunov; it also incorporates excerpts from press publications of various years and materials from the Antonov Company museum, for which we give special thanks to its executive director L. Ye. Ivasenko. Of great help in describing the current events was the Head of the Antonov Company's Public Affairs Office O. Yu. Trofymchuk. Of great value were also the accounts of the veterans of the 12th military aviation transport division of the Russian Aerospace Forces, Reserve Lieutenant-Colonels E. M. Kupchenko and V. N. Yudin.

Interesting and important information was given to me by the Antonov Airlines employees: Yu. V. Baitsur, A. V. Blagovisnii, Ye. A. Holovnov, A. N. Gritsenko, A. Yu. Dolenko, V. V. Zahynai, P. Yu. Kirzhner, V. N. Kulbaka, V. V. Nets, D. Yu. Patselia, V. V. Roman, V. M. Sudorhin, and, of course, K. F. Lushakov. I also greatly enjoyed working with the reminiscences of the Air Foyle team: Bruce Bird, Roger Clements, Christopher Fairchild, Paul Furlonger and Christopher Foyle himself. In a manner somewhat unusual to us, with bright details, these quotes, no doubt, brighten up the narration and, as I am inclined to believe, set it apart even more from the boring texts of traditional anniversary books. These records were delivered from the UK largely thanks to E. V. Kazantsev.

I would like to express my special gratitude to my counselors, the veterans of Antonov Airlines, I. D. Babenko and S. S. Halka, who not only provided me with a lot of important records and shared their personal reminiscences, but also took the time to clarify some points in the history of the airline company. They have done tremendous work in this regard, getting in touch with dozens of people in several countries. Besides, I. D. Babenko has also taken the trouble to read the manuscript and given many insightful comments to the whole text. He has also played a pivotal role in settling the question of the very possibility of publishing the book in the UK. All in all, he put no lesser effort bringing this book into being than I did.

I believe this book also to be interesting when it comes to the photographs used. Without any exaggeration, the photo content here is hugely diverse, which allows both the visualisation of the Antonov Airlines' history of the last 30 years, and the most important events in the lives of its aircraft. The photographs used, more than 450 of them, were taken not by professional photographers, but by people who were directly involved in the events described. Because of this they are not always of the highest quality, but they always truthfully convey the atmosphere of those events and are bright evidence of the company's accomplishments. The list of people who shared their photographs is given in the first double-page spread of the book.

On a final note, I have to say a few words of thanks to the Ukrainian aviation magazine *Aviation and Time*, with which I have been working for more than a quarter of a century. With the Antonov aircraft being a frequent topic on its pages, the team behind this magazine have collected extensive material, including about the airline company's operations, which also went into the book. Great tribute for help in working on the chapters about the airline company's aircraft goes to my colleagues from the magazine team, V. M. Zaiarin, who, sadly, has already passed away, and R. V. Maraiev. In fact, these chapters are the abridged and somewhat modernized articles from *Aviation and Time*. The blueprints of the aircraft included in these chapters were developed by A.V. Khaustov, who combined his work at Antonov and his work as part of the editorial staff of the magazine.

Overall, working on this book was an unforgettable experience. Owing to it, I have learnt a lot of new things and met some very interesting people. Now, when the work is finally complete, all that is left to do is to wish that the size of the publication would allow me to write about them in as much detail as they deserve. Then again, perhaps each and every employee of Antonov Airlines deserves a story of their own, as each of them dedicates their efforts to accomplishing those bright and important works the company has distinguished itself with.

Andrii Sovenko,

Antonov's veteran, member of the National Union of Journalists of Ukraine

Kostiantyn Lushakov

Let's reminisce!

There are things in life that we need to look back on from time to time. Simply so that they're not forgotten. So that no one is tempted to rewrite the history the way they like it, accommodating the immediate agenda. Unfortunately, it's not uncommon: for in recent years there have been a good many attempts to distort both the history of Antonov Airlines and its operations.

The company was created in the late 1980s – a turning point for both Antonov Airlines and the whole country. It was a uniquely bold move for that time, verging on the infringement upon the principles of the Soviet economy. Our plan to be involved in air cargo transportation – a thing unusual for a design-and-engineering organisation – seemed highly unnatural to many high officials. However, time has proven the case of those who stood up for such decision.

Antonov Airlines became a unique entity. It was Antonov StC's answer to the economic circumstances that have put the renowned firm into dire financial standing. And the airline company has done a great job of enabling Antonov to save its position among the aircraft manufacturers, and given Ukraine the right to call itself an aviation superpower.

Having entered the world transportation market, the airline company was the first to offer the services of the most capable heavy-lift aircraft in serial production – the An-124 Ruslan – laying the foundations for a new sector of that market, namely, the transportation of oversized and super-heavy cargoes. Today, several companies are operating in this sector, but if there is a need to perform some really unique transportation, then the authority of Antonov Airlines stays unchallenged.

The very appearance of the An-124 on the market and the subsequent continuous process of its improvement is the merit of Antonov Airlines. It was we who transformed a military transport plane into a wonderful commercial aircraft and by so doing, I would say, saved this truly unique machine, in which were invested powerful intellectual and financial resources of the whole aviation industry of the USSR. Since the beginning of the 1990s, the military were deprived of the opportunity not only to develop but even to maintain the airworthiness of the big fleet of Ruslans which they had at their disposal at the time. The An-124 as an aircraft type was endangered. But our airline company has found a new occupation for Ruslan, which went beyond its original design basis. It was the first to start using the aircraft for commercial transport and has achieved really remarkable results. Our example was followed by others, and gradually, part of the An-124 fleet found itself in commercial airline companies. And after its certification, which Antonov carried together with a number of interested organisations, the modified Ruslan An-124-100 received all the rights of a civil aircraft. Today, the high technical level of this legendary plane is confirmed by its ability to fly around the world without limits and its victories in numerous tenders on cargo transportation from high-profile international organisations, including the UN and NATO.

We were among the first in the former USSR to start working under real world market conditions. There was a lot we didn't know and couldn't do back then, but we learned as we went, our own inevitable mistakes included. It is hard to overestimate the significance of our partnership with the British firm Air Foyle, which played a very important role in Antonov Airlines' employees mastering the world market working practices. We also learned a lot of things from our next strategic partners from the Russian group of companies, Volga-Dnepr.

At present, the management, the flight and technical crews of Antonov Airlines are world-class professionals who have many years of hands-on experience of working with the most exacting customers, including famous industrial companies and high-profile international organisations. As to the airline company, in recent years it has increased the scope of work manifold, has performed unique, as well as record-breaking, air transportation, fulfilled numerous UN orders and requests of the Ukrainian government, and became the national air transporter.

Today, we are the only Ukrainian airline which does indeed have global reach. Flying all over the world, Antonov Airlines doesn't only carry with dignity the flag of Antonov StC, but also of our whole country. Quite often, the crews and aircraft are the only representatives of Ukraine in different parts of the world. Their high professionalism and outstanding performance capabilities became the outward manifestation of the international credibility of our company and our country. This alone gives grounds for treating Antonov Airlines as the national asset and honour of Ukraine.

I think of how, 30 years ago, with great enthusiasm, we embarked on organising the international air transportation of super-heavy cargoes, we being the world's first to step onto the untrodden path of this business. And today, when thanks to the efforts of my colleagues this narrow path has turned into a broad highway, and everything runs in the groove, there are new people coming who are willing to post there their own road signs, which mostly point the way the money we earn should go. A lie – blatant, barefaced, public, involving the media – has become an integral part of the campaign that those people started to lead against us.

What accusations didn't we face! Us appropriating the government-owned aircraft, inefficiency, theft, our selling out to Europe and NATO, our selling out to Russia and so on. The list of false accusations is so vast and paradoxical that it doesn't even demand an answer for each specific point. But still I am going to say: there is at least one irrefutable evidence that our work was effective and honest. It is the An-38, An-74-300, An-70, An-140, An-148, An-158 and An-178, which were created mainly using the money we have earned. Antonov Airlines is not an independent commercial entity, but it is a part of Antonov StC, one of its numerous divisions. Our strategic aim lies in providing the company with the opportunity to exercise its main function – to create new flying machines. In different times, from 70% to 90% of the expenses for designing, constructing and certification tests, licence tests of each new Antonov aircraft were covered by our funds.

But Antonov also doesn't exist for itself. In fact, it operates in order to provide the opportunity for the dozens of companies in Ukraine and abroad to participate in the series production of a competitive product, which meets the standards of the modern world. And no matter how many times we are told that it is wrong for design engineering to be funded by air transportation, that nobody else in the world does it, I see it as a verbal covering for the intentions to tear the airline company out of the Antonov StC structure and appropriate its income.

Looking back at the long way I and my colleagues have come, I notice that it is almost a sure thing for a successful business to have to face such attacks and struggle against them. And an important part of our struggle is to preserve the truth about our operations in the past and the present. Antonov Airlines has an honourable history and vast opportunities ahead. In fact, the idea behind this book was to get this message across to the general public. I am especially pleased by the fact that it is Christopher Foyle, the person who has done a lot for the establishment of the airline company itself, who is now helping us to publish it. I am infinitely grateful for that.

The book is to be published on the eve of the airline company's 30th anniversary. Preparing it for print, we wanted to summarize the first period of our active work on the international market, put on paper what has been done over those years. We also strived to have not only our achievements remembered, but also the hardships that we had to overcome (and there were not a few of them). In view of this, the book is written in a somewhat unusual manner for a commemorative publication, with bright episodes from the experience of flight crews and managers of various levels, with a great deal of reminiscences of the persons involved, with the author's digressions, with short reports on what has become of the main aircraft of the airline's fleet.

And although the book is entirely dedicated to Antonov Airlines, I believe that not only its employees would find it interesting – the former, the present, and the future. After all, the history of the airline company and the history of the establishment of the international market of air transportation of oversized and super-heavy cargoes went hand in hand, and moreover, in a way, they are the same thing. And so other specialists of the field, as well as the wide audience of readers who have a liking for aviation, are going to find in it a fair bit of interesting information.

Konstantin Lushakov,
Managing Director of Antonov Airlines (1991–2016)

Mr. Christopher Foyle

Foreword
by Christopher Foyle, the publisher and Chairman of the Air Foyle Group

I wish to congratulate Antonov Airlines and its parent company, Antonov StC, on its 30th anniversary of existence and operation. Without this commercial business Antonov would almost certainly not have been able to design and build its many new aircraft types over the last three decades. Indeed, without the airline company Antonov might have become almost moribund and dormant like some of the other previously great Soviet design bureaus.

I and my team at Air Foyle have been proud and grateful to have been associated with this great venture.

It was a curious coincidence of thoughts and events which brought us together, rather like a conjunction of stars.

Air Foyle had been an aircraft operator since 1978 and in 1982 became involved with outsize cargo by becoming the general sales agent for a German operator of Hercules aircraft. Always looking for a unique and unusual aircraft to market and represent, I became aware of the An-124 Ruslan aircraft in 1986 and tried to contact the owners in order to discuss a business relationship. Establishing it didn't come easily, but the persistence of Air Foyle and Antonov's willingness to do business made it possible to overcome all of the obstacles.

It was 1989 when we had our first joint Ruslan flights. In this regard, I would like to say a kind word about Antonov's leader of that time, General Designer Piotr Vasylovich Balabuev. It was he who conceived and implemented what was then a pioneering and innovative concept, which allowed the establishment of a business partnership between Antonov and Air Foyle and to make it effective.

Thousands of successful flights have been achieved by Antonov Airlines since then.

The enormous variety and range of different types of cargoes that have been carried, have been extraordinary – live chickens, tanks, railway locomotives, satellites, ostriches, generators, transformers, pressure vessels, other aircraft – the list is endless.

Without the Ruslan, many of these cargoes could never have travelled by air.

I salute the professionalism and dedication of the flight crews, the engineers and the maintenance support staff who have all worked together to have achieved this success.

We at Air Foyle have been proud to have played our part in this success.

In 2006, our businesses parted ways; however, I wish continued success and prosperity to Antonov Airlines.

Christopher Foyle

For 30 years now the phenomenon of Antonov Airlines has been generating great interest within a wide circle of aviation specialists, government officials, partner and competitor airlines, supporters, opponents and even people not associated with the aviation industry. Some admire how swiftly the Antonov team entered the market, how they made their way from the first tentative efforts at commercial air transportation of oversized cargo under Aeroflot's flag to become an internationally recognised airline that has its aircraft operating on every continent. Others, on the contrary, consider Antonov Airlines to be quite an unusual enterprise, and think that having found a convenient home for itself under the wing of the Antonov State Company (StC), its business is not transparent enough. But for the most part, people are surprised at the only example in the history of aviation of where an aircraft manufacturer receives the means for its main field of activity not so much from the serial production and sale of its products and know-how but rather from performing air cargo operations... All of these questions merit close study as any phenomenon is better understood by familiarisation with its history and examination of the circumstances under which it developed. With this in mind, this book offers readers the experience of a journey into the history of Antonov Airlines. As to conclusions ... let everyone make their own!

CHRONICLE OF ANTONOV AIRLINES: YEAR BY YEAR
Prehistory (1969–1989)

Prehistory

As a matter of fact, the decision to concentrate on unique cargo operations was more natural to Antonov StC than may appear at first glance as the company has been performing cargo transportations if not throughout its entire history, then, at least, for the last 50 years. At first this was not systematic but was rather the company carrying out one-off orders of the Soviet party and the government. The latter's reasoning was simple: who could have the most advanced airfreight technology? The only specialised design bureau in the country, of course! This is why, when some particular transport tasks arose, especially in the case of oversized cargo, the authorities almost always approached the Antonov Design Bureau. The bureau's services were not commercial in the conventional sense – they were not paid for, as everything was carried out as an order 'from above' – but as a result the Antonov team accumulated considerable experience in transporting all kinds of payloads under all sorts of conditions.

If we do not take into account the many earlier flights of the An-12, Antonov's involvement in cargo operations started with the An-22 transporting various cargoes for oil and gas reserves in Tyumen and diamond production in Mirny and Yakutsk regions. The first well of the rich Samotlor oilfield was drilled on 23 May 1965, and in four years' time this harsh region had produced about 22 million tonnes of oil. The next five years this figure rose to more than 100 million. Bringing this gigantic project to life required the involvement of air power, as it has always played an important part in the development of Siberia. The strongest heavy-lift aircraft in the world at that time was the An-22 Antaeus. Although its testing was still continuing, the demand for the aircraft proved to be so high that Alexei Kosygin, the Chairman of the USSR Council of Ministers, signed a special governmental decree on its temporary exemption from testing *"to accelerate the development of Siberia and the Far North"*.

A mobile generator being unloaded, Nizhnevartovsk, March 1969.

(1969–1989)

As a result, on 4 March 1969, following to the company's directive No. 178 and the Ministry of the Aviation Industry's (MAI) order about *"special cargo transportation for Tyumen Main Administration of the Oil and Gas Industry"*, the An-22 No. 01-03 set off to Siberia, with V. Terskii as commander of the flight crew and O. Kozhedub as chief of the technical crew consisting of eight people. A new directive, No. 198, came out in four days, and another aircraft, the Antaeus No. 01-01, set off to the distant territory, with Yu. Ketov as commander of the flight crew and I. Dubina as technical crew chief. By 21 March, Terskii's aircraft had carried out 16 flights from Tyumen to Nizhnevartovsk and two flights to Nefteyugansk. And Ketov's machine had flown seven times to Nefteyugansk. Altogether, they transported 12 mobile gas turbine generators, five excavators with combined weight of 625 tonnes and also large electrical equipment. Despite the harsh working conditions – temperatures of -50° C, short and narrow runways with frozen surfaces, the lack of

General Designer O. K. Antonov.

ground equipment – all the payloads were delivered to the destination points on time, i.e. before the onset of the spring thaw with its bad roads.

Since then, every year the Kyiv Antaeus aircraft have been making trips to Siberia. The aircraft were flown by test pilots V. Bohdanov, A. Halunenko, V. Zaliubovskii, V. Kalinin, Yu. Kurlin, E. Litvinchev, V. Samovarov, A. Spalvish, B. Stepanov, I. Titarenko and V. Tkachenko, with their engineering and technical crew chiefs being V. Tkachuk, V. Shelofastov, A. Eskin and other highly trained specialists. The crew of Soviet Union Hero Yurii Kurlin worked especially hard. While supplying the construction of the Aleksandrovskoye-Andzhero-Sudzhensk oil pipeline, they flew up to 240 hours per month. Striving to accomplish the assigned tasks as well as possible, the test pilots acted bravely and decisively, sometimes consciously putting themselves at risk. For landing on unfamiliar sites Yurii even developed a new method, the so-called 'conveyor' (equivalent to the 'touch-and-go' manoeuvre), for which he received an 'originator's certificate'. In 1970, Kurlin, while flying the An-22 No. 01-01 with a cargo of 60 tonnes (two excavators), took off in Surgut from a runway covered with a layer of snow more than a metre thick and he has also landed on a swamp frozen to only 40 cm. In the end, the work of the An-22 in these regions turned out to be highly cost-effective. In its issue of 18 May 1970, *Pravda* wrote, *"Just one Antaeus plane saved the Siberians a year's*

Vladimir Ivanovich Terskii.
Honoured Test Pilot of the
USSR.

A bucket-wheel excavator
being unloaded.

time and added no fewer than one million tonnes of oil". The romance of those difficult flights can be seen in poetry, which Yurii Kurlin composed at that time (in Russian):

Resembling the front line in an offensive,
Towards Nadym, Medvezhye and Urengoy,
The country of Tyumen to master,
The 'Antaeuses' soar up high, as if in combat.

In 1971, the aircraft and crews of Military Aviation Transport of the USSR joined the Antonov team to carry out transport operations such as these. However, according to Kurlin, the military aviators flew two to three times fewer flights per aircraft than the crews of the Antonov Design Bureau due to the fact that at that time the Armed Forces had only just begun to receive the Antaeus aircraft, and the flight and technical crews had not yet gained complete command of them. Besides, most of the flying missions involved such difficult conditions that they could only be performed by test pilots. And again, it must be noted that for their overtime work every crew member from the Antonov firm received additional pay of 20–40 roubles per flight – and this was big money at that time. Even a saying was

born in these trips: *"Difficult in Tymen, easy in the Crimea!"*, alluding to Alexander Suvorov's famous quote, *"Difficult in training, easy in combat"*. Apart from monetary rewards, the people also received free health resort packages and – however hard it might be to believe now – the permission to purchase around 150 Moskvich and Zhyguli automobiles (in total for them all) out of turn.

Almost everything in these Siberian flights was happening for the first time: items that were large and heavy being loaded into the fuselage, landing the world's biggest aircraft on deep snow-covered airfields, flying outside controlled airspace. Technical crews often had to introduce and develop new loading and unloading facilities right on the spot. For instance, after the first time in which excavators and pipelayers were carried in the An-22, an unfortunate flaw of the aircraft was revealed which prevented it being used effectively in this role – the caterpillar tracks were damaging the framework of the loading ramp. It is interesting to note that only civilian caterpillar vehicles caused damage to the Antaeus, while the military ones, according to earlier tests, could pass with no issues. The problem was solved with the help of steel drive-ons, placed on the ramp and serving as its extension. The idea originated with Yurii Kurlin and the senior technician Nikolai Vasilenko, the first syllables of their surnames forming the eye-catching name of the drive-ons, KurVa (a famous Polish swear word). With the help of specialists from Omsktruboprovodstroi (a building company dealing with the construction of gas and oil pipelines in the Omsk region), such structures were quickly manufactured and later introduced into serial production at Tashkent Aviation Plant, where the An-22 aircraft were built as well.

In some cases, the cargoes turned out to be so bulky and heavy that there was no established method of loading them into an aircraft. This is when the professionalism and creativity of the

The Antaeuses fly north

We have already examined the reasons why two An-22 crews flew to Western Siberia. The North, the region of the largest oilfields in the country, needed them to deliver mobile gas turbine generators and powerful bucket-wheel excavators. If it were not for air power, the vehicles would have had to travel there for almost a year. In the summer, they would have to go way up the Tobol, Irtysh and Ob rivers – more than 1,400 km – and then, when the swamps freeze,

they would have to take the winter road to the Samotlor, Pravdinskoye and other oilfields. Saving a year and delivering them earlier would give the country some additional hundreds of thousands of tonnes of oil. That is why these two air giants appeared at the request of the Tyumen Glavtyumenneftegaz company.

Vlamir Ivanovich Terskii's crew was introduced to the cargo that had to be taken aboard at the airport. The generators and the excavators were delivered there as

well. To outsiders it would seem impossible for such huge vehicles to be fit into the aircraft's belly, but for the aircrew who were long used to the abilities of their 'An', the task did not raise any doubts. But they were concerned about something else – the site where they had to land with this cargo. And their concern was justified, as it turned out on the next day.

The Antaeus' captain firstly flew from Tyumen to the little village, surrounded by bogs, as a passenger on the An-12.

Antonov team came into play. For instance, in November 1970, a 50-tonne diesel generator had to be delivered from Leningrad (now St Petersburg) to Cape Schmidt. It was impossible to lift it with the help of on-board overhead and then pull it into the fuselage through the tail loading door. And so everything was done the other way round. The aircraft was put into reverse and rolled backwards onto the generator, which was set on a dock deliberately built at the same level as the cargo floor. From this position the generator was pulled into the cabin with the help of barrows. This unique transport operation was performed by the crew of

Hero of the Soviet Union Ivan Davydov.

Another example of unconventional thinking when dealing with cargoes took place in 1977. Large Komatsu HD 1200 dumper trucks, purchased in America (the USSR didn't produce such vehicles) and shipped to Vladivostok by sea, had to be delivered to Mirny by the Antaeus and the crew of Yurii Kurlin. The trucks could not fit into the aircraft because of their size; they were dismantled, and their huge skips were cut in two halves lengthwise and then loaded into the aircraft. In Mirny, the trucks had their skips welded back together. During this time, the Antaeus aircraft were also involved

Two An-22 aircraft (Nos. 01-01 and 01-03) transported 625 tonnes of oversized cargo items for oilfield workers and geologists, May 1969.

D. Kiyanskii, a special correspondent for the *Rabochaya gazeta* (Worker's Newspaper)

Rabochaya gazeta, 2 April 1969.

Even before his Tyumen colleagues could execute the approach, having looked at the clearing cut out the taiga he realised that landing there with cargo would be one of the hardest challenges his crew had ever experienced. The site was barely large enough even for the An-12 and it was surrounded by swamps. One mistake, and the aircraft would land into the mire. After landing, these fears were confirmed. In a GAZ car, Vladimir Ivanovich went through the site where he would have to land his

Antaeus. The speedometer readout came as proof that the An-22 had never landed on such a short runway. Of course, it was impossible to expect that here, in a village amid swamps, they would specially build a concrete runway, but still he would rather not carry out such an experiment twice a day.

The first attempt was undertaken with the Antaeus unladen. According to crew calculations, the maximum landing deviation should not exceed 25 metres. To really grasp

what a distance like that meant, it is enough to note that the aircraft itself is more than twice as long. But according to the service instructions for the An-12 – which is an aircraft that is inferior to the Antaeus in many respects – the calculations anticipate a deviation of approximately 100 m. One more unfortunate circumstance was discovered before the departure. The landing field appeared to be covered with a snow-ice crust.

The whole population of the village

Yurii Vladimirovich Kurlin.
Hero of the Soviet Union.
Honoured Test Pilot of the
USSR.

Boris Vladimirovich
Stepanov. Honoured Test
Pilot of the USSR.

in another mission: they supplied Yakutia with food products, consumer goods, construction materials while the region was undergoing intensive development and the roads were either in a bad condition, or altogether absent. In his conversation with journalists, Oleg Konstantinovich Antonov said, *"Apart from having national economic significance, these flights were also important from a research perspective. They expanded the range of capabilities of our cargo giant and gave valuable resources for future transport aircraft design ... We aircraft designers have to keep up with technological progress. Perhaps, this isn't the last time our services will be called for."*

The 'first coming' of Antonov crews to Siberia lasted for 10 years – from 1969 to 1979. They were able not only to help to fully develop the Samotlorsk reserve, but also to create the large gas facility Medvezhye near the Arctic Circle, producing up to 65 billion cubic metres of gas per year. Over this period, the aircraft of the Design Bureau transported more than 20,000 tonnes of cargo, including pipelayers, bucket-wheel and single-bucket excavators, mobile gas turbine generators and pumping units, heavy special-purpose vehicles and buses, well heaters, geologist cabins, large-diameter pipes, valves for main gas pipelines and other equipment. At that, the peculiar conditions of Siberia made it impossible for 90% of these cargoes to be delivered to the destination points in any other way. Today, one can learn the geography of Western Siberia from the aerodromes where the Antaeus aircraft landed: Aleksandrovskoye, Igrim, Nizhnievartovsk, Medvezhye, Nadym, Salehard, Surhut, Tazovskii, Tarko-Sale, Tomsk, Urengoy, Hasaravei, Yangelskoye and others.

Describing the performance of the Antonov aircraft in his letter to General Designer O. K. Antonov, Viktor Muravlenko, the Managing Director of Glavtyumenneftegaz (Tyumen Main Administration of the Oil and Gas Industry), wrote: *"Siberian oilfield workers are well acquainted with the large family of*

Ans, beginning with the tireless An-2. The Antaeus aircraft, loaded with cargo for the Oil North, extend and strengthen relations between the Tyumenians and this powerful family. On behalf of the Tyumen oil workers, we ask you and your team of aircraft designers, constructors, test crews and engineers to kindly accept our deep gratitude for inventing this marvellous machine, for your kind-heartedness and participation in the great macroeconomic task of creating a powerful oil and gas industry in Western Siberia."

The passage above is quoted because it is highly representative of the words of acknowledgement which managers of different levels poured upon Oleg Konstantinovich and his deputies. Every year the leading newspapers published bombastic articles on the arrival of Antaeus aircraft in Siberia. The Antonov StC Museum still keeps dozens of these publications. But pleasant words were not the only reward for the intensive and creative work of the Antonov team. They obtained their first, truly valuable experience of transporting oversized and super-heavy cargoes and the no less important experience of generating profit from it for the Bureau (as far as it was possible in the context of socialist economy). Of great value were also the so-called agreements on economic exchange – instead of money the company was paid with building materials allocated by the government; in those days these were in short supply. This enabled construction work to start at a flight testing base in Gostomel, where, since 1959, people had been living cooped up in wooden huts. No flights were able to take place during the autumn and spring thaws due to the dirt runway becoming soft. During this time the distance between the village of Gostomel and the base gate had to be covered on foot as motor vehicles were getting stuck in the mud. Following the economic exchange, the Flight Testing and Improvement Base acquired a concrete runway and roads, the main territory of the Design Bureau acquired many facilities, and large numbers of employees were provided with housing. Even the

The Antaeuses fly north

came out to welcome the An-22. Hundreds of people witnessed another record, set by the remarkable aircraft. The giant machine touched the ground right at the intended spot, and when it stopped, the end of the runway was still another 300 metres away! But that flight was, so to say, a test one. The hardest part was to come: to land on a small snow-covered piece of land with an enormous load.

"... It had been snowing the day before.

That morning, it seemed, a blizzard was going to break out: the sky above the Tyumen aerodrome stood grey and low. The machines clearing the runway began to work before dawn. And the An-22 taxied to the start. The Antaeus made a circle above the town. It headed north-east. Up, from an aircraft, the earth is somewhat like a negative photograph. The islands of forest and woodland are black; the swamps stretching for hundreds of kilometres

are white. One can hardly discern the meandering river belts in between them, and the saucers of lakes frozen with ice.

"I tear myself away from the window and look into the cargo bay. The scene is so extraordinary. It's hard to believe that a huge, 23-tonne object – a bucket wheel excavator, which is standing still peacefully inside the hold – is actually flying at an altitude of over 8,000 m at a speed of 600 km/h! The crew captain is confident

Chairman of the USSR Council of Ministers Alexei Kosygin, famous for his progressive view of the economy, called the cooperation of the Antonov Design Bureau and the Tyumen oil and gas workers a 'socialist entrepreneurship'.

In the 1970s the territory of the Antonov flights was not limited to Siberia alone – they flew all over the USSR and even abroad. Here is how the first President of Antonov Airlines A. Bulanenko recollects one such operation: *"Once, the An-22 had to transport a nuclear accelerator from Switzerland to the Moscow region. Because of its large size, the accelerator couldn't be transported along the European roads, just like, for obvious reasons, it couldn't be cut into parts like the trucks, so that the only real option available was transporting it by air. The mountain airfield in the Alps was very difficult to approach, but Kurlin's crew have done an excellent job ... Gradually, we gained the reputation of being specialists in matters of transporting oversized and heavy loads. And we continued to carry out such transportations from time to time, as the need arose."*

Adding the An-124 Ruslan (a giant by the standards of that time) to the Antonov's arsenal boosted demand for the transport services of the company. Almost immediately after the aircraft's existence was declassified, it performed several pioneering transportations of civilian cargo under the direct command of the USSR government, and these were heavily covered by the press. The first of them was the delivery of a Euclid 152-tonne dumper truck from Vladivostok to Polarny (Yakutia) on Ruslan's first prototype in December 1985. As had happened eight years before, the vehicle could not fit into the aircraft because of its large size (the wheels alone were 3.5 m in diameter). However, this time it wasn't cut, but instead dismantled and transported in two flights, which were performed by A. Galunenko's crew. On 31 May the following year, the Ruslan carried a water turbine runner with

The crew of I. E. Davydov performed a unique transport operation, delivering a 50-tonne diesel generator with An-22 No. 01-06, November 1970.

in his colleagues: each of them is a highly qualified specialist ...

"The Antaeus lines up the runway. However, before I was told, it was hard to see the small clearing in the taiga as the aerodrome. Will the country's largest aircraft be landing on such a small patch, and with a cargo like this?! Yes, it will. Now the crew comes to the hardest part. I cannot see the faces of the pilots: I'm looking at them from behind. But even their postures betray how tense they both are right now. The huge aircraft starts landing. What surgical precision, what perfect calculation must be in place for the aircraft not to diverge from the intended spot by more than 25 metres at touchdown! It's only when you see the speed at which the snow-covered runway is rushing toward you that you realise what it means ...

"A soft bump. The Antaeus is running on the ground. But the run is unusually short. It seems that only a moment has passed but the aircraft is already standing still. As it turned out, the end of the runway was another 150 metres away!"

A Komatsu dumper truck
being transported from
Vladivostok to Mirny.
December 1977.

a diameter of 6 m and weight of 80 tonnes for Tash-Kumyr hydroelectric power plant from Kharkiv to Tashkent. In 20 days, another identical runner was sent by the same route. All of that stirred up interest in the aircraft's capabilities and Antonov, not only within the country but also beyond its borders.

Then there came a huge national tragedy – an earthquake in Armenia in December 1988. Relieving the consequences in the affected regions called for a quick transfer of around 3,500 tonnes of various payloads, including heavy machinery, e.g. a Liebherr 120-tonne crane had to be delivered from Germany. It turned out to be impossible without the help of Antonov and the An-124. A. Bulanenko continues, *"We instantly rushed to Armenia and were among the first to arrive. We used the An-22, An-124 and An-12. There was great confusion and chaos, the Humanitarian Aid Central Office providing assistance to the affected regions was in Moscow, while Leninakan had its own board, and every republic and every administrative entity also had one of their own, and all of them believed they had exclusive authority. After all, back then commands and orders were the only solution, they knew no other methods. We*

weren't allowed into Spitak, although the experience and competence of our crews made it quite possible for some landings to be carried out even there. In some cases, especially when we transported food, we were given landing clearance in Yerevan. According to sad accounts by crew members, everything they brought was immediately plundered – there were trucks arriving, and soon Ukraine's impartial help found itself in Armenian marketplaces. The plundering was done on a large scale. A bitter sight. And we remembered that no one, not even one of the numerous offices, paid for anything, neither kerosene, nor people's salaries, and not so much as a commendation or a letter missive was issued. But it's nothing, the main thing is that we were indeed able to help the Armenian people in trouble."

The string of tragedies in the USSR continued: a passenger train was damaged by a gas pipeline explosion in the Cheliabinsk region, and many people suffered burns. And again, Antonov was assigned to deliver burn care supplies and equipment to the site of disaster ... And little by little, things were becoming still more obviously abnormal: a section of the Antonov company and aircraft was almost

always distracted by new important governmental tasks and, as a rule, it was all done for free. At the same time, the government's financing of the firm became unstable. The company's management, headed by General Designer Piotr Balabuev (and this is one of his biggest merits), managed to evaluate the situation in time and make it the company's policy to finance itself by founding its own air transport department. Especially since the firm possessed the An-124, an aircraft with unique lifting capabilities, it would have been a waste not to use it for making money. In a few years, with the collapse of the Soviet Union and, consequently, the dissolution of the Ministry of the Aviation Industry (MAI) and the traditional funding sources, this move was nothing short of of the salvation of Antonov.

In 1987–88 many efforts had to be made to receive permission from the government to start earning money from flying the Ruslan. Among those who had been going to the authorities and receiving 'visas' (official approvals) from MAI, the Ministry of Civil Aviation, the Ministry of Foreign Trade, the State Planning Committee and the Ministry of Finance was the head of the company's Export Department Igor

The crew of Yu. V. Kurlin taking off from a runway covered with a layer of snow more than a metre thick with a cargo of 60 tonnes, Surgut, 1971.

A bucket-wheel excavator, delivered right to the Tomsk oilfield.

Yurii Nikolayevich Ketov. Honoured Test Pilot of the USSR.

The loading of a Euclid heavy dumper truck, December 1985.

Babenko. *"The last level of authority that we had to approach was the General Staff,"* Igor Diomidovich recalls, *"but Marshal Akhromeev didn't want to have any of it. Strategic MTA, the long arm of the Kremlin, and – all of a sudden – commercial operations?! It's out of the question!"* Still, despite all the difficulties, the year of 1988 brought the first agreement with Aeroflot, which granted us the right to operate commercial flights with their air operator's certificate with the only An-124 (its first prototype) that was then at the disposal of the Design Bureau. The agreement, though, covered only one domestic line, Moscow-Vladivostok, but now these operations were paid for.

It has to be said that Oleg Antonov himself believed the Ruslan to be a very promising commercial aircraft, and so he set about the task of upgrading it and making necessary alterations. However, Minister of the MCA Boris Bugaev held on to the opinion that the aircraft was not economically effective and therefore the An-124 was of no use to civil aviation in the USSR. But time soon changed that: the Moscow-Vladivostok route showed that the Ruslan had a great advantage over the previously used Il-76. It could lift three times as much cargo, it could fly at higher speeds, and it could operate with fewer landings along the way or could do without them altogether. At once, Aeroflot felt threatened. Taking advantage of its monopoly,

its directors adopted harsh tactics toward the emerging rival: they made it fly empty across the whole country, they set low tariffs; in short, they did everything they could to make Antonov voluntarily abandon the route.

Because of this, the idea of mastering the international transport market began to gain in popularity, all the more so as the company was in dire need of hard currency for technical re-equipment, especially for the purchase of computers, and the prospects for obtaining the necessary sums from the ministry became quite illusory. By that time, almost no one doubted that the An-124 could expect to have a great commercial future. The aircraft had already passed most of the tests and been exhibited at several international air shows, including the Paris Air Show at Le Bourget in 1985 and 1987. There it caused a stir, and in 1985 the Paris newspapers even reported *"the Russians stealing the show"* with their An-124. It was at these events that the company's chiefs started receiving offers from Western businessmen who wished to either purchase the Ruslan aircraft or lease them for various purposes, including the transportation of payloads to the north of South America, where large oil fields had been recently discovered. The Company's General Executive, K. Lushakov, recalls that these offers often were quite specific, e.g.

The loading of a turbine runner for Tash-Kumyr hydroelectric power plant, May 1986.

one of them was about transporting helicopters to Europe on the way from the Singapore Air Show. As a rule, the enthusiasm of those making the offers subsided a little upon hearing that this was only a prototype of the An-124 and the aircraft had not yet been certified and introduced into serial production; but the demand for such aircraft was made clear. Another aspect that facilitated the Ruslan entering the global market was the USA government limiting its C-5B Galaxy's usage in commercial operation. It had proved itself too costly for taxpayers, especially after the entire fleet of these aircraft had had their wings replaced. Thereby, the Ruslan's only potential rival was 'ruled out'.

To the credit of the Antonov team, it must be noted that in their hopes for international transport operations they were fully aware of their lack of vital business experience, an established customer base and commercial reputation outside the USSR. For future operations to be commercially effective, it was absolutely critical firstly to find a business partner who would have already had these attributes. And then they would be able to decide whether or continue working with them or whether the company should try to operate independently. However, the veil had not yet been completely from the An-124, just as the notorious Iron Curtain was still firmly sitting in its place, although Gorbachev did slightly shift it. To initiate business contact with western cargo companies and engage them with the Ruslan's capabilities ('the long arm of the Kremlin!'), then meant walking on thin ice.

Yet, when the soil was prepared, the fruitful grains fell into it themselves. In 1987, one of the most influential cargo carriers, British HeavyLift, participated in the Paris Air Show and exhibited its SH-5 Belfast, the carrier of the largest oversized cargo in western commercial aviation. On one of the exhibition days, HeavyLift General Executive McGoldrick, its commercial manager Graham Pearce and cargo traffic manager Jones set off for the Ruslan, which was parked nearby, with the aim of having a word with the Antonov team about the future. On board they were met by Anatolii Bulanenko. He reflects:

"Not consulting with anyone, I decided to get

Vladislav Arsentyevich Bogdanov. Honoured Test Pilot of the USSR.

The process of loading a giant turbine, 1986.

in touch with HeavyLift. At that time they only had three Belfast and several Hercules aircraft in working order, but the market demanded more than that. 'We have one or two "Ruslans",' I said, feeling uncertain how many of them could be introduced into commerce. But it appeared absolutely clear to me that the British would not be able to master the flight operation and technical maintenance of the An-124, insomuch as our planes still were test vehicles in many respects, with no manuals for a good many of the equipment components and with all captions being in Russian etc. Only our people knew the secrets to these planes' functioning. Therefore, I offered them wet leasing. That evening

Thank you, Ruslan!

It seemed that the giant had frozen above the runway. With the four powerful engines strenuously roaring, it seemed that it was hovering in one spot merely a few metres above the ground. Only the concurrently landing jet aircraft helped to show that the speed of the giant Ruslan was not any lower. Created by Kyiv Antonov Design Bureau, the heavyweight An-124's long-awaited landing at the Kharkiv aerodrome became a curtain-raiser to the unique transport operation, which started out in the Ukrainian city and was completed in Middle Asia.

For several months in a row, the workers of the S.M. Kirov Turbine Plant had been making water turbine details and assemblies for Tash-Kumyr hydroelectric power plant. Its construction was planned during the 27th Congress of the CPSU. At first, the plan was to transport the unit (the weight of only one of its runners was 80 tonnes) on land to Zhdanov, and then by water – through the Volga-Don Shipping Canal and the Caspian Sea. Then again along roads through deserts ... Experts estimated it would have taken four months to deliver it.

But by that time, the news of the first flight of the world's largest cargo aircraft reached the Arctic Circle and the Far East, and the Kharkiv engineers turned for help to the Kyiv aviation experts ... Together with the specialists from Dnipropetrovsk [Dnipro], they developed a cargo-loading method into the aircraft, using towing vehicles, cranes and other machinery. And finally the water turbine runner, assembled, ready to be installed at the hydroelectric power plant, was loaded into the belly of the modern air giant.

I reported everything to Piotr Balabuev and asked him: what shall I do next? His answer was: continue, despite the possible restrictions on the part of offices responsible for secrecy; something might come out of it, indeed. However, at the time any economic independence of the company was out of the question. For this reason, at the exhibition we only reached a basic agreement with the British, but they promised to come to Moscow, to the MAI, and there engage in more detailed discussions."

Indeed, on 9 December 1987, the HeavyLift representative team comprised of the people mentioned above appeared in Moscow and had several meetings with the representatives of

Sending heavy construction machinery into the earthquake-affected Armenia, December 1988.

V. Dolganov, staff reporter of *Komsomolskoye znamia* [*The Komsomol Banner* newspaper]

Komsomolskoye znamia, 1 June 1986.

Antonov's Deputy General Designer A. G. Bulanenko said, *"The operation is unique because the transported assembly is relatively small in diameter, only 6 metres, therefore the aircraft load is uneven, and is accumulated at one part of the cargo hold ..."* All the more reason for them to be proud of their success. This first experience opened up broad prospects of further aircraft usage for transporting assemblies of energy transforming machines by air. Not only would it save the transportation time, but

would be labour-saving for the assembler crews.

At Kharkiv airport I met Nikolai Gubanov, the foreman of the Komsomol youth team of assemblers of the Spetsgidroenergomontazh [plant producing equipment for water power stations], who are escorting the multi-tonne cargo. The assembler is highly appreciative of the novelty of the solution, created as a joint effort by engineers and aviation specialists. *"It is clear even now that it will help greatly to enhance the quality of the assembly*

work," the foreman said, *"because now we don't have to adjust and match all kinds of large details of all dimensions ..."*

Finally, a short command comes through the pilots' headsets – the takeoff clearance. The Ruslan flies up into the sky, to touch the ground again two and a half thousand miles away from Kharkiv.

Deputy General Designer
of Aircraft Maintenance
A. P. Eskin.

Antonov, Aviaexport, the Ministries of Aviation Industry and of Civil Aviation. Babenko recalls, *"The discussions concluded with a dinner at the Hotel Ukraina restaurant, but in terms of business they were unfruitful, as we still had our hands tied."* Most likely, it is the latter circumstance, i.e. the confusion over who exactly he was trying to settle a deal with (the Antonov firm, the foreign trade organisation Aviaexport, one of the ministries or both of them at once), that alarmed the HeavyLift's chairman. However, McGoldrick proved himself to be a determined businessman. Despite the discussions being unsuccessful, he continued to send requests to Aviaexport, where they were, however, immediately readdressed into a bin. The reason was the same as before – the aircraft remained military and still, in many respects, secret.

Fortunately, there are many determined people in the business world. In September 1988, when the An-124 was on display at the Farnborough Air Show near London, the first meetings with the English businessman Christopher Foyle were held. Since in the future the name of this person will be repeatedly mentioned in this book, we will now speak about him in more detail. William Richard Christopher Foyle was born on 20 January 1943, into a family of booksellers. The family business was founded in 1903 when Chris's grandfather with his brother opened a London bookshop, W & G Foyle Ltd. His father and aunt continued the business which soon flourished. The family bookshop became one of the tourist attractions of the British capital – the overall length of its bookshelves reached almost 50

km! Christopher's mother came from a family of Hungarian emigrants. Foyle's maternal grandfather, a reserve officer in the Austro-Hungarian Army, was called up at the beginning of the First World War, and after a stint on the eastern front, was posted to a staff job in Vienna. When the war ended in 1918, the family remained in Vienna and became Austrian, Foyle's mother went to London in the early 1930s to improve her English. There she met Richard Foyle, son of William Foyle, the founder of Foyles, and they were married in 1937. Chris became interested in aviation as a boy and commenced gliding when aged 15. Having got his private pilot's licence on powered aircraft in 1975, he decided to try his hand in the aviation business, founding Air Foyle in 1978.

In the aviation field, Foyle proved himself to be quite an unusual and even talented leader. First of all, he didn't try to break down closed doors and to start his business in those segments of the air transport market that had already been sufficiently occupied by numerous peers. Instead, he preferred to look for new areas where he could channel his efforts and bravely decided to enrich the market with a couple of new segments.

Commencing in 1979, Foyle had been operating small cargo aircraft within the UK and into Europe at night for TNT, the Australian overnight transport integrator. In 1985 TNT's entrepreneurial CEO, Sir Peter Abeles, decided to purchase a fleet of 72 BAe 146 aircraft from British Aerospace, converted to freighters. The BAe 146 was then the quietest aircraft in existence. Being an Australian company, TNT could not own or control an airline in the UK or Europe.

General Designer P. V. Balabuev telling General Secretary of the CPSU Central Committee M. S. Gorbachev about the advantages of the An-124 Ruslan, Kyiv, June 1985.

One of the most impressive transport operations performed by the company at the very beginning was the Tu-204 fuselage being transported from Ulyanovsk to Novosibirsk for testing, 1988.

Foyle negotiated a contract with TNT to manage and operate its aircraft on Air Foyle's Air Operator's Certificate and licences, with Air Foyle employed crews. Air Foyle commence operating its first TNT BAe 146 aircraft in May 1987 and this soon grew to 12 aircraft. The aircraft operated a night schedule around Europe TNT. The aircraft were on the ground during the day, so Foyle found additional cargo charter work from other shippers during that period.

Having thus succeeded, Foyle applied the principle of managing aircraft in this way to passenger aircraft for charter airlines and ultimately operated a fleet of Boeing 737, 727 and Airbus A300 and A320 aircraft throughout Europe including Iberia, the Canaries and the Mediterranean, for EasyJet, Sabre Airlines, Airworld, Debonair, Air Scandic and Color Air. These flights were operated from Luton, Gatwick and several provincial UK airports. In 1982, Christopher took up air transportation of oversized cargo with American Lockheed L100-30 Hercules aircraft, and in in 1994 won the prestigious contract with Oil Spill Response Ltd to provide a Hercules and an Il-76 aircraft on 24/7 standby 365 days a year, at Luton Airport.

He also founded CFALCo a leasing business owning a variety of assets including tanks and

Agreement on cooperation has been reached. At the foreground: Piotr Balabuev, Anatolii Bulanenko. Christopher Foyle, Bruce Bird

1989: one more difficult flight completed.

Tractor T-800 being loaded into the An-124 No. 01-03 to be sent to Polarny, Chelyabinsk, April 1990.

containers and a fleet of training aircraft leased to flying schools, Air Foyle Escapade, an upmarket incentive travel and corporate hospitality business using executive aircraft to take groups of customers to small airports serving interesting European destinations, banner towing advertising, and an airport ground handling company at Luton Airport.

Naturally, a business-minded person of this kind could not just skip over the excellent opportunities offered to him through such useful aircraft as the An-124. Here is an excerpt from the reminiscences of Christopher Foyle, written specifically for this book: *"In June 1987 I saw the aircraft for the first time at the Paris Air Show and on visiting the*

Aviaexport chalet was told that anything was possible and discussions were welcome. A dialogue then started by telex between myself and Aviaexport in Moscow. This culminated in an invitation to Moscow and I and one of my colleagues had our first meeting on the 1st April 1988. Across the table from us were representatives of Aeroflot, Aviaexport and of Antonov Design Bureau, Anatolii Bulanenko and Igor Babenko. Naturally, many questions were asked of us as to our interest in the An-124 aircraft, the reasons for it and how we perceived the worldwide market potential for this aircraft. I was invited to write a study on the potential market and this was produced by Bruce Bird who joined Air Foyle at this time and the report was sent to Aviaexport before our meeting in September 1988 with Apollon Systsov, the Minister for Aviation Industry, at the Farnborough Air Show. Following that meeting, there were more visits to Moscow in 1988 and early 1989, to discuss different types of business relationship, including joint ventures and a general sales agency. Unbeknown to me at this time, Antonov had been seeking to become an independent operator of the Ruslan with its own air operator's certificate but had not made much progress with the Moscow bureaucracy."

As with HeavyLift, the discussions with Air Foyle took place in Aviaexport's building. Antonov was represented by deputy general designers Ya. Goloborodko and A. Bulanenko. This was an important stage with the first joint documents being drafted to become the framework for future partnership, but in practice things were moving quite slowly, with miles of red tape constraining the flights' launch. Babenko remembers:

"And then came the February of 1989, Kyiv was to be paid a visit by Mikhail Sergeevich Gorbachev. First Secretary of CC CPU [the Central Committee of the Communist Party of Ukraine] V. Shcherbitskii had Mriya taken to Borispol to be shown to Gorbachev as one of Ukraine's accomplishments. The company's employees decided to take advantage of the situation and prepared a semi-detective script, which P. Balabuev later brilliantly acted upon. After Mikhail Sergeevich and Raisa Maksimovna (his wife), accompanied by Shcherbitskii, boarded the plane, Balabuev made a secret sign and the air stairs behind them went up. The entire suite was left outside. Here, in the cargo hold, the General Designer and the General Secretary of the CC CPSU [Central Committee of the Communist Party of the

The An-124 performing a commercial flight.

USSR Council of Minister's decree No. 520r becomes a landmark in Antonov's history.

Soviet Union] *had a conversation without being interrupted. Eventually, Shcherbitskii received an order to draft a proposal for transferring the aircraft to Antonov and lay it on Gorbachev's table in two weeks."* At that time, the orders of such kind were executed on the double, and on 23 May 1989, exactly a month after the visit, the USSR Council of Ministers held a meeting, where they examined the question of allowing the Kyiv Antonov team to perform independent commercial operations with the An-124. The Council invited Piotr Balabuev, and he reported the company's aspirations to use the earned money for technical re-equipment. But the plan received mixed response from those present in the room. The Defence Minister and the Minister for Civil Aviation opined that the country already had structures (MTA, Aeroflot) whose aim was to perform flight operations for state purposes, while 'designers should design'. In this tense atmosphere, Chairman of the USSR Council of Ministers Nikolai Ryzhkov exhibited great wisdom and finesse by noting that, in his opinion, the company's initiative was worthwhile. He also informed the opponents that Gorbachev was rather in favour of the project. Soon this pivotal question was answered in the affirmative.

USSR Council of Minister's decree No. 520r was thus issued on 24 March 1989, becoming a landmark in Antonov's history. Its very first paragraph started with the long-awaited phrase: *"To accept the proposal ... on granting O. K. Antonov Kyiv Mechanical Plant the permission to perform flight transportations of oversized cargo on the An-124*

aircraft on international and domestic lines under Aeroflot air operator's certificate, commencing from the year of 1989 ..., to conclude agreements with foreign companies ..." Later on the document determined that during the first six months of 1989, MTA of the USSR had to lease to Antonov two Ruslans, another two machines were to be purpose-manufactured at the Kyiv Aircraft Plant in 1990–91, and the loan for their purchase for the amount of 100 million roubles was to be issued by Promstroybank of the USSR. The company assumed full economic responsibility for commercial flight operations, but it was also allowed to keep all the income, including foreign currency, and freely (!) use it for production purposes. The exclamation mark here is used because it is hard, from today's view point, to recognise that no more than 30 years ago, for the company to freely use its own well-earned profit, it needed a special paragraph in an exceptional governmental decree by one of the two global superpowers!

However strange the quoted document would seem today, we should give credit to it signifying one of the key plot twists of this story. It legalized the long-deserved right of the Antonov team to perform commercial cargo operations. It left behind for ever the time when unique transport operations were performed virtually free of charge. It empowered the company to derive its money not only by asking for it from the state, but also by earning it, which ultimately enabled its survival during the next highly challenging years. It has become one of the corner stones of the foundation of Antonov Airlines.

Air Foyle Chairman Christopher Foyle and General Designer P. V. Balabuev.

CHRONICLE OF ANTONOV AIRLINES: YEAR BY YEAR
The first steps (1989-1991)

The first steps

Having received the long-awaited permission to perform commercial flights, Antonov didn't waste time and at once began to form an entity specifically designed to perform them. Here is an excerpt from the order of General Designer P. V. Balabuev of 11 April 1989, by which the airline company was established. *"To create a self-supporting foreign trade firm, affiliated to the KMP* [Kyiv Mechanical Plant was the then conventional name for Antonov StC], *and name it Ruslan, with it being responsible for:*

• *providing air transportation services on international air routes on a contractual basis with 'Aeroflot' and foreign firms;*

• *day-to-day marketing of air transportation services within the USSR and abroad;*

• *developing and working out the operational procedures and the ways of using the aircraft, performing actual transportations and thus demonstrating the unique transporting capabilities, operating performance and cost-efficiency of the Antonovs for the purpose of selling them."*

A. G. Bulanenko was appointed as the director of the newly formed entity, and I. D. Babenko was appointed as his deputy. For seven years, the subdivision operated under the name of Ruslan, borrowed from the aircraft. Starting from 1997, the company was more and more often referred to as Antonov Airlines, as it better reflected its nature. And in 2001, this name was registered as its official trade name.

As you can see, even this first document that directly concerned the airline company has already determined two important features which distinguish it from the 'classical' airlines. First of all, it wasn't an independent commercial entity, but instead it was a part of Antonov StC, i.e. one of its many subdivisions. Secondly, its strategic aim wasn't so much to improve its own economic performance as to provide the Antonov firm with the opportunity to perform its main function – to create new aircraft. Except that in order to achieve that aim, the airline company had to demonstrate top performance. That was the reality. Otherwise they wouldn't earn enough either to create advanced aircraft or to maintain the airworthiness of their fleet. That is how the market works.

However, in economic terms, there is nothing strange in the design bureau choosing the airline company as a source of financing, rather than the serial production plant. That was the economic environment of the time. In the late 1980s, the country could already sense the approach of a major

Anatolii Bulanenko, head of the Ruslan firm, and Igor Babenko, his deputy. Kyiv, 1989.

(1989–1991)

economic crisis, and the demand for aircraft kept on steadily decreasing. But conversely, the demand for air transportation kept growing, especially abroad. Besides, at that time Antonov almost exclusively possessed the unique means of performing special operations through the An-124. It would have been very strange not to try to take advantage of this. Finally, it was probably impossible to form an economically efficient affiliation between a design bureau and a serial production plant in the context of the state-run economy and command-and-control government. In the decades to come only a few successful aviation businesses emerged from the former USSR but the creation of this airline company did work out, albeit with great difficulty. However, we can leave the generalities behind, and continue the story of those historic events.

Encouraged by the support of the government, the Antonov team was very optimistic and bravely looked ahead. As prescribed by Decree No. 520r, the aircraft fleet of the Ruslan firm dramatically expanded. In addition to the first An-124 (the An-124 with serial number 01-01, registration USSR-680125), two military An-124s (No. 01-05 and 01-06, USSR-82007 and -82008) were leased from the fleet of the 566th Military-Transport Aviation Regiment based in Seshcha in Bryansk Oblast. At the same time, the Kyiv Aviation Plant started building two more Ruslans (Nos. 02-08 and 02-10, USSR-82027 and -82029) using the loan provided by the state. The firm was able to start performing flights, but for that it first needed to find customers. I.D. Babenko recalls: *"We started off by meeting up with the representatives of the 'Aeroflot's International Sector, and we received a warm welcome. When I say 'we', I mean myself and Head of Economic Research Brigade L. V. Rudakov, and later we were joined by Lead Engineer A. N. Naumenko and translator I. E. Smirnov. As our aircraft's fuselage read 'Aeroflot', we had no problems submitting flight requests and getting them approved. We were perfectly safe behind this word like behind a granite wall."*

First Aeroflot allowed us to transport the luggage of Kazakh German repatriates that were leaving the USSR at that time. The Kyiv crews performed a few flights from Moscow to Hannover and Leipzig, which gave them the most happy memories. First, the luggage was packed into 6-metre shipping containers, which were very easy to load, and secondly, these were the first profitable flights, even

though Aeroflot didn't give Antonov the full sum. Soon afterwards, a concert of the famous rock band Pink Floyd was going to take place in Moscow, and so 120 tonnes of stage equipment had to be delivered from Athens. Furthermore, the concert in Moscow was to take place two days after the concert in Athens. Rosconcert had already given up on the idea of the concert happening. Aeroflot flatly refused to perform the transportation in such a short period. That is why the Ruslan firm's offer was received with joy and the agreement was signed the next day. But in truth, this time the loading process was very difficult: everything went in bulk, and the Greek freight handlers drooped after three hours of work, with the aircraft only one-third loaded! Thanks to the help of the guys from the An-124's technical crew, the loading was finished on time; the Athenian flight operations officers had already allowed for the start and taxying ... but then they learned that the Ruslan engines needing a warm-up of four minutes at lineup, and were really shocked – they would have to stop a busy capital airport for that length of time, where there is an aircraft taking off or landing every 30–40 seconds! As a result, the Ruslan had to stand with engines turned on for about an hour, waiting for a gap in the schedule. This was the first example of how some of the technical characteristics of the An-124 in its initial military transport version were incompatible with the exacting requirements the market sets for commercial aircraft. Many other problems such as this were discovered over time, and the airline companies (Antonov StC and other airline companies) had to begin work to eliminate them.

Another revelation was brought out by the

The flight is performed by the An-124 of the Ruslan firm.

Samovarov Vasylii, class 1 testing pilot

The loading of Pink Floyd's stage equipment, Athens, 1989.

African flight. It was agreed that the payment would partially consist of dollars and partially of roubles. However, the letter of advice from the Vneshekonombank of the USSR showed that only the so-called 'transferable roubles' made it into the company's foreign currency account, and there was no sign of the dollars. This was despite Antonov StC having already received special permission from the Council of Ministers to freely take the proceedings in foreign currency! Despite all the efforts of the company's management, justice in this issue could not be achieved; however, it became an eye-opening lesson on the Soviet banking system. The latter was especially ruthless regarding foreign currency – 40% of the money went to the so-called 'presidential' tax, some sums were remitted to the Soviet Union's budget, and some to the national and republican fund, and then they were topped by a classified tax into the local budget and, thus, the state took around 80% of the money. That is why, not because of any particular greediness, many of the first Soviet entrepreneurs and chiefs of state-run enterprises sought to keep the laboriously earned foreign currency in foreign banks.

In the same year (1989), one of the Ruslans delivered the yacht Fazisi from Sukhimi to London, where it was to participate in a round-the-world regatta, while the crew of the test pilot V. I. Terskii performed the first cargo transportation between two foreign states – Spain and Iraq. All these largely successful flights were performed under the flag

The loading of the yacht Fazisi is completed, Sukhumi, 1989.

of Aeroflot; however, gradually, with the company becoming more and more experienced, the protecting shield of this powerful airline company began to turn into a hindrance. Not only did Aeroflot demand significant percentages for its services, but its huge, inert structure turned out to be completely ill-adjusted to working in the dynamic conditions that the market dictated. Here is what K. F. Lushakov had to say about it: *"Working with Aeroflot meant sometimes up to two weeks of waiting to receive flight clearance, and we were desperately losing customers. The realities of life made us look for another partner, a Western partner. Because in the eyes of the world to where we were going to fly and earn money, all of us were 'Russians'; that is, according to the general public opinion, by no means*

Ruslan's management meeting with the representatives of Aeroflot: the attempt to find common ground, Hostomel, 1989.

The loading of 35-tonne cable reels to be sent to Zambia, Oslo, 1989.

could we be trusted. We knew that the Western cargo dispatchers would far more readily approach a fellow firm, and we hoped that such a firm would act like a guarantor for us."

The need for an experienced partner became more obvious after the company realized it was getting involved in a business that its employees knew nothing about, that they had no other means of communication apart from telegraph, and nobody had the faintest idea of where to look for customers. When we look at how far the company

has come, the inevitable conclusion is that almost all the transportations of that time happened by mere chance. The Ruslan firm's services were called upon mainly on those occasions when a delivery schedule was at risk and the shipper could face a large fine, or in the event of wars or natural disasters when large quantities of cargo had to be promptly transported. We had to immediately establish systematic procedures to identify customers around the world. It was impossible to do this without the help of Western businessmen.

Russians to launch all-cargo airline

A SECOND Soviet Union international airline – a pure cargo carrier concentrating on heavy, outsize premium-paying freight and operating fifth freedom international charter services – is likely to commence operations early in 1991, writes Bob Murphy.

Provisionally named Antonov Airlines, its formation depends on the widely expected redrafting later this year of the USSR's air law, which currently stipulates that any of the country's civil aircraft operating outside of its borders must do so under the legal

auspices of Aeroflot. It is anticipated in Kremlin circles that this proviso will be scrapped over the next six to eight months, disclosed Igor Babenko, head of the Soviet Ministry of Aviation Industry's Kiev-based Antonov Design Bureau (ADB) in an exclusive interview with *ACN*.

And this will clear the way for Antonov to set up the new carrier, whose charters will be operated mainly by the massive 150-tonne-capacity An-124, dubbed the Ruslan, which ADB designed and produced.

The unloading of the reels, Zambia

Fortunately, Christopher Foyle displayed exemplary persistence – he was not going to give up. Not only did he not lose interest in the idea of becoming a sales agent of Antonov StC on the charter service market after half a year of discussions, which took place after Farnborough '88, but he also made a great step forward in creating the documentation for the future partnership. He came to be more energetic than Michael Hayles, who took over as General Executive of HeavyLift after McGoldrick left. Speaking figuratively, HeavyLift slept through

the moment, when the USSR Council of Ministers' decree gave Antonov its long-awaited independence of action, while Foyle came to Moscow on the 1 April 1989, only a week after the document was signed, and had another meeting with the Antonov team. Foyle recalls:

"During our meetings in Moscow, facing us across the table were representatives of Aeroflot, the Ministry of Civil Aviation, Aviaexport, the Ministry of Aviation Industry and Antonov, and so it was not clear to me with whom we would be dealing until,

Air Cargo News, **May 4, 1990**

"Although Antonov crew operate and maintain the aircraft for commercial operations, charter contracts must be directed through the Aeroflot bureaucracy, said Babenko. *Aeroflot then applies for the required traffic rights and negotiates fuel contracts and handling arrangements.*

"Basically, we have to fly under an Aeroflot registration but as soon as the law is changed we will establish a new airline."

Although the Soviet Air Force has about 25 to 30 Ruslans, Antonov operates just

two for commercial purposes and three for testing. Additionally, it has control of the prototype 250-tonne-capacity An-225, the only one in existence.

Bruce Bird, special projects manager for Air Foyle, which has been Antonov's general sales agent for Europe, North America and the Middle East since July last year, said that obtaining fifth freedom rights for the proposed new Ruslan Airlines should prove to be no real problem. *"For example, Singapore-Amsterdam is a route*

we are interested in developing for An-124 services and neither the Singapore nor Dutch governments object to this plan," he stated. *"We also see good potential in North America."*

Inside the Ruslan's cockpit –
Anatolii Naumenko, one of
the first managers of the
airline company.

at last, this became clear and we were invited to
lunch at the Restaurant Prague in Moscow in April
1989 by Antonov represented by Mr. Goloborodko
and Anatoly Bulanenko."

Obviously, the lunch was rewarding because in
early May, Christopher Foyle came straight to Kyiv, to
Hostomel, brought a draft contract and negotiations
went at full speed. For detailed elaboration of the
legal issues, a lawyer from Kyiv University was
involved – V. I. Ryzhyi. A month later, during the
Paris Air Show, the first personal meeting took place

between Christopher Foyle and Petro Balabuev
during which the leaders of the companies, as the
saying goes, dotted the i's and crossed the t's in the
draft future agreement.

A full-scale agreement between the partners
was signed on 19 July 1989, and from then Antonov
Airlines began to run as a professional business.
Air Foyle Ltd took over the functions of marketing
the transport services of Antonov Airlines, and
advertising, insurance, etc. Most importantly, in
the relationship with the new partner there was

The Bumerang yacht
delivered to Honolulu to
take part in the regatta.
1991.

established a strict discipline in financial issues, which had not been possible before. Christopher Foyle opened an account in one of London banks, from which Antonov StC received money for the transportation services it performed. A seamless process of searching for the most suitable niche for Ruslan aircraft in the world's airlift market began. Konstantin Fedorovich remembers:

"Chris's energy and our enthusiasm allowed us to quickly find common language and work in the market. Foyle was a great help to us in doing so. Watching his people, we comprehended the methods of work adopted in the West and started using them ourselves. We, certainly, already had some experience in international flights, to exhibitions for example. But in those cases many organisational issues were solved from Moscow. And flying under commercial contracts is quite another story. We learned to act on our own. To some extent, Foyle's help cannot be overestimated. For example, charter flights require some financial operations which for Soviet banks were impossible in principle, and Western banks had already mastered them long ago. Ultimately, this cooperation allowed us to learn how to react quickly to market demands."

The first flight under contract signed by Foyle took place in November 1989 – Ruslan aircraft under the command of Yu. V. Kurlin brought from Helsinki to Melbourne a printing press die weighing 53 tonnes on a 12-tonne trolley and five escalator sections for one of the local supermarkets, 8 tonnes each, and Christopher himself was on board. Commented Foyle, *"Captain Yu. Kurlin invited me on to the fight deck and as I held a pilot's licence, albeit a private*

one, put me in the co-pilot's seat and told me to fly the aircraft – an awesome experience."*

From Australia the aircraft went to New Zealand with television equipment weighing in total 75 tonnes – including six special buses and several big broadcast towers.

During the return flight the aircraft carried rolled aluminum. The very first joint flights showed that not only the Kyivans had much to learn from their British colleagues, but the opposite was also true. Foyle continues,

"One particular flight I remember, and on which I flew myself, was the one where we carried a nose cone of the Ariane 5 space vehicle from Emmen in Switzerland to the United States. We were told by the Swiss authorities that it was imperative that the aircraft should take off at exactly 12:00 noon, no earlier and no later. We were all very impressed to see the loading carried out successfully on time, the engines started and warmed up, and to be on board the aircraft as it sped down the runway and the wheels lifted off at exactly 12:00 noon."

Christopher Foyle.

Loading two pressure vessels for L'Air Liquide at Paris Charles de Gaulle, bound for Budapest, November 1990.

Melbourn. The Australian flight participants near their aircraft. From left to right: V. Mason,
S. Strelnykov, V. Kazachanskyi,
V. Ivakhnenko, Ye. Soroka; standing are: M. Tupchiienko, V. Rieka,
B. Levenchuk, A. Maistrenko,
I. Kalyta, S. Zhovnir, V. Soloshenko, M. Sliez, V. Tkachenko, S. Horbyk, V. Petrenko, A. Bocharov,
V. Petrychenko, V. Veresoka.

Tkachenko Volodymyr, the Honoured Test Pilot of the USSR.

And yet, despite the successful start of flights, there were many difficulties. Foyle continues, "During the first 12 months business was very slow, and we had the added complication of flights being operated under the Aeroflot flag and with Aeroflot competing with us to make the contracts with customers. I and my colleague Bruce Bird travelled to Moscow on several occasions to meet with officials from the International Commercial Department of Aeroflot. Meetings several hours long took place in their smoke filled conference room with sealed windows and no air conditioning. The heavy cigarette smoke became so thick, you could barely see one end of the room from the other. They were obdurate. Agreement and compromise were impossible." This was one of the reasons why the completed flights could be counted almost on one hand.

At the turn of 1989–90, Antonov Airlines fulfilled the contract with the Volkswagen concern for transportation of manufacturing equipment from Germany to Mexico. At the same time, the very first flights ordered by the UN took place. At the only hydroelectric power plant on Zambezi River, a large fire occurred, as a result of which Zambia and Zimbabwe almost completely lost electricity, and the international community decided to assist them in doing repairs. With the help of Ruslans, huge 35-tonne coils with cable were delivered to the site of the accident from Oslo.

The participants of these flights remember them with passion. That was the time when everything was for the first time – the unique airlift operations

and a flow of new impressions from visiting foreign countries and unusually large earnings were clear reasons for feeling proud about the aircraft, the company and the country. A. N. Naumenko, who became one of Antonov Airlines' first flight managers, says about that period: "We worked from 8 a.m. to 10 p.m. seven days a week and without holidays. The working day was crazy – phones, meetings, work with crews. By the end of the day I came home having no voice and literally could not talk ... But the enthusiasm was great." For British guys it was also a hard time. Bruce Bird remembers, "It would take 30 or 40 frustrating minutes of constant telephone dialling before being able to make a connection from England to Kyiv in the early days, ... how most of our business was done by telex ... how different it is now!" Despite the difficulties, everyone involved in the new venture was experiencing a huge upsurge. As a result, aircraft of the newly created airline flew 694 hours on commercial flights by the end of 1989, while the freight turnover amounted to 57.373 million tkm.

However, Air Foyle only acted as Antonov Airlines' sales agent in Europe, North America and the Middle East. The tempting markets of Australia and the Far East with its 'banana-lemon', Singapore, remained desirable but still inaccessible. Several attempts to work with these regions through the mediation of Chinese companies turned out to be not very successful, since the money again went through Aeroflot and was very difficult to extract. But soon, A. N. Naumenko, at behest of the Director of Antonov

StC V. N. Panin, brought to Kyiv Viktor D'Jamirze, an Australian businessman and philanthropist, an Adygei by nationality, famous in the whole of the Soviet Union by the fact that he presented to the Russian Orthodox Church an icon studded with precious stones. Anatoly met him during an air show in Australia, and the brothers D'Jamirze (seven in total and their sister) were recommended by the ambassador of the USSR himself in Australia. In 1988–89 the newspaper *Pravda* wrote about this family every week. For example, after the earthquake in Armenia, the children of D'Jamirze played violins on the streets of their city – they earned money to send to Armenian children.

Viktor arrived with a spirit for the organisation of transportation and received permission to fly to Australia by registering Antonov Airlines Cargo and Service Ltd with a registered capital of $1 (one dollar). He offered to start doing transportations to Japan, Southeast Asia and Europe from the Australian continent, which required sending of the Ruslan aircraft there for a long period. In the following years, a similar form of organisation, when an aircraft and its crew would fly around the world stand-alone and not return to base for a month or two or even more, became Antonov Airlines' main style of work. Such a method is enabled by the highly qualified crews and the high level of operational efficiency of the An-124, at the end of the day, making it possible to almost eliminate deadheading and to increase profits. But on the first Australian mission not everything went smoothly. As the pilot in command, V. A. Tkachenko, recalls: *"We could not dispatch for a long time – we had significant opposition from the authorities. We managed to overcome it only by the New Year of 1990 by taking the opportune cargo – equipment for the mausoleum of Ho Chi Minh in Hanoi, similar to Lenin's mausoleum. From Hanoi we went to Singapore, from there it was necessary to fly to Australia but permission was not granted again. The local representative of Aeroflot for a long time tried to persuade us against flying there, even threatened. And the manager was not with us, all the responsibility was on the captain. We had to fly at our own peril and risk."*

The active opposition of Aeroflot and the weakness of D'Jamirze's managers led to the loss of many contracts. There were few flights. In order not to waste time, Tkachenko engaged in advertising supermarkets, products, etc. by photographing them against the background of the aircraft. Volodymyr Andriiovych continues: *"For a month and a half spent in Australia we performed only 19 flights. We transported within the continent and to New Zealand expensive horses, fresh fish, elite calves, other cattle. After the first flights there emerged an unexpected problem – it was impossible to enter the aircraft because of a terrible smell: it turns out that the animals urinate during the flight. To wash the Ruslan, we had to buy a whole barrel of shampoo, 250 litres, and book a fire truck. We washed all day long; half the aircraft was covered with foam. Then they made special pallets and everything went ok. In these flights over the unfamiliar continent the airborne inertial navigation system proved itself particularly successfully. Generally speaking, the Ruslan aircraft generated much interest in Australia. As a rule, we just started the approach procedure and people were already running to look at the aircraft. I did not anticipate that aviation would be so popular among ordinary people. The expedition was very interesting but eventually proved to be poorly organised and showed us that cooperation with Western companies is necessary in such deals, since they have experience, connections and advertising. On our return on 8 March we brought an orchid for each of the women at Antonov Airlines – a gift from D'Jamirze."*

The aircraft returned with a cheque for US$100,000 (at that time it was a lot of money), but when it was taken to the bank the cheque had been stopped. From the explanation of the businessman it appeared that the Antonovans were to blame for everything, since when he almost signed a contract for transportation of thoroughbred sheep to the USSR, they took the aircraft away. In fact, the order for transportation of sheep was lost as a result of a provocative statement by the representative of Aeroflot saying that the An-124 had an unpressurized cabin and sheep would inevitably perish in flight.

(This was published by the newspaper *Pravda* in an article titled "Where did the US$100,000 go?") Nevertheless, D'Jamirze's explanations were accepted at the time and once again an aircraft was made available to fly to Australia but the result was the same: Ruslan returned with two cheques and neither was honoured on the grounds of breach of contract. After this, relations with him were severed, Antonov brought a claim in the Australian court, but Viktor D'Jamirze escaped from responsibility.

Antonov Airlines then made a bitter but very important conclusion for practical business: as a rule, local judges do not sue their own people. *"The story with D'Jamirze taught us a lesson,"* K. F. Lushakov summarizes, *"Now we see that in such a short period of time of 2–3 months it was impossible to create a market in such a vast region. We were too impatient. And it's even good that we*

Antonov Airlines' first air operator's certificate and ICAO's letter of assigning the company a three-letter code, ADB.

The Ruslan is a very beautiful aircraft.

broke up relatively early with him and did not suffer any more losses."

As a result, the D'Jamirze brothers turned out to be on thin ice: having the airline but not a single aircraft. They urgently needed a new partner ready to provide aircraft in exchange for simple promises, since the brothers could offer nothing else. At the very end of 1991, Viktor came to the USSR and started negotiating with the Minister of Civil Aviation E. I. Shaposhnikov and Air Force Commander P. S. Deinekin. The D'Jamirzes set serious sights on the Soviet military An-124 and Il-76 aircraft, but they were hampered by one event: the quarrel with Antonov severely undermined their reputation in the USSR.

He sent a letter to the Ukrainian media, full of declarations of love for Ukraine and a list of the merits of his family. Further, the letter said (quoting from *Vechirnii Kyiv* newspaper): *"And now I consider it my duty to inform the public that one of our former Ukrainian partners Petro Balabuev hides almost US$20 million in one of the London banks. The money is used by the English partner of Balabuev – Mr. Foyle."* The letter ended with an explicit threat: something like, if I tell that you [the Ukrainians] hide currency then the Ukrainian diaspora in Australia will stop helping you.

For those who do not remember those times, it is difficult to imagine what it means in a crisis-stricken country to spread the word that some bad guy is hiding US$20 million from the people! This could result in more than one trial, however

the big uproar collapsed. It was shadowed by events much more significant: at that time the Soviet Union was breaking apart. Either for this reason or because his anti-Antonov propaganda did not achieve its goal, D'Jamirze's attempted collaboration with the Soviet Military Transport Aviation did not succeed.

The aviation business of the brothers ended unfortunately, but not unexpectedly. In 1992 they rented an aircraft from HeavyLift having effected an advance payment amounting to 50% of the cost of transportation, and the second half they promised to pay after transportation on the pledge of personal property of one of the brothers – Vladimir. But after the flight the money was not paid and the property was re-registered under the names of other relatives. Judging by the available documents, after this, HeavyLift had a hard time with the brothers who behaved defiantly to the British company and threatened to appeal to the UN and personally to Boris Yeltsin. I wish I could quote more of the correspondence and tell the whole tale as a detective story but we've already gone far away from the main topic of the book so it's time to stop! But I'll add one small quote. This is an excerpt from the official press release from the Australian Court of Justice on 6 February 1995: *"The court forbids the former directors of the company – Viktor and Vladimir D'Jamirze – for four years, and Nikolai and Alik D'Jamirze for three years to do business and hold senior positions."* Well, we can conclude that justice was served.

However, let's return to the air transport department of the Kyiv Design Bureau. By the end of 1990, without receiving assistance from Aeroflot, and indeed often encountering direct opposition from them, the department gained sufficient independence in matters of organising commercial transport services, searching for customers and partners, optimizing financial flows and other components of their business.

For Antonov to cease flying under the flag of Aeroflot, and its control, Christopher Foyle came up with the idea of Air Foyle his British cargo airline which held a UK Air Operator's Certificate and valuable international licences and traffic rights, to wet lease all Antonov's An-124 Ruslans into its own fleet and operate on British, not Soviet traffic rights, around the world. Antonov agreed with the idea and discovered an obscure piece of Ukrainian legislation that permitted state enterprises to lease out equipment. Christopher Foyle drafted a wet lease agreement which Antonov signed. In June 1990 Air Foyle applied to the UK Department of Transport for a permit to wet lease these aircraft into its existing fleet of BAe 146 cargo aircraft. This was granted. Antonov then removed the Aeroflot insignia from its aircraft and repainted them with Air Foyle – Antonov. Juri Chuprinin the head of cargo at Aeroflot's International Commercial Department flew to Kyiv to tell Antonov that they could not do this, but he returned to Moscow with a flea in his ear. From then on, Air Foyle became responsible for applying for all international traffic rights, permits and diplomatic clearances. Aeroflot's obstructiveness

was removed at a stroke. Air Foyle, not Aeroflot, also became solely responsible for negotiating and making contracts with customers on a worldwide basis and managing finances. That, coupled with the first Gulf War following Saddam Hussein's invasion of Kuwait, meant that the commercial business then took off. From then on until 1993 the An-124 Ruslan aircraft operated on the Air Foyle ICAO designator 'UPA', until 1993, when the wet lease permit ended and the aircraft then operated on Antonov's designator – 'ADB'.

Having obtained the UK wet lease permit Air Foyle then went about applying for the very important US Department of Transport 402 permit. This was ultimately granted and Chris Foyle went to Washington DC in late 1990 where Jeffrey Shane the Assistant Secretary of Transportation presented it to him in a ceremony in his office. The first flight performed by Antonov under this permit was from Houston to Dhahran carrying oil skimmer boats.

In 1990, the flying time of Ruslan aircraft increased to 2,082 hours, and cargo turnover reached 72,894,000 tkm. That year Antonov crews performed flights to Australia, Bangladesh, Great Britain, Hungary, Vietnam, Germany, Zimbabwe, India, Jordan, Iran, Italy, Kenya, Libya, Luxembourg, Netherlands, New Zealand, UAE, Papua New Guinea, Saudi Arabia, Singapore, Syria, the United States, France, the Central African Republic and Yugoslavia. For pilots and technicians – Soviet people who grew up behind the Iron Curtain – such a rapid penetration into the rest of the world has

From the beginning of the 1990s, more and more flights were performed in partnership with Air Foyle.

Antonov StC test pilots had to develop the skills of civil airline pilots.

become one of the most unforgettable periods of their lives. I think that the people reading these words in the second decade of the 21st century, who are accustomed to simply wander for a week somewhere to Egypt or Thailand, particularly the British, simply cannot imagine the powerful explosion of emotions and impressions that overwhelmed the participants of those flights.

As business success in Kyiv grew, Aeroflot increasingly began to consider Ruslan as its direct competitor. As a result, the Ministry of Civil Aviation of USSR demanded that Antonov StC formalized an air operator's certificate, ie legalized the existence of airline independent of Aeroflot.

It was a truly Jesuitic step, because no one at Antonov StC had any idea how to register an airline. And not only at Antonov StC! After the formation of Aeroflot in 1933 no other commercial airline had been created in the land of the Soviets! It was necessary to travel a lot to Moscow, establish new contacts and find mutually acceptable solutions to a number of issues with the officials of the Ministry of Civil Aviation and the Ministry of Aviation Industry. The case was particularly complicated by the fact that the An-124 had not yet been certified as a civil aircraft. In the end, the necessary document was issued. However, in order to fly on international routes Antonov StC was required to receive its own three-letter call sign instead of Aeroflot's sign and the prerogative of issuance of such call signs belongs exclusively to ICAO. Here is the story of Antonov Airlines' leading engineer, S. S. Halka: *"Before applying for a three-letter code we thoroughly studied all necessary documentation,*

both Soviet and ICAO, and communicated with the aviation authorities. What's interesting is that we did not encounter any obstacles from the officials in Moscow – at that time their attitude to Ukraine was much better than now. Together with Igor Babenko in March 1991, we wrote a letter and sent necessary documents to ICAO headquarters in Montreal. Imagine: we received a positive answer in some 10 days! Apparently, the popularity of the Antonov brand played its role and some 'kinship' between Canada and Ukraine did the trick. Without any problems, we were given exactly the three-letter code that we requested – ADB, which means Antonov Design Bureau (under this code Antonov aircraft are flying until today). Everything went well, because when a person on a daily basis systematically and professionally does his job then the need for heroic deeds simply does not arise."

By mid-1991, the air transport division of Antonov StC had all the attributes of an airline: aircraft and service facilities, crews and a base for their training, a network of commercial agents, national air operator's certificate and international three-letter code. But this was only the beginning. It was vital that the Ruslan company began to realise the goals for which it was created. With money from air transportation, Antonov StC was able to deploy a large-scale programme of technical re-equipment, purchase of personal computers and powerful design workstations. The introduction of information technology into the process of designing new aircraft began; in particular, the centre wing and An-70 outer wing were designed using equipment purchased at that time.

CHRONICLE OF ANTONOV AIRLINES: YEAR BY YEAR
Formation (1991–1992)

Formation

Ruslan heading for Jordan. September, 1990.

By 1991 the airline established as part of Antonov StC began to show its first results. However, this period already described brought not so much real achievements as an awareness of the immense prospects that were opened up by the almost exclusive possession of such a unique aircraft as An-124 Ruslan. In addition, it was understood that air transport is a very specific and complex activity with strong competition and a host of difficulties, both purely technical and organisational. In short, it became clear that this business needed to be arranged seriously. And it was necessary to begin, obviously, from decisions about the personnel.

Firstly, considering the significant increase in the volume of work, it was necessary to increase staff numbers. But it so happened that the first four managers who started up all the practical work on the organisation of transportation immediately

after the order of USSR Council of Ministers dated 24 March 1989 came into force – I. D. Babenko, A. N. Naumenko, I. E. Smirnov and A. S. Syrkina – left the company for various reasons by the summer of 1991. K. F. Lushakov, who was appointed as the Executive Director of the airline and Deputy Director of A. G. Bulanenko for flight test and certification, suggested the formation of a new team to the leading test engineer of An-124 and An-225 M. G. Kharchenko, who recalls:

"This was already the second proposal to be involved in the business of Airlines which I received. The first one came from Bulanenko back in March 1989. But then we had just started flight tests of Mriya aircraft, there was a lot of work and I did not see for myself a real opportunity to combine this work with commercial activity. However, in 1991, when Mriya was practically parked due to termination of tests funding, with clear conscience

(1991–1992)

that I did not leave aviation, I accepted Lushakov's proposal. I proposed to form the backbone of the airline's staff from people whom I had learned well during 10 years of teamwork on development of An-124 – from leading engineers to test crew on this aircraft. I proceeded from the fact that people who perfectly mastered the intricacies of flight and testing work were able to master any kind of intellectual activity, including marketing of air freighting services. Nevertheless, the selection was thorough and the most difficult issue was a good knowledge of English. As a result, permanent jobs in the air transport unit went to S. N. Gavrilov, S. S. Galka, B. V. Gorobeyko, A. Y. Dolenko, V. S. Mikhailov, V. M. Sudorgin. However, soon they also could not cope with the increased volume of work and a second wave came to assist them – N. Y. Vasiliev, V. N. Kulbaka and others. The team undertaking economic analysis and calculations comprised of V. S. Maksimova, . S. Onopchenko, L. V. Babina.

"There was a lot of speculation about how to organise the work of flight and technical crew. One of the most obvious at that time seemed to be the way typical of any classical airlines – to recruit a permanent staff of civil pilots and engineers and 'link' them to specific aircraft. In fact, such a way would have meant the gradual separation of the air transport unit from the design bureau and, at the end of the day, led to the formation of a separate subsidiary structure. Another possible way was to involve from time to time, for commercial flights, our company's test pilots and technical crew from the flight test department. For this approach the main difficulty was that laws regulating test and commercial flight activities are different. Thus, the rules of civil aviation are very strict, even draconian, and they regulate all actions of crews in any situation, literally 'from A and to Z'. At the same time, test rules are more democratic, since this type of flight activity has a creative nature and allows experimentation within certain limits. It is difficult to teach the same people practically simultaneously to follow so different rules. And after all, these are the questions of the crew's flight coordination and, at the end of the day, the safety of flights.

"Exactly for that reason at first I was a strong supporter of establishing a subsidiary airline; however Lushakov and the company's management did not share this idea of mine. Flight and technical

crews involved in commercial flights remained in those units where they had been before. Although they studied flight rules at international airways and obtained corresponding permits, they completed courses of English language and they remained testers. Over time, I realised how correct it turned out to be in our particular situation."

It should be noted that decision-making of fundamental issues related to the organisation of The airline's operation took place in conditions of quite intensive flights. Volga-Dnepr Company – the main competitor and then the partner of Antonov Airlines – did not exist at that time, and the crews of Antonov StC satisfied the whole world's demand for transportation of oversized and extra-heavy cargoes. Only occasionally the crews from Military Transport Aviation of Russia, the main operator of Ruslan aircraft, were involved in this process. But due to military specifics, Russians could not seriously compete with the Antonovans.

Flights related to the Persian Gulf War of 1990–91 stuck in the memory of the people of Kyiv. Without exaggeration, this war became the hour of triumph for both the Antonov Airlines and its main aircraft – An-124. Kuwait, like other well-developed Arab countries, extensively used wage labour of third world country nationals, in

M. G. Kharchenko (on the right) contributed much dealing with the airline's operational issues.

Refugees from Kuwait entering the life-saving Ruslan. Jordan, September, 1990.

The sky over Kuwait was black due to numerous fires which precluded flying.

particular Bangladesh, Pakistan and India. When, on 2 August 1990, Iraqi troops invaded Kuwait, a large mass of wage-workers rushed to flee the war. Many of them found shelter in Saudi Arabia and Jordan, where refugees concentrated in tent camps. There, experiencing an acute shortage of food and water, they caused a number of problems for the countries they stayed in. Asking for help in exporting these people to their homeland the UN functionaries approached Air Foyle, who at that time together with the delegation of Antonov StC had participated in the demonstration of An-225 at the air show in Farnborough. Foyle discussed this request with Balabuev who replied that An-124 was not a passenger aircraft and it was simply impossible to ensure a proper level of comfort when transporting people on it. However, at that

time comfort was not a matter of priority and the UN only required a written confirmation that during the flight the evacuees would have enough air to breathe. Christopher Foyle recalls, *"When I told Petro Vasilievich about the enquiry, in September 1990, we were sitting round a small table in the enormous cavernous cargo compartment of the An-225 at the Farnborough Air Show, he asked for a piece of paper and as the Head of Aircraft's Design Authority, wrote and signed, then and there, a certificate permitting the aircraft to carry passengers seated in the cargo compartment."* Christopher immediately ordered the purchase of mattresses to cover the aircraft floor, and chemical toilets to be placed along the sides. In a few hours, two Ruslan aircraft departed to the Middle East: one to evacuate people, the other to deliver gas masks and other necessary goods to Saudi Arabia.

As remembered by Bruce Bird, Executive Director of Air Foyle by that time, Christopher agreed on a contract for the transportation of refugees using only a mobile phone. He definitely had to talk a lot. *"I think he singly kept the telephone battery industry in profit that year,"* Bird characteristically described the intensity of his president's work.

For the refugees the aircraft had to arrive in Amman, the capital of Jordan. Foyle continues: *"I was in the office in Luton. It was a Saturday. I received a telephone call from the UN official in charge in Geneva to say that various VIPs were assembled at Amman airport, but that there was no sign of the aircraft and it was overdue. A few minutes later I received a telephone call from the Flight Manager on the aircraft to say that the aircraft had arrived at the airport at Amman, to which*

According to recollections of the participants of those flights, the Ruslan accommodated up to 1,000 people.

they had been instructed to fly, but there was no sign of any officials or passengers. The airport was deserted. What should they do? I knew that there were two airports at Amman and realised that our Ops. Officer had instructed them to fly to the wrong one. I told the Flight Manager to take off as quickly as possible and fly immediately to the correct airport, which they did."

It is reported that loading of refugees in Ruslan aircraft was an impressive sight, worthy of featuring in any Hollywood blockbuster about the end of the world. In the pictures in the British newspapers of those days, the An-124 is seen with its nose cone raised and a huge queue to the horizon of bearded men entering the aircraft (women and children were taken out by Boeing aircraft). Having entered, they, like true Muslims, sat on mattresses. There were attempts to count them but they never tallied. Today, participants of those flights quote different numbers – from 600 to 850 and even to 1,000 people per flight. They did not have luggage with them which is why all these figures are possible. When the last person settled himself on the last free centimetre of the floor, the ramp was closed, and Ruslan took-off for Dhaka, the capital of Bangladesh. On its return journey the aircraft took 80 tonnes of rice and 5 tonnes of tea to feed refugees remaining in camps. As recalled by the pilots, at the beginning of flight they did not close the hatch to their cabin, ignoring instructions and being guided by ethical considerations, but the smell in the cargo cabin soon became so terrible that they had to shut the hatch. A. V. Tkachenko's crew performed eight such flights.

The second Ruslan, in addition to gas masks, delivered American Patriot anti-aircraft missile systems to the combat area, carried humanitarian supplies and performed other urgent work. Then UN experts clearly saw the impressive capabilities of An-124 and came to the conclusion that in terms of operational flexibility this aircraft simply did not have competitors. Later, when there was a need for urgent transportation of humanitarian supplies to areas of natural disasters and military conflicts, the UN constantly approached Antonov Airlines.

After the Allied forces defeated Hussein, the work for Antonov's Ruslans only increased. Ordered by the Americans, with the help of Foyle like almost all the orders of that period, the aircraft performed flights from Chicago, delivering heavy equipment to Kuwait to extinguish the burning oil wells: huge bulldozers, earth-movers and special fire extinguishing cannons. M. G. Kharchenko remembers:

The refugees returned to their native land successfully. Bangladesh, 1990.

S. S. Galka was one of the organisers of flights for national currency transportation to Ukraine.

"The forecasts were very gloomy. Many believed that the planet was facing a global environmental catastrophe. When approaching the Gulf, a very impressive picture opened up: black sky from countless fires on wells burning day and night. Bad visibility obstructed landing, which was performed visually, since all ground radio aids were ruined. And again the military origin of An-124 aircraft helped us a lot: its flight and navigation suite allowed us to fly on a designated route in a stand-alone mode and reliably reach a specified point. To clarify the aircraft position we used an onboard surface surveillance radar. Not only flights were complicated and dangerous – in airports where the Ruslans landed, we repeatedly found unexploded ordnance and mines. But despite all the difficulties we managed to quickly deliver to Kuwait all the necessary equipment, thanks to which the fires were defeated."

However, participation in international conflicts was not the only memory of that period. At the turn of 1990s, significant historical events also took place within the borders of USSR, the key events being the collapse of the Soviet Union and the proclamation of independence by Ukraine. For Antonov Airlines, the change of political authority meant a change in aviation authority. The Department of Aviation Transport was urgently established in the country, which, however, could not clearly formulate its powers or responsibilities. A long and difficult process of forming a new regulatory basis for the implementation of various forms of aviation activities, including freight transport, began. In this process, the employees of Antonov Airlines, who by that time had considerable practical experience and who knew the key points of relevant legislation in foreign countries, took an active part.

It is necessary to pay tribute to the new government – even in the heat of political battles and in the rush of the first period of establishing a state, it did not forget about the air transport department of Antonov StC and often approached it for help. Stepan Safonovich Galka tells about one of the very first and most important assignments of the new state: "Soon after adoption of the Declaration of Independence, in September 1991, the Cabinet of Ministers of Ukraine issued a resolution on transition to its own currency. The first version of national currency was coupons, printing of which was ordered from England, France and Spain. We had the task to deliver coupons to Ukraine. The very first flight when Ruslan went to bring the money took place on 3 December. A. G. Bulanenko supervised the whole operation and I was on that flight as a manager. Ten special squad soldiers protected us led personally by the head of Security Service of Ukraine, E. K. Marchuk. In Paris we loaded 130 tonnes (!) of coupons into the aircraft and unloaded them the same night in Boryspil. Until January 1, we made eight such flights, and

Night time unloading at Stansted airport. January 1991.

altogether our An-124 took-off about 30 times to transport the entire money (in the direct sense of the word) of the country. The most important state order was fulfilled impeccably."

There were other instructions too, also important and responsible and sometimes dangerous. During the period of Armenian-Azerbaijani conflict over Nagorno-Karabakh, the aircraft of Antonov Airlines delivered humanitarian supplies to this trouble spot and carried out other flights under direct orders of the government. During the first years of Ukraine's independence, a new entry was added to the list of tasks undertaken – humanitarian aid. These flights earned a special place in Antonov Airlines' story, because, first of all, they were free of charge (at least initially) and, secondly, a little later, they came back to bite the company with a huge international scandal. No good deed ever goes unpunished!

At first, things went so well: Ukrainian emigrants in America decided to help young independent Ukraine as much as they could and alleviate its third-rate products, shabby clothes, etc. The diaspora was very fragmented and different groups requested the government of Ukraine to send aircraft to take their donations. Each group had its own leader, in the central part of the United States this turned out to be a highly qualified doctor Zenon Matkivskii. He contacted directly the Vice-Premier of Ukraine K. I. Masik, who gave the direction to P. V. Balabuev, and Ruslans performed a series of free flights to

America. Having, apparently, a well-developed business acumen, Zenon quickly recognised the huge market potential of these An-124 aircraft coming for his cargoes. And though he had little knowledge of aviation, especially in such a specific field as air cargo transportation, he – like Foyle – decided to become Antonov StC's sales agent, and for that purpose he set up the Ventrex company in the US. Matkivskii recruited several specialists who left other air transport companies and soon 11.4% of all income from air transportation was received by the Antonovans under contracts signed by Ventrex. (In parenthesis, we note that Foyle's share in that period was 66.8%.) However, the enterprising physician was not satisfied with the commissions that were due to him as an intermediary, and he soon came to think of picking up the main source of income – the aircraft of Antonov Airlines itself.

In order to transform this idea into reality, Matkivskii chose a rather effective path. Since Antonov StC itself, and everything that belonged to it, was the property of the state,* Zenon did not waste time talking with the company's representatives and directed all his efforts to 'achieving mutual understanding' with representatives of the highest echelons of state government, including some influential members of Ukrainian Parliament. He said: *"You own excellent aircraft and fine crews but you do not know how to work in market conditions. As a result, Ukraine loses a lot. It is necessary that*

Long after the end of the Gulf War Ruslans were carrying heavy vehicles for extinguishing oil well fires in that region. Kuwait, June, 1991.

* Technically, this is not quite true. Already at that time two Antonov Airlines Ruslan aircraft were bought out from the state by Antonov StC team.

By Ukrainian government instructions, regular batches of humanitarian cargoes were delivered. Gostomel, 1992.

the Ruslan company was managed by American managers." As it is usual in such cases, 'work at the top' was supported by loud patriotic appeals through TV, demagogic publications in the press and the like. As the days grew longer, the storms were stronger: Ventrex launched a heavy campaign to prepare a draft of a corresponding resolution of the Cabinet of Ministers of Ukraine, which

was handed to the country's Vice-Premier V. N. Shmarov. In fact, this document was never signed, and therefore does not deserve much attention, but it was so unprecedented in its nerve (not to say impudence) that it is difficult to resist quoting at least the first and last of its points:

"1. The Ruslan company should be removed from Antonov Design Bureau.

Love and dollars or behind the scandal

As was mentioned previously, the scandal involving the transportation of the equipment for pop star Michael Jackson turned out to be a pure and simple bubble. Blaming Antonov StC for losing a profitable dollar contract, People's Deputy of Ukraine Vladimir Yavorivskii and the American Nadia Matkivska clearly had overdone their argument. Their plan popped with a loud noise, and the spatter flew right into the accusers.

The journalists of the mainstream periodicals, who witnessed the unpleasant meeting of Vladimir Yavorivskii and Nadia Matkivska with the employees in Antonov

StC's hall, said unequivocally that foul play was going on.

Foul play, indeed. A play on the people's patriotic feelings, which 'Garth' studio presented not only as bungling of the aircraft company led by General Designer Piotr Balabuev but forgery also on the brink of sabotage. Here one could suspect the beginning of a quest for new enemies instead of those 'commies' which everyone was fed-up with and which were hated so much by the Democratic deputies.

But the dispute started not so much for a new election image, although that could be helpful for a member of the bankrupt

Supreme Soviet, as for a specific profitable business. The fuss over what might-have-been to service Michael Jackson's concert tour was just an excuse to discredit the 'Antonovans' as amateurish businessmen.

The question of how an aircraft designing company could have a commercial business had been answered even during the Soviet Union times when Balabuev expressed at the highest level the idea (seditious at that time, but as subsequent events showed a heaven-sent opportunity for Ukrainian aviation) of an independent, autonomous existence. The General Designer must have had foresight. The rupture of allied ties would

11. All existing leadership positions should be abolished."

According to the draft document, the business had to be led by the employee of Ventrex, Mr. John Dror, who previously worked in Canada as a representative of Air Foyle.

Naturally, with such radical intentions, direct talks with Antonov StC's team were not included in Matkivskii's plans, but organisers of the Ruslan aircraft expropriation still had to explain themselves.

On 16 September 1993, in the company's conference hall there was a meeting with one of them, Mr. Zenon's wife Nadiya, the people's deputy of Ukraine V. A. Yavorivsky and the leadership and labour collective of the factory. In the course of

Loading of three transformers with a 42-tonne mass for shipping to New Caledonia. Barcelona, January 1991.

Lyudmila Menzhulina
Pravda Ukrainy, 5 October 1993

have ruined what was said at the meeting with the aircraft company by People's Deputy Yavorivskii: *"Only with advanced aircraft will Ukraine be able to force its way through to the world economic area."*

This breakthrough was prepared in advance and with great deliberation by Balabuev and his many thousands of workers, engineers, pilots, and scientists. First of all, it was based on aircraft that are second to none in the world – Ruslan, Mriya, others – and then on development of the entire aircraft design and manufacturing complex, which actually was inherently the property of the republic, as well as its pride.

The funds that the government could allocate for these purposes were clearly insufficient. Advanced scientific research and development required advanced technologies for its implementation so the company had to earn its revenue itself, and this revenue had to be significant and in dollars.

This is how the Ruslan business unit (and not a commercial company) of Antonov StC was born and started its business of cargo transportations, which of course was not free of charge. For this purpose, the An-124 military transport aircraft was converted by Antonov StC into a civil transport 'heavy

draft horse'. Then they bought their own developments – several Ruslan aircraft – on credit from the state.

In order to fight its way to the world transportation market, they needed to find agents/representatives, and learn the business. The first steps in the air transportations business were not easy for Antonovans, and not always successful. Over time, they gained both experience and income. The loans/credits were paid back from the income, and the lion's share was spent on equipping Antonov StC.

Today the complex is fully equipped with computers, and has its own laboratories. More than US$14 million was spent on

this long and very heated discussion, in which the author of this account participated, there emerged very interesting information. In particular, the actual financial results of Ventrex's activities as a sales agent turned out to be much worse than Air Foyle's, and even worse than Antonov StC's own managers to whom Mr. Zenon intended to lecture. In addition, statements about a missed three millions-worth contract for transportation of stage equipment for Michael Jackson's world tour due to Antonovans' incompetence were nothing more than hogwash.

As a result, the collective strongly rejected Matkivskii's initiative as an attack on the integrity of the company and an attempt to deprive it of one of the main sources of funding for that period. As Balabuev expressed himself during the meeting, *"Making the transport department leave the company's structure during these rough times is the same as depriving the peasant of a working horse ..."*

However, the defeat in Kyiv did not stop the Americans who, by hook or by crook, continued to look for approaches for the precious Ruslan aircraft. Soon the leadership of Antonov StC had to defend its interests in the international arbitration court of New York. As an aside, representatives of Antonov Airlines insisted that the case should be considered in the court of the country of the defendant-company (Ventrex). This surprised the judges, who were accustomed to the plaintiff, as a rule, insisting on holding proceedings in his or her country. The American judge even said that this case would be included in textbooks on jurisprudence. To cut a long story short, the attempt of American 'well-wishers' to take possession of the aircraft failed.

However, adversity is the school of wisdom. This story, like the Jamirze lesson, taught the airline's staff a lot. In later years its Executive Director K. F. Lushakov said: *"Matkivskii's team, posing as patriots of Ukraine, pursued their personal interests to a huge extent. In air transportation they were amateurs and tried to rely on the services of amateurs. Having established Ventrex, they recruited those managers who were fired by Foyle and other well-known companies. They tried to break down our relationship with Christopher, but they failed ... This story allowed us to look at ourselves through different eyes – we were not so poor and unfortunate, we have a value if they are fighting for us so desperately."*

A new challenge presented itself as a result of two events. Following the break up of the Soviet Union and Ukraine's declaration of independence on 24 August 1991, Ukraine decided to issue its own currency instead of the Soviet Ruble. In January 1992 it introduced the Karbovanets and Kupon. Until then Antonov had been paying the An-124 engine Progress design bureau and Motor Sich production plant in Zaporizhzha in Ukraine in Rubles for engine overhaul and maintenance, so this could not continue. Furthermore, Progress and Motor Sich, noting that Antonov was earning US dollar revenue from its commercial flying, wanted to share in that revenue. Antonov could not agree with them the quantum of that dollar amount, nor, in any case, would Antonov be permitted by government regulations to pay another Ukrainian entity for its services in a foreign currency. A deadlock which could ground the aircraft emerged.

Piotr Balabuev asked Chris Foyle to go to Zaporizhzha and negotiate a solution with them. Chris Foyle recalls: *"Antonov lent us an An-74 and*

Love and dollars or behind the scandal

the latest technologies – millions that the company earned alone! This allowed the aircraft businesses of Ukraine to stand on a level with the world's leading aircraft designing and manufacturing companies, to obtain airworthiness certificates for their aircraft.

The most important factor was a certainty that despite the political and economic storms, the scientific potential of Ukrainian aviation would survive. The company's team with its long history was kept from falling apart and even in difficult, inflationary times aircraft bearing the Ukrainian national symbols have been designed and produced. Although given life by Russian and Uzbekistan plants, the profit

that they make is for Ukraine.

Examining the question of profits, the reproach to Balabuev by Yavorivskii's question *"How many dollars did you earn for Ukraine?"* was a strange and tactless one. The People's deputy was persistently hinting about a luckless US$3 million Michael Jackson contract but the net price of that contract was only US$800,000. As was proved by documents presented by Anatolii Bulanenko, Deputy Chief Designer and responsible for commercial cargo transportations, at the meeting with Antonov StC, it was Ventrex company, the agent of Ruslan, who let the contract slip. Or rather, that company simply deceived the Antonovans, making them believe until the very last day that

the contract was signed. Having held two aircraft in anticipation, Ruslan actually lost other, no less profitable contracts. It then, on its own, paid off the down time by earning US$500,000 in two weeks (and not in two months as under Jackson's contract).

This, then, is the essence of what happened. Ventrex was headed by Zenon Matkivskii, the physician from the USA who had been recently engaged in the aviation business. Of all Antonov StC's partners, his company was the weakest (this is confirmed by a number of documents) but it was also the most pushy aggressive partner. The Matkivskiis, who became famous in Ukraine as suppliers of humanitarian aid for Chernobyl victims, decided that they wanted no more

crew for the day and I and Bruce Bird flew down there. We walked into a large meeting room to be met by Mr Muravchenko the General Designer of Progress and Mr Boguslayev the General Director of Motor Sich, together with a large number of their acolytes, and, surprisingly, Alexei Isaikin the Chairman of our new Russian main competitor Volga-Dnepr Cargo Airlines. Initially, the atmosphere was tense but the discussion settled down and we managed to negotiate and conclude a mutually acceptable agreement as to what Air Foyle would pay Zaporizhzha in US dollars per flight hour flown for engine life and overhaul. We came back to Kyiv and a satisfied Antonov."

Meanwhile, co-operation with Foyle continued to expand. In 1991, the volume of transportations increased by 61% and reached 117,584,000 tkm. Commercial flying time of Ruslan aircraft for the year exceeded 3,080 hours. During this period, Antonov Airlines was actively searching for its niche in the world transport market, and for that reason

the list of cargoes was extremely wide: starting from unique manufacturing equipment that simply could not be transported by any other kind of transport to 'general cargo' – small packages packed on standard pallets for transportation, for which even passenger aircraft are suitable. The number of flights between foreign countries increased significantly. In January 1991, three transformers of 42 tonnes each were brought from Barcelona to New Caledonia during one flight. To move them inside the fuselage, for the first time roller beams – now widely used – were employed. In that flight, with its range reaching half the length of the earth's circumference, the total weight of cargo exceeded 140 tonnes.

Among the first contracts, a special place is held by an agreement with the large Luxembourg cargo carrier, Cargolux, specialising in the transportation of 'general cargo'. Firstly, it was a big and profitable contract; secondly, it clearly demonstrated the drawback of the Ruslan's inability to use modern airport handling equipment, and thirdly, it forced

From 1991 the inscriptions "Antonov" and "Air Foyle" appeared on the airline's aircraft.

---

unconditional arrangements with their historical homeland and wanted to convert the relationship onto a business footing.

Through the people's deputy Yavorivskii, the Cabinet of Ministers received recommendations for the establishment of a special Ukrainian Cargo Airlines company based on Ruslan. In the proposals (exclusively in English) explained that the aircraft must be taken from Antonov StC and renamed – because 'Ruslan' was a very pro-Russian name. All the old specialists in cargo transportation should be replaced with new ones and the leadership also had to include an ally of Matkivskii – presumably an American! There was no information on where the earned money would go.

The Antonov StC staff rebelled against this. "We won't let you take Ruslans away!" proclaimed the posters in the hands of workers. Today Ruslans are their only breadwinners. There is no point explaining what the people's deputies-demagogues have fed the country with. We would like explanations from elsewhere too. Why do our overseas guardians love only that in Ukraine which is clearly profitable? Their efforts are aimed in that direction only. And the local flag-waving patriots help them with everything.

The very same Matkivskiis established in Odessa a close connection with the Filatov Institute, known for its unique eye lenses used throughout the world. When a journalist asked 'Lady Nadia' why she didn't

return to Ukraine to direct her enthusiasm to the poor agricultural sector, Matkivska took offence. And Yavorivskii also took offence on behalf of his protégée. Indeed, how can you compare sugar beet and aircraft? This is something that cannot be compared!

The same is true of love and dollars.

Two 65-tonne gas-turbine generators are being prepared for shipping to Kuwait. London, January 1991.

serious changes to the organisation of Aviation Airline's aircraft and crews work by making them more adapted to conditions of the world market.

Cargolux had put one of its cargo Boeing 747s in for repairs and Mr. Foyle proposed to replace it with Ruslan. Looking ahead, the partners would have

had good opportunities for contracts for dozens of trips between Luxembourg and Singapore with computers and mass-produced items on board. As the speed of An-124 is slightly less than the Boeing's, during the first trial flight An-124 departed an hour ahead of the Cargolux's aircraft, but both aircraft

One of six giant excavators during loading operations at Stansted Airport, on route to Kuwait City. June 1991.

landed almost simultaneously. The unloading also began simultaneously; the Boeing had 90 tonnes of cargo on board, Ruslan 40 tonnes. In four hours the unloading of the Boeing was completed, in another four hours they loaded with new cargo, changed the crew and performed a return flight. For Ruslan similar operations took three days! During this time, Boeing flew back and forth several times and its pilots when returning from the next trip and seeing Kyivans still doing the same, began joking about them and their aircraft. The reason for this more than embarrassing situation was that the An-124 cargo floor did not have roller tracks and, as a result, international type pallets that were perfectly suited for Boeing 747 were not suitable for Ruslan, and the aircraft had to be loaded almost manually. The Chinese loading workmen could not work any faster and there was another problem – no material incentives for the crew to accelerate the loading and unloading process. Like all Soviet people abroad, the crew received a daily allowance regardless of whether they worked or were idle. It should be admitted that many were abroad for the first time and wanted to earn more and simply killed the clock.

Anatolii Naumenko, who performed the flight-manager's duties in that flight, on his return reported the situation to A. G. Bulanenko. As a result, there appeared a proposal to create a new payment system which would not slow down but

stimulate the work. Jointly with test pilot A. V. Galunenko such a proposal was prepared. The essence of it was to pay people extra money for real flight hours. A new system was quickly developed but great powers and outstanding courage were needed to implement it. After all, it absolutely did not fit the existing Soviet practice and violated the holy of holies of accounting instructions on calculating payments in foreign currency! *"We*

In the first flights of the contract with Cargolux, huge Ruslans were being loaded manually. Singapore, 1991.

In the spacious cargo cabin of the Ruslan autoloaders operate as in a warehouse. Luxembourg, 1991.

Organisers of the An-124 certification met at MAKS-2007 airshow. Left to right: General Designer D. S. Kiva, A. G. Kruglov, I. K. Mulkidzhanov, V. D. Kofman. Moscow, 2007.

Christopher Foyle in Washington DC in December 1990, obtaining the US permit from Jeffrey Shane US Assistant Secretary of Transportation allowing Antonov to fly to/from and within the United States.

reported to Balabuev," Naumenko said. *"Everyone was very afraid that the General Designer would have objections. But he understood us in a couple of minutes and gave his approval."*

The new payment system quickly yielded results – flight hours rose sharply, everyone at once became filled with ambition not to stay on the ground but fly. In order to accelerate the loading and unloading work, large pallets were made on which several standard pallets could be placed and all these were loaded into the aircraft with the help of overhead cranes. As a result, the time required for loading and unloading Ruslan aircraft was substantially reduced. However, in order to start flying under the contract with Cargolux, it was necessary to solve another important problem. In compliance with the established medical regulations, if the crew crosses

four time zones, it should rest for 24 hours, if eight time zones, two days' rest is required. When flying from Luxembourg to Singapore 10 time zones were left behind, so even if loading and unloading could be carried out quickly, the airport health control would still not let the crew make the return flight. The challenge was solved by taking on board an enlarged, so-called 'one-and-a-half' or 'reinforced' crew consisting not of two but three pilots, allowing two pilots-in-command, two navigators, etc. In addition, all aviation authorities were informed that Ruslan had separate compartments where crew members who were not busy could rest and therefore all medical norms were observed. In addition, they had a fully fledged onboard kitchen allowing for good nutrition.

As a result the contract with Cargolux was executed brilliantly. Two Ruslan aircraft belonging to Antonov Airlines made 62 flights on the Luxembourg-Kyiv-Singapore-Abu Dhabi-Kyiv-Luxembourg route, spending 33 hours flying time for one such trip, plus two loading/unloading cycles of eight hours each. During this period the efficiency of the An-124 usage reached peak levels. Thus, the monthly flying time on each aircraft exceeded 270 hours. For ramp-equipped cargo aircraft this is an incredibly high score. Pilots worked out their medical standard quota (80 hours flight time per month) in just three cycles; in other words, in a week! But fortunately, managers of the company's flight base took time to train enough pilots. After three trips the crews changed and Ruslans again went into the sky.

The apparent success achieved by during the first years of commercial operation of Ruslans had at least two serious consequences. Firstly, it inspired a group of employees from Ulyanovsk Aviation Industrial Complex to create in 1991 Volga-Dnepr Airlines – the second carrier, relying on using the unique capabilities of the An-124. Secondly, Western cargo airlines realised that they were dealing with an emerging competitor. It turned out that the Antonov Design Bureau (as they called Antonov Airlines according to its ICAO three-letter code) was actively creating a new sector of the freight market, offering services for airlifting such cargoes that none of western companies could fit into their aircraft. Rapid growth of Volga-Dnepr's fleet in the next few years further accelerated this process.

The first concerns of the leaders of the air freight market coincided with the request of the US Federal Aviation Administration (FAA) to the Aviation Register of the Interstate Aviation Committee (IAC) of the Commonwealth of Independent States (CIS) on the availability of type certificates of Soviet aircraft. This was due to the sudden influx of these cheap aircraft to the western transportation markets that followed immediately after collapse of the USSR. FAA seriously feared that all these An-12, Il-76 and Tu-134 did not comply with the requirements for safety established in the West. In response, the deputy chief of Aviation Register, V. V. Sushko, sent a list of those aircraft that were certified in the USSR as civil. An-124 was not on that list. All hell broke loose! FAA decisively stood guard over flight safety in the airspace of its country, and at the same time the interests of its own airlines, and in July 1992 banned flights of Ruslan aircraft in the United States. Diligently following the example of 'big brother', the same action was taken urgently by the aviation administrations of many other states.

It goes without saying that commercial aircraft must meet airworthiness requirements and the certification of An-124 aircraft at that time was already in progress. It was initiated by airline's managers who in real life faced problems caused by a lack of certificate. In a number of cases it was difficult to obtain permits to fly over territory and land, and sometimes Ruslan was simply blocked from entering the airspace of this or that country. In such situations only the unique capabilities of the aircraft saved the situation – the authorities had to turn a blind eye to formalities since there was no alternative to Ruslan. Employees of Antonov Airlines repeatedly posed this problem to the management. As a result of these appeals, in 1990 the General Designer P. V. Balabuev allowed part of the money being earned to be spent on purchasing

Brüel & Kjær equipment, which was placed along the runway in Gostomel and, following to American practices, measured the noise levels produced by An-124 during takeoff, landing, takeoff run, taxying, etc. These tests became a first milestone in the process of civil certification of Ruslan.

The ban on flights forced a significant intensification of these activities, which now went into full force. Besides IAC, the leading certification centres of the CIS and itself, also participating in this processes were the An-124 manufacturers – Ulyanovsk Aviation Industrial Complex (UAIC, now OJSC Aviastar) and Kyiv Aviation Production Association (KiAPO, then Aviant Kyiv State Aviation Plant, then Serial Plant Antonov), developers and manufacturers of D-18T engines – Zaporizhzha Machine-Building Design Bureau Progress (ZMKB, now the Ivchenko-Progress SE) and Motor Sich JSC, and the developers of avionics equipment, Volga-Dnepr Airlines.

D. S. Kiva, who in that period held the post of the First Deputy General Designer and supervised the aircraft certification process, said: *"The American ban affected both us and Volga-Dnepr, but they already had more Ruslans than us, and pushed them harder. Therefore, the management of Volga-Dnepr made a great effort to ensure that the Russian authorities, the IAC and its Aviation Register regarded the An-124 certification as an important task at state level. The Ulyanovsk airline, as well as*

The appearance of the An-124-100 marked not only a new stage of the airline's activities but also of the whole commercial aviation cargo business.

the Ulyanovsk Aviation Industrial Complex itself, took part in financing the activities. This money seriously helped fast and high-quality certification, since we had to rely only on our own resources, there were no government support. It should be emphasised that all practical work including actual development of a civil modification of the aircraft and its testing was carried out by the Antonov Company.

"The civil version of Ruslan is characterized by serious improvements in the cabin, availability of additional equipment, absence of a number of purely military systems, generally speaking – a full list of changes takes many pages. All this we reflected in the certification developed on the basis of *NLGS*-3 airworthiness requirements applicable at that time and validated in the IAC. Then during half a year we performed test flights of our aircraft, prepared correspondence tables. In order to speed up the certification procedure we used a lot of materials that were developed during official tests of An-124 as a military transport aircraft ... We certified a huge Ruslan without any discounts and indulgences. It was a huge job, the severity of which our partners shared with us. But it turned out that the costs incurred by Antonov Company were incomparably large. I'm not talking about money – during the certification process we lost aircraft and people in an accident. It was a severe loss for the company. However, it was not in vain – tests are meant to find the weak points of design and prevent the emergence of dangerous situations in real operation. Having analysed the causes of the accident we strengthened all the Ruslans, making them even more reliable."

For its part, the developer of the D-18T engines installed in the An-124, ZMBK Progress, also carried out extensive work on engine certification. Here is the story of the General Designer of aircraft engines F. M. Muravchenko: "Transformation of Ruslan into civilian aircraft posed many serious problems for us as well – the creators of the D-18T engine. It took about 40 additional activities, lots of new tests and checks, before the engine was ready for civil aviation." The civil version of Ruslan got the designation of An-124-100 – all the An-124s that were in commercial use were converted over time into this type, and all newly constructed ones were also manufactured in this version. On 30 December 1992 the Chairman of IAC T. G. Anodina presented to General Designer P. V. Balabuev the Type Certificate No. 24-124-100 for the An-124-100 as a civil transport aircraft. The D-18T engine also received Certificate No. 23-D.

"But even after the certificate was issued," D. S. Kiva continues, "the Americans still doubted the airworthiness of Ruslan and requested a number of documents to confirm it. I had to go to the FAA together with A. I. Isaikin and V. V. Sushko. For several days we negotiated, and demonstrated evidence. But even after that, the Americans did not lift the restrictions, and they sent a delegation of experts to us led by FAA Chief Executive Tony Broderick. Only having familiarized himself with the Antonov Company and being personally convinced that we had everything necessary to create aircraft that fully met modern requirements, did he call the US directly from us and instructed them to lift the ban. It was early 1993."

The importance of this event cannot be overestimated. It's fair to say that Aviation Airline's regained its wings. And then there was nothing to stop spreading them over the whole planet.

Ready for takeoff!

CHRONICLE OF ANTONOV AIRLINES: YEAR BY YEAR
Under market conditions (1993–1994)

Under market conditions

The Cargolux general cargo contract described in the previous chapter is only one episode on the hard and risky path that the airline has travelled in search of its place within the worldwide system of freight operations. This path began with the very first commercial flights performed by the Ruslans, if not earlier, and continued through the first period of Antonov Airlines' activity. One can say that this period ended when the company at last had found its own specific place in the market that hadn't existed before. Probably, the historic milestone described earlier can be compared to the human coming-of-age: indeed, a person feels mature, when he/she has found his/her true identity, his/her place in this life.

The airline approached the market with a unique aircraft of which the world was unaware and as a consequence had no idea how to use it in an effective way. Managers of Air Foyle and the Ruslan Company declared that they were capable of transporting cargoes of almost any size and weight but they received very few orders for such flights. The business environment had not yet got used to the fact that very heavy pieces of industrial equipment, transport systems, equipment for extraction of mineral resources etc could be shipped by air. Moreover, many people did not understand what they could do with this facility. As a result, the market situation was contrary to the classical one: the supply bred demand. However, something similar happens from time to time in aviation history. If we remember when the Boeing 747 was presented for the first time, very few people believed that it would be possible to find enough passengers for the aircraft. But today everyone knows that it became one of the most successful aircraft in history! The same happened to An-124: this aircraft created its own marketplace.

Perhaps the most important lesson learned from the Cargolux contract was understanding the fact that the Ruslan is not suitable for general cargo transportation (though all the problems that emerged during this transportation were solved). A. G. Bulanenko, who had the idea to use pallets which could be loaded using aircraft cargo handling equipment and installed roller tracks used for aerial delivery of military vehicles, played a large part in this. He assigned Y. V. Baitsur, the head of aerial delivery systems testing team, to prepare the corresponding design and establish manufacturing of such pallets at the Antonov flight test base in Gostomel. They produced three sets of rigid pallets 6 m x 2.8 m with load capacity of 10 tonnes each. These pallets could be lifted up by overhead cranes and moved along the fuselage using aerial delivery roller tracks. Twelve of these preloaded pallets were loaded into the aircraft within a few hours, but the pallets were too heavy: more than 1,000 kilos each. The habit of using all the space within the cargo cabin had led to the situation in which pieces of cargo were placed on the pallets, one on top of another, with the total height of up to 4 m, and as a result the lowest layers of the pile (boxes with computers, for instance) were in some instances smashed by the weight of the multi-layer pile on top of them. The problem was solved by buying 200 plywood sheets 10 mm thick which were placed between layers of boxes at the height of 1.3 m and 2.6 m. In some instances, low pressure in the An-124 cargo cabin (compared to passenger aircraft) caused cargoes to be damaged – some

The agreement between Antonov StC and Air Foyle company has been extended. From left to right: Dmitrii Kiva, Bruce Bird, Christopher Foyle, Piotr Balabuev, Arkadii Zharovsky and Anatolii Bulanenko, Kyiv, 1993.

(1993–1994)

packages opened in flight and consignees claimed for damages. In other words, experience in this business had proven that the Ruslan lost out to the Boeing-747-200, let alone the Boeing 747-400F. The main reason for the success of Cargolux contract was effective work management plus relatively cheap fuel that at that time was available in Kyiv, apart from on one occasion when the fuel delivery train disappeared – probably stolen!

"The very first years of operation revealed not only the high efficiency of the Ruslan but also some weak-points," wrote V. I. Tolmachev, Chief Designer of An-124, in 1991, "And the main problem was lack of general cargo transportation equipment meeting standard international requirements. Self-sufficient cargo handling equipment of the aircraft did not match cargo handling terminals of well-equipped international airports. This increases the time of loading of palletized cargoes." Later on, the possibility of equipping the aircraft with roller tracks like in *Boeing* aircraft to transport fruit, vegetables and flowers from warm countries, Colombia and Israel in particular, was studied thoroughly. But it turned out that these roller tracks are quite expensive to manufacture and each time the experts came to a conclusion that in this particular case the Ruslan would not be able to compete successfully with B-747 or DC-10. To the present day, general cargoes are transported in the Ruslan only in order not to fly empty on the return flight.

Step by step the marketplaces where An-124 effectiveness was doubtful were rejected and those market places where the aircraft was beyond competition stayed. One market selected was the transportation of low density outsized cargoes. Here is a fragment of A. N. Naumenko's memories about one of the flights made in 1989: "We had to carry 120 tonnes of rolled aluminum (by the way under the contract concluded by Jamirze) for the side of a supermarket in Melbourne. It took 30 huge trucks to bring the cargo to the aircraft. When all the aluminum was unloaded from the trucks and stocked around the Ruslan it seemed that its volume was three times as big as the aircraft itself. Aerodrome personnel were making bets on how much aluminum we would be able to load inside: there were different opinions 50%, 60% and 85% maximum. I fell under their influence and having grabbed the tape measure started measuring the cargo which turned out to be more than 900 m ^{3}.

But our team headed by V. I. Veresoka showed their excellent work (while the head of the team was like an orchestra conductor) and in 12 hours a hundred and a half of airport employees were standing open-mouthed and refusing to believe that there was enough space inside the fuselage for all that aluminum to fit in. No less admiration was caused in Melbourne: even 40 trucks were not enough! Many Australian and New Zealand newspapers dedicated their front pages to the Ruslan, Kurlin, Veresoka."

Australian interest in the aircraft is understandable: Boeings, which they had used previously, were not capable of doing such job! The An-124-100 and Antonov Airlines were spoken about in the most glowing terms for transporting various outsized pieces of equipment, including super-heavy self-propelled vehicles, but those are the very cargoes that the Ruslan was designed for.

Yu. V. Baitsur put a lot of effort into the development of the airline's cargo handling devices.

Unloading of general cargo pallets from the Ruslan, Luxembourg, 1990.

L.V. Zhebrovskii, An-124 maintenance senior engineer.

General cargo pallets were loaded using cargo handling cranes and moved along standard aerial delivery roller tracks.

The capability to carry such cargoes, along with broad multi-purposeness and long-term autonomy of operation are the huge advantage of An-124-100 over other heavy aircraft. Ever since this advantage became clear, Antonov Airlines has done everything to translate it into practice. Giving the floor to K. F. Lushakov: "We switched to specialisation in air transportation of outsized cargoes requiring special transportation preparation both of the cargo itself and the aircraft that is to transport it. This type of transportation service is a business area in which those who already have experience of such work and use aircraft designed for such operations feel the most confident. The appearance of the An-124-100 on the commercial transportation market had led to remarkable increase in worldwide demand for air transportation of outsized mechanical engineering products, manufacturing equipment, single-piece cargoes of up to 120 tonnes and more because this aircraft provided for consignors unprecedented capabilities.

Quickly spreading information about the aircraft has fed further growth of this market. Such companies as Lockheed Martin, Boeing, Loral, Volkswagen, Siemens, General Electric and others, whose main criteria for large-size cargo transportation were speed and range, became regular customers of Antonov Airlines. If during the first years the market of heavy and outsized cargo transportation was the market of urgent transportation or was driven by intention to avoid penalties for late delivery then later the intention of major manufacturers of outsized cargoes to plan ahead their usage of air transportations was clearly visible. For instance, Lockheed Martin, one of the most powerful airspace companies, signed a long-term contract for the transportation of outsized components of satellites and rockets inside the USA and between the USA, Europe and China. Moreover, its engineers started to take into account the dimensions of the Ruslan's cargo cabin as early as at the development stage in order to ensure that large-size structural components could be transported by our aircraft."

In addition, Boeing ordered Antonov Airlines aircraft for delivery of the engines of its newest airliner, Boeing 777, to the factory in Seattle where the main assembly line is located. In this time, An-124-100 crews have learned the routes connecting Boeing Field with the locations of General Electric and Pratt & Whitney engines assembly lines. When Rolls-Royce engines were to be installed onto the 777, Antonov Airlines flew them from Birmingham, England. Today, when there is a need to replace an engine on a Boeing 777 at any airport around the globe, Antonov Airlines is approached.

Thus, over the years the An-124-100 has become an essential link in the manufacturing chain of 'manufacturer-carrier-customer'. In its market area – single-piece cargoes with dimensions that do not fit any other aircraft in the world and weighing up to 150 tonnes – this aircraft is second to none. It was this type of transportation that made its name. For instance, Antonov Airlines holds the record for single-piece cargo air transportation, carrying a 135.2-tonne electrical generator made by the Siemens company from Dusseldorf, Germany, to Delhi, India. In 1995 this fact was listed in the Guinness Book of World Records. In 1998 a 132-tonne steam turbine from the same company was delivered to Chile and became the second heaviest cargo ever transported by an aircraft. In April that year the aircraft carried a 72-tonne water distillation plant to the Marshall Islands. The government of this island country was so impressed by this event that it issued a collectors' postage stamp to commemorate it. A 93-tonne axial steam turbine wheel was transported from Delhi to Kuala Lumpur (Malaysia) and everyone in the region was talking about it.

Gradually, these nearly unique transportations became the methodical work of Antonov Airlines

in the world market. Starting from 1993–94, 70% of flights performed by its Ruslans were shipments of non-standard outsized cargoes that do not fit other aircraft and which had been transported by ground or water before the An-124-100 was introduced. A list of these cargoes includes heavy energy generating equipment (turbines, generators, transformers), oilfield equipment for oil extraction and refining, chemical reactors, aerospace cargoes (space vehicles, aircraft components and engines, helicopter, launch vehicles), yachts, locomotives, stage equipment etc. The nature of these cargoes, is that either their large size makes air transportation more profitable or the cargo must be delivered to the destination very urgently or the profit that is to be lost in case of ground transportation is higher than aircraft rental costs. In short, the costs of air transportation of such cargoes are paid back to their owners with interest.

Antonov Airlines pays special attention to the preparation of such cargoes for transportation. The company specialists developed a package of special software for computer-aided modeling of An-124-100 and An-22 loading. Nowadays 3D mathematical models of the cargo cabin and large-size cargoes enable the development of a highly reliable loading procedure. Years of operation at this market have brought unique experience of different loading and unloading activities and the airline's aircraft get everything needed for the transportation of very wide assortment of cargoes.

It is necessary to say some words about the step-by-step improvement of aircraft cargo handling equipment. As with everything else in the Ruslan, this equipment initially was intended exclusively for military cargo handling and didn't match standard civil cargoes. The problems that were revealed by this threatened commercial operations many times, especially at the initial stage of Antonov Airlines' activity. In such cases only the quick-wittedness and professionalism of the aviators who discovered new capabilities of cargo handling equipment and the whole aircraft in critical situations saved the day.

One such episode is mentioned in the second chapter of this book. When in the winter of 1990 a large fire occurred at a hydroelectric power plant on the Zambezi river, two countries, Zambia and Zimbabwe, were left almost completely without electrical power. The United Nations decided to help the countries with repairing the power plant. The Ruslan Company was hired for the transportation of 35-tonne cable reels more than 4 metres in diameter. Ostensibly, this should have presented no problems. The An-124 payload capacity allows it to carry three reels in one flight. But immediately the question arose: how to load them into the aircraft? Carrying them inside using two overhead cranes was not possible: at that time their total tractive power

was limited to 20 tonnes. Rolling them inside was impossible too: the floor-concentrated load would be too high. If they tried to roll them along the ramp with covering plywood boards then the reel would have run into the cargo cabin ceiling. Of course, the reel could be placed horizontally and rolled using logs but even this variant would cause problems. The solution was found by L.V. Zhebrovsky who proposed to install four overhead cranes instead of two and lift the reels using this double set of cranes. There was some opposition to his proposal: such a variant of fuselage loading had not been considered when the An-124 was designed so it would require very careful calculations. But there was no time for these calculations as the contract was under deadline pressure so P. V. Balabuev, General Designer, agreed an experiment. In order to detect possible diagonal deformation of the fuselage, paper strips were glued to the skin. The 35-tonne cargo was lifted using four overhead cranes and all paper strips were undamaged. Everything was OK! Promptly, the aircraft flew to Oslo, loaded the reels in short order and delivered them to the destination point in time.

V. I. Bogaychuk,
Deputy Chief Designer.

Four-crane cargo handling system used for loading of 35-tonne power cord reels.

Deck for water turbine wheel loading, Kharkiv, 1986.

British partners of the airline also drew attention to the necessity of upgrading the cargo handling system of the Ruslan. As recollected by Bruce

Bird: *"I remember one of our early loads with large pressure vessels of 25 tonnes and 37 tonnes from Paris to Budapest. There was no*

Development of super-heavy and outsized cargo handling system

The An-124 aircraft was designed according to the military operation requirements of the Ministry of Defense of the USSR which required the possibility of loading into it only a clearly defined assortment of military cargoes. That list did not include non-self-propelled vehicles heavier than 20 tonnes which would need to be accommodated in the fuselage with the help of on-board cargo handling devices. Consequently, the maximum designed load of overhead cranes of the OCHE (onboard cargo handling equipment) was 20 tonnes. A wheeled or caterpillar vehicle with a mass of 50 tonnes maximum could enter through the nose loading ramp, and the axle weight could not exceed 12.5 tonnes. The aircraft was also equipped with two electric winches with

tractive power of 3,000 kg/ft for loading wheeled non-self-propelled vehicles. However, the very first transportations in the area of national economy ordered by the USSR government proved that these capabilities of the OCHE were absolutely not enough.

The first and truly unique transportation (because a unit of such size and weight hadn't been delivered by air before) took place in the summer of 1986. An 80-tonne hydroturbine wheel of 6.3 metres in diameter and 3.6 metres in height had to be delivered from Kharkiv to Tashkent. The designers faced the following problem: how to pull this single-piece cargo through the nose cargo ramp and then along the cargo cabin floor to the centre of gravity of

the aircraft? It was impossible to drive in a trailer with a turbine, because their total height was greater than the height of the cargo cabin, and the total weight of the trailer with the turbine was more than 120 tonnes.

Specially for this transportation, an external transfer and elevation deck and floor boards for the cargo floor were designed and manufactured, which then became the prototype of all further special systems for solving similar problems. The turbine itself was installed on 'skis' to move along the grooves made in the cargo floor boards and distribute its pressure on the floor. The device technical specification and drawings were developed by Designing Department 9 of our Design Bureau, and

loading system at that time and I was guessing at what advice to give to the customer. We received instructions from Kyiv to lay steel sheet on the *floor and fit the cargo with rollers. The customer equipped the cargo with the latest technology in rollers made of nylon. But at that time*

Loading of Mriya with the help of 'Foyle's loading deck', New York, USA, 2003.

I.D. Babenko,
veteran of Antonov Airlines

this device was manufactured by Kharkiv Turbine Plant. In order to protect the nose ramp of the aircraft from excessive loads, the deck connected to floor boards directly on the cargo floor, passing over the ramp lowered to the ground as during the normal 'kneeling' of the aircraft. The angle of the ramp was equal to the slope of the cargo floor, i. e. 3 degrees. The two side winches were to pull the load upwards with this angle. The main question was: how to reduce the frictional force between two steel surfaces – the skis and the grooves of the floor boards. To solve this problem Kharkiv turbine manufacturers proposed to add graphite powder to the grooves. Unfortunately, this was not enough: when moving, the powder was squeezed out

of the grooves causing an increase of the friction force, and consequently of the temperature at the contact points. There was a real risk that surfaces would weld together. To eliminate this, they decided to mix the powder with grease, which is used for the lubrication of loaded bearings. The pulling force was very high, but the two airborne winches of the aircraft managed to do this, and the loading was more or less successful. When the turbine loading was finished, the deck with a total mass of 40 tonnes (including floor boards) was disassembled and loaded into an aircraft for unloading in Tashkent.

There were two of such airlift missions which gave us invaluable experience. In future, when we faced similar problems we

tried to use the rolling approach rather than slipping by placing something with a round shape between the skis and the decking grooves including pieces of water-pipes.

The P-16 aerial delivery platform, 2.8 m wide and 6 m long with 20 tonnes loading capacity and equipped with wheels to move around the airfield, was used for the transportation of the Fazisi yacht from Sukhumi to London. Since its mass was within the limits the platform with the yacht installed on it was loaded into the aircraft with the help of winches. After that we used P-16 and P-7 aerial delivery platforms many times for various cargoes, which could not be lifted by cargo handling cranes due to different reasons.

Four cargo handling cranes were

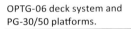

OPTG-06 deck system and
PG-30/50 platforms.

none of us understood the realities of loading the An-124 and the slight differences in angles between the ramp and aircraft floor produced very high loading on the individual rollers. The rollers began to shatter explosively beneath the cargo with nylon shrapnel whistling past our ankles. There was only

one way to deal with the situation and that was to keep on going, it is always easier to get the cargo off than get it on. Things are different now.

"There is another story involving this difference between the ramp and aircraft floor. Once an An-124 arrived at London Gatwick to deliver helicopters for a

Development of super-heavy and outsized cargo handling system

required to load 35-tonne power cord reels for delivery from Oslo to Lusaka since, as was already mentioned, the tractive power of two standard cranes was 20 tonnes only. We had to manufacture four special load distribution beams, each pair of which was lifted by two cranes. The reel was placed on these beams in the truck, then the truck drove closer to the aircraft and the beams were hooked to the cranes. In the years that followed, this four-crane loading system was rarely used because the load on the ceiling rails was high and it was difficult to synchronize operation of all hooks during cargo lifting, as well as the movement of the cranes along the fuselage. The three-cranes system was also used, but now the most widely used is the pulley block and

tackle system which allows an increase of two cargo handling cranes with tractive power up to 30 tonnes.

The very first year or two of the airline's activities had demonstrated that the majority of cargoes and equipment that were proposed for freighting required special loading racks. When the aircraft squats at the nose, the angle between the cargo cabin floor and horizon is 3 degrees, and the angle between the horizon and nose ramp is 8 degrees. This dog-leg prevents tall self-propelled vehicles from loading because their protruding parts hit the cabin ceiling before the vehicle passes the dog leg. This is especially noticeable when loading truck cranes with a long boom or excavators. The solution was found

when transporting three transformers from Barcelona to New Caledonia. The aircraft at 'squatting' position lowered the nose ramp not to the concrete pavement itself, but onto the supports, so that the ramp's plane was in line with the plane of the floor. And the deck, the length of which varied with the size of the cargo, was attached to the front edge of the ramp, which turned out to be at a certain height above the concrete pavement. Initially these decks were makeshift, the supports under the ramp, too, were made of locally available materials.

However, even in the days of the USSR, preparations began for the transportation of a 96-tonne axial turbine wheel from Leningrad to Tashkent for the hydroelectric

helicopter show in England. A truck was reversed into the aircraft to help with the offload. The driver was careless when leaving the aircraft and drove too fast so that the underside of the truck hit the aircraft ramp with a load bang. Everyone rushed to the aircraft to inspect the damage ... but it was the truck that was *damaged, not the aeroplane. An early lesson in the robust nature of Antonov aircraft."*

The adaptation of the Ruslan to cargoes has been an ongoing process for 30 years, starting from the time of the events described. Much work has been done by engineers and technicians and

The so called 'Foyle's loading deck' for self-propelled vehicles.

power station being built in Central Asia. Having experience of transportation of a turbine wheel from Kharkiv, the team of designers under the supervision of V. I. Bogaychuk designed a special deck that allowed the loading of this wheel without kneeling the aircraft nose landing gear. The deck was a U-shaped truss structure, on top of which was a two-lane roller system with guide rails along the entire length and a continuation along the cargo cabin floor.

This transfer and elevation deck was made at the same Leningrad Electro-Mechanical Plant and was a powerful 37-tonne structure. Its assembly took 10–12 hours. Despite all its weak points, this deck helped to deliver a turbine wheel to Tashkent in August 1992.

Initially, the airline rented this deck but later it was bought and used several times. The most successful transportation carried out with its help was the delivery of a new electric locomotive produced by General Motors from Canada to Ireland in 1994. The weight of the electric locomotive itself was 102 tonnes, so that along with the deck the total weight of the cargo on board was more than 140 tonnes.

Eventually, it was decided to make special sectional decks of two types – for self-propelled vehicles and for non-self-propelled single-piece cargoes. The deck for self-propelled vehicles was manufactured in England through an order from Foyle, and it was henceforth called 'Foyle's deck', unlike other ones

manufactured in Kyiv. The flat top surface trimmed with corrugated aluminum plates enabled the entry of any vehicle whose height was less than the height of the cargo cabin. The deck consisted of three-metre sections, which were easily placed in the cargo cabin next to the cargo. Some sections of this deck were used to load the Rolls-Royce engines into An-22 aircraft when they were transported from England to France, to a plant in Toulouse.

The loading of transformers, stators and rotors of turbines and other similar cargoes without wheels that could not enter the fuselage by truck because of their size required another solution. A universal cargo loading system was designed for this purpose. It included a deck, which was a

142-tonne transformer placed on OPTG-120 deck.

a deep experience of commercial transportations has been gained to allow the Antonov Airlines' executive director to say with full authority: *"Today each aircraft of Antonov Airlines is equipped with everything needed for loading and unloading of cargo in 95% of cases. Situations when we need to invent something new are very rare these days."*

The heaviest cargoes and the cargoes with the largest size are loaded into the aircraft through the nose cargo door using special transfer and elevation decks. These sectional structures are transported

Development of super-heavy and outsized cargo handling system

continuation of the forward ramp of the aircraft, floor boards for the cargo floor and roller sections. Roller sections, each having six rollers 100 mm in diameter connected to each other, enabled the rolling of the load. The platforms with the cargo on them were placed on rollers. This system called OPTG-06 had two disadvantages — it was very heavy (17,325 kg without the platforms of 2,500 kg each, since all components were made of steel), and very high (about 200 mm without platforms), which limited the dimensions of the cargo being transported. As the cargo moved, the free roller sections had to be moved forward and laid in the groove.

A new deck system called OPTG-120 was designed and manufactured in 2000. It was made of aluminum alloys using rollers from aerial delivery roller tracks. This reduced the weight of the system without platforms more than three (!) times — down to 5,150 kg. Two sets of this system are currently in use, while OPTG-06 was put into storage. OPTG-120 has four fixed roller tracks, two in each line, a 12-metre-long deck and eight platforms each 3 metres long and weighing 186 kg. Four platforms, connected together, can carry a cargo of up to 120 tonnes. The overall height of the system with a platform is about 115 mm.

Each shipment of a super-heavy and

outsized cargo requires careful preliminary study, because in the form in which it is transported along the road, it often cannot be loaded on the aircraft. The Airline specialists from time to time travel to the customer and on site develop a loading technology, discussing the specifics of using special loading systems. This is especially true for transformers, since with small base dimensions these devices have a high weight, which must be distributed in accordance with the strength of the cargo floor of the aircraft. A vivid example of such a transport operation was the transportation of a transformer by An-225 aircraft using freighting framework with

Loading subway cars at Schwerin airport (West Germany).

on board the Ruslan. Then they are installed: they look like extensions of the cargo floor but go far beyond its overall dimensions. Powerful motorized cranes can lift a single-piece cargo up to 150 tonnes and place it on the deck and then the cargoes are rolled along the rollers inside the fuselage. The decks are the last-resort solution. The time required for their installation and removal increase the total time spent for loading/unloading and requires additional effort. They also require a place inside the fuselage for storage. That is why the designers of Antonov StC are constantly working to enhance

a total mass of 142 tonnes from Austria (Linz) to the USA (Phoenix, Arizona). The freighting framework was equipped with two 'skis' each 15 metres long and loaded with the help of OPTG-120.

Another example was the delivery of six subway cars from Germany to China in three flights. Initially six flights were planned since the fuselage of the Ruslan could accommodate only one car at time. However, after careful study of this transport problem, the specialists of the airline (D. K. Kurko) found that removal of the bogies from the cars would make possible the loading of two cars next to each other, placing the bogies along

with them in the free space, which was what they did. A special deck was built, since the subway car was 24 metres long, and the cars were equipped with low transportation trolleys. Despite these additional costs, the customer got significant benefits because the number of flights was halved.

propelled vehicles up to 30 tonnes. In addition, the airline's aircraft are equipped with special devices which allow for both lengthwise and crosswise movement of cargoes inside the fuselage, using the available useful volume in a more efficient way.

Improvement of the An-124-100 cargo handling equipment has become an important part of a wide range of activities aimed at bringing the former military transport aircraft into compliance with the commercial operation conditions of the world market. Alongside the enhancement of expertise of the airline's management and its general commercial agent, this has enabled it to increase steadily the volume of transportation services provided for customers across the globe. As early as in 1993 the airline managed to overcome the negative effect of the six-month grounding of the previous year caused by the absence of civil type certification for the Ruslan. The airlift tonnage of 122,397,000 t*km exceeded not only the 1992 level but also that of 1991. By the end of the next year, 1994, the cargo turn-over reached 143,512,000 t*km, and total flight time of the fleet was 5,968 hours.

In those years Ukraine was struggling with the hardest period of the 1990s crisis connected with

OPTG-120 deck floor boards.

Very long cargoes required two sets of OPTG-120 decks.

the capabilities of the standard Ruslan's cargo handling equipment which in particular includes two overhead cranes moving along the ceiling of the cargo cabin. Currently these cranes are the only means of loading different types of non-self-

the collapse of the USSR, and the air transportation division of Antonov StC was one of very few Ukrainian enterprises which experienced some stability of operation. But even it required support. It was fortunate that the state didn't forget that it was the owner of Antonov StC and, notwithstanding the ominous economic situation, was trying to do what it could do. One of the strongest measures that were put in place by the Ukrainian government was the decree of the Cabinet of Ministers No. 477 dated 17 August 1992. The document's name was *"Measures aimed at implementation of the order of the President of Ukraine dated 3 July 1992, Ukraine aerospace industry development programme"* which was signed by the then prime minister V. Fokin. Item ten of the decree stated: *"Make a provision for additional funding of the Programme in line with public funding. In view of this leave to Aviation the scientific and technical complex named after O.K. Antonov for permanent perpetual use the An-124 aircraft Nos. 01-05, 01-06, 01-08 ... for commercial operation by Ruslan freight company with the following use of income for Programme implementation."* Therefore, the above-mentioned aircraft transferred from being rented by the airline

to being owned by it.

For the sake of fairness, we need to emphasise that the above-mentioned programme was implemented for the most part; moreover, it was the only programme of this nature among all the other programmes for the

The Siemens 135.2-tonne generator was listed in the *Guinness Book of Records*.

Transporting Boeing 777 engines.

The Marshall Islands' postage stamp issued in honour of the Ruslan.

Anything can be loaded into the Ruslan, and the Ruslan can carry anything!

Intensive commercial operation of the Ruslans allowed the founding principles of the Ukraine aerospace industry development programme to be put into action.

development of other branches of Ukrainian industry! In those years, several types of new competitive aircraft were designed, a number of older aircraft were retrofitted, and work on advanced aircraft started. This is the best proof of the fact that the decree of the Cabinet of Ministers mentioned above was put into life wholeheartedly by Antonov StC employees! Also, that the money earned from air transportation was invested exactly in that business, as was provided for by that document. During the time of writing this book, the author examined the evidence and has become convinced that without the contribution of Antonov Airlines the Ukraine aerospace industry development programme would remain ink on

paper, as happened to the majority of the post-USSR countries. That is why even at that time in the mid-1990s P. V. Balabuev with good reason said:

"After the collapse of the USSR the Antonov Company started intense commercial operation of the Ruslans and the inflow of foreign currency driven by this operation was used for the implementation of the Ukraine aerospace industry development programme. This money allowed us to keep the scientific and engineering potential of our enterprise during the transition period of the 1990s, to continue working on the development of the new generation aircraft An-70 and An-140 and eventually kept the aviation industry of Ukraine safe from complete devastation."

CHRONICLE OF ANTONOV AIRLINES: YEAR BY YEAR
World fame (1995–1996)

World fame

Having entered the world market and accomplished their first noteworthy achievements, the next concern for Antonov Airlines was the necessity to increase labour productivity caused by the growth in competition. The middle of the 1990s was a peak of the other airlines' activities that followed Antonov Airlines and Volga-Dnepr with operation of An-124-100 aircraft. Rossia State transport company, Magistralnyie Avialinii, Antonov Air Track, Trans-Charter, Titan, Ayaks and Poliot airlines started operating at that time. All of them aimed to repeat the success of the pioneers and gain their own market share using different and

The An-124-100 has been the main Antonov Airlines aircraft type for 30 years.

sometimes dubious methods. In order to retain its leading position under such circumstances, the aviation transport subdivision of Antonov StC had to work hard to improve all the components of its aviation transport business.

First, great attention was paid to enhance the main means of such business – the An-124 aircraft. As mentioned before, Antonov Airlines entered the market unique in its capabilities but poorly adapted for commercial operation. The Ruslans were in fact military transports, which was why the first task was to enhance the An-124 to comply with the market standards, to introduce the aircraft to those conditions the An-124 had been operated under.

(1995–1996)

Primarily, they removed all the equipment for military applications that had become unnecessary – radio-electronic and para-dropping – and they changed the composition of the oxygen equipment. They installed the equipment necessary to perform flights on international routes – radio stations with civil frequency wavebands, flight-control instruments scaled in feet, collision avoidance systems, etc. The extension angle limit of the flaps was reduced from 40 ° to 30 °. After the crash of the Ruslan during certification tests, the nose cone of the aircraft was modified. As the airframe life expectancy rate for commercial operation is 1.7–2.2 times higher than that for military aircraft,

they developed a new system for prolongation of airframe life expectancy which guaranteed safety even under very high intensity of aircraft operation. For the civil certification of the An-124-100 aircraft, they implemented the following important modifications: refinement of crew rest compartments; organisation of recreation areas for technical crew; vital instructions in English; installation of buffets, refrigerators, toilets, etc.

As an aside, the toilets, which were so important during long-haul flights, were not stipulated at all in the initial military versions of the aircraft for quite valid reasons, which we need to go into here. However, the absence of toilets in a commercial aircraft would have been acutely felt, with unexpected consequences. Anatolii Naumenko reminisces about this: *"November 1989. Our Ruslan was to become the first Soviet aircraft flown to New Zealand. We were preparing to deliver television equipment from Melbourne to Auckland to illuminate the British Commonwealth Games (in total, 34 countries!) that were under preparation in Auckland. On 8 November, in the morning, when we had already been ready for takeoff, a car drew up to the runway and we were passed the latest newspapers. It turned out that the mayor of Auckland had appealed to the Ruslan's crew with a request. As it would had been not only the first Soviet aircraft over their city but also the world biggest transport, the mayor requested it to circle over Auckland at low altitude to let citizens better scrutinize the giant. Moreover, in order to describe the event from within, 20 New Zealand journalists embarked in our forward cabin of the upper deck. Not to be bored during the flight they thoroughly stocked up with beer, which had been drunk to the last drop within 4 hours. And here I reach the crux of the tale: the Ruslan wasn't equipped with a toilet at that time. I set down two buckets, which became completely filled up by the end of the flight.*

"While approaching Auckland we requested permission for a demonstration flight. The air traffic control tower approved it. Kurlin (Yurii Vladimirovich was the captain) said: 'Even though we have 75 tonnes aboard, we will perform our standard demonstration flight as we usually do during exhibitions.' We performed the entire programme at 270–300 m altitude: eight aerobatic maneuvers in both directions, turns at zooms, etc. Everyone was in wild rapture on the ground.

A. G. Bulanenko – a patriarch of air cargo transportation.

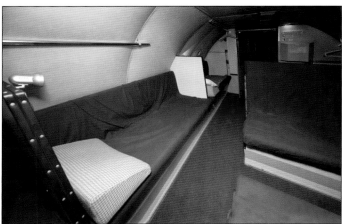

All necessary conveniences for effective work and good rest for flight and technical crews are provided on board the An-124-100.

Next day the morning newspapers reported that the Ruslan's arrival had paralyzed all the traffic in the city for half an hour. They published pictures – hundreds of people standing on the roofs of their cars looking into the sky. While landing I put on a headset and heard someone engaged in a crew conversation with the tower. He said he had been a pilot of Boeing, he had been piloting for 30 years but had never seen such a miracle yet. Everything was ready for an important meeting in the airport; a happy mayor headed a group of officials.

"It should be noted that Yurii Vladimirovich piloted the aircraft so expertly that not a single drop spilled from the buckets. He also landed the aircraft very carefully. I sighed with relief but it was premature. We started taxying, trying to get as close as possible to the people meeting us. As we got closer, the flight engineer suddenly screamed: 'Yurii Vladimirovich, the tow bar doesn't fit.' We had a tow bar more than 10 m long and we also needed to have a spare space for the towing tractor. And Kurlin jammed on the brakes! As a result, both buckets toppled over ... Everyone, crew members and journalists, instantly raised their legs and some of them even closed their noses and froze like that. It was only I who walked – I did not care anymore. A ruckus began. Crew members accused Kurlin: 'It is your fault so you have to clean up!' He appealed to

me: 'Anatolii, do something about this! I understand that you are a manager, but I am dressed in a suit, so I cannot. Take a rag!'

"Time passed. The people meeting us were worried about why we did not open the door, why we did not leave the aircraft. In about 10 minutes, our technicians managed to get down from the rear cabin, make their way through the cargo compartment and open the aircraft entrance door. Immediately local television representatives started climbing the aircraft board. A horrible situation ... Fortunately, we managed to hush up this unpleasant episode at the time, but on our arrival in Kyiv, I told Balabuev everything. He was very angry with me, but after that accident our Ruslans became the first to be equipped with toilets."

Such things happen ... Due to the measures taken, the aircraft corresponded more and more to its new commercial conditions of operation, although some of its shortcomings persisted. Unreliable engine operation was the biggest shortcoming at that period. Veterans of Antonov Airlines said that the D-18T engines failed so often that we considered the situation to be permanent failure. That was a problem of all the Ruslans, not only Kyiv's ones. Here is one of the cases of failure, witnessed by I. D. Babenko: "At Christmas 1992, one of the Ruslans, owned by Volga-Dnepr

Airlines, performed a charity flight to Sarajevo with gifts for children. The aircraft arrived at Liverpool in the morning and started loading procedure in the presence, probably, of thousands of English children who had come to see off their gifts. In 4-5 hours, the aircraft was completely loaded and the crew started the engines up. The engine #2, located on the same side as the audience, failed to start up. An hour later, after numerous and unsuccessful attempts to start the engine, this procedure was stopped. The audience was asked to go home. At night another aircraft flew to Liverpool, the gifts were reloaded into it and the aircraft flew away without witnesses. Sometimes a crew had to take off with only three engines in operation as for one reason or another it was impossible to replace the engine at the time of its failure."

However, D-18T engines failed in the air even more often than on the ground; such failures happened not only during takeoff but also at other flight stages, including landing. At the beginning of 1990 Antonov Airlines fulfilled a contract with Volkswagen involving the transportation of processing equipment from Germany to Mexico. The destination aerodrome was located at an altitude of 2.2 km, and the heat there reached +46°C. According to the contract, both the Ruslans flew away almost simultaneously. The first aircraft, piloted by A. V. Galunenko, arrived at this aerodrome in the afternoon, at the hottest time of the day. Having activated reverse thrust during the landing run, one of the engines 'caught', as they say. There was a colossal surge, with flames emanating from the rear of the engine. An hour later, the second aircraft arrived and exactly the same thing happened. So, both the Ruslans of Antonov Airlines were grounded in Mexico and there wasn't a specialist available who could make qualified decision as to the engines. A profitable contract for 15 flights was in jeopardy.

However, Alexander Vasilyevich was not only an excellent pilot but had a solid reputation as a good engineer. He proposed the following plan of action. Initially, the idea was simply to inspect the engines visually first. If no obvious faults were found, he proposed to take one of the aircraft off without cargo at night, when the heat had reduced. He proposed to slightly 'run' the engine during the test flight. *"I have a feeling that everything should be fine"*, said Alexander Vasilyevich. He explained his plan to the Design Bureau specialists on the phone. Those specialists, in their turn, consulted ZMBK Progress and P. V. Balabuev allowed the flight to take place. The plan succeeded – the engine operated normally. Both aircraft came back to Germany without even flying to Kyiv as it could have delayed the contract fulfilment. Having been loaded, these aircraft performed flights to Mexico

F. M. Muravchenko, General Designer of engines, and Ivchenko-Progress State Enterprise, headed by him, work continuously to further upgrade the D-18T engine.

D-18T engines are in compliance with modern requirements on noise level and emission.

Cargoes, transported on the UN request, were of a huge variety.

combined with high temperature and reverse thrust caused a surge. If we perform a landing like that again, we will have the same surge. That is why I invented a new method for landing and I was going to test it right at that moment. And then I intended to inform the second aircraft whether I had succeeded or not." He activated reverse thrust at increased speed mode when the aircraft was still in the air, just before touchdown. It helped – all engines operated steadily. Of course, officially, an activation of reverse thrust while in the air is a violation of the aircraft flight manual. However, the decision of the first-class test-pilot A. V. Galunenko should be considered an example of a creative approach in a critical situation caused by unreliable engine operation in extreme climatic conditions. Such a decision made it possible to avoid a much greater risk. In this way they performed 13 more landings, each with a 100-tonne cargo – and there were no problems!

As was found out later, the reason for the low gas-dynamic stability of the 0- and 1- series D-18T engines was the increase of clearances between turbine-blade tips and stator during engine operation. There were other reasons for the power plant failures. However, due to the efforts of the engine developer, ZMBK Progress from Zaporizhzha, the detected shortcomings of the D-18T were successfully eliminated. From 1997 they started producing engines of the 3rd series, which absorbed the long-term experience of D-18T engine operation; they applied a whole series of steps in order to increase engine reliability and economic efficiency and to prolong service life. The assigned service life of these engines reached 24,000 hours. All the 0- and 1- series engines installed on Antonov Airlines' aircraft, were upgraded to 3- series levels during planned refits. As a result, the improved engines turned into the so-called H-profile engines, which meant reliable!

However, bringing the reliability of the engines to the required levels was only half the battle. It was important that they fully met all the requirements imposed on them by operation as commercial aircraft, including noise level requirements. In order to ensure compliance with the requirements of Chapter 3 of Annex 16 to the ICAO Convention on noise level, the nacelles of all the An-124-100 aircraft were equipped with sound-absorbing elements. Moreover, at the time when this book was being prepared to be published, they were working to ensure compliance with the requirements of the next Chapter 4 noise certification.

As for other aircraft systems and equipment, the reliability of their operation was generally satisfactory. There were some failures of hydraulic pumps, power generators and elements of electronic equipment, but due to multiple back-ups

again. Just before an approach Galunenko said: "I believe a combination of rarefied air at altitude

they did not lead to serious consequences. Onboard they always had spare units for those which failed most often. Technical crew members were highly professional, so the majority of such faults were eliminated immediately after landing and unloading at airports around the world.

As time has passed, the ICAO's requirements for aircraft, flying on international routes had been constantly getting tougher. In order to meet such requirements the equipment of the An-124-100 aircraft was permanently upgraded. Thus, at the very beginning of the 2000s the aircraft were equipped with 3MGPS satellite navigation system. When vertical separation intervals for aircraft flying over the Atlantic were reduced to 300 m, they provided the necessary modification and got the Type Certificate Supplement. They also equipped the aircraft with TCAS-2000 traffic collision avoidance system, manufactured by Honeywell, as well as SPPZ-3 Terrain Awareness and Warning System. In accordance with Eurocontrol requirements, the aircraft were equipped with new radio stations with 8.33 kHz frequency grid. However, the process of improving the Ruslan's type design is still ongoing. Taking into account the experience of the aircraft operation, some elements of the wing and fuselage are being reinforced and the front ramp and cargo floor are being improved for the convenience of land fork lift operation. They are also perfecting anti-corrosive protection for some vulnerable areas, etc.

In August 2004 Antonov Airlines developed the An-124-100M-150B – a model of the Ruslan with increased maximum payload up to 150 tonnes, increased maximum takeoff weight from 392 to 402 tonnes, and increased flight range, including while loaded with a cargo of 120 tonnes, from 4,750 to 5,300 km. An important advantage of the An-124-100M-150B was the simplification and acceleration of the loading of single-piece cargoes of up to 120 tonnes. In accordance with Eurocontrol requirements on Precision-Area Navigation (P-RNAV) in terminal areas, the renewed Ruslans were equipped with upgraded navigation equipment that made it possible to reduce the number of flight crew members from 6 to 4. In August 2009, based on the results of additional fatigue tests of aircraft units, calculation and research work, and having taken into consideration their individual utilisation during the service life of each aircraft and analysed the operational experience of the Ruslan's airframe, the aircraft was assigned a service life of 50,000 flying hours, 10,000 flights and 45 calendar years.

The process of further development of the An-124, its systems, equipment, methods of application and maintenance, did not stop for a minute. Modernisation of the aircraft continues

and nowadays a significant proportion of its equipment, totalling more than 100 items, has been replaced with upgraded equipment produced by leading Western companies. The aircraft's avionics gradually became completely digital; the same applying to the power plant control system, where the principle of Full Authority Digital Engine Control system (FADEC) has been implemented. At present, instruments with a pointer indication in the cockpit are being replaced with multifunction displays.

The management of Antonov StC and Antonov Airlines has always paid, and still pays, considerable attention to the Ruslan, considering this outstanding aircraft to be one of the cornerstones of maintaining its competitiveness in the global air cargo transportation market. As a result, Antonov Airlines' aircraft are always ahead of the Ruslans

The UN's cargoes have been delivered to Monrovia, the capital of Liberia.

A. V. Galunenko,
Honoured test-pilot of
the USSR and the Hero of
Ukraine, with P. V. Balabuev,
General Designer.

it allows, without excessive formalities and delays, the entire production and scientific potential of the Company to be used for the constant airworthiness maintenance of the aircraft. In particular, the presence of highly skilled specialists on board the Ruslans, many of whom took part in development of these aircraft, allows confident autonomous operation of the An-124-100 for long periods at a considerable distance from the main base of Antonov Airlines, located in Gostomel town near Kyiv. As mentioned previously, the typical operating mode of the aircraft stipulates a stay away from base for periods of up to three months. Secondly, this ensures that Antonov Airlines remain technological leaders compared to other operators of these aircraft. Thus, the An-124s of Antonov Airlines were the first to be converted to the An-124-100 type and then went through a set of improvements to meet the requirements of Chapter 3 on noise level. In addition, they were upgraded with collision avoidance systems, regional navigation, equipment for flights with reduced vertical separation intervals and many other advances prior to such enhancements being implemented on other Ruslans. The status of this part of Antonov StC guarantees Antonov Airlines technological leadership in the future market of large-sized super-heavy cargo transportation due to the priority of the An-124-100M-150 and the An-225 aircraft being incorporated into the fleet. Thirdly, it enables the company to carry out really unique transport

of other companies in terms of the number of improvements implemented on them. By 2001, the advances achieved had allowed Antonov Airlines' aircraft to increase the routine maintenance period to 500 hours. And this is only one of the favourable consequences of the fact that Antonov Airlines' aircraft are under constant supervision by the leading experts of the Design Bureau, which, like Antonov Airlines itself, is a component of the unified Antonov StC.

In general, the unified identity of Antonov Airlines and Antonov StC has many positive aspects. First,

Antonov Airlines' aircraft are
frequent guests in the 'dark'
continent.

The helicopters, repaired in Ukraine, delivered to Sri Lanka.

operations that require the use of all the capabilities in the aircraft's design, because only the aircraft's developers understand these reserves. Additionally, transport operations such as these, require the development of special methods for loading and unloading, as well as special equipment. In such cases, the assistance of the Design Bureau allows the contract to be executed in the shortest possible time, with the safety of the cargo guaranteed and that it will be correctly transported. Fourthly, after decades of teamwork, Antonov StC has developed a stable system of partnerships with developers and manufacturers of engines, equipment and other units, that, of course, helps Antonov Airlines to deal quickly and reliably with the issues of spare parts supply, repair and service life prolongation.

Transportation of a locomotive weighing 140.1 tonnes, produced by General Motors, from Canada to Ireland. June 1994.

V. V. Nets is one of the most experienced load-masters of Antonov Airlines.

However, we will not tire the readers with stating the obvious. A representative of any competing airline can easily continue this list, recognizing that his or her enterprise is deprived of such support and that the Kyiv air carrier is known to be the most profitable in this market. For us, who are trying to judge the phenomenon of Antonov Airlines as impartially as possible, it is interesting to ponder such observations ... In truth, this does give certain benefits to Antonov Airlines. Its commercial structure does have trump cards in the market game. The support of other sub-divisions of Antonov StC has become a trump card for Antonov Airlines. However, the air transport sub-division has to pay in full for such an advantage, in the literal sense, being an important source of financing for the Company's core business – aircraft development. Competitors do not include such factors in their list of the benefits of Antonov Airlines' position. Here again they make a mistake, considering Antonov StC's air transport sub-division by criteria typical for classic airlines. But for us it is quite obvious: Antonov Airlines is a unique structure. And what other people consider as the compulsory handing over of money earned, is in fact the main mission of Antonov Airlines.

As an aside, within the period described – 1995–96 – a special responsibility was allocated to Antonov Airlines. The next phase of the economic crisis was raging in the country, and the Antonov StC team had just survived a terrible loss – the first prototype of the new generation An-70 transport had crashed. Antonov StC's specialists put all their efforts to build a second prototype of this aircraft without stopping the An-140 regional passenger aircraft development. The lion's share of financial support for both promising programmes fell at that time on the shoulders of Antonov Airlines, and it fulfilled its duty with admirably, doing its best to make the future of its Company more secure. To

S. I. Kogut is an employee of the commercial department of Antonov Airlines.

support a world-famous aircraft manufacturer with more than a half-a-century history at a difficult time – can any of the other, classic airlines boast of such an achievement?

It is interesting, to note the fate of the airlines mentioned at the beginning of the chapter, which were all established with a more classic commercial set up. Except for Volga-Dnepr and Poliot, all of them, after having worked for a year or two, 'went off stage'. It turned out that with only one or two An-124-100 aircraft, it was hard to survive in the market: the airworthiness maintenance system of this aircraft is too complicated. The agent network also needed to be wide enough to provide the aircraft with business. Experience has shown that it is possible to resolve problems smoothly by operating at least seven or eight Ruslans but Antonov Airlines, having at first only two aircraft, had successfully entered the world market and firmly established its position in it. Only the comprehensive support of such a heavyweight company as Antonov StC allowed Antonov Airlines to reach such a dominant position.

Having traversed high in the world arena, by the mid-1990s Antonov Airlines had earned a reputation as an exceptionally reliable air carrier. For example, by that time Antonov Airlines had already performed flights to 347 airports in 138 countries of the world; even in the USA the Ruslans of Antonov Airlines had visited 52 cities! The majority of states recognized the right of Antonov Airlines to fly with the so-called fifth freedom rights, which permits the operation of commercial flights between two countries by a carrier registered in a third country. Not every airline is awarded this but experience has demonstrated that Antonov StC can deal with the most difficult situations. The second half of the last decade of the twentieth century was full of exactly such situations. Civil wars and ethnic conflicts, man-made and natural disasters continually arose in various parts of the world. In response to these cataclysms, the United Nations at that time significantly intensified its activities, which led to a growth of its demand for air transportation of a wide variety of goods. Taking into account the positive experience of cooperation with Antonov Airlines in the beginning of the decade, the UN significantly increased the amount of business for its services in 1994-95.

This wasn't just a matter of its good reputation. One of the most important reasons for the increased number of contracts was the availability of large-capacity aircraft like the An-124-100 in Antonov Airlines' fleet. Such aircraft were an irreplaceable means of delivering to 'hot spots' large-sized cargoes, such as heavy trucks, camp kitchens, field hospitals, helicopters, construction equipment, rescue and cleaning equipment, etc. At the same time, thanks to the large volume of the cargo compartment and availability of autonomous loading and unloading equipment, these aircraft were well suited for transportation of ordinary humanitarian goods – tents, medicines, food, light vehicles, generators, everything that victims may need. When flying to airports with infrastructure destroyed by disaster or war, the Ruslans' capacity for extended autonomous operation became especially important.

Another important reason was that having transport aircraft of various classes, Antonov Airlines always offered a comprehensive solution to the task, ensuring the delivery of goods directly to their addressee almost regardless of the airport conditions or even without a landing field available at the destination. The cargo was transported by the An-124-100s or the An-22s to the major airport nearest to the disaster point, and from there to the disaster area by smaller An-12 and the An-32 aircraft capable of landing on short unpaved runways. In addition, if the situation required, the cargo could be airdropped by parachute from any type of aircraft, including the Ruslan; and this was another significant advantage of cooperation with Antonov Airlines. Other civilian airlines were unable to perform such missions because either their aircraft were not provided with the necessary equipment or the pilots were not trained in parachute airdropping methods. The An-32 aircraft, in the fleet of Antonov Airlines until 2003, were equipped with special fire-fighting equipment that allowed them to be used for firefighting missions in Ukraine, Russia, Spain and Portugal. Due to this special equipment, the An-32s were able to deliver drinking water to disaster areas.

And there is one more important point. Usually, in case of various crises, a very quick response was required from the international organisations working under the patronage of the United Nations. Therefore, it was so important to resolve all legal formalities that arose when sending aircraft to a disaster area in the shortest possible time. Antonov Airlines had a permanent agreement with the relevant UN Authorities, which allowed, at the right time, the mobilisation of its aircraft without excessive loss of time. Due to this fact, aircraft were constantly close at hand and involved in the fulfillment of UN flights more often than those of other companies.

The period 1994-95 was remarkable for the large number of such flights to African and Middle Eastern countries, Angola, Yemen, Congo and Sierra Leone, due to the troubled situations there – civil wars, droughts, epidemics. Mostly, they transported humanitarian aid and various cargoes for the UN military contingents. Sometimes, although very rarely, the aircraft were loaded on the return flights, and then fish and some manufactured goods were

delivered to Europe. Everyone who participated in those flights remembered them. D.Yu. Patselia, one of Antonov Airlines' flight-managers, tells: *"Africa is a particular 'dark' (as it is called) continent. It is very specific: heat, neglected airports, runways in poor condition. There you cannot be confident of anything. You can fly to a destination having booked*

V. A. Borisenko, one of the first load-masters of Antonov Airlines, is guiding the loading process.

A representative of a consignee is observing the unloading process.

The first foreign press photographers inside the Ruslan's cargo compartment. Farnborough, Great Britain, 1986.

Christopher Foyle travelled the world promoting Air Foyle-Antonov Airlines. Here he is with Sheikh Ahmed bin Saeed Al Maktoum of Dubai, Chairman of Emirates Group, at the Dubai Air Cargo Conference and Exhibition, October 1996.

a hotel, ordered fuel there in advance and so on, and they tell you: we do not know anything. The one who promised you all this has already left. That is all. The price of fuel can change at any time. You can fly to the country and find out that you have to pay for the possibility of working there, although there is not a word about it in any document. To cut it short: there are countries one very wants to come back home from. In Africa, there are many such countries."

As V. V. Nets, an aircraft and engine operation engineer, tells, sometimes the troubled nature of a region turned out to be a very real risk, as, for example, in South Yemen in 1995. *"A civil war was coming to an end in that country,"* Valery Vasilievich recalls. *"We landed, unloaded. We were about to fly away, when suddenly we heard thunder. We looked out from the aircraft and saw a column of sand on the left side – that was an bomb explosion? The pilot ordered us to leave the aircraft.*

However, as soon as the attack was over and it became clear that the runway was not damaged, we immediately started the engines and took off. Sometimes it happened that the airfields, that our aircraft landed at, were shelled but, fortunately, our planes were not damaged. In general, it seems to me that in those cases they were more likely trying to frighten us rather than cause real damage. However, who knows?"

The operation of Antonov Airlines in Africa was highly appreciated by the UN experts. In the following years, they increasingly invited Antonov Airlines to provide the UN activity; one-off contracts for transportation turned in to long-term ones. The volume of transportation on such contracts increased constantly within the last years of the past century, when the United Nations carried out many special operations in different parts of the world: 1,947 million t*km in 1998, 6,976 million t*km in the following year and 39,316 million tonnes in 2000. A lot of work was carried out in Central and South Africa, including Sierra Leone and a large volume of cargo was delivered to East Timor (Indonesia) and Split (Macedonia). After a passenger version of the An-74 aircraft was included in Antonov Airlines' fleet, Antonov started transporting not only cargo with accompanying personnel, but also groups of people, such as the UN mission to Kosovo in 2000. *"On the one hand, we are contracted to UN programmes by the government of Ukraine,"* K.F. Lushakov concludes on this theme, *"but on the other hand, we independently participate in the tenders announced by the UN in order to confirm constantly our right to carry out this prestigious work."*

Taking into account the commissions from the United Nations, within the 1995–96 period Antonov Airlines' aircraft performed a total of 12,482 commercial flight hours and the freight turnover exceeded 331,078 million t*km. During this period, Antonov Airlines confidently flew around the world, operated frequently in the domestic market of the United States, performed transportation for the benefit of prestigious European customers and participated in a number of major international projects at that time.

Information about Antonov Airlines entered all the world's reference books, advertisements periodically appeared in the leading aviation publications, and the top managers of Antonov Airlines and Air Foyle continually briefed the most authoritative journalists. A completely new era had entered the history of Antonov Airlines. Near worldwide fame was a feature of this new stage.

This meant that one more function was added to the numerous roles of Antonov Airlines – the representative one. Antonov Airlines' crews and aircraft with their long-term productive operation in the public eye had earned the right to fly the flag not

only of its company but also of its country in all the continents, in the remotest corners of the planet. Today, in many places, especially where Ukraine is perceived as a distant country, it is known mainly in connection with the three word combinations: Dynamo Kyiv, the Klitschko brothers and Antonov Airlines.

In fact, Antonov Airlines, albeit unofficially, had always played such a role, starting from the very first years of operation in the world market. At that time any arrival of Soviet aircraft, especially such as the Ruslan, was perceived abroad as the most important political event, a visual indication of the end of the Cold War. Hopes for a better future, the joy of new meetings and pride in the company's achievements were important elements of the romance of those years. I. D. Babenko tells: *"I was lucky enough to demonstrate the An-124 at several international aviation exhibitions, including Oshkosh (the USA) in 1989. It happened this way: We transported some cargo from Luxembourg to Montreal, and simultaneously – by request of Aviaexport – we took two Su-26 sport planes to this exhibition. Since the return load from Montreal was expected a few days later and we had to pay for the parking there, we accepted an offer from the organisers of the exhibition to stay with them for free.*

"*The Americans perceived the aircraft amazingly enthusiastically. For several days, from morning to night, a continuous stream of people entered the aircraft though the front ramp along the port side, reached the rear ramp and returned along the starboard. That was a spectacle – a queue like the one to the mausoleum of Lenin in Soviet times! At the end of the exhibition the organisers asked us to perform one demo flight; they paid for the fuel. The crew was very strong – V. I. Terskii, G. A. Pobol and others. Jeana Yeager and Dick Rutan, who were at the zenith of their glory after their round-the-world flight with Voyager, joined us on that flight. After landing, Jeana opened the vent light in the cockpit and leaned out up to her waist, waving the American flag. A hundred thousand Americans rose to their feet and screamed with delight. They were ready to buy an empty bottle of the Obolonskaya spring water as a souvenir. It was a very strong blow to the Cold War.*

"*Former compatriots, who by chance turned out to be abroad, came to meet us at many airports we transported cargo to. I remember a guy in the very south of Argentina, who was born there after the war, but spoke Russian excellently. He proudly told everyone around that this magnificent aircraft was built in his homeland, which he had never seen.*"

Something similar still happens nowadays, despite the thousands of landings carried out in recent years in dozens of countries, but maybe to a somewhat lesser extent. Wherever the Ruslans

World mass-media always pay great attention to Antonov Airlines.

Su-26 sport aircraft, purchased by a flying club, have been delivered to the USA. Oshkosh, USA.

of Antonov Airlines fly, it is always an event for an airport. The local authorities always come to see the aircraft, and ordinary employees try to come near and take pictures with the Ruslan in the background or at least drive past on the airfield transport. It became ridiculous. The author witnessed in 2001 at the Italian Lamezia airport near Naples, local firemen drove up to the aircraft several times in their huge fire truck. The individual firemen alternately changed, but did not dare to get out of their truck. Sometimes we met braver audiences. Such people usually ask for permission to look inside, and when they see with their own eyes how much cargo the Ruslan can accommodate, they invariably get excited. In cases when the cargo is particularly important, an arrival of Antonov Airlines' aircraft deserves to be reported in the local press as well as to be shown on television. The capabilities of the Ruslan and Antonov Airlines still seem to be fantastic and keep on exciting the imagination of people around the world.

The end of the Cold War. Oshkosh, USA. 1989.

CHRONICLE OF ANTONOV AIRLINES: YEAR BY YEAR
Throughout all continents (1997–1998)

Throughout
all continents

The An-22 Antaeus, a veteran of remarkable transportations, is in the air again!

Having started operating just two the Ruslans, allotted to Antonov StC in accordance with the decision of the government of the USSR dated 24 March 1989, very soon Antonov Airlines faced an urgent necessity to expand its aircraft fleet. It was caused by several reasons; first of all by the increase in demand for services. However, it was impossible to involve the first prototype of the An-124 aircraft in commercial operations due to State requirements and the certification test process. That was why the completion of construction of the first of two aircraft, ordered earlier, in 1990 at Kyiv Aviation Plant (serial No. 02-08, aircraft number USSR-82027) came just at the right time. In addition, in 1991 the An-124 aircraft, serial No. 01-08, was upgraded and added to Antonov Airlines' fleet with USSR-82009 number assigned. This aircraft had just completed the test programme for airdropping troops and cargo. Taking into account this aircraft, the commercial fleet of the enterprise now reached a total of four Ruslans, which received the numbers UR-82007, -82008, -82009 and -82027 after the disintegration of the USSR.

(1997–1998)

During that time, the market for super-heavy and large-sized cargo transportation was growing rapidly, and in 1992 the top management of Antonov StC decided to lease the An-124 UR-82066 aircraft, serial No. 03-01, from the Kyiv Aviation Plant. In the following year, the second Ruslan UR-82029, serial No. 02-10, built to order, entered flight operation.

Then in 1999 the number of the Ruslans of Antonov Airlines increased by two more: No. 07-05, number UR-82072 and No. 07-06, number UR-82073) *"Any airline should constantly evolve, constantly expand its fleet,"* V. S. Mikhaylov, one of the most experienced managers of Antonov Airlines, commented about this event. *"That time they did not produce new Ruslans any more, but even if they had done so such aircraft would have been too expensive. Russian military aircraft were in rather poor condition; it would require an unacceptable amount of money to restore their airworthiness. Two aircraft of Rossiya State Airlines, those planes that served Yeltsin before, were of a great interest to us. Those aircraft were good, almost new ones, with less than 1000 logged flight hours each, but their operation was actually cancelled. For example, one of them had not lifted in to the sky for more than a year by the time of purchase. One of the Russian leasing companies proposed those aircraft to us and we agreed. We ferried the first plane to Gostomel in July 1999, carried out necessary works on the aircraft, and in two months it had flown away to commercial flight. But the second aircraft became the one we took more trouble over: we transported engines and spare part kits for it, sent specialists ... so, we 'revived' that aircraft. Now both these aircraft are our property."*

The second reason for the expansion of Antonov Airlines' fleet was the expediency to involve in its operations not only the An-124-100s, but also other types of aircraft. *"We started operating the Ruslans,"* K. F. Lushakov explains, *"but as soon as you get involved in operations, you get such orders where aircraft of smaller dimension are more effective. For this purpose, we hired the aircraft remaining at the disposal of the Antonov Company after the completion of various test programmes."*

The An-22 UR-64460 became the first of the new aircraft Antonov Airlines started commercially operating from 1992 (the aircraft performed 53 commercial flights within that year). The Antaeus UR-64459 joined the An-22 the following year, and the aircraft, UR-09307 entered Antonov StC operation a year later. Many suitable transport missions were found for the Antaeuses – veterans of national economic transportations – and these aircraft demonstrated reasonably high efficiency while fulfilling these tasks. Due to lower fuel consumption and, generally, the lower cost of the An-22's flight hour in comparison with that of

V. S. Mikhaylov,
Head of the subdivision
of the Technical Support
Department of Antonov
Airlines.

the An-124-100, transportation of some types of helicopters, engineering and combat equipment, or humanitarian cargo with a total weight of up to 55 tonnes, turned out to be more profitable. The Antaeuses were also used when it was necessary to urgently deliver D-18T engines to replace those failed on the Ruslans of Antonov Airlines in countries of the Middle East and Latin America, including Argentina. In some cases, when choosing an aircraft to perform a contract, the balance tipped in favour of the An-22 due to the less strict airfield requirements demanded of the aircraft. This was an important role in the choice of the Antaeuses for the government-ordered transportation of different military cargoes from some African countries to be repaired in Ukraine. In general, the An-22 was heavily used across Africa especially in 1995–96. The planes transported industrial equipment to Cairo, Luanda and Johannesburg and frequently fresh fish by return flights. Later, due to the large fuselage volume, the Antaeuses gained popularity also among the so-called 'shuttle traders' who transported consumer electronics from the United Arab Emirates to Ukraine.

Unlike the Ruslans, the Antaeuses of Antonov Airlines were given missions not only in the foreign market but also within the borders of the former USSR: fulfilling orders of the government of Ukraine, they transported food, clothing and other humanitarian goods to the zone of the Armenian-Azerbaijani conflict, and delivered equipment for rebuilding the zone. However, the best days of the Antaeus had already passed. All three An-22s of Antonov Airlines belonged to early production batches, their lives were coming to an end, and for safety reasons their maximum payload was limited

by 53 tonnes. "When it happened," V. S. Mikhaylov said, "the An-22 became a little inferior to the Il-76 which was more modern in terms of equipment and economic efficiency. Only in those instances when the cargo was not heavy but its dimensions did not fit into the narrow 'Il's' fuselage and, at the same time, was too small for the Ruslan, did the Antaeus beat the competition." However, the number of such instances turned out to be too small, and when the service life of the two An-22s expired, it was not extended.

Since 2001 Antonov Airlines's fleet comprised only one Antaeus, and this aircraft has coped well with all the missions that fell to its lot. As it is regulated by modern ICAO requirements, the aircraft is upgraded with new equipment, including the Buran-A meteo-navigation radar, the TCAS-2000 Traffic Collision Avoidance System and the SRPPZ-2000 Ground Proximity Warning System. In the mid-2000s, the aircraft flew to Osaka, Seoul, Australia, many European countries and carried out six flights to deliver humanitarian aid to the earthquake-affected areas of Turkey. This aircraft was widely used by aircraft manufacturers to transport aircraft units, produced at different factories within the cooperation structure. For example, the aircraft carried tail fins and tail parts of the fuselages of the An-148 prototypes from Voronezh to Kyiv and wing boxes and fuselage central sections from Kyiv to Voronezh. The same aircraft delivered almost completely assembled fuselages and other An-140 units from Kharkiv to Isfahan (Iran). As a rule, such flights were performed by crews under the command of V. V. Goncharov and technical crews, headed by N. V. Shein. N. I. Onopchenko, Deputy General Designer, made a great contribution to the success of such flights. It should be noted that flights to Iran almost always imposed additional moral responsibility on Antonov Airlines: the Ukrainian-Iranian contract for production of the An-140 aircraft in this country and, accordingly, the payment of wages to Kharkiv aircraft builders depended on the timeliness and quality of such flights being fulfilled. Realising this, the personnel of Antonov Airlines always did all their best to avoid failing their Kharkiv colleagues.

The famous An-12 aircraft, capable of carrying up to 20 tonnes, became another aircraft type which allowed Antonov Airlines to react much more flexibly to the changing market demands. The first such aircraft, designated as UR-11315, started commercial operation in 1993: the UR-11765 and the UR-21510 aircraft joined it in the following year. The high economic efficiency of flights carried out by these aircraft encouraged the management of Antonov Airlines to enter the An-12 UR-11348 into the airline's fleet in 1996 and lease the aircraft UR-11322. The 'twelfth', along with the Ruslan, became another workhorse – for a long time it occupied second place after the An-124-100 in terms of the number of flights performed. Thus – such are the vicissitudes of fate! – it always remained in the shadow of its more powerful 'colleague'. So impressive flights, entries in the record books and sensational events are not reckoned to the An-12 account – these aircraft just worked conscientiously and modestly making an important contribution to the collective success of Antonov Airlines' business.

The An-12s have flown to the countries of Europe, to Israel and Sri Lanka. Flights to deliver decked helicopters, repaired in Sevastopol, to India were an interesting story. They had to fly through Africa, too. Under the agreement with Ukraine International Airlines, the Antonov's An-12 performed regular cargo flights (twice a week) between Kyiv Boryspil airport and Luxembourg, Amsterdam and Frankfurt am Main as well as transporting Ukrainian 'shuttle traders' from Italy and Turkey. In this general, routine and, for the majority of readers, mundane work, from time to time one can find flights that capture the imagination of even the most indifferent to aviation. On one such flight, in 1997 under the contract signed by Air Foyle, the An-12 delivered an important cargo from England to the Falkland Islands (they are located almost in Antarctica). In the same year, one of the An-12s of Antonov Airlines in strict secrecy transported the latest model of the Audi car from Germany to the North Magnetic Pole of the

Earth (located in the north of Canada) to be tested. In July 2001, this aircraft participated in the provision of Elton John's concerts in Berlin, Izmir (Turkey) and St. Petersburg. Although these performances of the star were considered chamber ones, they required the transfer of 12 tonnes of music and broadcasting equipment, including devices for on-line streaming of the concerts via the internet.

The An-12s continued to work as a part of Antonov Airlines in the first decade of the new century, although it became more and more difficult to operate these aircraft meeting all the modern ICAO requirements. The reason was general obsolescence of these veterans of cargo aviation, especially obsolescence of their on-board equipment. Nevertheless, Antonov Airlines endeavoured to maintain them in operating status and provide the required level of airworthiness. At least one aircraft was equipped with a new radio station, collision avoidance systems and other systems as required by ICAO. And yet, the effective commercial operation of the An-12 in the Antonov Airlines' fleet became impossible within a few years. The reason was the high cost of the propellers' service lives extension but there were other mixed technical-economic issues. As a result, today there is a vacancy for an aircraft with a carrying capacity of up to 20 tonnes Antonov Airline's fleet ...

Along with the three main types of aircraft listed above, the airline also operates the An-26 and the An-74T lighter-class aircraft, which also remained at

A fuselage of the An-140 is being loaded into the Antaeus to be transported to Iran. Kharkov, December 2007.

The An-22 is transporting the An-148's wings for further assembly at Voronezh. Kyiv, August 2008.

Loading the Trent 900 engine of the A380 passenger giant into the An-22. Great Britain, July 2004.

the disposal of Antonov StC after termination of a number of test programmes. These aircraft are re-equipped in accordance with their new role and are used to transport small consignments of cargo and fulfil some special missions. The intensity of flights, in comparison with the An-124, is small. For example, within the described period, the An-26 carried out only a few dozen flights a year. The 74th flown in order of magnitude of intensity. The majority of such flights were carried out within European and CIS countries. In this nearby theatre of transportation, these aircraft carry the flag of Antonov Airlines with pride, releasing the Ruslans for global operation as one of the drivers of the world economy. In the second half of the 1990s these words, as well as the International Cargo

Transporter inscription which appeared at the fuselages of the An-124-100s, perhaps most fully reflected the essence of the airline's activity.

However, during those years the crews and aircraft of Antonov Airlines remained the representatives of Ukraine, and remained its citizens and its aircraft, no matter what global tasks they had to solve. Bearing this in mind, and wanting to take care of flight safety, the management of Antonov StC and Antonov Airlines always attached great importance to compliance with all requirements of the aviation regulations of their country and to creative development of relations with the aviation authorities of Ukraine. A. N. Gritsenko, who made a lot of efforts to establish and strengthen mutual understanding between The State Aviation Administration of Ukraine (as it was called at that time) and Antonov Airlines, tells the following account of these efforts.

"The State Aviation Administration – formerly known as Ukraviatrans and before that as Ukraviatsia – and the Department of Air Transport – began its activity after the collapse of the Soviet Union, when Antonov Airlines had already been working hard. We immediately fell into the sphere of close attention by the department, and since then our relations have been constantly developing. It should be noted that our relations have not always developed smoothly, and I associate the difficulties that sprung up from time to time with a number of circumstances, primarily due to the fact that the leading positions in the State Aviation Administration were always occupied by the people from the Ministry of Civil Aviation, but we always belonged to the Ministry of Aviation Industry. We simply did not know each other, did not know many regulations of civil aviation we had to meet while operating our aircraft. However, at present we no longer have such problems; we perform commercial flights in full compliance with all the fixed requirements. Another difficulty was caused by some tensions between Ukraviatrans and Antonov in general. There were many subtle reasons for this but I will only note that many representatives of our aviation authorities considered cargo transportation to be beyond a design bureau's business. They considered classic airlines, for example Ukraine Airlines, and military aviation transport to be suitable for such purpose. Besides, the failures that befell the company at the turn of the decade, first of all the crash of the An-74 in Lensk and the An-124 during certification tests in 1992, played their negative role as well. After the crash of the first An-70 prototype we came to the aviation authorities but they closed all the doors to us. Nobody believed we would be able to gain the momentum we have nowadays ...

"Indeed, our aircraft fly away from the base, having one or two contracts, and then 'string shish-kebab' without returning home for a month or a month and a half. But the aviation authorities did not understand this. It reached the point of absurdity: we were forbidden to fly to a country based on the fact that there had already been the carrier assigned to that country. But, in fact, those carriers had just Tu-154s, Boeing-737s or, in the best case scenario, An-12s in their fleets. How could they compete with the Ruslans? Many people agreed with our position but there were not any real shifts for months or even years! We were given permission to perform commercial flights only to the countries with no designated carriers, but we needed the whole world! And one another point: the most important task of the aviation authorities of any country is flight safety but this task does not always have the same solution. For example, it is always easier to prohibit a flight: it will provide one hundred percent flight safety! Unfortunately, the salary and career of an official do not depend on the success of the commercial activities of the air carriers, therefore we lost a lot. Moreover, not only we lost. There were some cases that caused certain damage to the international prestige of Ukraine. For example, in May 1998 we sent one of our Ruslans, that had just completed another commercial flight in Tashkent, to the Berlin Air Show. However, the aircraft managed to fly just to Ukraine, and we failed to get permission in time from the aviation authorities of Ukraine to leave the air area of our motherland, Ukraine. So, this prestigious air show lost the chance to meet the promised An-124-100 aircraft.

"It should be noted that both Antonov Airlines and the aviation authorities have been constantly working all these years to overcome these emerging problems. It is remarkable that the reason for many of them was simple – employees of the aviation authorities had been never engaged in this kind of business and did not understand that we were adjusting to commercial life. Several their leading specialists had to take part in some flights performed by our aircraft. They saw themselves the way we worked, how we had really mastered in the USA alone dozens, even hundreds of airports. They seemed to gradually grow up with us. As a result of joint efforts, quite positive relationships were established between the aviation authorities and Antonov Airlines. Representatives of the aviation authorities had to assure themselves that we had turned, figuratively speaking, from an ugly duckling into a beautiful swan."

Stepan Safonovich Galka continues the account of Alexandr Nikolayevich. Stepan Safonovich also gave a lot of efforts to strengthen Antonov Airlines' business relationship with aviation authorities of Ukraine: "Indeed, our airline and aviation authorities of our country developed in parallel, and this process still continues nowadays. For example, constant improvement of the legal framework for the realisation of all types of aviation activity is still underway. Our employees also take part in the important work that Aviation Authorities carry out. Their great practical experience in international flight operation is embodied in the normative documents which are developed. And yet, Antonov

V. V. Zaginay,
Head of the Technical
Support Division of Antonov
Airlines.

The An-12 of Antonov
Airlines is taking off in
Gostomel.

The An-74 of Antonov Airlines is mainly operated for passenger charter transportation.

Airlines is the only airline in the country that has fifth freedom rights to and from the USA, Australia and Canada; that is, we are authorized to carry to these countries cargoes belonging to third countries as well as operate our aircraft within these states, known as cabotage. Such experience can be called unique without exaggeration."

As time passed, the achieved level of organisation and fulfilment of flights, and the level of qualification of flight and technical crews, allowed Antonov Airlines to obtain Ukrainian and British licences to transport dangerous goods. Those were the aircraft that in 1994 took out nuclear fuel from Iraq following the UN Security Council resolution. These complicated flights were carried out between Habania and Yekaterinburg (Russian Federation). Moreover, Antonov Airlines became the Ukrainian designated carrier of military and special-purpose cargo. A special result of many years of hard work, deserved recognition of Antonov StC's merits were stated in the decree of the Cabinet of Ministers of Ukraine of 8 December 1997, No. 1365, signed by the Prime Minister of the country V. Pustovoitenko: *"To assign to the Aeronautic Scientific and Technical Complex named after O. K. Antonov the status of national air cargo carrier"* (that was the name of Antonov StC that time).

It should be stressed, that this high rank did not come to Antonov Airlines from heaven but was the result of hard and conscious work. Let's start with the fact that it was a necessity in the life of the company to obtain the status of a national carrier. In the mid-1990s, competition in the air cargo transportation market became considerably stronger. Older and more experienced market players, seeing the success of Antonov Airlines and Volga-Dnepr Airlines, realised that they had to take action immediately and as a result, in some countries, both the 'young tigers' began to encounter obvious difficulties in obtaining commercial rights for cargo transportation.

Partners from Air Foyle suggested to Antonov StC specialists the way to avoid the approaching crisis. It turns out that one of the conditions to simplify the procedure for obtaining permissions for commercial transportation for foreign companies in some world leading aviation countries (UK, Canada, China, the USA, France, etc.) is the status of national carrier. Having received such information, K. F. Lushakov appealed to Aviation Authorities of Ukraine for clarification of the conditions and procedure for such status assignment. However, this procedure was also new for the Aviation Authorities, and after a time they started developing the Ukrainian National Air Carrier Regulations but the process was obviously delayed ...

Without waiting for the completion of the official document, the specialists of Antonov Airlines themselves prepared and sent to the Cabinet of Ministers of Ukraine a set of documents confirming, in Antonov StC's opinion, the right to be assigned this proud status. The document, entitled *Strategy. Goals. Target Programmes,* stood out amongs the other documents. It comprehensively covered all the main components of the successful operation of Antonov Airlines for the future. First of all, the document clearly defined the main target of Antonov Airlines – to become integrated into the world air transport system. The realisation of nine (!) target programmes would lead to the achievement of the goal. The programmes, in their turn, were divided into subprogrammes devoted to an individual component of operation.

The issues of operation in the market, consistent and persistent formation of 'its own' share of the air transportation market, in which Antonov Airlines would remain beyond competition, were thoroughly covered in the *Strategy* ... Great attention was paid to flight safety, aircraft fleet development, achievement of the maximum level of aircraft technical readiness, compliance of the aircraft with ICAO requirements and improvement of maintenance methods. The important points of strengthening business relations with partners, agents, authorities, the public, etc. were not forgotten either. In addition, all the components of increasing the economic efficiency of transportation found their proper reflection in the

document.

This list could be continued, but it is already long enough for a reader to properly perceive the remarkable nature of this *Strategy* ... So, the most amazing thing is practically everything that was outlined in the document was finally fulfilled! Well, not quite everything, but certainly 90–95%. For modern Ukraine such figures are truly phenomenal.

Captains and test pilots V.V. Goncharov and A.A. Kruts.

The An-26 of Antonov Airlines mainly flies within CIS-countries.

A. N. Gratsenko,
Head of Antonov StC
representative office in the
Ruslan-SALIS company.

Therefore, Antonov Airlines was deservedly assigned the status of National Air Carrier. But getting such status meant not only getting a well-deserved recognition of past achievements, but also assuming the burden of responsibility for reaching a high level in the future. For this it is necessary for it to constantly improve its work, gaining advantages over competitors and giving exemplary service to partners. In reality, this process has been running throughout the whole history of Antonov Airlines. In accordance with the *Strategy* ... they have always put an emphasis on enhancing the organisation of flights, raising the professional level of personnel and upgrading of forms and methods of aircraft maintenance. For example, while fulfilling a Cargolux contract, the question arose of what to do, if by the time regular routine maintenance was required, the aircraft was away from its base? Carrying out the work in advance might increase maintenance costs; carrying out the work later would be a violation of the Flight Crew Operation Manual regulations. They made an optimal decision from the point of view of the maximum possible reduction of the aircraft idle time: to take technicians and necessary equipment on board, and perform routine maintenance during unloading-loading, whether in Luxembourg, Singapore or Gostomel. After the accidents with engine failures in Mexico, specialists from ZMBK Progress, provided with the necessary tools, often accompanied the Ruslans. They inspected the D-18T engines and, in case of necessity, were authorized to extend their service life. As a result, by the mid-1990s, during each trip the Ruslan was an actual complex focused on obtaining the maximum commercial efficiency, consisting of an aircraft, a set of spare parts and personnel.

The search for an optimal form of work arrangement for the technical crew had the same goal. Initially, Antonov Airlines practised the rotation of technical personnel, although chief technicians and engineers (the 'masters' of an aircraft) were still assigned to their aircraft. The reason for such rotation was the desire to financially support a larger number of people, since their salary was higher when flying along international flights. But later the Ruslan fleet had grown and such practice became senseless. Technical crews in full were fixed for a specific aircraft determined by the state of the equipment.

The formation of permanent flight crews had an equally positive effect. People who know each other well work more efficiently, understand each other better under difficult circumstances, and, if necessary, can provide effective support to a colleague. The psychological climate of the crews has improved significantly, which was of great importance during long flights.

As far as we can judge, the management of Antonov Airlines has always been very attentive in recruiting personnel, considering the successful allocation of people as one of the necessary conditions for effective and safe operation of an aircraft. As a result, the crews of Antonov Airlines consist of highly qualified specialists who have wide experience in testing and flying the aircraft almost all over the world in both simple and adverse weather conditions all around the clock. All crew members have standard certificates confirming the right to perform international flights in accordance with the current legislation of Ukraine and ICAO regulations. Technical crews, accompanying aircraft in flights, are well experienced in autonomous operation of aircraft at remote airfields for a period of up to three months. All the members of technical crews have received appropriate training; they are very experienced in the most difficult loading and unloading processes. At least one technical crewmember is fluent in English. In case of aircraft failure at a foreign airport, Antonov Airlines possesses a well-established system for the delivery of spare parts and everything that may be needed to maintain aircraft airworthiness to any point of the planet. But the repair must be carried out by the technical crew of the damaged aircraft. In

general, it should be noted that the well-coordinated professional work of the team is the basis for proper aircraft operation, and therefore, the guarantee of the successful completion of the entire transport operation.

Pilots and flight crews in general are the 'gold fund' of Antonov Airlines. The majority of them are professionals of the highest qualification. As A. V. Galunenko, the chief-pilot of Antonov Airlines and the Hero of Ukraine, notes, all captains of the An-124-100 aircraft have a total flight experience of not less than 5,000 hours, including on-type flight experience of the An-124-100 aircraft of not less than 900 hours, instrument flight experience – not less than 2,000 hours – and flight experience at night of not less than 1,800 hours. All the pilots have on-type flight experience of the Ruslans of not less than 100 hours. At least three people from the crew (as a rule, the captain, navigator and radio operator) are fluent in aviation English and are able to conduct radio communications with ground control towers. Each pilot of Antonov Airlines performs 700–800 flying hours per year on average. These figures look impressive even against the background of a general growth in the volume of air transportation and an increase in the flight experience of pilots

of many airlines in the CIS countries. But what is behind these figures? Here is an extract from the author's conversation with A. N. Kulikov and V. A. Bezmarternyh, the first-class test pilots and the captains of the Ruslan aircraft.

"Artem Nikolaevich, you are a pilot with great experience who piloted different aircraft for different organisations. What is the specificity of flight work for Antonov Airlines?"

"Our work, of course, differs from the work of the civil airline pilots, those who carry passengers and cargo along regular air routes. They always know exactly where they will fly to today, tomorrow and in the nearest future. The number of airfields each pilot performs landing at is rather limited. It is necessary to take a captain to each new airfield in advance. It is performed by another pilot who has already landed there or who is simply more qualified, this is a law of flight work. Then the crew passes there as along a well-trodden path. But we fly all around the world; we can land at three or four airfields per day, and at many airfields for the first time. This is a great difficulty, but our crews are ready for such work, including psychologically – that is especially important. Often we have to make landings at short intensively landed airfields at night,

Evening in Gostomel. People and aircraft are resting.

V. A. Bezmaternyh,
captain of the Ruslan.

and such a task has to be done by the aircraft of the Ruslan type. For such work, the crew should be very well prepared, and that is really the case in Antonov Airlines. It is obligatory that one of crew members is a test-pilot. As a rule, it is a captain."

"The most important thing is that flight laws are not violated in these situations," Vladimir Arkadievich joins our conversation. "The Commercial Department of the airline applies to the flight service prior to making a contract. We have a pilot and a navigator on duty available at any time; they calculate the possibilities of the landings at each new airfield, maximum cargo and fuel weight admissible, and make preliminary conclusions. Moreover, they creatively join the process of commercial deal forming. Piloting different types of aircraft, they often suggest to managers the optimal terms for carrying out a flight."

"And what happens in those cases when the preliminary conclusion shows the impossibility or problematic execution of the required

A. N. Kulikov,
captain of the Ruslan.

transportation? Do you immediately reject the contract?"

"Specialists of Antonov Airlines try to use the maximum available means to fulfil a contract. As far as crews are concerned, they really do their best. Sometimes it is necessary to determine right on the spot whether it is possible to perform takeoff or landing and under what conditions. Sometimes it happens that according to the Flight Crew Operation Manual, the aircraft can take off, but for various reasons, crew members are in doubt about this. A captain makes a decision in such cases. He must correlate the capabilities of the aircraft, the crew, current airfield conditions and, finally, guarantee safety. Periodically special, unique cases happen in Antonov Airlines' contracts, which have to be carried out exceeding the Flight Crew Operation Manual instructions. Before such flights, it is obligatory to conduct consultations with designers, carry out a joint in-depth evaluation of the forthcoming mission and come to an agreed decision. Usually the General Designer approves the agreed decision. It is his right, as he knows all the resources inherent in the aircraft's structure. And it is our task, a task of test-pilots, to realise such resources. Once we carried a 132-tonne crankshaft, damaged as a result of an accident at the power plant, from Port-au-Prince in the Caribbean Islands to Portugal, to the manufacturing plant, while according to the Flight Crew Operation Manual the maximum carrying capacity of the An-124-100 was 120 tonnes only. Moreover, the weight of the mono-cargo was limited to 50 tonnes. As a result of the measures taken, the transport operation, which required seven intermediate landings, was completed successfully."

"The Antonov pilots are not attached to any specific type of aircraft. Today they are on a commercial flight by the An-12, tomorrow – a flight by the Ruslan, the day after tomorrow they participate in tests of the An-148 or the An-70. Does this fact have a negative effect on flight safety?"

"I practise, our pilots alternate commercial flights with test work. For example, A. V. Galunenko and V. Y. Gorovenko were leading test-pilots of the An-70, A. A. Kruts was engaged in tests of the An-74TK-300, A. K. Khrustitskii and S. M. Troshin worked on the An-140. But pilots always pass through selection to become test-pilots. They selected only those who adapt well to aircraft of different classes, who are ready to pilot any aircraft with a high safety level. The crews proved the right to pilot different aircraft by passing special exams. It means that changing the aircraft type does not negatively affect safety. Moreover, with this practice, pilots gradually acquire the ability to take into account the individual particularities of each aircraft, even within the same type. After all, each aircraft has its own customs, its own habits – one has a slightly higher fuel consumption, another's centre of gravity position differs, the third plane has peculiarities while landing. To get the best results, each aircraft requires an individual approach."

"And which flights are more difficult: commercial or test ones?"

"Both commercial and test flights have their own specifics and their difficulties. You can't compare their stresses. For example, after an hour of a test flight a pilot can get as tired as after 10–12 hours of a commercial flight. However, flying the Ruslans of Antonov Airlines, a pilot stays away from home for month or two, constantly changing time and climatic zones. As a result, tiredness accumulates and it seems sometimes, that commercial flights are even more difficult."

In addition to flight and technical personnel, each flight of the airlines is accompanied by a flight manager (chief of transportation), whose duties are vast. L. Y. Patselia, a representative of this profession, explains about the duties: "We have a lot of work – preparation of financial documentation, monitoring of current flight information, participation in preparation for a flight: drawing up plans, briefings; tracking of weather-reports. Besides, we have to contact a customer's representatives, work with all airport

services, customs, border services, etc. In general, there are three categories of managers in Antonov Airlines. The first one is the commercial managers – they search for contracts, make contracts, calculate prices, do their best to connect flights for place and time in order to get the so-called 'shish-kebab'. The goal is to minimize idle time, ferry flights and costs. Everything that is connected with the specific planning of flights, like the receipt of diplomatic permits, especially if a peculiar cargo is transported, provision of landings, booking of hotels, is the work of the operational service or, as these specialists are called in the West, 'operations'.

Technical crew of Antonov Airlines can make their aircraft ready at any point of the planet. Kabul, June 2003.

1998 became the most intensive year in terms of cargo transportation from China to Ukraine: 6,600 tons of consumer goods were carried to Gostomel in 233 flights.

Mecheria (Morocco) to Luton/Virgin Round the World Hot Air Balloon Gondola for Richard Branson. January 1997.

Flight managers, being on-board, implement all the preliminary preparation actions on a certain flight, in effect they realise the plans.

It is natural that when such a complex mechanism works, some discrepancies occur, as happens in any work. I recall one of the flights in the last days of December 1999, when a rather strong discrepancy happened. According to the contract signed by Air Foyle's businessmen, the consignee had to pay for all airport fees and provide the necessary vehicles for unloading at the point of destination. The cargo was particular – 100-tonne generators. On arrival we asked if everything was ok. They answered – yes. We deployed the platform, rolled out the cargo, and then the customer representative said he was sorry, they had not got a crane and could not take

the cargo. We spent one and a half days in this situation. It was awful. This is one of the reasons why we sometimes take our commercial managers aboard so that they can see how their plans are realised. It lets them gain practical experience."

Continuing the story about managers of Antonov Airlines, M. G. Kharchenko, in the early 2000s, was pleased to draw the following picture: "We have grown out of short trousers. We have strong, highly experienced commercial managers, who easily outstrip many Western managers. Our employees are much more educated than some of them. The only advantage our Western partners have is the fact that they are a part of the world banking system. But we had problems even with credit cards. Many things still need to be solved but

In the second half of the 1990s large sections of the Arian-5 European rocket-carrier were transported several times from Switzerland to the USA.

obviously, progress had been made in the second half of the 1990s. Now up to 60% of contracts are signed by our employees."

Fairness requires us to give some kind words here to the flight managers from Air Foyle too, who, in most cases, had been flying at the Ruslans of Antonov Airlines for 16 years. They decided the most important matters of the flight arrangements and shared with the rest of the crew members all the difficulties of multi-day flights. In this, the British showed no less devotion to their work than their Ukrainian colleagues, and often they demonstrated enviable ingenuity. Here is a story from Christopher Fairchild, one of Air Foyle's managers: *"We called Margo Burgers 'Cargo Margo' – the only woman flight manager so far employed to work on the An-124 aircraft. In order to look her best after a 14-hour flight on the Ruslan (with few/no bathroom facilities!) she invented something quite original. While on one of our trips to the Far East she had her eyelids tattooed with black eyeliner. Hence, no need for makeup! What interesting things a woman can do in order to be beautiful!"*

The author was lucky enough to be personally familiar with many of the employees of Antonov Airlines mentioned in this book. I saw many of them working too, often at times of stresses. I do not know whether it is necessary to repeat once again the words about their high professionalism, resourcefulness and other wonderful qualities to reiterate message to the reader. Maybe it is better to just set some examples, just within the period of 1997–98.

On 19 July 1997, while taking off from the airport at Genoa (Italy) toward the sea, Ruslan UR-82029, collided with a flock of cormorants just at the moment of lift-off from the runway. The aircraft was flying to Karachi (Pakistan) with 100 tonnes of cargo on board. Takeoff weight was maximum. As a result of a collision with 48 birds, each weighing up to 8 kg, the aircraft and engines were significantly damaged. Engine No. 3 surged and had to be switched off. Engine No. 2 reached a critical level of vibration. Due to failures in the power plant, the operation of the hydraulic and electric systems was disrupted and the control system of the aircraft switched to redundant channels, which limited the crew's capabilities. The situation was complicated by bad weather and low altitude above sea level – less than 100 metres. The situation did not become critical due to the fast and decisive actions of A. M. Shuleschenko, flight engineer, who managed to localize quickly the failures of the aircraft systems and restore their efficiency in the manual control mode to an extent that allowed the aircraft to be turned and brought to the runway. N. S. Bogulia, the captain, accomplished this complicated task. Psychological burdens in this 11-minute flight

were so high that while landing the co-pilot made a mistake in controlling engine reversal. Again the situation turned into an extreme one, as the runway ended in the sea, and with such a weight

What different cargoes for transportation were Antonov Airlines faced with at the threshold of the 21st century!

After a successful flight. From left to right: S. F. Nechaev, navigator; A. V. Galunenko and A. Z. Moiseev, pilots, A. V. Shuleschenko, flight engineer.

the aircraft could not stop at that runway without activating thrust reverse. Shuleschenko left his work station and, together with the captain, completed the actions using reverse thrust. The Ruslan stopped 30 metres before the end of the runway.

The following year, on 5 December, A. M. Shuleschenko again saved the aircraft, but that time Alexander Maksimovich was on the ground. That day, one of Antonov Airlines' crew performed a training flight in the An-12 aircraft in the airfield zone. A failure occurred while extending the landing gear. The crew performed all the actions on main, redundant and emergency landing gear extension stipulated by the Flight Crew Operation Manual, but none of that helped. The fuel reserve allowed the aircraft to stay in the air another half an hour. A. M. Shuleschenko was invited to the Flight Control Tower for consultation. He quickly evaluated the situation, talked to the crew and found an original solution, not prescribed in the Flight Crew Operation Manual, showing the highest skill of a test flight engineer. By radio, he recommended the crew members to cut off some units in a certain sequence, and the crew managed to extend the landing gear. The flight was completed by a successful landing.

I would like to stress that there are many examples of competent and cool action by the Antonov Airlines' crews in difficult situations – such as A. K. Khrustitskii's flight in a Ruslan with two idle engines; the takeoff performed by V. A. Shlyakhov in Novosibirsk after an engine failure while carrying more than 120 tonnes of cargo; or the landing in Toronto performed by E. E. Luchko when the synchronisation shaft of the flap

extension fractured. All these cases are extremely interesting, especially the last because it demanded extraordinary action not only from the flight crew but also from the technical crew. It happened like this: in 1997, a Ruslan piloted by Evgenii Evgenievich Luchko, headed to Toronto to pick up cargo. When approaching landing, during flaps extension, the warning system activated signalling that the flaps on the right and left half-wings had extended in different ways. Then the protection system went on and the anti-retraction brakes fixed the inner flaps in different positions. The outer sections of the flaps had to be extended manually using the emergency system. In this event the crew coped with the situation with coolness, and the captain landed the damaged aircraft superbly.

Inspection showed that the synchronisation shaft had burst. The damage was serious; however, the cargo had been already delivered and so it was impossible to cancel the contract. They asked the Canadians to help them. When the Canadians found out that it was a control system element they had to deal with, they resolutely refused to help, asserting they were not authorised to interfere in the units directly affecting flight safety. So, the technical crew of the An-124-100 had to fix the yoke themselves within a night, and then the designers in Kyiv had to approve the decision made by technical crew members.

In this way – due to the hard work of all its employees – Antonov Airlines finished the first decade of its history with impressive results and by continuing to rely on its employees' professionalism and dedication, would continue to reach new heights.

CHRONICLE OF ANTONOV AIRLINES: YEAR BY YEAR
Between two eras (1999–2001)

Between two eras

Antonov Airlines entered its second decade looking ahead with confidence. A strong brand, an effective management system, skilled personnel, a sufficient fleet of aircraft with unique freight capabilities and strong support from the 'big Antonov' – these were the characteristics of the airline at the turn of the 21st century. Although this list looks like a list of compliments, it is a statement of facts. The proof is easy to find if we have a look at the typical flights of one of Antonov Airlines' Ruslans at that time. A brief description would be non-stop work: arrival, unloading-loading, one or two days' stay to rest the crew and then moving to the next point. One day the aircraft is in USA, the next day Europe, then in Africa – a work pattern that continues even today. On average each aircraft achieves 100–150 flight hours and around 20 landings each month. An aircraft might go to the USA and stay working there for a month despite the fact that USA is a powerful country and has enough of its own aircraft. The cases when a foreign company is able to enter its domestic market and work there are exceedingly rare.

A typical flight of the Ruslan takes place in a month or a month and a half of self-contained operation.

In order to get a better understanding of a Ruslan's typical commercial flight, look at this of destinations and dates of landings of one of the aircraft (UR-82029) during spring 2001. The aircraft left Gostomel on 26 March and then landed in the following airports: Marseille (France) – 26 March, Dakar (Senegal) – 28 March, Marseille – 29 March, Dakar – 30 March, Marseille – 31 March, Dakar – 31 March, Marseille – 1 April, Dakar – 2 April, Marseille – 3 April, Dakar – 4 April, Ostend (Belgium) – 5 April, Liege (Belgium) – 5 April, Skopje (Macedonia) – 6 April, Hahn (Germany) – 6 April, Malaga (Spain) – 8 April, Bamako (Mali) – 9 April, Hahn – 9 April, Prestwick (Great Britain) – 13 April, Keflavik (Iceland) – 13 April, Gander (Canada) – 13 April, Newborg (USA) – 14 April, St. Louis (USA) – 14 April, Monterrey (Mexico) – 16 April, Houston (USA) – 17 April, Newark (USA) – 18 April, Houston – 19 April, Syracuse (USA) – 20 April, Tulsa (USA) – 21 April, Panama (Panama) – 26 April, El Yopal (Colombia) – 27 April, Panama – 27 April, Orlando (USA) – 28 April, Lyneham (UK) – 29 April, Stansted (United Kingdom) – 29 April, Stephenville (Canada) – 3 May, Paraguana (Venezuela) – 4 May, Trinidad

(1999–2001)

and Tobago – 5 May, Luton (United Kingdom) – 6 May, Bozel (France) – 6 May, Gostomel – 8 May.

I want to underline that this list is typical, and there are examples of much longer and much shorter flights as well. From the list one can see that during 44 days of autonomous flight the aircraft landed 39 times at the airports on four continents: Eurasia, Africa, North and South Americas. During its next period of flying, which ended on 30 June, the aircraft visited five continents. And this is how all Antonov Airlines aircraft worked! All this allows us to declare that the business of the airline became stable and global. And the geography of service sales speaks volumes. For instance, in 2000 the major proportion of all transported cargoes were cargoes from European countries – 26%, India occupied the second place with 18%, then Far East countries with 16%. The cargoes transported from CIS countries constituted 10%. As for the destinations to which these cargoes were delivered, the majority of them were in Africa – 39%, 19% were delivered to customers in North America and 12% in Europe. These numbers have not changed significantly over the past few years. The CIS countries continue to be less favoured with consignors: the import to these countries is only 3% of the annual freight traffic of Antonov Airlines.

It is worth emphasising in this regard that no matter in which part of the world the aircraft were, they were always cared for by Antonov Airlines' real-time aircraft management service – within this entire period headed by Vladimir Mikhailovich Sudorgin. Not a single Ruslan took off without specialists of the service having performed all necessary formalities for its flight: they submitted applications and got the overflight permits to fly over foreign countries' aerospace and diplomatic authorisations for landing, arranged aircraft servicing at the intermediate airports and destination airport, ordered fuel, booked hotels and performed much other necessary work. However, when the contract was signed by the Air Foyle managers, part of this work was taken over by them. But when the contract was signed by the Kyivans the specialists of Vladimir Mikhailovich had very little time for rest. And indeed, how could they rest if they had the whole world as their area of responsibility?

Obtaining overflight permits in time is the prerequisite not only of successful business but also a guarantee of aircraft and crew security and safety. At the very beginning of joint work with

the British there were several cases of delays in getting such permissions due to various unforeseen circumstances, which required flight managers and pilots-in-command to get themselves out of very delicate situations. Christopher Fairchild, an Air Foyle employee, has a very interesting story about such a situation: *"During December 1990 and the early part of 1991 I made a number of flights on the An-124 between Luxembourg and Singapore. I remember on one occasion arriving into Abu Dhabi for a fuel stop and being advised that our next stop, Kiev, was to be changed. Fuel was in short supply in Kiev and could not be guaranteed. After some considerations, the captain decided that it would be possible to fly direct Abu Dhabi to Luxembourg missing out Kiev. We took on more fuel, filed a revised ATC flight plan and departed. While en route I decided to put my head down and promptly fell asleep. My sleep was broken by the radio operator tugging on my leg and shouting 'Turkey, no permission, no permission. You must speak to Ankara controller.'*

"Taking up the radio operator's position I spoke to the Ankara controller. The controller stated that we didn't have permission to overfly, we were violating Turkish airspace and that he would report us to the head of Turkish civil aviation. He also advised that we were to re-route avoiding Turkish Airspace. Explaining the reasons why we were routing through Turkish airspace I also asked the controller to give my best regards to Izmit Bey Director General of Civil Air Turkey. 'So you know Izmit Bey?' asked the controller. I replied, 'Two years earlier I was renting his apartment in Istanbul and he was my very good friend.' There was a short pause then the controller said. 'I shall pass your good wished to Izmit Bey but … nevertheless you are violating Turkish airspace and I will report you to him. You should expect to receive a fine.' Again there was a short pause and the controller said 'You are clear to cross Turkey direct with final destination Luxembourg.' We never did receive a fine."

However, the global nature of the airline's activities, being tied to the economy of not just one state but the planet as a whole, has not only positive aspects. Any negative processes in the world economy affect inevitably the activity of Antonov Airlines. Thus, the 1998–2000 crisis in Southeast Asia caused a significant decrease in demand for transportation. In addition to that, in 2000 a number of negative macroeconomic factors

V. M. Sudorgin – Head of operation of Antonov Airlines.

As you can see on these pages, Ruslan can make around 20 landings on one route making a shish-kebab of a wide variety of cargoes.

cause is a consolation, as well as understanding that many other airlines around the world suffer from such crises.

The management of Antonov Airlines has always considered the planned expansion of business ties with business partners to be the factor that can reduce losses caused by world economic crises. For instance for 17 years Air Foyle was side by side with the Kyivans on the difficult road of the development of the air transportation market for super-heavy outsized cargoes. As mutual confidence continued to grow, cooperation technologies developed, and international authority gained, the sphere of cooperation expanded more and more, and the agreement between partners periodically renewed. At the same time, the British company carried out a wide range of work on the marketing and organisation of charter flights of Antonov Airlines and provided quick financial services for flights. In particular, the British were responsible for relations with the UN, namely for preparing tender bids, for signing of contracts and obtaining all types of permits, and they provided their flight managers for participation in the Ruslan flights and the ongoing coordination of the airline's activities with UN representatives. At the same time, employees of Antonov Airlines worked in the office of Air Foyle. It is worth mentioning here that in 2000, the United Nations topped Antonov Airlines' 20 largest customers.

Christopher Foyle recalls the period 1997–2000: *"The UK MOD had decided to re-equip its RAF cargo fleet with the then yet be completed Airbus A400M, as well as the Lockheed C-130 J Hercules. As an interim measure they put out the STSA (Short Term Strategic Airlift) requirement, inviting those in industry to bid to supply a suitable aircraft until the arrival of the A400M. Following the first invitation to bid, working with our Antonov partners we offered the An-124 but retro-fitted with Rolls-Royce engines and highly modernised to be based in the UK. This together with other bids were turned down as being too costly, and a new invitation to tender was put out. During the first bidding process the UK MOD sent a large team of specialists from DERA at Boscombe Down to Antonov's headquarters design bureau and machine works, to evaluate their design and manufacturing capabilities. They were very impressed by what they found, stating that the Antonov system of stress testing to finality was much superior to western aircraft manufacturing techniques and practice.*

Following the new invitation to tender put out by the UK MOD, Air Foyle-Antonov offered a version of the An-124 to be based at an RAF aerodrome in the UK, to be flown by reserve RAF officers, with aircraft instrumentation in the English language, a delegated design authority from Marshall Aerospace in Cambridge, and a big stock of spares and engines

became evident, in particular the average price for aviation fuel in the world doubled. Although the airline was trying to reduce the impact of such circumstances, it was unable to counteract them completely. As a result, the cargo turnover in 2000 compared to 1999 decreased from 217,293 to 180 million ton/km, and the flying time reduced from 7,153 to 6,400 hours. In 2001, terrorist attacks posed a major setback to the activity of air carriers. The fact that these ongoing processes have an external

kept on site at the UK base. Once again the MOD sent a team of specialists from DERA to Kyiv, and again they came back with a glowing report as to Antonov's capabilities. We had an excellent government lobbying agency working with our special team, staffed by ex-senior RAF officers. Together with Air Commodore Owen Truelove who was our consultant, we had an in-depth knowledge of the internal decision-making process within the MOD, and it was not a pretty sight. We had been specifically told during the bidding process that manoeuvrability on the ground would not be a deciding factor in the competition, as the An-124 cannot reverse or turn in very tight circles on the ground like the Boeing C-17, its competitor in this process. However, in terms of capability, cost and efficiency, we were streets ahead of the C-17. We could fly twice as far with double the payload at half the price, but it was not to be. The then Chief of the Air Staff Sir Richard Johns was desperate to get four C-17s, even prepared to trade a Tornado squadron. The story goes that it was decided during a bit of horse trading on weapons systems at a meeting between the Prime Minister Tony Blair, Gordon Brown the Chancellor of the Exchequer and Geoff Hoon, the Defence Secretary. Some months later I bumped into a friend in the men's room at an aviation dinner, Sir Peter Squire, who by then had become the new Chief of the Air Staff. As we were using the facilities, he told me that the decision had been taken on the aircraft's manoeuvrability on the ground, not what we had been assured at the outset of the bidding process! No wonder that ex-Soviet countries become cynical about western preaching on the moral high horses of probity, integrity, transparency, fairness and the rule of law! Eventually having chosen the C-17, the poor old MOD had difficulty in financing them, ending up with an expensive lease for only four."

But Antonov Airlines and Air Foyle were connected not only by a business relationship. Little by little they became real friends based on mutual respect and a sense of responsibility for the result of their joint efforts. "How it used to be when we visited Antonov so many years ago?" Bruce Bird asks himself. "Everything was so basic or even nonexistent. The difference now in the ability of Antonov to upgrade their facilities to efficient installations of all kinds and to express their natural hospitality, usually to excess! The feeling of pleasure that I might have contributed in some small way to this change in just a few people's lives."

And as shown by the following quote, Bruce Bird was not only working wholeheartedly for the sake of a common goal but he was glad with all his heart when they reached it. "I remember our fifth anniversary celebrations when the intake of vodka exceeded my capacity and I took a walk outside to cool off. It was a warm evening, the grass was

cool so I lay down to examine the star spangled sky. When my friend Konstantin Fedorovich arrived he wanted to talk to me but I refused to talk to him unless he lay down with me. They tell me my behaviour was strange ... but it was Konstantin who lay down on the grass to talk to me ..."

Christopher Fairchild recalls: "I remember our tenth anniversary. Arriving on the boat chartered by Antonov at the island in the Dnepr where the

Bruce Bird and Christopher Foyle congratulating Antonov StC's team on the 55th anniversary of its founding. Kyiv, 2001.

From the early 2000s there was a steady development of business relations between Antonov StC and Volga-Dnepr Group. On the far left is A. I. Isaikin, President of Volga-Dnepr Group; to his left is D. S. Kiva, General Designer.

Christopher Foyle at one of the English clubs and we had a conversation about the extraordinary background of this charming man. A combat aviation pilot, he fought at the side of Baron Mannerheim – a friend of his father – during the Finnish Civil War; later, fighting against fascists as a member of the Royal Air Force, he was one of the first pilots to land a Spitfire on Sicily. After World War 2 he worked as a civil pilot and at the end of the 20th century was working as a consultant for Air Foyle.

Another fragment of Christopher Fairchild's memories about a funny adventure he experienced in 1996 is a good example of comradeship between Ukrainian and Russian companies' employees: *"In 1996 I was the Air Foyle Flight manager who flew from Penang, Malaya to Zhuhai in China. The AN124-100 delivered four small stunt aircraft which were to be displayed at the air show. On arrival all the crew and myself were driven by bus to the nearest available hotel. The journey took six hours and we eventually arrived at the city of Shenquan, bordering with Hong Kong. During our stay of approximately six days I arrange one evening to take a walk with one of the flight engineers. Our intention during the evening was to find a restaurant to experience the local cuisine. At about 7pm we set off from the hotel, towards the bright lights and centre of town. After forty-five minutes we found what seemed to be a very popular restaurant and found ourselves a table out on the street. A very pretty waitress came to our table and presented us with a menu in a language neither of us understood. We laughed and asked if she spoke English or Russian. Her reaction was negative. Looking around at what other people were eating we pointed to one table. 'Some of that' I said, pointing at a prawn like dish and 'Some of that' pointing at some chicken. My colleague said it wouldn't be enough and we should choose another dish pointing to a large metal pot on another table with beef and cabbage leaves.*

After some time our order arrived with rice, chop sticks and two small glasses. We toasted the meal that we were about to eat. We were both proud that we had communicated so well that we now had a splendid meal before our very eyes, and not too expensive either. The prawns were excellent, the chicken was very tender and the beef a little tough but cut into pieces very manageable. After about 20

picnic was prepared, to find a string quartet in black tie and tails playing classical music in the woods. Surreal ... And I remember many social occasions with our good friend, Emanuel Galitzine, now 84 years young, when he took over Kiev and Moscow musicians and instructed them how to play and sing in the old way. He has at last now obtained his Russian passport with the double headed eagle and takes pleasure in confusing the authorities by alternating his British and Russian passports." The author was lucky enough to meet Prince Galitzine at the Farnborough Air Show in September 1998. There was a small evening reception arranged by

"My friends, our union is great!

"Since 1992 among the founders of the Volga-Dnepr Airlines there are two very important shareholders: Antonov Company and ZMKB Progress. Even though their shares in the charter capital are small, the

role of these companies and their teams cannot be overrated. After all, they are the designers of An-124-100 aircraft and D-18T engine. This speaks for itself.

"We all owe them, first of all for the

very existence of our main aircraft, secondly, for continued airworthiness of the aircraft and the engine and, thirdly, their further improvement. It is due to their creative input, intellect and utter devotion to our

minutes our waitress came to our table. We thought she was asking if we were enjoying our meal. I explained that everything was excellent. The chicken (animating my words with a CLUCK ! CLUCK !) was very tender but, the beef (animating my words with a MOO ! MOO! and horns with my hands), was a little chewy.

The waitress then led us over to another part of the restaurant, 'Cluck ! Cluck !' she said pointing to a very large snake in a cage and 'MOO! MOO!' pointing another cage containing a wild dog. We didn't bother to ask her about the prawns ..."

But let us leave pleasant memories and return to the main topic of our account. We stopped at the expansion of the airline's business relations. This was a continuous process, and one of the most important steps aimed at increasing the number of orders for the services of Antonov Airlines was made in 2001. On 23 February Air Foyle and HeavyLift, which previously competed with each other, reached an agreement in principle regarding the establishment of a Joint Venture in order to promote the services of Antonov Airlines to the world market. Negotiations over details of the agreement lasted for more than two months and finished in Kyiv at the international conference of air cargo carriers. On 15 May Christopher Foyle and Michael Hayles, the presidents of the companies, announced that they were going to initiate the procedure of joint venture registration, and on 1 August this joint venture started its official operation under the name of Air Foyle-HeavyLift. Since that time, the network of agents engaged in the search for orders for Kyiv's Ruslans has almost doubled, and the reputation of HeavyLift has been added to the authority of the alliance Air Foyle-Antonov.

The result achieved was highly appreciated by the partners. For instance, Konstantin Lushakov noted then: *"Antonov Airlines is satisfied with the expansion of its operation worldwide and establishment of cooperation with two British companies which not only have 30 years of best practice in the area of outsized cargoes transportation but also enjoy authority over the world market. Antonov Airlines is well pleased with the long-term cooperation with Air Foyle and hopes for the same fruitful relationship with the newly established company."*

Christopher Foyle made a point: *"Since 1989 Air Foyle and Antonov Airlines worked in close cooperation and achieved considerable success. Nowadays the demand for air cargo transportation continues to grow and both our companies believe that the business opportunities of outsized cargoes transportation are really huge. We always noticed the supreme competence of HeavyLift that recently used to be our main competitor for the An-124-100 services market and we are happy that we are joining our efforts now. We are sure that cooperation between our Joint Venture and*

Bruce Bird, Christopher Foyle and Emanuel Galitzine at the Antonov StC's museum. Kyiv, May 2001.

The Agreement for the establishment of Air Foyle-HeavyLift joint venture is signed. Michael Hayles, Christopher Foyle and Dmitry Kiva, Evgenii Golovnev and Andrii Sovenko are behind. Kyiv, May 2001.

Viktor Tolmachev, Technical Director of Volga-Dnepr Airlines
Volga-Dnepr corporate newsletter, July-August 2000.

common love – aviation – that today both the aircraft and the engine are living their second lives. The two well-known interstate programmes on upgrade of D-18T and An-124-100 are keystones for our joint

successful work.

"All of them – Piotr Balabuev, Fedor Muravchenko, Dmitry Kiva, Vladimir Kolesnikov, Anatoly Vovnyanko, Leonid Martynenko and many and many other

employees of both Antonov Company and ZMKB Progress – are excellent people, reliable partners, great enthusiasts of aviation and An-124 -100 Ruslan aircraft."

Transportation of a ship's engine crankshaft from Hamburg for a tanker under repair. 2001.

Border guard patrol boat about to be loaded into the Ruslan. October 2004.

Antonov Airlines will help it to boost its position and its reputation as one of the world leaders of the air cargo transportation market".

Graham Pearce, commercial director of HeavyLift, agreed with him: "I'm glad that my company has established a joint venture with Air Foyle. HeavyLift has no doubt that the outsized cargo market expansion will continue. As a result of establishment of the joint venture the customers worldwide will get considerable advantages resulting

from the huge experience of arrangement of such cargo transportation owned by all three partners."

Expansion of partnership contacts was important, but still only a part of the policy pursued by the air freight unit of Antonov StC in the market. After all, market players include not only its partners but competitors as well. For example, during the period under review here, in 2000 33–35% of the total air freight volume was taken by An-124-100 aircraft of Antonov Airlines, while more than 50% of this market was controlled by Volga-Dnepr, 8% was taken by the Russian airline Polet and there were also smaller operators. Despite the fact that all these airlines had different areas of business, they still had much in common, in particular the general task of maintaining airworthiness of the Ruslan and searching for the most acceptable ways for its further modernisation. In order to solve these problems there is a reasonable need to join the efforts of all An-124-100 aircraft operators. There are other reasons that require competitors to coordinate their efforts in solving many of the issues that the emerging air freight market is currently bringing up.

The most constructive approach in this regard was adopted by the Volga-Dnepr Group. After its leadership realised that any confrontation was a dead end, they took a number of steps in 2000 in order to resolve some controversies that had previously

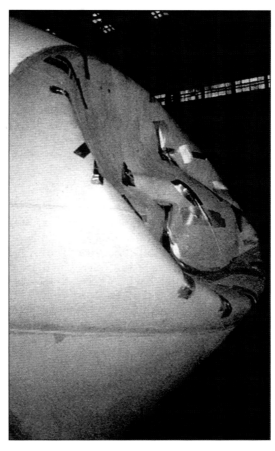

An-124-100 UR-82007 radome after ball lightning strike. December, 1999.

Technical crew of Ruslan UR-82029 inspecting damage caused by ball lightning strike. Ostend, Belgium, October 18, 2000.

occurred between Volga-Dnepr and Antonov StC. These steps found a most welcoming response among the leadership of Antonov Airlines. Here is the opinion of K. F. Lushakov: *"Since the establishment of Volga-Dnepr we proposed to them to work together in order to avoid unnecessary competition. It took them 10 years to reach similar conclusions. We are sure that we need to work in concert in the market. If we work this way we would achieve great results. It would allow us to focus the financial assets on improvement of an aircraft to use it more effectively in future."* In fact, in almost two decades Volga-Dnepr has been consistently upholding the idea of joining the efforts of different airlines to upgrade the Ruslan and resume its serial production.

The idea of resuming the production of the An-124 aircraft family that emerged at the turn of the century had quite solid grounds; first of all the ever-increasing demand for transporting cargoes by these particular aircraft. All Ruslan's operators tried to expand their fleet by adding existing aircraft manufactured in previous times that had become of no interest to their owners. Needless to say, all active carriers kept a close eye on such aircraft immediately as they appeared on the market. Such a case happened in 1998–2000, when one of the Russian Ruslans (serial No. 07-03) was abandoned by its owners (the Ajax airline) and the Dutch authorities placed a lien on it in the city of Maastricht. As a designer of the aircraft, Antonov StC was concerned about the fact that its creation was rusting in one of the European airports and causing unhealthy excitement among the mass media and various competitor companies. The company's leadership had always been sensitive to such cases and so that the reputation of an aircraft carrying the brand 'An' would not be injured they helped many times to 'drag' other airlines' aircraft out of all sorts of critical situations. For instance, the military An-22 which got stuck in Aden after an emergency landing was repaired in very difficult conditions; a Volga-Dnepr An-124 was reconditioned and ferried back to Russia after an emergency landing at Gander. On 4 December 2000 the governmental authorities of the Netherlands in accordance with rules of international law organised an auction sale of trapped Ruslan, Air Foyle as a general sales agent of Antonov StC won the auction and entered into an agreement with Antonov Airlines for joint operation of the aircraft. Bruce Bird explains: *"I remember when I attended the auction of An-124 RA-82070 in Holland. We never expected to win the auction but were attending just to see what happened. My surprise when the auctioneer's hammer fell with a sharp crack with the announcement that I had just bought an An-124 . . !"*

After this, specialists from Kyiv performed the required checks and a reconditioning repair of the 'Maastricht prisoner' and on 3 February 2001 the aircraft landed successfully in Kyiv. Bruce Bird continues: *"I was watching from the flight deck of 82070 as we taxied at Maastricht before the first flight of the aircraft for three years. Seeing the hundreds of people who had come to watch the final departure of this aircraft that had been so much in the news. Some slight trepidation at this first flight but my determination that if I was the instrument for buying the aircraft then I was also going to deliver it."* That's how the Ruslan was actually helped out of overseas imprisonment. Alas it was not destined to become a part of the Antonov Airlines fleet.

The fact that the aircraft registered as RA-82070 was already in flying condition in Kyiv, and not somewhere in Europe under arrest, aroused a sudden interest in the aircraft from numerous Russian institutions that were one way or another connected with its previous owner. However, well-informed people say that this is a common practice – until the item is sold at an auction everybody keeps silent, but as soon as it finds a new lawful owner out of nowhere all kinds of creditors, claimers, straw man, etc. start to demand something from the owner. Numerous legal proceedings were initiated in Russia, Ukraine, the United Kingdom and the Netherlands, involving various firms, state institutions of several countries, ICAO experts and even scientific institutions. Little by little this problem evolved from a mere economic dispute into a major interstate Russian-Ukrainian conflict, which was absolutely not in the interest area of Antonov StC, which at that time considered Russia to be its strategic partner for development of a number of new competitive aircraft. In this situation, the management of Air Foyle, having consulted with Antonov StC, considered it better to conclude an amicable settlement with the Russians, in accordance with which the Ruslan returned to the manufacturing plant in Ulyanovsk, and costs incurred by Kyivans and the British were compensated. *It was a very unfortunate and frustrating experience, Christopher Foyle recalls: "We, mainly in the person of Bruce Bird, had worked hard in the top commercial courts in London, the Hague, Moscow and Kiev to retain the aircraft for Antonov, against the opportunistict predations of Center Capital a Russian company controlled by a smooth, plausible businessman Rashid Mursukaev, but the court got confused as to who owned the aircraft. Owing to this confusion and conflict of instuctions, the aircraft had to be released to Center Capital for a modest sum of money. A bitter experience."*

Yet, no matter how important the aircraft, trade connections and so on are for airlift services, the main asset of the airline was, and always will be, its people – lovers of their craft, professionals who have repeatedly proved their ability to act without hesitation and efficiently in the most improbable situations. A. N. Gritsenko then flight manager in that memorable flight of Ruslan UR-82007, tells us about one such case, which took place in December 1999:

"It was a very usual flight. The airfield of the Algerian city of Busfer, where we loaded the cargo to carry it to Belarus, is surrounded by mountains like a horseshoe. There you can take off only in one direction – towards the Mediterranean Sea. At first, the weather was beautiful, but then clouds appeared, it started to rain, and then a thunderstorm began. When it was time to take off, the rain stopped, only the clouds remained. At line up Artem Nikolayevich Kulikov, pilot-in-command, looked at the weather radar screen and saw no signs of thunderstorm activity. But as soon as we entered the clouds, the cabin was lit by the brightest flash, and there was an explosion – as was later determined, ball lightning hit the second engine. Later, the guys from the aft cabin told me that they had never seen such a bright light in their life. The engine parameters went beyond extreme limits, all the annunciators started flashing, and the senior flight engineer shut it down. After thinking over the situation, we came to a conclusion that it was pointless to go back: we would have had to return to the lightning area again. Therefore, we continued to climb with three engines. However, about four minutes later there was another explosion and such a strong flash that we all lost sight for a while – the second ball lightning struck the nose fairing. Then the brightest bundle of light which seemed to me a half a metre thick hit the pilot-in-command's side of the windshield. A jet of fire was flowing very slowly, like lava from a volcano. There were dark dots inside that flow: the melted remains of the metal lightning protection stripes installed in the nose fairing of our Ruslan. Almost without seeing anything, the second pilot-in-command Volodya Bezmaternnykh continued to pilot the plane. So passed 15 seconds, then the fire stream suddenly stopped.

"As soon as the crew checked the on-board systems, the second navigator Valera Nakonechnii asked me where we were going to land. After a short consultation with the pilot-in-command and navigators, we made a joint decision not to return to Africa, but to continue the flight along the route. The aircraft behavior was, in general, normal. At the moment of lightning strike circuit breakers in some of electrical circuits became actuated, but after the necessary switching the aircraft electrical system operation was restored. The navigation complex also functioned OK. Of course, we knew that the nose cone was damaged, but there was a metal partition behind it introduced in all Ruslans after the accident during the certification tests.

"We managed to contact the base with the help of the An-140 crew, which was at the time in the test flight zone. We reported the incident and asked permission to change the route – to go home, to Gostomel, instead of Belarus. However, our management after they realised that that the flight was continuing without additional problems gave an instruction to fly to Baranovichi, in order to avoid customs problems.

"After landing and taxying to the parking area in Belarus we saw all the people who happened to be nearby were running to the nose of our aircraft. We also went out of the aircraft and saw a really impressive sight – the aircraft nose was smashed, the fiberglass fairing had eight through ruptures each 200–600 mm long. Almost two and a half metres of lightning protection stripes were completely melted and metal droplets penetrated deeply into the windshield, and they still remain there today. We roughly fixed the ruptures in the fairing and left for Gostomel for repair."

It is interesting that exactly one year later, in December 2000, another Ruslan (UR-82029) experienced a ball lightning strike. This happened during approach to the Belgian city of Ostend. As in

RA-82070 piloted by Antonov StC's flight crew departing to Kyiv, Maastricht, Netherlands, 3 February 2001.

Organisers of all kinds of rallies, including the most famous races, have asked for the help of Antonov Airlines more than once.

the Algerian case, the clouds were blurry, and there were no signs of thunderstorm activity. Despite the unexpectedness of the incident, the crew under the command of S. M. Troshin were able to come out of the difficult situation with pride.

The customers, partners and competitors respect not only the high professionalism of the Ruslans' crews as the excellent reputation of Antonov Airlines in the business world has been developed by the tremendous working capacity, responsibility and reliability of all the company's personnel. This is shown by the words of D. Y. Patzelia who is already familiar to us: *"The Paris-Dakar rally takes place every year. It is very popular, and leading car manufacturing companies send their latest models to undergo this test. And the start and finish dates of the rally are strictly fixed, they are not changed for any*

reasons. This is done to demonstrate that regardless of the heat or the showers, cars always finish on time. However, in 1999, the racing drivers faced a new problem – some Muslim tribes in Nigeria located in the territory through which the rally route passed, suddenly stood up against the race and began to threaten its participants with terrorist attacks. In light of this the organisers decided to transport cars over dangerous areas by air with the help of Antonov Airlines. It was very hard work: three Ruslans were flying from N'Djamena (Republic of Chad) to Sebha (Libya) and made about 60 flight hours in five days. It was required by the schedule of the rally. Neither the crews nor the aircraft failed – the job was done in full accordance with the contract. Following that a website called 'Saint Antonov' appeared on the Internet."

CHRONICLE OF ANTONOV AIRLINES: YEAR BY YEAR
Hot spots (2001–2015)

Hot spots

As the readers will already know, flights to various hot spots, recently affected by natural or man-made disasters, droughts, epidemics or armed conflicts, have always been an important part of Antonov Airlines 's activities. It is sufficient to recall the flights to eliminate the consequences of the 1987 earthquake in Armenia, the rescue of refugees from the front line zone during the Gulf War in 1991, flights under UN orders to Angola, Yemen, Congo, Namibia and Sierra Leone over the 1992 to 1995 period. In these and dozens of other cases, humanitarian aid and various cargoes for the UN peacekeeping contingents, delivered by Antonov Airlines to the right place at proper time, saved many thousands of human lives.

It should be noted that flights to hot spots are a common activity for Antonov Airlines. Performing such flights, the operator convincingly demonstrates its advantages over other market players because all Antonov Airlines' aircraft are in fact 'demobilized' military transports. Of course, now all its aircraft meet civil requirements as high as those for specially designed aircraft but their military origin remains one of their advantages. As a result, Antonov aircraft demonstrate their best qualities precisely at those places where the aerodromes are not functioning properly, where there is no ground equipment available, where it is necessary to deliver the most diverse, often unpredictable goods, including oversized self-propelled and non-self-propelled machinery. And as long as such places remain on the planet, Antonov Airlines remains ahead of the competition.

Its reputation as an extremely reliable partner for transportation to such places, gained by Antonov Airlines during the 1990s, resulted in the fact that in the autumn of 2001, after the UN had issued a mandate to carry out an anti-terrorist operation in Afghanistan that created the necessity to deliver a huge amount of cargo to the country, applications for work rained on Antonov Airlines. However, the operator could not immediately start flying to the war region. There were several reasons. First, nobody could really calculate the extent of the threat to such flights posed by the large-scale battles taking place in Afghanistan. Secondly, the largest aerodromes, including Bagram, Kabul and Kandahar, had been bombed and could not receive the An-124-100 aircraft. Thirdly, the Aviation Authorities of Ukraine strictly prohibited flights to Afghanistan. At the same time, L. D. Kuchma, then-President of Ukraine, repeatedly expressed in the media his support for the anti-terrorist operation in Afghanistan and promised that Ukraine would assist the coalition forces, including the aviation transport support.

Thus, an ambiguous situation arose about the possible flights of Ukrainian aircraft to Afghanistan. Some Ukrainian airlines, having had transport aircraft and also having received invitations to participate in the transportations, actually had to refuse to participate. They were afraid of penalties in case they would not be able to obtain a permit

(2001–2015)

for a flight from the State Aviation Authorities of Ukraine. In that situation, the management of Antonov Airlines, having consulted with representatives of the Ministry of Foreign Affairs, the Cabinet of Ministers and lawyers of the Presidential Administration, nevertheless decided to take a chance for the world community. They started preparing for transportation, forming price policy and searching for a compromise with the Aviation Authorities. This work lasted until December 2001, when the time came to make the decision: to fly or not to fly to Afghanistan? Three of the Ruslans flew to Cologne, took on board German army trucks with food and then transferred to Baku where the aircraft started waiting for permission from the Aviation Authorities of Ukraine.

"I had to go to the Department of Aviation Transport; the working day was coming to an end," A. N. Gritsenko recalls. *"I was sat in the office of the Chief of the Aviation Security Department surrounded by about ten people from different departments. They started rebuking me full-tilt, telling me that it was very dangerous and Antonov Airlines would not get any permission, and if Antonov Airlines flies without permission, it would lose the Air Operator Certificate. In reply to all my arguments about the necessity to carry out that work, which would not only bring Ukraine*

Antonov Airlines' aircraft landed in Afghanistan for the first time at the very beginning of 2002.

Delivery of a heavy mine-breaching vehicle to Kabul from Cologne, Germany, 2002.

V. V. Goncharov, captain of the An-124-100.

profitable contracts, but also would correspond with the policy of the President of the country, I heard just one answer – no. I was looking for the slightest clue for compromise, but, unfortunately, the Department's employees were adamant.

"At one point, it seemed to me that a compromise could be found: to deliver the Department's specialists to Afghanistan by our aircraft, which would be the first to fly there, in order to let the specialists estimate the state of aviation security at Bagram Airport we were going to fly to. Having talked to K. F. Lushakov I proposed to them to urgently go to Gostomel and take our An-26 aircraft to fly to Baku for further transfer to the An-124-100 aircraft. They agreed, but at that moment a phone call sounded and the Chief of the Aviation Security Department was summoned to his boss. We had been waiting for him for a long time. And when he returned, he said that nobody would fly. Moreover, the Chiefs of some Ukrainian airlines were invited to the Ministry of Foreign Affairs for a meeting on this matter to be held by the Deputy Minister the morning of the next day."

K. F. Lushakov went to the meeting. There, in a working atmosphere, they managed comprehensively to examine all issues related to the possible participation of Ukrainian airlines in Afghan transportation. As a result, certain plans were adopted for the implementation of the proposals, which were made by Antonov Airlines. That is, the ban was actually lifted.

Antonov Airlines made the first flights to Afghanistan at the turn of 2001–02. These were six from Cologne to Bagram when Ukrainian aviators delivered about 500 tonnes of the most needed cargo for the German military contingent in that country. Strictly speaking, it would have been more convenient for the Germans to land the aircraft in Kabul, but the runway of the airport had been destroyed by bombing, so at that time the airport could not accommodate the heavy Ruslans. The first wheels that touched Afghan land were the wheels of the An-124-100 aircraft commanded by A. K. Khrustytskii with I. A. Belozerov as a flight manager. In Bagram, as well as in other places, where the Antonov Airlines' crews started flying to, the breath of recent battles was still felt. Just a few steps aside the taxiway strips the craters gaped, there were blackened remains of burnt-out trucks and armoured vehicles and vast sections of the airport's territory remained mined. But the staff of Antonov Airlines demonstrated the highest level of organisation and discipline, operating quickly with well-coordinated loading and unloading procedures that made it possible to minimize the potential risk and avoid any serious incidents.

The second aircraft to arrive to Bagram was the one led by D. V. Antonov with E. A. Golovnev as a flight manager. This is what this highly experienced flight manager, who performed more than 50 flights to Afghanistan, recounts: *"The situation was complicated by the fact that we hadn't trustworthy information as to the situation in Kabul and Bagram. Even the runway coordinates were written down not completely correctly. When we flew up to Bagram for the first time, through the lacerated clouds Dima Antonov saw the runway, which was a little bit shifted from the place we were expecting to see it according to GPS indications. He had to perform a sharp roll of the aircraft and approach along a quite steep glide path. By the way, later such landings became a common practice, but was required by the desire to stay within the protected area of the airport rather than through any mistakes. When approaching, we clearly saw the state of the runway – five bombed craters were hurriedly patched up and that was a cause for concern. However, the landing and the next takeoff were successful ... O!*

The most important thing was to fly away from there before sunset. During one of the subsequent flights we delayed, so we had to take off in almost complete darkness. Being afraid of attracting fire, we didn't switch on floodlights and navigation lights. What else do I recall? Perhaps the well-coordinated actions of the military men while unloading our aircraft. All of them were under arms and in full marching orders, but they worked very intensively and effectively unlike those locals who were sometimes hired for such work. Besides, we remembered there were a lot of mines in the ground around the taxiway strips and parking places, so we always had to be careful and try not to leave the concrete areas. One day, I saw how an Afghan, who decided to cut a corner between taxiway strips, tripped a mine. An ambulance arrived promptly, but it didn't make any difference to the careless wanderer."

The flights to Afghanistan, especially the first ones, were carried out under very difficult conditions and demanded the highest professionalism of the flight crews. When entering the country's air zone, it was necessary to identify the aircraft through the American AWACS long-range radar surveillance aircraft which was constantly on duty. In addition, instrument landing equipment was still not available in Kabul even after the runway had been repaired, and the time allotted for landing was strictly limited to 15 minutes. If the crew did not fit into this narrow slot, it was obliged to return. The reason was there was a large 'anthill' in the Kabul area with many aircraft from the United States and other countries in the air simultaneously. Nevertheless, despite completing hundreds of flights, the Antonov Airlines' crews never had to return because of a

A. B. Ablulayev, navigator.

Unloading the CH-47 Chinook transport helicopter. These vehicles were one of the main American 'workhorses' in Afghanistan.

A. V. Krents, radio operator.

delay, they always stayed within the slot limits.

Even the first flights demonstrated that the scale of the operation carried out by the Allies in Afghanistan would be exceptionally large. Thus, it was going to be necessary to transport a truly myriad number of cargoes, so, it was important to look to long-term contacts with the main participants in the antiterrorist coalition. The United States, Great Britain and the Federal Republic of Germany were the first to be contacted. Since the United States had their own military transport aircraft, they did not need the services of commercial airlines. As for the UK, its Ministry of Defence had already had a valid contract with Volga-Dnepr, and was quite satisfied with the volume and quality of the

The intensity of Antonov Airlines' flights to Afghanistan was such that while one Ruslan is unloaded, the next one is landing. Outskirts of Kabul airport, 8 September 2003.

services provided. Therefore, the managers of Antonov Airlines decided to pay special attention to the cargo transported by the Bundeswehr, as they understood that for the first time since the end of the World War II the Germans were taking their armed forces outside Germany, and that

Repair work on the taxiway strips of Kabul airport and unloading the Ruslans are undertaken simultaneously. Autumn 2003.

would inevitably entail the transportation of a huge quantity of cargo for various purposes. So it happened.

For the first five months of 2002 the Ruslans of Antonov Airlines carried out 182 flights to

Afghanistan. 12,971 tonnes of cargo had been transported from several airports located in Europe to Bagram as well as to the rebuilt airports of Kabul and Kandahar. In addition, the Federal Republic of Germany and the Defence Departments of Poland and Great Britain were customers for the flights. Humanitarian aid was the main part of the cargo transported. The Germans completely justified the forecasts of the managers of Antonov Airlines: they carried almost everything by the An-124-100 aircraft, from drinking water to helicopters and tanks.

The sharp increase in the intensity of flights to Afghanistan caused a lot of new problems for Antonov Airlines, first of all the necessity to comply with an accurate schedule of all the procedures associated with maintenance of dozens of 'boards' at different airports. *"We realised that the success of our work depended on how accurately and harmoniously all the participants of the transportation process adhered to the general rhythm."* A. N. Gritsenko continues his story about the organisation of those flights, *"In order to avoid organisational failures, we decided to send our specialists to Baku in order to dispatch all the Afghan flights at that key airport. The aircraft of Antonov Airlines performed up to eight landings per day in Baku on those hot days. For the benefit of the Bundeswehr alone, we carried out more than 500 flights with cargoes for various purposes and almost all of them were performed without any frustration. Just due to that work, done on demand of the Federal Republic of Germany, we subsequently received an offer to participate in the SALIS programme."*

Not only the intensity of flights grew within the first half of 2002. As the winter turned into the spring and then the summer came, the air temperature at the main Afghan airports steadily increased. Moreover, all of the airports mentioned were located at a significant height above sea level (Bagram – 1,620 m, Kabul – 1,790 m, Kandahar – 1,010 m). These factors adversely affected the operation of the An-124-100 aircraft's power plant resulting in limitation of the takeoff weight at those airports. In some cases they even had to postpone the start of engines till early morning when the air was still cool. According to B. V. Gorobeyko, who devoted a lot of energy to efficient organisation of Afghan flights, in such cases the aircraft remained at the destination airports for the night, waiting for the better conditions for takeoff. There was not much that was positive in that situation: a proper rest in a hotel in a rebellious country was out of the question. Crew members set up for the night in nearby small trailers, or simply stayed on board, napping at their usual places and taking turns in going out to patrol the approaches to the aircraft.

One quiet Afghan night the author of these lines had to walk several times around Mriya along deserted taxiway strips of Kabul airport. I believe these impressions will be etched in my memory for a long time: the dark crown of mountains against the backdrop of the sky illuminated by the moon, German armoured vehicles, continuously cruising along the barbed wire around the airport, the nervous beams of searchlights coming from Belgian checkpoints, faintly audible shooting near the former town of Soviet specialists, and the majestic silhouette of the An-225 aircraft over all this scene – the giant patiently waiting for dawn to come.

As the Allies became familiar with the region, a demand arose to transport cargo not only to Afghanistan, but also to return it. In fact, the return traffic was meagre, 8–10 times less than the direct transport. For example, for the whole year of 2002 Antonov Airlines' aircraft performed 217 flights to the country and transported 14,936.6 tonnes of cargo; in the opposite direction they flew loaded just 25 times and carried 1,169 tonnes. Such trends continued the following years. The consignments sent to Europe mainly consisted of various equipment and property arranged in standard containers, as well as military equipment that required repair as a result of combat damage or simply breakdowns.

If the equipment remained in running condition, as a rule there were no problems during the loading process. In most cases, they managed to drag the broken combat vehicles into the cargo compartment by means of onboard winches. However, sometimes it was not so easy to solve the problem. An example is the story of Vitaly Róman, one of the load masters: *"That flight, Bagram-Wroclaw, was carried out in the interests of the Polish contingent. They brought us an armoured vehicle by trailer. We asked about the weight. They said the weight was 23 tonnes. The armoured vehicle was broken. The engine was out of order, so the hydraulic control system was dead. The wheels did not turn, so we could not drag the armoured vehicle in by means of the winches. Our onboard loading equipment was all that could help, but in order to lift 23 tonnes it was necessary to assemble a combination of cranes with a 30-tonne carrying capacity. Such a crane combination has height limitations for the location of the hoist fittings – no more than 1,800 mm from the floor of the cargo compartment. The armoured vehicle's hoist fittings were located at a height of 2.3 metres, plus the height of the trailer. We decided to put nylon slings under the bottom of the armoured vehicles. Each such sling was designed to lift 20 tonnes. So, four such slings had to bear 80 tonnes. We started lifting, but the lower edges of the armoured body cut the slings, and the armoured vehicle flopped down to the ground. We asked them to send a lower trailer, but the Poles answered they did not have such a trailer, and they were not going to ask the Americans for it. In short, it took*

A. N. Polischuk and M. I. Rasshivalov, flight engineers.

Mriya is forced to spend the night in Kabul. September 2003'

The staff of Antonov Airlines consist of truly universal specialists. In the three pictures – E.A. Golovnev, Head of Financial and Analytical Department of Antonov Airlines.

us more than 10 hours to tinker with that armoured vehicle, although such a loading procedure usually took us one and a half to two hours. It seems to me that the armoured vehicle was considerably heavier, since a 30-tonne forklift truck barely lifted it off the ground."

From 2003, the 'air bridge' between European countries and Afghanistan, built by Antonov Airlines, ran as a well-oiled machine. Of course, the intensity of transportation was not constant. The peaks of flights occurred in 2003 and 2008–12, when 350–450 flights were performed per year

with the highest peak of 482 flights in 2011. The majority of requests for quotations for flights were sent three to five days prior to the date of departure, that made it possible for both Antonov Airlines and customers to prepare properly for the flights. However, during the many years of work in the Afghan sky, cases happened when a cargo had to be delivered much more urgently. Then the whole system worked much faster, providing a minimal period from the receipt of a quotation request to the departure – around three hours. But sometimes the aircraft were redirected while in the air. In such

Hot autumn of 2003. Kabul.

To Afghanistan by a charter flight

On Saturday, exactly at 18.00, the first super-powerful An-124 aircraft took off from the Wroclaw-Strachowice airport; the second aircraft took to the skies 10 minutes later. As well as special equipment, 24 Polish soldiers were allocated to the decks of the Ukrainian

Ruslans. This is the first group of the contingent that will participate in the combat operation code-named as 'Indestructible Freedom', held in Afghanistan under the general command of the United States. The Polish contingent must be at the place on

April 22, namely at Bagram airbase.

The Polish contingent will fly to Bagram in six groups of two aircraft each. Lieutenant-Colonel Marek Mahezinski is the commander of the Polish contingent. He is a head of the soldiers from the 1st Brigade of sappers from

cases the crews coped brilliantly with the situation.

The vast experience of the flight crews, the professionalism of the specialists in the operational service, the enviable self-sufficiency of the Ruslans are the most important factors that ensured success even under the most difficult conditions. As a result, of 1,977 flights performed by Antonov Airlines to Afghanistan from the beginning of 2002 to the end of 2015, as well as the 1,494 return flights, not one was abandoned! And it should be noted that the total amount of cargo transported reached a colossal total of 215,028 tonnes! To my mind, such a quantity of cargo, intended to support the actions of troops in a foreign combat theatre, has never been transported by the air either before or after the Afghan events.

Being involved in the Afghan transportations, and moreover being involved on such a scale, Antonov Airlines quickly became one of the important elements of a complex logistic system that enabled the the coalition forces to function. Moreover, the exceptional reliability Antonov Airlines demonstrated in fulfilling its contractual obligations made the carrier a very desirable partner for the future operations by Europeans in the region.

Therefore, when in 2003 a demand arose for transportation of large batches of cargo to Iraq, the coalition command again turned to Antonov's staff.

They started getting requests through a number of commercial companies which were authorized by the Ministries of Defence of the coalition countries to arrange transportations in their interests. In addition, from the spring of 2003 the demand arose to deliver cargoes intended to restore the economy of the country destroyed by the war. Thus, in April-May Antonov staff were offered to transport a large batch of building construction material and equipment to Baghdad, initially for the US Embassy in Iraq. Skylink Air and Logistic Support Company won an international tender for the administration of such air transportations and offered Antonov Airlines very profitable terms for implementation of the task. However, once again Antonov Airlines did not have the ability to accept the offer. The reason was the same as two years before on the eve of flights to Afghanistan – the ban issued by the Aviation Authorities of Ukraine and the vague position of the Ministry of Foreign Affairs of Ukraine, which rhetorically supported the anti-terrorist struggle, but did not take any practical

E. I. Naumkin, navigator.

Ya. I. Kashitskii, navigator.

Damaged military vehicles, which often could not drive any more, were brought out from Afghanistan by return flights.

Radoslaw Biczak, Artur Bilski
Polska Zbrojna, No. 12 (271), March 24, 2002

Brzeg, the 10th Transport Team from Opole and commandos of the GROM subdivision. The Polish military will be engaged in reconnaissance and engineering activity at the destroyed airport. They will operate together with Americans, British, Canadians and Australians ...

Poland rented charter flights by the transport aircraft of Antonov Airlines, which operates seven An-124 Ruslan aircraft with a maximum carrying capacity of up to 150 tonnes.

These aircraft are capable of traveling a distance of 5,000 km without refueling.

Mriya lands within the protected zone of Kabul airfield.

According to B. V. Gorobeyko, who directly arranged the first flights to Iraq, the number of quotation requests and, consequently, refusals grew. The pressure of the appeals to Antonov Airlines and their trading agents in the United Kingdom was gradually becoming more and more intense, until it came to open threats not only to refuse further cooperation but also to break the existing contracts. Trying to save the situation, A. G. Bulanenko, the President of Antonov Airlines, wrote several letters to the Ministry of Industrial Policy and the Ministry of Transport of Ukraine. Many Ukrainian officials also realised the acuteness of the situation. For example, on June 2, V. P. Kazakov, the State Secretary for the Defence-Industrial Complex and Machine Building Sector of Ukraine, addressed a letter to the Ministry of Foreign Affairs, and, referring to the real threat of contract loss, urged them to make up their minds about the possibility for Antonov Airlines flying to Iraq.

During the first few days of June 2003, the situation had escalated to a peak. On the June 3, P. V. Balabuev got an alarming letter from Foyle, in

steps. Of course, the officials' first care was for the safety of Ukrainian crews, but their inactivity didn't encourage success for the commercial activity of Antonov Airlines.

particular the following passage: *"Because of the signs of a decline in the economy, the business of oversized cargo transportatios for industrial and commercial companies has significantly weakened ... Currently, still available is still the business connected with peacekeeping forces and recovering works in Basra, and – in the near future – in Baghdad. However, we are very worried about the current situation. According to our information, the Ministry of Foreign Affairs of Ukraine does not want the planes of your company to fly to Basra, although other operators, including passenger airlines, such as Virgin Atlantic, fly to Basra on the order of the British government. I am writing to inform you that if we are prevented from performing the proposed work this way, it will have serious negative financial consequences for our business, as well as shatter confidence of our customers who simply will not offer us such work in the future. I, with all due respect, ask you to apply to the Ministry of Foreign Affairs to change this policy, which differs markedly from that of other countries ..."*

The next day, the General Designer took a number of decisive steps towards a compromise between the need to save the business and the proper level of safety of Antonov Airlines' crews. Among these actions, he sent a letter to the I. P. Smeshko, Chairman of the Commission on Military-Industrial Cooperation and Export Control under the President of Ukraine, where he indicated the following: *"The Ministry of Defence of Italy warned our agents that they would break the contract, previously signed with us, regarding air transportations to Kabul if our company refuses to fly to Iraq. The Italian side considers this matter as an integrated contract for the provision of Italian forces in the Middle East countries and Afghanistan. Further delays in making the decision to allow Ukrainian airlines to fly to Iraq will cause significant financial losses to our airlines and undermine the political prestige of the country that has declared its support to the world community in the anti-terrorist struggle."*

The pressure of all these factors, as well as the UN Security Council Resolution No. 1483 of 22 May 2003 which lifted the embargo from the Republic of

B. V. Gorobeyko contributed greatly to the effective organisation of flights to various hot spots.

German soldiers accept the cargo intended for them.

Some of what they had to carry to Afghanistan ...

Iraq, led the Ministry of Foreign Affairs of Ukraine and then the Cabinet of Ministers to remove all political restrictions on cooperation with Iraqi programmes. Just two days after Balabuev's call, Smeshko replied to him that there were no more fundamental issues and that he should immediately apply to the State Export Control Service and the relevant Ministries to obtain a permit for flights. By the time such appeals were sent out, they had already had sufficient clarity in the evaluation of the level of security at Iraqi airports. In addition, a special crew manual was drawn up to minimize all possible risks.

However, when the necessary permissions had been received, and on June 11 the first Kyiv Ruslan UR-82072 took a course from Rome to Basra with a cargo for the Italian military forces, some

One of the regular batches of humanitarian been delivered to Afghanistan. August 31, 2005.

doubts still remained. In order to ensure further the sufficient safety of the transportation and to establish this for other aircraft departures to Iraq, the leaders of Antonov Airlines needed detailed reports from the first crew. Such documents were received on the same day. That's what V. N. Kulbaka, the flight manager of that flight, wrote: *"In my opinion, the airport provides quite a high security level. The airport is patrolled by helicopters from the air and by soldiers on the ground. The UK's troops, which include a professional group on loading/unloading of aircraft, are based in Basra. There is enough equipment for unloading of all types of aircraft ... An opportunity to arrange crew rest has not been provided yet."* At the same time, the report of A. N. Kulikov, the captain, was not so optimistic: *"The military campaign is under way, so civilian aircraft may run a high risk. Missiles are still launched ... As for approach systems, just VOR DME and approach threshold lights are in operating status. Runway, taxiway and apron lights are out of order. Approaches to the Basra airport are free ... condition of pavement of the runway, taxiways and parking places is good."*

The crew members of the second Ruslan, UR-82073, which went the next day along the same route loaded with the same cargo, were also given the task to write reports. As with the first flight, the second aircraft performed visual landing. Then the aircraft was unloaded within less than two hours and sent on its return flight without refueling in order to cut time in a potentially dangerous zone. A short stay in Basra left D. K. Kurko, the flight manager, with quite favourable impressions: *"... the aircraft was unloaded completely. They did not use special equipment for unloading ... There was not a handling agent, in the usual sense of the word,*

Unique powerful loader sent to Afghanistan. 17 January 2009.

available in Basra – we were met by American and Italian military personnel. There were no civilians observed near the aircraft during the unloading. Basra airport is an American military base. It was not possible to estimate the security system in detail within such a short time, but I have reason to suppose that it is at quite a high level and corresponds to the standards adopted for the US military bases."

Such standards stipulated complete control not only over the territory of the airports themselves but also over vast adjoining areas of the takeoff/landing zones. Both pilots and managers of Antonov Airlines perfectly understood the importance of this. For this reason, they would only start flying to Iraq when it was guaranteed that such a control had been established, which included the approaches and takeoffs within those zones, in accordance with the so-called 'Afghan' scheme with the steep-gradient approach repeatedly tested by Soviet pilots during the 1980–89. Such flight modes demanded high flying skills from Antonov Airlines crew as well as crew integration since civil aviation did not stipulate such 'aerobatics'. However, it was exactly for this reason that Antonov Airlines crews comprised test-pilots capable of going beyond the possibilities of ordinary airline flight, brilliantly fulfilling these most difficult tasks and safely returning home.

I do not know what the American and British soldiers felt when a Ruslan or Mriya was bearing down over them along a steep spiral with a special whistling sound, but the Antonov staff experienced the most vivid impressions during those moments. I remember the feeling: it was as if you were sitting not inside the world's biggest and heaviest cargo carrier but inside a manoeuverable aircraft performing complicated aerobatics. Through a

starboard window I could see just the sky, through a port window rotating as in a kaleidoscope I could see the the Basra air terminal building, the sea port with huge oil tanks, the patch of desert slashed to pieces by caterpillar tracks, oil derricks burning distantly and the concrete parking of British helicopters right under me ...

The flights to Iraq, which started in mid-2003, ran at quite a high rate. By the end of the year Antonov Airlines had performed 70 flights without any serious problems from security point of view. Thus, the intensive joint work of the Antonov Airlines, the State Aviation Administration of Ukraine, international organisations and coalition forces was crowned with obvious success. However, in the following years the Ukrainian authorities renewed their ban on flights to Iraq several times, but in

Teal Braune, State Secretary of the Federal Ministry of Transport of Federal Republic of Germany, expresses gratitude to K. F. Lushakov, Managing Director of Antonov Airlines, for excellent work on the cargo delivery to Afghanistan. Berlin, 11 May, 2004.

In the foreground, the An-12 and the An-124-100 of Antonov Airlines; in the background, the An-124-100 of Volga-Dnepr. Kabul, October 29, 2007.

Mobile power plants are delivered to Iraq. Basra, September 2003.

each instance the reasoned position of Antonov Airlines prevailed. Despite the vigorous start of the transportations, the following year their intensity began gradually to decrease: in 2004 there were 36 flights, in 2005 31 flights and the trend continued downward. In all, by the end of 2015, they had carried out 268 flights to the country, and the total weight of the transported cargo had reached 18,756 tonnes. As we can see, these figures were far lower than those for Afghanistan. The reason is simple – once the Allies had established firm control over the seaport of Basra and the main transport arteries of the country, they started sending most of the cargo via those entry points as it was less expensive. As

a result, Antonov Airlines, like other carriers, dealt only with urgent or especially valuable cargo. Basically, they carried from the United States and the European Union countries the equipment necessary to restore the oil-mining and oil-refining infrastructure destroyed in the course of military operations.

Of course, flights to Iraq soon became a routine practice. The methods and means to ensure flight safety were perfectly worked out, but this does not mean that their danger completely disappeared. From time to time, situations arose that no one could foresee or prevent. And then much depended on simple luck or good fortune, which, fortunately, did not desert the Antonov Company. One such case happened in August 2005, when the Ruslan UR-82072, commanded by A. Z. Moiseyev, was flying to Baghdad. The crew performed the descent and approach for landing along a steep glide path within a small protected area, limited by the two runways of the airport of the Iraqi capital. They stopped near an Arab An-12 aircraft, which stood near a large hangar. Everything indicated that on that day the situation at the airport was tense, so the flight crew members did not leave their work stations for the short time necessary for unloading the delivered self-propelled equipment. *"The unloading had almost finished,"* Anatoly Zakharovich recalls, *"suddenly I felt the aircraft seem to slightly to jump and stagger, and then it happened again. I quickly stepped out of the aircraft to see what was going on.*

Having walked out onto the concrete, I saw a dust cloud from an explosion. Everything became clear – shelling. But then the American helicopters took off, other means of airport defence were activated and the mortar fire on our parking place stopped. And in a couple of minutes we got a command to finish unloading quickly and fly away. We obeyed the command immediately and with pleasure."

One more hot spot – Chad – has been part of the geography of flights of Antonov Airlines for almost two decades. A civil conflict of ethno-religious reasons has been periodically fading and then reigniting in this Central African country for more than half a century. When Chad was a colony of France, Christianity spread over the south of the country while the north continued to be Muslim. After gaining independence, the Christians, supported by the French, came to power in the country. The Muslims launched an armed struggle against them. This situation has been aggravated by the never-ending interference of the neighbouring countries in Chad, who in every possible way have been helping the rebels.

The international community has repeatedly drawn attention to this conflict and tried to find effective ways to resolve it. To prevent the bloodshed, peacekeeping contingents were sent to the country. From time to time Antonov Airlines were engaged to support the activities of the peacekeepers. Thus, Antonov Airlines fulfilled the first four flights to Chad in 1991. Later there was a relatively low

annual intensity of flights with a peak in 2002, when 25 flights were carried out. They carried literally everything to the belligerent country: from food products to oil-mining equipment. Although the total number of flights performed during that period cannot be considered high, each of them was very difficult and required the most thorough preparation demanded by many factors, including a very high air temperature and insufficient runway length at the airport of N'Djamena, the capital of the country. Therefore, every time when planning a cargo transportation, all the participants in the process approached the decision very carefully and constantly monitored the situation in the country.

New helicopter arriving in Liberia to equip the UN peacekeeping forces. Monrovia, 5 January 2006.

Transportation of unique cargoes is always a huge undertaking for the technical crew.

Italian contingent in Iraq receive another helicopter. Basra, 29 October 2007.

Loading patrol cars for the Iraqi police.

to N'Djamena. A. N. Gritsenko gives an account of that period: *"One operation transporting cargo for the Swedish peacekeeping contingent in the Republic of Chad in the winter of 2008 is still fresh in mind. The request for the operation was received at the end of January. We had repeatedly flown to N'Djamena with different cargo before, but in January the situation in the country began to change rapidly. They reported on armed uprisings of various tribes. The fighting detachments of the opposition organised an armed campaign against the capital in order to depose the constitutional government. The situation sharply deteriorated. It became rather dangerous to fly to N'Djamena, so we stopped flights.*

"Battle actions were already underway in the capital, including the airport area. The mass media gave contradictory reports on their progress, and we could not rely on them while deciding on the resumption of flights. On the other hand, customers continued to insist on the necessity to perform those flights to Chad as they had made applications for them in advance. In order to get independent and objective information, we contacted British insurance companies and international organisations. First of all, we wanted to obtain intelligence, collected from

The comparatively steady run of flights to Chad was disrupted at the beginning of 2008, at the time of an unusually sharp aggravation in the civil conflict. At that time, the rebels had shot down a governmental Mi-24 helicopter, using portable anti-aircraft missile systems, and it became clear that a new serious threat loomed over the aircraft flying

various sources. But even the obtained intelligence was contradictory. If the peacekeepers claimed the situation in the capital and the airport area was safe and secure, then the insurance men sharply raised the rates of fees. At least the only point both were unanimous about was the fact that the situation in N'Djamena varied with each passing hour.

"In the morning of 1 February 2008, we received information that the situation was under control and it was permitted to fly, but two hours later the information came that N'Djamena airport was closed and all flights were prohibited until a special permit was issued. Following this, the Aviation Authorities of Ukraine issued a decree banning flights to the Republic of Chad until a special order was issued. A couple of days later, we were again informed that everything was quiet in the airport of N'Djamena, and that Air France had already started transporting passengers there. We checked that information and it turned out to be true, with the only proviso that Air France's passengers were soldiers of the French contingent in the Republic of Chad.

"In the meantime, the pressure from the Swedes increased. We were given many examples of the fact that the airport was safe and that all the bans had already been lifted. As evidence, they provided the official statement of the Aviation Authorities of the Republic of Chad. After that statement the

French military reported that they were preparing the first charter flight to N'Djamena in the evening of 10 February.

"We were ready to fly, but demanded that the French implement additional measures to ensure the safety of transportation. On 11 February, the Head of the French Coordination Centre informed us that an air traffic control specialist with his call sign and frequency would constantly stay at the

American equipment for oil mining is ready to fly to Iraq.

Mortar fire over parked aircraft. Baghdad, 31 August 2005.

Accommodation modules are delivered to the ruined country.

Equipment of the Canadian peacekeeping contingent delivered to Macedonia. Skopje, June 1999.

Unloading machinery of the peacekeeping contingent in Yugoslavia. Pristina, 16 May 2003.

control tower of N'Djamena Airport for constant contact with the An-124-100 aircraft's crews. Having entered the contact zone, our pilots would receive from him the latest information about the situation for a descent route directly to the airport. Additionally, that promise was confirmed by the French through diplomatic channels, but even after that the ban of the Aviation Authorities of Ukraine was not lifted.

"On 12 February, after talking to representatives of our Ministry of Foreign Affairs about possible procedures for lifting the ban, I received a reply that they required an official approach by the Ministry of Defence of France. Having reported this point of view to the French, I received the answer that the Republic of Chad was a sovereign state and was not under the control of France. Moreover, I was informed that Air France and Air Gabon had already performed three flights each with passengers to N'Djamena. However, the Aviation Authorities of Ukraine ignored the information.

"On 15 February we received an official notification from our Customer that if we did not agree to fly to N'Djamena, the contract would be broken. On the same day, Idriss Deby, the President of Chad, introduced a state of emergency and a curfew throughout the country. As a result, government control was restored, and the Aviation Authorities of Ukraine finally gave permission to prepare for the first flight, subject to special aviation security requirements being followed. In order to verify their implementation, an inspector was sent to Chad. He boarded our aircraft. Having arrived at N'Djamena with the very first flight, he personally evaluated the situation at the airport. After that the bans on the flights of our aircraft were lifted, subject to strict compliance with safety precautions."

Since then, all Antonov Airlines flights to Chad have been carried out exclusively with the permission of the Aviation Security Administration of the State Aviation Administration of Ukraine. This has had a very positive effect on the level of flight preparation and implementation. In 2008 alone, Antonov Airlines carried out 90 flights in the interests of the EU peacekeeping forces in that country, and all of them were performed in accordance with the plans without any serious problems. E. A. Golovnev tells us about one such flight to N'Djamena from Athens on 26 April 2009. "Although no firing at the airport area was observed during that voyage," he says, "but the locals say the calm will not last long. In general, the whole of Central Africa is very uncomfortable from the point of view of the crew's stay. Heat, dust, lack of loading-unloading infrastructure plus the local population, which is not very eager to work, cause real difficulties."

Of course, we would add the permanent war. The war, which sometimes abates a little, but never entirely stops. Entire generations are born and die there, not having lived in peace for a single minute. And often the only help they saw in their lives was that delivered by Antonov Airlines. However, Antonov team members, although they descend from the sky, are not angels. They are just professionals who famously do their altruistic work. For example, to the end of 2015 Antonov Airlines aircraft had performed 264 flights to Chad, having

Repaired Mi-24 helicopters were brought to the capital of Chad, N'Djamena. 26 April 2009.

delivered 18,098 tonnes of cargo to the destitute country. One can only imagine how many people were saved from hunger, disease and war due to such activity!

But Afghanistan, Iraq and Chad are just the tip of the iceberg, the most noticeable part of the world's problems. But there were flights to Sudan for the rotation of the Indian peacekeeping contingent as well. There were flights to Mali to support the operations of French troops against radical Islamic groups. Support was provided to the UN peacekeeping missions in Angola (104 flights, 8,260 tonnes), East Timor (27 flights, 1,822 tonnes), Congo (161 flights, 10,964 tonnes), Kosovo (38 flights, 1,407 tonnes), Sierra Leone (70 flights, 5,402 tonnes), Rwanda (31 flights, 2,055 tonnes), Eritrea

Soldiers of the government troops of the Republic of Chad unload the Ruslan.

Crew of the Ruslan operating the loading in the area of the Ebola fever epidemic. Central African Republic. Bangui. October 2014.

(15 flights, 969 tonnes) and other similar places on our planet, up to the end of 2015. How many people were saved as a result of this truly titanic work? How many complicated political and ethnic conflicts were settled? How many material assets were saved? There are no precise answers to these questions. And the answers are not really relevant, because even if they managed to help just one person, then all the applied efforts were not in vain.

Loading of AH-64A Apache American attack helicopters. Afghanistan, Kandahar. November 2014.

In connection with the flights to hot spots in the interests of military contingents from different European countries, let's not forget that after 1992 Ukraine also sent its military units to participate

in international peacekeeping operations, and the transport operations to provide such missions were performed by Antonov Airlines ... Here I want to add the word 'naturally'. I mean, it is natural that the Ukrainian airlines carry out transportation in the interests of Ukrainian peacekeepers. But according to the status of these flights, they were operations of the United Nations rather than Ukraine. Accordingly, the United Nations announced tenders for the right to carry out these flights, as for all other flights, and Antonov Airlines had to bid for those tenders and fight for the right to carry out transportation in the interests of their own peacekeepers. However, these are the rules made by the international community, and there are no exceptions to the rules.

In 2000, Antonov Airlines carried out first flights to Kinshasa (Democratic Republic of the Congo) and Pristina (Kosovo), where Ukrainian peacekeepers were carrying out their difficult duties. In order to support their activities, 22 flights were carried out to those places up to 2008. Antonov Airlines aircraft delivered various military equipment, helicopters, armoured vehicles, cars and spare parts. In addition, from 2004 they performed more than 40 flights to Monrovia (Liberia). Food products, power stations, conditioners, communication and reconnaissance equipment were added to the list of cargo mentioned above. Over the 2012 to 2014 period, flights to support contingents to the Congo were carried out with stop-overs in Kisangani, as well as in neighboring Uganda (in particular in Entebbe). At least 16 flights were made to those airports, and to the list of the transported cargoes were added barreled fuel. Needless to say, those flights were vital for the maintenance of the normal functioning of the Ukrainian troops in the UN peacekeeping forces.

However, the activities of Antonov Airlines, even during the periods of the highest intensity of flights to the hot spots, were not limited to them only. Even in the peak years (2001–03, then 2008–12), the share of flights to such places did not exceed 35-40% of the total flight numbers. The bulk of the work the company continued was in its traditional global market of super heavy and oversized air cargo transportation. At the beginning of the new century this market faced hard times. So, 2001, for the first time after a long recovery, was marked by a significant decline in the global air transportation industry. At the year-end, all leading airlines in Europe and America announced a fall-off in traffic volume by of 14–21%. This recession appeared in the middle of the year and was caused by a general decline in the global economy, primarily a decline in industrial production in the US. The events of September 11 worsened the situation even more, having provoked a real panic in the air transportation

Large crowds of impoverished people gathered in expectation of humanitarian aid delivered by Antonov Airlines.

market. However, despite the impact of such negative factors, the volume of work performed by Antonov Airlines in 2001 remained practically at the level of the previous year and amounted to 24,576 tonnes transported in 566 flights (in 2000 the figures were: 22,431 tonnes and 519 flights).

That was a real success, the achievement of which was positively influenced by the formation in mid-2001 of Air Foyle HeavyLift Joint Venture, which united two British companies with vast experience in performing non-standard transportation and with long-standing ties in the market. At the beginning of 2002, this alliance of Antonov Airlines' trading partners completely proved itself and made it possible to further increase the efficiency of the joint work. For example, over the January 1 to June 1 2002 period, the aircraft of Antonov Airlines carried out 302 flights and transported 19,253 tonnes of cargo, exceeding the level of the same period in 2001 by 63%. In particular, the company continued the transportation of oversized industrial equipment. Thus, having performed eight flights, they then carried oil-mining equipment of GE Energy Germany from Europe to the capital of Chad, N'Djamena. In addition, they completed a series of flights from Southeast Asia to Europe loaded with electronics for household and industrial purpose. They started a programme to transport the products

Helicopter departure from Kyiv to Sri Lanka.

Capabilities of the Ruslan in over-sized cargo transportation seem simply fantastic.

of smelters from Japan to Canada by means of the Ruslans. The An-12 aircraft of Antonov Airlines also continued their regular flights along the Kyiv-Brussels route.

Intensive work at an ever-increasing rate continued throughout 2002. Recalling that period, I would like to mention a number of unique transportations. Two generators of General Electric Company each of 100 tonnes were transported from Cologne (Germany) to Turkmenbashi (Turkmenistan). Antonov Airlines delivered a rotor

of the ALSTON generator with a weight of 76 tonnes from Ostend (Belgium) to N'Djamena (Chad), and a rotor of the same company weighing 110 tonnes was carried from Macao to East Midlands airport in the UK. Three motor boats were transported in one flight from Simferopol. Along with a large number of Afghan orders, all these operations meant that 2002, with 43,655 tonnes of cargo transported, and 2003, with 55,281 tonnes, became the most successful in the history of Antonov Airlines.

This huge fire helicopter will be transported to Greece. Kuala Lumpur, June 2001.

CHRONICLE OF ANTONOV AIRLINES: YEAR BY YEAR
On Mriya's wings (2002–2015)

On Mriya's wings

Since the mid-1990s, the market for super-heavy and oversized cargo transportation started actively developing. The air transport subdivision of Antonov StC augmented the volume of air transportation, and the fleet of the Ruslans expanded. However, from time to time, the office of Antonov Airlines received applications for the transportation of such goods which were beyond even the Ruslans' capabilities. Such proposals had to be abandoned, although an aircraft that could lift almost any cargo stood still only a couple of hundred metres outside Antonov StC's office in Gostomel town. The aircraft stood motionless.

From the standpoint of today, the decision to restore the airworthiness of the An-225 aircraft and bring it to the market, adopted by P. V. Balabuev, General Designer, was inevitable. But, at the same time, according to K. F. Lushakov, Executive Director of Antonov Airlines, such a decision had come at a price. Repair-and-renewal works, as well as upgrade of many elements of the An-225's

No other air carrier in the world has an aircraft equal to the An-225 Mriya in terms of cargo capacity.

(2002–2015)

structure, required a level of investment that should not affect other areas of Antonov StC's activity. However, the real prospects that opened up to the owner of such a unique vehicle as Mriya tipped the scales in its favour and in May 2001 the aircraft again took to the sky. Once it had received a Civil Aircraft Certificate and had become technically ready, the aircraft started operating as a part of Antonov Airlines. Since then, Antonov Airlines has been able to transport cargo nobody else in the world could carry!

When the An-225 was almost ready to enter the market, the world was shaken by the tragic events of 11 September 2001, which had vast negative consequences for air transport all around the world, including in the field of cargo transportation. The volume of orders for the services of Antonov Airlines as well as many other airlines began to decline. This fact not only reduced the inflow of funds for the completion of works at the An-225, but also, in general, cast doubt on the expediency of commercial operation of the cargo giant.

Humanitarian freight is in the An-225's cargo compartment.

Mriya performs containerized transportation.

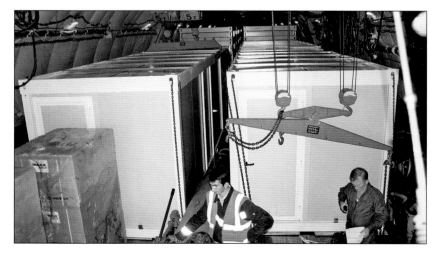

world aircraft fleet only Mriya could provide, were still in demand; and that such demand in the future would increase. At first, the volume of this demand would be sufficient to justify putting into operation the only available aircraft.

This conclusion was confirmed by the first commercial flights which the An-225 had to perform before the completion of all the planned works on board. On 28 December 2001, the aircraft flew from Gostomel to Stuttgart (Germany) to be loaded. It took on board food, clothes, blankets and other humanitarian cargo of 187.5 tonnes total weight. The customer – one of the UN departments – planned to deliver this cargo to addressees in the Sultanate of Oman on the same day – on 28 December. The cargo had to be carried further, right 'from the wheels'. However, during the mission, the consignee informed that it would only be able to get the cargo on 2 January 2002; so, as a result, the An-225's crew headed by A. V. Galunenko, its permanent captain, had to stay to celebrate the New Year in Germany.

On 2 January, having made an intermediate landing in Cairo, the aircraft unloaded at one of the Omani military air bases, then flew to Muscat airport, refueled and headed to Munich. As Michail Kharchenko, the flight manager of that flight, says, in that ancient German city the An-225 *"was met with pomp, there were a lot of press, officials and representatives of aviation authorities. They attentively followed us, tried to understand if the aircraft would fit into the airport, how maneuverable the plane was on the ground, how it taxied, etc. Everybody was satisfied with what they had seen, for we did not need outside assistance."* In Munich, the An-225's fuselage was loaded with 200 tonnes of cargo of a similar nature. It is remarkable that the contract was signed for the transportation of 230 tonnes, but in Bavaria such amount of humanitarian aid was simply not available in time for the loading. Therefore, a part of the cargo cabin of the aircraft remained unoccupied. Having refueled in Gostomel, Mriya delivered its cargo to Bishkek (Kyrgyzstan) on schedule. In the history of aviation such a quantity of payload had never been transported before by an aircraft for one flight.

In June 2002, after the completion of all the works on board, commercial flights of the An-225 continued, and such work became for Mriya its usual mission, albeit not frequently. Basically, at that time Mriya performed flights to deliver humanitarian aid to help civilians in zones of various military conflicts. One flight from New York to Entebbe (Uganda), carried out in early December 2002, was notable due to its originality. The An-225 delivered to that African country 80,000 boxes of Christmas gifts for children with AIDS. The gifts

Nevertheless, the managers of Antonov Airlines, showing high professionalism, managed not to overestimate the significance of those extremely negative but still temporary trends. A careful analysis of the real market situation showed that those unique services, that amongst the entire

were collected by American kids, many of whom came with their parents to Kennedy airport to hand over their presents and see off the world's biggest aircraft. *"Those were shoe boxes,* Anatoly Moiseyev, the captain of the An-225 crew, says. *"A child put there his or her best toy, some clothes, sweets, and even sometimes a precious thing begged from a father or a mother ... I saw a four-year-old girl laying down her favourite doll assigned for a similar little girl in Uganda. The children stood in a chain singing songs. The boxes were stacked in large containers and loaded into the fuselage. Simultaneously with loading they arranged a meeting beside the aircraft with the participation of senators, popular singers and the children themselves. They loaded in total 140 tonnes of cargo but it took much space in the cargo compartment and, because of the long distance of the upcoming route, the takeoff weight of Mriya reached 630 tonnes! Just for the second time the An-225 climbed into the sky with such weight ... There was a meeting in Entebbe too, we were met by the President and the Ministers of Uganda, they said words of gratitude."*

In December 2005 the world's biggest aircraft again took part in a charity event. The An-225 delivered Christmas presents to needy children in Ukraine. Those gifts, also placed into 70,000

Seeing-off ceremony of the An-225 to the flight with Christmas gifts for children of Uganda. New York, December 2002.

shoe boxes, were collected by the children of Great Britain. The flight for delivery of such holiday surprises to Ukraine was carried out at the request of *Samaritan's Purse,* the international charity organisation. This organisation delivers the joy of a Christmas present to many thousands of disadvantaged children in different countries of the world and for many years it has been using the services of Antonov Airlines. *"The deed that Antonov Airlines and Samaritan's Purse do,"* Dave Cook, the founder of the Samaritan movement who arrived at Mriya, said, *"is very important, because these consignments are intended for children. In*

Mriya has brought a 138-tonne transformer from Austria. USA, March 2003.

Kabul: loading the property of the Italian contingent of peacekeeping forces in Afghanistan.

Reliable working security was provided while loading Mriya. Kabul, September 2003.

many places of the world children are deprived of many absolutely necessary things, they starve, they are in need. We must help them, as the Bible tells us. And Antonov Airlines shows us an example in this deed."

Watching the successful operation of this unique aircraft, consignors all over the world realised that application of the An-225 opened up new prospects for them. After all, Mriya is able to take off with 250 tonnes of payload into the sky – that exceeds almost twice the capabilities of any other aircraft! Moreover, as a matter of

Restless night abroad. Technical crew members patrol the parking place.

principle, a cargo on this aircraft can be located not only inside the fuselage, but also outside it with special hinge fittings. This makes it possible to transport by air such oversized and heavy elements of industrial equipment and building structures as never before. At the end of March 2003, Mriya transported a huge 138-tonne industrial transformer of 4.3 metres high and more than 11 metres long from the city of Linz (Austria) to Phoenix (Colorado, USA) with intermediate stops in Gander and Montreal, as well as other equipment of 175 tonnes total weight. This broke

Evening in Afghanistan.

96-tonne trailers with power equipment are transported from the USA to Iraq. Basra, September 2003.

Mriya is loaded with prefabricated houses to be delivered to disaster areas.

The heaviest commercial cargo ever carried by air – 247 tonnes. June 17, 2004.

the world record for mono-cargo transportation that had been set by the An-124-100 aircraft in 1995. The truck that the transformer was placed in at Phoenix had more than 50 wheels and a length comparable to the Boeing 747. Thousands of Americans watched this unique operation. In that week, on 29 March Mriya delivered 135-tonne industrial air conditioners from Houston in the south of the USA to Dubai (UAE) and on 10 April the reliable wings of Mriya carried 168 tonnes of medical equipment to Bahrain. Similar orders for the services of the aircraft still came, but all of them were single orders; such orders were performed within several days and after that Mriya returned to the base again. Antonov Airlines did not manage to arrange so-called 'shish-kebab' from the orders similar to the one the Ruslans strung during their flights. However, the management of Antonov Airlines did not despair: the experience of arranging transportation performed by the Ruslans clearly showed that at the very beginning the number of orders was always small, but when a new transport entered the market and proved to be reliable, the number of orders started growing. Therefore, the main priority at that time was to inform consignors about new opportunities, which were opening due to the An-225's entrance into operation and to demonstrate convincingly the aircraft capabilities in real missions.

The efforts soon brought benefits. In September 2003, for the first time in the aircraft's history, they managed to 'string a shish kebab' while operating Mriya. Having departed on 9 September from Gostomel, the aircraft performed a programme of 41 flights with a total duration of 170 hours for 29 days. The unique aircraft was operated by flight crew headed by A. Z. Moiseyev; the technical crew, which comprised the author of these words, was headed by S. Y. Pyatak and V. V. Nets, leading engineers. That time Mriya performed several circular flights between the United States, Iraq, Afghanistan and Italy, carrying oversized industrial equipment from New York and Houston to Basra, as well as the property of the Italian contingent of peacekeeping forces in Afghanistan from Kabul to Rome. The weight of cargo transported in these flights ranged from 80 to 193 tonnes.

It is important that in almost all those cases the cargo would have required two Ruslans to lift it under those conditions. Especially, it became evident at Kabul, located at an altitude of 1,600 m above sea level, where Mriya could take on board up to 90 tonnes, while the Ruslan only 40 tonnes. So, the An-225 surpassed the An-124-100 in terms of economic efficiency, although Kabul cargoes were not unique – they were ordinary trucks, trailers, containers. Much more unusual were the goods, carried from New York to Basra: 96-tonne trailers with power equipment. Mriya's cargo compartment accommodated two such trailers although the Ruslan could carry just one.

Despite the obvious success, the September series of flights revealed the urgent need for further improvement of the aircraft, especially in terms of its adaptation to the conditions of modern airports. First of all, it was necessary to equip the An-225 with a new, lighter and more compact towing bar. The new towing bar would save the volume of cargo compartment for commercial cargo and, most importantly, would significantly facilitate the work of the technical crew. Soon the new towing bar took its place aboard Mriya. Later on, during numerous downloads, it turned out that the 'outer space' history of the An-225, initially optimized for the transportation of rocket system elements mounted externally, resulted in certain inconveniences when dealing with ordinary terrestrial cargoes. Thus, in accordance with cargo floor strength limits, while loading a technical crew often had to place the heaviest cargoes closer to the tail part of the aircraft. However, sometimes it was impossible to do like this without installing temporary ballast in the nose part of the fuselage, since the aircraft could 'topple' backwards. Searching for ballast at an unknown airport took precious time, and not always were they able to find ballast. In addition, the absence of a rear cargo ramp caused certain difficulties while loading and unloading.

In general, 2003 can be certainly called the year of Mriya: this aircraft carried out 38 commercial flights and transported 3,708 tonnes of various cargoes. These figures include 180 tonnes of construction equipment which were delivered from Prague to Tashkent on 18–20 July, and a series of flights between Kabul, Eindhoven and Cologne started on 31 July. However, the most striking achievement was waiting for the aircraft in the following year: on 16–18 June 2004, the An-225 transported the largest commercial cargo in the history of aviation! That was a transportation of four pipe layers with a total

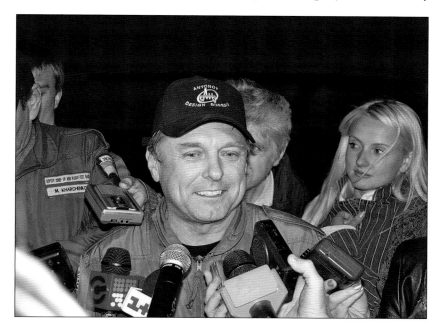

weight of 241 tonnes, as well as 6-tonne loading equipment, by the order of the Government of Uzbekistan. The flight was performed from Prague to Tashkent with intermediate landings in Gostomel and Ulyanovsk. The pipe layers were intended to construct a pipeline. The aircraft was piloted by a crew under the command of A. Z. Moiseyev. *"All the parameters that were documented during this flight were the record-breaking ones. 630-tonne takeoff weight was entered in the Guinness Book of Records,"* M. G. Kharchenko, the head of this

Intermediate landing of the An-225 in Gostomel. A. Z. Moiseyev, captain, gives an interview to the Ukrainian media. 17 June 2004.

Mriya's crew on the record-breaking flight, 16–18 June, 2004.

Heavy American trailers are located in two rows in the cargo compartment of the An-225.

The An-225 became the first flying art gallery in the world. On September 27, the aircraft set a record for the *Guinness Book of Records*, having lifted 500 paintings of 120 Ukrainian artists to an altitude of 10,150 m.

transportation, told the Ukrainian journalists.

In the same year, on 10–11 November, the An-225 demonstrated another unique achievement – it transported eight (!) M-18 Dromader agricultural aircraft and Cessna 188-B aircraft from Adana (Turkey) to Tripoli (Libya) in one flight. Those aircraft were necessary to combat the large-scale invasion of locusts in Libya. The cargo of such volume could only be placed only in the fuselage of Mriya. When loading, the outer wing panels of the transported aircraft were detached. Anatoly Moiseyev commanded the crew, and Vladimir Mason was in charge of loading and unloading operations. The aircraft were delivered in exact accordance with the schedule agreed with the customer – Societée Ligne Verte, a Libyan company.

The flight of Mriya, performed from Vatra (France) to Ras-al-Khaima (UAE) in March 2007, continues the list of shining transportation missions. During that flight Mriya carried to the Emirates the elements of equipment for a cement plant with a total weight of 194.5 tonnes. In December of the same year, the

An-225 transported a new container loader weighing 55 tonnes along the route Skrydstrup (Denmark)–Geilenkirchen (Germany)–Baku (Azerbaijan)–Kandahar (Afghanistan), and 46 tonnes of cargo for a contingent of German troops that were based in the high-altitude region of Afghanistan. In 2007–08 Mriya carried out 45 flights, being loaded with 100–200-tonnes of cargo. Gradually such work became habitual for the aircraft, and the flights, which had been considered to be unique before, ceased to excite the imagination of the public.

Nevertheless, those and subsequent years became the period of full realisation of the really extraordinary capabilities of the aircraft. They performed many dozens of not simply flights but really unique transport missions, each of which required the most thorough preparation and highly professional execution. As a result of one of them, in August 2009, the An-225 crew received a Certificate proving the inclusion into the *Guinness Book of Records* of the transportation of the heaviest monocargo in the history of aviation – a generator with a special frame with a total weight of 187.68 tonnes.

This generator was transported from Frankfurt (Germany) to Yerevan (Armenia), where it was needed for a new electrical power station. Negotiations with the customer of the operation, the South Korean GS Engineering & Construction Company, which had won the tender of the Armenian government and become the general contractor for the construction of the electrical power station, had been going for more than a year. All that time specialists of Antonov StC had been carefully preparing for the transportation. During the preparation they faced a number of complicated technical problems.

For example, as the original height of the generator did not allow it to be loaded onto the aircraft, it was necessary to dismantle the control unit, located on the top. A thorough calculation of the flight along the upcoming route showed that the initial weight of the generator – 176,400 kg – had to be reduced. They removed all possible elements from the generator's body. As a result, the weight declined to 174,000 kg. But even after this, the load on the running metre of the cargo floor of the aircraft was 19,333 kg/m, which was almost twice as much as permissible. In order to reduce the load, it was necessary to install the generator on a special 13,700 kg frame of about 17 m long. Because of the design features of the generator, during the flight the G force in the forward and backward directions should not exceed 1 G, which was almost impossible to provide in real flight. In order to stay within the required constraints, they developed special instructions for the crew as well as formulated strict requirements for flight conditions.

The mission was brilliantly performed by the crew of Mriya headed by A. Z. Moiseyev, captain, E. A. Golovnev, head of the transportation, and V. V. Mason, loadmaster. After the mission completion, the aircraft had become an absolute world heavyweight record holder: a new record was added to the absolute payload record as well as the record for the maximum commercial cargo transportation in the history of aviation.

The An-225 holds another record – in June 2010 it transported the longest cargo in the history of air transportation. Two 42.1 m-long wind turbine blades were delivered from China to Denmark for Geodis Wilson A/S, one of the world leading logistic companies. Although the total weight of the blades did not exceed 15 tonnes, only the An-225 aircraft could carry a cargo of such dimensions due to the length of its cargo compartment which was 43 m long. As the blades had to be urgently delivered for special tests, transportation by sea or by road was not considered expedient. For example, transportation of this cargo by sea would take the whole month. Mriya took just 12 hours to perform the mission … And yet, not every flight of Mriya was crowned with an entry in the record books. What yesterday was a record, today is usual routine everyday work for this aircraft.

The An-225 was, and still is, beyond competition in the market of oversized and non-standard cargo transportation. Often, this aircraft is the only transport able to effectively fulfill the task. In support of this claim, in June 2013 the aircraft carried out a series of flights between Manchester (Great Britain) and Seoul (South

Solemn cutting of the cake in honour of arrival of the An-225 in Hyderabad (India).

Industrial equipment of such dimensions and weight can be transported only by the An-225.

Gifts for Ukrainian children are delivered. Mriya's nose cone is raised. It snows in Kyiv. December 2005.

Organisers of the charity event delivering gifts. From left to right: K. F. Lushakov, D. Cook, D. S. Kiva, V. N. Kulbaka.

the next Siemens transformer, total weighting with a loading frame of 155 tonnes, from Zagreb (Croatia) to the city of Cebu in the Philippines. In June 2014, Mriya delivered a huge 139-tonne boiler from Leipzig (Germany) to Edmonton (Canada). Together with loading equipment this unit weighed 147 tonnes.

Another use of the An-225 should also be noted, which is not as prestigious as record-breaking transportation but is extremely important in this present-day uneasy world. This is the participation of the An-225 in rescue operations to counteract the consequences of various natural disasters, catastrophes and armed conflicts.

We have already mentioned the hundreds of landings Mriya performed in Afghanistan and Iraq, but other episodes are also worth mentioning. In October 2009 the An-225 performed several flights to deliver the generators to Samoa which were necessary to restore the Satala power station damaged by the tsunami. The volume of Mriya's cargo compartment could simultaneously accommodate 10 12-tonne generators, each of a sea container size. In February 2010, the aircraft carried out a series of flights to deliver oversized construction equipment (bulldozers, trucks, tractors and loaders) to liquidate the consequences of the earthquake in Haiti. At the request of the Government of Japan, these valuable cargoes were carried from Tokyo (Japan) to Santo Domingo (Dominican Republic) by air, and then were transported to the capital of Haiti, Port-au-Prince, by road. Only a year later, Japan needed help having been hit by a terrible tsunami. In March 2011, Mriya delivered to Tokyo humanitarian goods, generators and other equipment with a total weight of 140 tonnes, which were sent by the government of France.

It is clear that such flights, although they are not record-breaking ones, attract no less interest from the general public. As a result, Mriya is destined for glory: it is constantly in the field of view of

Korea). During this mission Mriya transported oversized equipment for the shipbuilding industry. In order to load and unload this equipment they used special tools also developed by Antonov StC specialists. Having completed the series of flights, the aircraft delivered outsized 140-tonne industrial equipment from Seoul to Basel Airport located on the border between France and Switzerland. At the end of the year, the An-225 transported

On strong wings – from heart to heart

At first, we heard the roar of six turbojets and then we saw the An-225 itself through the thick veil of snowfall.

While frontier guards and customs officers were performing the obligatory control procedures necessary after the completion of an international flight, standing near the air stairs I took a brief interview with Anatoly Moiseyev, the commander of the flight detachment

of Antonov StC, who headed the crew of Mriya during that flight. Anatoly Zakharovich informed that a charitable cargo had been loaded on the aircraft at East Midlands airport, a British airport located approximately 160 km to the north of London. It took the aircraft 3 hr 5 min to cover the considerable distance to the Kyiv-Antonov base airfield in normal operation mode.

Meanwhile, they raised Mriya's nose cone and in the depths of the cargo compartment we saw huge stacks of 70,000 boxes with Christmas presents for children from poor Ukrainian families. Together with the cargo, the aircraft carried to Ukraine a group of Britons, who organised the collection of the gifts. The group was headed by David Cook – the founder of Samaritan Wallet, an international

ANTONOV

ALSTOM

the world's leading media, it periodically 'flickers' in the news and from time to time participates in air shows, all of which has provided the aircraft truly worldwide fame. In 2005 British specialists included the An-225 among the 13 most significant aircraft in the history of aviation. Images of selected aircraft were placed on 13 silver coins that were issued by the British Mint. This series of coins of nominal value of $25 of the Solomon Islands, a part of the British Commonwealth, is dedicated to the 100th anniversary of the history of world aviation. Recognition indeed!

In fact, the domestic Mint also did not ignore the An-225. In 2002 coins with the image of Mriya became the first in the Aircraft of Ukraine series, issued by the National Bank of Ukraine. The An-225 is depicted on a convertible coin with a face value of 5 hryvnas and on a silver coin with a nominal value of 20 hryvnas, which, however, that time already cost more than 200 hryvnas.

V. N. Kulbaka, Commercial Director of Antonov Airlines, and a representative of the customer of that record-breaking transportation – GS Engineering & Construction South Korean company – give an interview to German television.

Electrical generator transported by the An-225 from Frankfurt (Germany) to Yerevan (Armenia).

Vadym Feldman
Demokratychna Ukraina, 7 December 2005

charity organisation. Being a successful businessman he saw on TV a BBC report about the Armenian-Azerbaijani conflict in Nagornii-Karabakh, and, in particular, about the suffering of children in that Transcaucasian region. The report so shocked Mr. Cook that he founded a charity organisation, which started Christmas Child events for deprived children.

David Cook and Simon Barrington,

Executive Director of Samaritan Wallet, said that for many years their organisation has been providing for Christmas gifts for thousands of children in different countries. Konstantin Lushakov, Executive Director of Antonov Airlines, Valery Kulbaka, Commercial Director of Antonov Airlines, and Michail Kharchenko, Deputy Head of Antonov Flight and Test Base, told that air delivery of charity gifts to different

addresses had been carried out by Antonov Airlines for 12 years.

Gregory Comendant, President of the All-Ukrainian Council of Evangelical Christian-Baptists, was among those who met the charitable cargo that day. He said that the gifts would be distributed among needy children in all regions of Ukraine in accordance with a pre-made claim list.

Loading agricultural aircraft to be delivered to Libya. Turkey, 10 November 2004.

British and Ukrainian coins with the image of Mriya.

Mriya departs on its next flight.

According to the *Catalogue of Coins of Ukraine*, in 2018 the market value of this coin has multiplied many times, and true collectors are ready to pay for it 11,000 hryvnas. Even if we take into account the fivefold decrease in the national currency rate over the past period, the value of the coin has increased at least 10 times! Impressive, is not it? However, there is nothing surprising about this. Simply, this is another reflection of the fact that the An-225 itself is of huge value that should be valued and carefully cherished. And thus the legendary Mriya will again and again go into the sky in order to confirm with every flight the justice of the motto of Antonov Airlines: *"No other name carries more weight!"*

CHRONICLE OF ANTONOV AIRLINES: YEAR BY YEAR
Tranquility is but a lovely dream (2003–2005)

Tranquility is but a lovely dream

The year 2003 did not start badly for the airline. A smart market policy aimed at the largest customers, and a full-scale use of all partners' capabilities within the framework of Air Foyle-HeavyLift, had convincingly shown its effectiveness. Despite the decline in transportation in the world's air transport triggered by 'September 11 syndrome', Antonov Airlines showed a growth of nearly 100 per cent growth of all its indices in 2002. Thus, commercial flying time in 2002 compared to the previous year increased from 5,572 to 10,114 hours, and the quantity of carried cargo from 24,607 to 43,924 tonnes. By and large, this was a phenomenal result. And although it is not so difficult to find an explanation for it due to a dramatically increased number of orders for transportation to Afghanistan and Kuwait, this did not detract from the merits of the airline's managerial department who managed to get these orders, and all the other personnel who succeeded in fulfilling them.

(2003–2005)

This positive trend towards further growth persisted in the first half of 2003. This is evident from the statistics of air freight of that period. For example, for the first four months alone, Antonov Airlines' aircraft flew 2,571 hours and the amount of delivered cargo reached 20,554 tonnes, which is almost the same as for the whole of 2000! No need to have special mathematical skills to be able to calculate that the efficiency of using the available aircraft fleet almost tripled! During this period, the 'hottest'

direction, as before, was Afghanistan. However, in general the airline demonstrated an extremely wide geographical range of flights. In the Middle East alone, there were flights to Bahrain, Jordan, Qatar, Kuwait and the UAE. In the total table of flights for the first four months of 2003 it was possible to count more than 100 geographical names on different continents. During the same period, several remarkable shipments were operated by Mriya aircraft (An-225), which gave rise to massive public interest. That meant, in general, that the market situation for Antonov Airlines and the prospects for its further development were very optimistic.

Suddenly, like a thunderbolt from a clear sky, on 26 June 2003 Ruslan aircraft UR-82007 was arrested at Canadian Goose Bay Airport, Newfoundland. How? Why? What for? After all, from the very beginning of its activity, the airline strictly observed all international laws and regulations avoiding debts in payment for services related to flight operations, obtaining necessary diplomatic clearances and duly executed all certificates for transportation of specific and delicate cargoes. And regardless of all that – the aircraft was arrested!

Taking advantage of modern communication lines, the duty staff of Antonov Airlines in Ukraine and England immediately started searching for trustworthy information about the incident, while airline's management began assessing the current situation. Gradually it became clear that the aircraft that had flown to Canada carrying a load of equipment for Italian Air Force units to conduct their annual military drills there, was detained not because someone was lodging any claim on the airline or Antonov StC itself. It turned out that the Ruslan aircraft was arrested because of the claim of Cypriot company TMR Energy Ltd on the State Property Fund of Ukraine (SPFU), while Antonov Airlines had absolutely nothing to do with that dispute! The significant point was that in 2002 the Stockholm Court of Arbitration delivered a judgment obliging SPFU to pay in favour of TMR US$42.3 million. However, the Ukrainian organisation did not rush to satisfy the judgment. Then TMR decided to bring pressure on Ukraine, starting arrests, as it claimed, of the state property. Having figured out

O. P. Korshunov – flight department senior navigator.

S. N. Gavrilov – power plant leading engineer.

Ruslan UR-82007 was
unexpectedly arrested in
Canada, June 2003.

this so-called logic the lawyers of Antonov StC
immediately lodged a complaint to the Federal
Court of Canada protesting against identifying the
property of the company being a state-owned legal

entity (Antonov StC) with the property of the SPFU.
Thus, in the legal proceedings between TMR and
SPFU the company turned out to be in the position
of a third party which suffered the greatest losses.

Prior to bringing the aircraft
to life again it was necessary
to free it from a snow
blockade.

So began the exhausting 19-month (!) struggle for release of the aircraft in various judicial jurisdictions, requiring huge efforts from the airline and the entire Antonov StC. Probably, now, there is little purpose in describing it in detail. However, a brief summary of the parties' positions should be given.

The SPFU treated its debt negligently, simply not considering it to be its own. There is a grain of truth in this. The debt appeared as a result of a number of problems in changing the form of ownership of the state-owned Lisichansk oil refinery, conducted during 1992–94 by Marc Rich and the Russian company TNK. It can be said that the debt was simply 'saddled' on the SPFU. However, even after the decision of the Stockholm Court of Arbitration, the SPFU did not start looking for ways to solve the problem but preferred to continue to turn a blind eye to it, ignoring international law. The SPFU continued its ostrich-like behavior during the trial of the Ruslan case having lumbered Antonov StC with the responsibility of struggling for release of the aircraft.

TMR's position was intended to draw out the case, to use the judicial proceeding itself to put pressure on Ukraine. 'Suspended' situation in court satisfied TMR managers as they did not want to further aggravate relations with the government of Ukraine. From Canada came news that the *"actual interests of TMR and personally Marc Rich are in friendship with the government of Ukraine because* this allows the company to participate in exploitation of its energy resources. This is their genuine strategic long-term policy and the aircraft has nothing

The keys from the released aircraft are being handed over. From left to right: sheriff of Goose Bay Deif, head of the brigade M. Kharchenko, senior technician of Ruslan V. Khatin, 26 January 2003.

To dig Ruslan out of snow it was necessary to use heavy vehicles.

Assessment of the technical condition of the aircraft which had been parked in harsh conditions for 19 months. It was ferociously cold in the cockpit.

The joyful moment of the meeting. Ruslan's pilot-in-command A. V. Likhoded and the head of technical team M. G. Kharchenko report to General Designer P. V. Balabuev about the difficulties which they managed to overcome.

to do with that. They need the aircraft simply as an instrument of pressure on the government of Ukraine, as means of attracting public attention to, in their opinion, unfair treatment of the company and creating hysteria around the whole case."

Realising that the airline had become hostage to someone's big game, the leaders of Antonov StC took a clear and hard-line stance in court: *"Antonov Airlines are irrelevant to the essence of the dispute and we demand immediate release of the aircraft!"* They stated: *"SPFU and Antonov StC are different legal entities established in accordance with the law of Ukraine and the arrested An-124-100 cannot be alienated to repay debts of any government agency of our country. Notably, in accordance with the Law of Ukraine 'On Property', the considered An-124-100 aircraft is allocated to Antonov StC and belongs to it under full economic jurisdiction. The property*

transferred in this way is dissociated from the state of Ukraine. Aside from that, according to Articles of Incorporation of Antonov StC registered in 1993, its property belongs to employees and the company itself, like other state-owned companies, is not liable for obligations of the state and the Ministry of Industrial Policy, in whose jurisdiction the company was at that time. Thus, the only parties by decision of Stockholm Arbitration Court are: the claimant TMR and the defendant SPFU."

Casting back to the time of those events, it is crucially important to note that Antonov was fighting not only for its aircraft. In fact, it acted as a consistent and strong-willed defender of the interests of all Ukrainian state enterprises involved in international cooperation. After all, if the Cypriot company won, then such a judicial decision would, first of all, establish a precedent in Canada, and secondly, it would be vigorously used as an example of judicial practice by lawyers conducting cases against Ukraine in other countries. Activities in the legal war in the Federal Court and the Federal Court of Appeal (Canada) were headed by Dmitry Kiva and Konstantin Lushakov. *"Our position remains unchanged,"* Dmitry Kiva said in January 2004. *"Our company should not be liable through its own property, in this case An-124-100 aircraft, neither for Ukraine's debts, nor for debts of other state-owned companies or institutions. And we will further keep on proving our position in all judicial authorities, up to international courts."*

It should be noted that the line of defence based on proving the impossibility of covering SPFU's debts by alienating the property of Antonov StC, was not the only one. Rather quickly after commencement of the proceedings, the company's lawyers discovered weak points in the procedural moments of implementing the order in recognition of the Stockholm Arbitration Court decision in Canada. Early in 2004 they lodged with the Federal Court of Canada an action for invalidation of the very decision in the territory of that country. It was no longer a defence but an offensive that threatened TMR with a complete termination of case.

Understanding that their position in Canada was seriously shaken, TMR's lawyers decided to ramp up pressure on Ukraine by expanding the area of possible arrests. The crucial matter was that according to the New York Convention, decisions of the Stockholm Court are recognized by more than 100 countries around the globe. However, formal procedures for implementation of court decisions in different countries are different, therefore the list of countries where arrests could take place expanded gradually. In 2004 it already included Belgium, Israel, Italy, the United States, France and Germany. In March 2004 accounts of the Ukrainian Embassy in Tel Aviv were arrested and on 7 April, in the French port of Honfleur, a Fatesh bulk-carrier belonging to Commercial Fleet of Donbass, LLC (a company based in Mariupol), was arrested. Taking into account the escalated threat of arrests, Antonov StC refused to demonstrate its aircraft at air shows in Farnborough and Le Bourget, almost stopped flights of An-225 aircraft, and significantly narrowed the geography for An-124 aircraft operation, which badly affected the flow of currency earnings from freight activities. The company suffered losses while the legal processes, which absorbed huge effort and money, progressed extremely slowly. The decision to fly to any country constituting a potential threat was now taken only after a thorough assessment of the situation. The same happened with the flight from Brussels commissioned by NATO. Customers persuaded representatives of Antonov Airlines that loading of vehicles would take place in a military zone, that it would not take long and that the aircraft would depart to Kabul without problems.

On 17 August 2004, An-124-100 aircraft UR-82073 landed at airport in Brussels. Approximately ten minutes after loading started, the NATO agent, responsible for this process, informed the pilot-in-command – Dmitrii Antonov – that a court enforcement officer and police officers had appeared at the airport gate to arrest the Ukrainian aircraft against the claim from Cypriot company TMR Energy Ltd. Seven minutes later Dmitry Antonov requested clearance for takeoff due to changed plans. The pilots started the engines and had already begun to taxi the aircraft out, but the aircraft failed to take off. The air traffic controller ordered it to stop. The pilot tried to establish the reason for this order but the air traffic controller did not really know anything, saying only: *"You have some problems with the police."* The crew had telephone contact with its base in Gostomel, and partners in London, but they also had no clear information. Having held consultations, the decision was taken to hold position until there was clarity. Thus, the Ruslan aircraft waited about an hour in suspense, with engines running.

Then Dmitry Antonov decided to return to the military parking area – there was still hope for NATO protection and that it would be possible to resolve the situation. However, the management of Brussels airport began to bring strong pressure on the crew trying to force them to move to the civil zone. Dmitry was threatened over the radio that if he did not immediately obey, force would be applied and in this case airport authorities would absolve themselves of any responsibility.

By this time, the lawyers of Antonov Airlines and representatives of the Ukrainian embassy joined the scenario. Negotiations with Belgian aviation authorities were initiated and lasted for about a day. All this time the crew was on the aircraft prohibiting anybody to get in. Eventually, Ukrainian diplomats came to the conclusion that the aircraft would have to be moved to the civil area anyway since the military area was partially blocked and 12 hours later the royal family's aircraft had to depart. The threat of a serious international incident was in the

UR-82007 is back in Gostomel again, 29 January 2005.

air ... Due to this, it became possible to arrest the airline's second Ruslan. And again – this time in Belgium – the heavy judicial mechanism began to turn: the process of searching for lawyers, preparing documents, proceedings in the Supreme Court, etc., was launched.

Meanwhile, at the 'Canadian battlefield' success was obviously on the side of the Ukrainians. In this country the case of Ruslan's arrest was considered four times in various courts. At different stages of case consideration, as well as the lawyers of Antonov Airlines, specialists from many state legislative authorities and legal departments of Ukraine were involved. Finally, on 24 September 2004, the Federal Court of Canada reversed its decision to arrest the Ruslan and resolved to release the aircraft. The aircraft was released, but ... was arrested again right away because TMR lodged a lawsuit in the Provincial Court which took the case into review. Hearings were held during October–November 2004. On 17 December, the Provincial

court also confirmed the unlawfulness of the aircraft arrest. Thus, two Canadian courts – the Federal Court and the Provincial Court – made a judgment in favour of Antonov StC. However, the Ukrainian aircraft was not allowed to leave Canada until consideration of the appeal claim that TMR had filed with the Federal Court of Canada immediately after September's decision was announced. Hearings on this appeal claim were held in January 2005 and on 24 January the Canadian court delivered the final judgment in favor of Antonov StC.

So, justice had been done! Without losing a minute, Antonov sent to Canada a team comprising of 19 specialists led by the head of the flight test base M. G. Kharchenko, including the head of department V. N. Kulbaka, pilots A. V. Likhoded and I. G. Volovik, navigator V. A. Ulyanenko, flight engineers V. M. Leshchenko and Y. A. Kurmaz, aircraft radio operator A. V. Krenz, senior engineer Y. A. Rudko and nine aircraft technicians. In addition to the company's employees, a representative of

the State Aviation Administration of Ukraine A. S. Tarasov also joined the team. Having reached Goose Bay on an An-74 aircraft, the team received the keys to the released Ruslan aircraft from Sheriff Deif of Goose Bay. But before assessing the condition of the aircraft and preparing it for the flight, it was necessary, literally, to make their way to the snow-covered Ruslan. It took half a day to bring the external power source to the aircraft. And only then did the team start working in accordance with the programme prepared. The frost during those days reached -30–35°C! As remembered by the participants of aircraft 'reanimation', the icy wind burned with fire. Drifting snow covered the smallest cracks. But the team carried out its task perfectly: all planned activities were accomplished.

Then there was the long-awaited moment: 29 January, 12:30 pm – Ruslan's wheels touched the runway of native Gostomel! Those who had made so many efforts to unchain the aircraft came to meet it there – General Designer P. V. Balabuev, his First

Deputy D. S. Kiva, General Director of Antonov StC V. N. Korol, CEO of Antonov Airlines K. F. Lushakov, First Deputy Minister of Industrial Policy of Ukraine V. P. Kazakov, Head of Department of the Ministry of Industrial Policy V. P. Kovtun, as well as numerous employees of the company and representatives of Ukrainian media. Slowly, almost solemnly, the entrance stairs of the aircraft were extended. *"Comrade, General Designer,"* Kharchenko's thunderous voice rang out. *"Mission accomplished! The Ruslan which was detained in Canada has now been returned to its base!"* "Congratulations on the safe return to the homeland! Thank you for a good job!" Balabuev shakes his hand joyfully. A moment later Kharchenko, Likhoded and the whole crew find themselves embraced by those who came to meet the aircraft.

Journalists immediately rushed to the crew asking questions on how the flight was and what challenges they had to overcome. *"An-124-100 is an excellent aircraft!"* answers Aleksandr Likhoded. *"A year and a half at the parking apron, including two winters, a thaw period, and it's still in perfect condition. A real fighting machine! Therefore, we won't be able to about heroism of the crew. The technical team prepared the aircraft for the flight so well that nothing extreme occurred during it. We flew in the normal way."*

Thus, a difficult but well-deserved victory was won. However, it was incomplete: the joy was clouded by knowing that the second Ruslan continued to languish at Brussels airport and the threat of new arrests, although significantly reduced, was still not completely eliminated. As ill luck would have it, the hearings in Belgian court were appointed only for the end of April 2005 – the ponderous mechanism of European justice could not work faster. But the enforced pause was used for a diligent and precise preparation for the trial. Having weighed up all pros and cons, the company's management at this stage of the struggle passed, so to say, from the specific task of releasing the aircraft to a strategic attack on all fronts. The goal was to completely resolve the threatening situation

UR-82073 returning from Belgium and landing in Gostomel in heavy fog conditions, 7 December 2005.

The first to come down the stairs of the released aircraft was acting General Designer D. S. Kiva. He is welcomed by the Chief Engineer of Antonov StC S. A. Bychkov.

for the whole state when Ukrainian property was arrested abroad. *"I believe,"* said D. S. Kiva from the pages of the authoritative periodical *Zerkalo nedeli*, *"that the whole point is that someone has developed a detailed and well-thought out scheme for appropriating Ukrainian property. And the arrests of Ruslans are only exploratory moves in its implementation."*

It should be mentioned that indeed the problem with TMR was not the only case in Ukraine. There was, for example, Norsk Hydro company which also demanded repayment of debts and initiated arrests of Ukrainian sea vessels. To resolve these conflicts, first and foremost, required the political will of the Ukrainian leadership, which would be based on economic calculation: what is cheaper for the country – to pay due invoices and wait for new arrests or pay lawyers but in such a way as to resolve this problem once and for all? Finally, this political will was manifested and from 2005 high-ranking officials from the State Property Fund, the Ministry of Justice and the Ministry of Industrial Policy of Ukraine joined the process of resolving these conflicts. With their involvement it became

possible to direct negotiations with TMR in a more constructive way and involve new concerned parties, in particular the new owner of Lisichansk refinery – the company *TNK-BP Ukraine* – and eventually to conclude a settlement agreement with Marc Rich's company in November 2005. After registering this agreement and passing all necessary formalities, the preparation could begin for the return of An-124-100 UR-82073 aircraft from Brussels to Kyiv.

As in the Canadian case, a qualified technical team and flight crew headed by Dmitry Antonov, who was the pilot-in-command of the Ruslan aircraft at the time of its impounding, were dispatched to the capital of Belgium. All preparations on the aircraft which had been grounded more than 15 months were accomplished within two days and on 7 December the 'Belgian captive' landed safely at its home base.

December 7, 2005 turned out to be grey and hazy in Gostomel. But the faces of the people saluting the aircraft glowed with such joy that it seemed as if the sun emerged from the clouds. Two and a half years of persistent struggle against injustice had culminated in a complete victory. There in the meeting hall of the Antonov flight base was held a press conference with the key participants fighting for the aircraft's freedom: D. S Kiva, K. F. Lushakov and an employee of the law firm Ilyashev & Partners – R.V. Marchenko, and also M. G. Kharchenko and D. V. Antonov. Perhaps the most long-awaited statement at this press conference was made by Roman Marchenko who said that the conflict between the Cypriot and Ukrainian companies was completely settled. *"TMR Energy Limited and Antonov StC have sent applications for termination of claims to countries having obligations to implement the decisions of the Stockholm Arbitration Court,"* he said. *"From now on, Antonov Airlines' aircraft get the opportunity to fly again around the globe without the tiniest threat of arrest."*

Thus, one more difficult period in the history of Antonov Airlines was left behind. We have here focused on the resolution of the conflict with TMR but this does not mean that the airline did not have any other concerns. Although with limitations, commercial flights continued to be carried out and it would be unfair not to mention at least some of them. For example on 29 October 2004 one of the An-124-100s belonging to Airlines delivered a patrol boat from Kyiv to Termez (Uzbekistan). This ship was manufactured by the Kyiv plant Leninskaya kuznitsa by order of the State Border Protection Committee of the National Security Service of the Republic of Uzbekistan to prevent drug smuggling. Its dimensions together with transportation frame (width 5.3 m, length 20.335 m) did not allow

At the aircraft stairway the Head of Antonov StC responds to the first questions of journalists.

the use of any other vehicle except Ruslan for its transportation to its destination. The loading of the boat into the aircraft was achieved with the help of a specially designed system for loading and unloading large-sized cargoes weighing up to 120 tonnes. And on 1 December another such boat was delivered to Uzbekistan.

On 10 December, four Mi-8 helicopters from the Ukrainian contingent of peacekeeping forces were transported from Sierra Leone to Kyiv. Within a few days, aircraft of Antonov Airlines carried out six flights by the order of the Chapman Freeborn company from Germany. They delivered power-generating equipment and humanitarian supplies from Berlin and Prague to Baghdad, carrying 80–110 tonnes per flight. A 60-tonne turbine was brought from Turkey to Iraq for the construction of an electrical power plant there. On Christmas Eve, Antonov Airlines carried out a pleasant mission delivering about 1,600 tonnes of gifts and various goods for the upcoming holidays in 15 flights from Macau to Budapest and Prague. Much work was carried out for the United Nations: from Karachi (Pakistan) to Bujumbura (Burundi) the Ruslans flew 17 times, each time taking on board 80 tonnes of food supplies and other cargo. Just before the New Year, Antonov Airlines performed two flights from Tallinn (Estonia) to Khartoum (Sudan), transporting two engines of 50 tonnes each.

However, there was a truly extraordinary airlift operation that Antonov Airlines was honoured to perform during the period 18–25 April 2005, when a really unusual cargo was delivered from Ethiopia to Italy ... And the story is thus: having conquered

Abyssinia (the former name for Ethiopia) in 1937, the troops of Mussolini received an order to take something valuable to Italy. In the city of Axum (north of the country) – the ancient capital of the once powerful kingdom – there was a sacred place where the kings were buried and granite obelisks were erected over their graves. It was decided to send to Rome one of them which had fallen on the ground centuries ago and broken into several parts. In 1939 it was placed near the Colosseum.

In 1949 Italy and Ethiopia signed a peace treaty, one of the articles of which provided for the return of the stolen shrine. However, it turned out that there is no practical means to transport an almost 170-tonne obelisk. This situation continued until 2001 when the request for the obelisk's transportation was received by Antonov Airlines. But when the company's managers began studying

A detailed report about the elimination of the threat of aircraft arrest. From left to right: K. F. Lushakov, D. V. Antonov, D. S. Kiva, M. G. Kharchenko and R. V. Marchenko.

Even with the constant threat of arrests, Antonov Airlines did not stop active work in the market. Gostomel, October 28, 2004. Loading the patrol boat Gurza for shipment to Uzbekistan.

Loading a mobile power station for shipment to Iraq, 29 September 2003, New York.

conditions of transportation it turned out that the runway in Axum was only 2,400 m long while the aerodrome elevation above sea level was 2,100 m and it was not fitted with radio aids and lighting equipment. A careful calculation showed that the An-124-100 could land there with a cargo of 60 tonnes but at an ambient temperature of +15°C maximum. Therefore, it was decided to perform the transportation within the period of October to February and land in Axum early in the morning with the sunrise.

Meanwhile, the Italians demounted the obelisk, having divided it in the places of the ancient cracks.

This work took more than three years. Thorough weighing of the pieces showed that they weighed 59.8 tonnes, 58.4 tonnes and 46 tonnes respectively. Every day at sunrise in Axum specialists measured air temperature. Finally, all the problems were resolved. On 18 April, Ruslan aircraft UR-82072 landed at an Italian Air Force base near Rome. The aircraft was met by the Minister of Culture and Monuments of Italy, the Ambassador of Ethiopia, the representative of UNESCO and other officials. Loading was performed in an orderly way and the next day at 5:30 GMT the aircraft was already circling over Axum. The sun had not yet risen,

Captive bird regains the sky

The aerodrome in Gostomel met the Ruslan aircraft with such a dense fog that journalists who dreamt of filming its landing could see the aircraft only after it touched the ground. It smoothly taxied to us and was right next to another former 'prisoner' that had returned from Canada (where it was held for 18 months). It seemed, if they

had arms instead of wings, they would embrace like brothers ...

"I'm very pleased that I returned the aircraft home," said the crew commander Dmitry Antonov, who during the confinement of the Ruslan did not leave it for more than 24 hours at the airfield in Brussels. "We were so worried – after

all, our bird was parked for a year and a half. But our mechanics, headed by the head of flight test department Mikhail Kharchenko, prepared it in two days and got flight permission from the Ukrainian and Belgian dispatcher service. The engines of Zaporizhzha Motor Sich company and all systems worked perfectly, however one

it was still twilight, air temperature +17°C. By dawn's early light the pilot-in-command Anatoii Moiseiev skilfully landed a heavy aircraft at the very end of the runway, vigorously braking, and a huge crowd of people, amongst which were many clerics in colourful clothes, approached the aircraft with reverence. The cargo was accepted by the Ambassador of Italy in Ethiopia. Prayers began to resound, the crowd was jubilant ... And on 20 and 24 April, the second and third parts of the obelisk were delivered to Axum. The shrine of the Ethiopian people was returned to its home ...

Now the restrictions are history and the freedom of flights has been re-established. Although it formally happened in November 2005, when a settlement agreement was signed with TMR, the critical decision to unblock the conflict occurred in September. Its most important result was elimination of the threat of aircraft arrests, ensuring the opportunity for Antonov Airlines to fly again all over the world without restrictions. The first flight under the new conditions was the flight of Ruslan UR-82009 to the USA on 13 September 2005. The aircraft brought 90 tonnes of humanitarian aid from Europe to the areas that suffered from devastating hurricane Katrina. And one week later, on 20 September, another Ruslan delivered to New Orleans 100 tonnes of cargo also intended for liquidation of consequences of the hurricane. The customer of this flight was the Ministry of Emergencies of Ukraine. From that moment Antonov Airlines began gradually to restore the lost positions in the world market of air transportation of heavy and bulky cargoes.

The Airline attempted to go back to its previous mode of operation, trying to cover the losses caused by the arrests. The cost of the arrests can be estimated based on the number of goods transported during this period. In 2003 the airline transported a total of 55,391 tonnes making 1,080 flights, then next year only 32,151 tonnes with 806 flights, which means the volume of production dropped by 42%. The situation in 2005 remained cheerless – 32,354 tonnes of cargoes were transported in 707 flights. Apart from the missed

profits there were expenses for conducting judicial battles, storage of the arrested aircraft and, after their return from 'captivity', expenses for their restoration. The loss of some traditional customers,

Ancient obelisk – the shrine of the Ethiopian people was returned to its original home. April 2005, Axum.

Nikolay Patsera
Kievskie vedomosti, 9 December 2005

system had a small malfunction but it was eliminated in the air."

Acting General Designer Dmitry Kiva noted that the return of the aircraft became possible thanks to efforts of President Yushchenko who helped to solve the problem through a settlement agreement. The company had to pay about

€300,000 for aircraft parking at the Belgian airport and total losses amounted to more than US$100 million. Then the Ruslan had to go through the necessary scheduled maintenance according to a special programme and within a month it was able to resume operation.

Then all seven Ruslans and one super

heavyweight Mriya were gathered in Antonov StC's squadron with a backlog of orders waiting for them. Once again they could fearlessly fly in any country and participate in NATO transportation ...

Loading a yacht for shipment from Lisbon to Cape Town, 27 November 2005.

who during this period were forced to turn to other carriers, was also very painful for business. The gradual comprehension of all the negative consequences of the arrests could not but give rise to questions about causes of the situation.

Almost immediately after the arrest of the first Ruslan in Canada a theory emerged that Antonov Airlines hadn't become involved in the conflict between TMR and SPFU by coincidence, and this conflict was a smokescreen intended to disguise the main significance of the arrest: it was a manifestation of a competitive war in the market of large-sized air transportation, primarily for the NATO contract for strategic transfers of military cargo of allied countries which will be discussed in detail in the next chapter. Analysing the situation with the benefit of hindsight, we have to admit that this theory has much convincing evidence: first of all, the fact that the Cypriot company which obtained the decision

of the Stockholm Arbitration Court as early as May 2002 had not taken any steps to implement it for more than a year and began taking active action only after 12 June 2003 when a memorandum of understanding was signed between NATO and Ukraine intending to rent Ruslan cargo aircraft. This memorandum was the culmination of the NATO tender for the selection of cargo aircraft from two main candidates: the Antonov An-124-100 and Boeing C-17. Boeing lost at that stage but apparently did not intend to surrender.

This theory is also supported by the fact that the Ukrainian aircraft was arrested at the time when it was transporting NATO cargo in Canada – the most important transshipment point in the entire transport system of the North Atlantic Alliance. Obviously, the expectation of the authors of this action was simple – the arrest of the Ukrainian An-124-100 would inevitably discredit the very

Free as a bird!

Blues skies for Antonov as 'ban' in the West lifted

Air cargo heavyweight specialist Antonov Airlines has LIFT OFF again.

After two years of being under the threat of arrest at all airports in the western world, the airline has been given the all clear to seek business worldwide.

The seizure threat was imposed on

Antonov's seven-strong fleet of An-124s and giant 250-tonne capacity An-225 as the result of a dispute between the Ukraine State Property Fund and Cyprus-registered TMR Energy.

But Air Cargo News has learned from industry sources that, on 1 September, a preliminary verbal agreement was reached between TMR and the Ukrainian

Government and the 'ban' was lifted pending further talks.

The news was immediately transmitted to the Stansted, UK, headquarters of the airline's joint venture partners Air Foyle HeavyLift.

Although commercial director Graham Pearce was reluctant to make an official statement, he told ACN: "At the moment

Shipment of a gas-pumping unit from Kyiv to Bukhara, 3 October 2003.

ability of the Ukrainian side to fulfil smoothly its obligations under the NATO contract. There is another irrefutable argument. The Sheriff of the Canadian province of Newfoundland made a final decision about the arrest of Ruslan aircraft upon the testimony of Anatoly Dovgert, head of the department of international private and customs law of the Institute of International Relations, Taras Shevchenko National University of Kyiv. These testimonies are dated 5 June 2003 and contain a positive response from the professor to a direct question about the possibility of arresting Antonov StC's property in aid of a claim execution against The State Property Fund of Ukraine.

Despite the persuasiveness of this 'competitive' version, the author is forced to admit with bitterness that it is not the only possibility: it turned out that Antonov Airlines had aroused envy in those who were ready to 'cut the wings' of the exceedingly

successful Antonov StC team. The next theory we'll call the 'domestic' one, meaning that the orchestrators of the aircraft arrests could have been within Ukraine itself.

The basis for this theory is the repeated attempts that occurred both before and after the described events originating from various political forces in Ukraine and even individual magnates aimed at gaining control over Antonov StC. And since the main source of financial independence of the company was the activity of the Antonov Airlines, the main attacks in a number of cases were aimed directly at it. In the long chain of all these checks, legal proceedings, bans, etc., the arrests of the aircraft do not seem to be out of the question. The logic of such actions was also obvious: preventing Antonov Airlines from flying, depriving it of income, bankrupting it, changing the leadership or making it more docile ... The 'domestic theory' is

Stan Elston
Air Cargo News, 16 September 2005

things are looking good but until the deal is finalised we can't be 100 per cent sure about anything. However, I understand the negotiations are going well and we can fly anywhere with immediate effect."

It is understood that all parties hope that all outstanding problems will be resolved within a month.

Industry sources confirm Antonov

Airlines UK, through Air Foyle HeavyLift, which retained all its staff working on 24/7 basis, is now quoting for all destinations.

It is believed a job from Germany and one in the USA have already been confirmed.

At present, one of Antonov Airlines' An-124s is still under arrest in Belgium but it is likely moves are being made to have it

released and flown back to Kyiv as soon as possible.

It is clear that there is a new mood of optimism at the Stansted base. A person close to the airline said: "All the staff look as they have just woken up from a nightmare."

Loading an electric generator for shipment to Khartoum, Tallinn, 25 February 2005.

of alienating Antonov aircraft was a reference to excerpts from the book *Theoretical and Practical Commentary on Civil Legislation of Ukraine* edited by V. Medvedchuk, at that time the First Deputy Chairman at Verkhovna Rada of Ukraine (Ukrainian Parliament) and a member of the family of Russian President Vladimir Putin. This book was published on the eve of proceedings in Stockholm. A strange coincidence. Generally speaking, there was at times an impression that Antonov StC was fighting not so much with a western company that had arrested its aircraft but with Ukrainian organisations that were eager to take possession of the property of a disobedient company.

In the following years the struggle for Antonov StC in Ukraine, for the separation of Antonov Airlines, calmed down several times and then flared up with renewed vigour. The account of these truly dramatic events is still waiting its time and has no direct relation to the subject of this book. What is important is that all these attempts have so far failed and that in the course of this struggle P. V. Balabuev, the General Designer of the company, who did so much to strengthen the position of Antonov StC and the aircraft industry in Ukraine as a whole, was forced to leave the leader's chair and soon afterwards passed away. In the dark time of those years Dmitry Kiva took charge of the company's destiny. A new era in the history of Antonov Airlines began ...

supported first of all by the absolutely passive (or worse) position of the State Property Fund and other government agencies in the settlement of relations with TMR. Because of this, the case was lost in the Stockholm Arbitration Court, which opened the possibility of arresting aircraft. For the author, who observed all these events happening, it was difficult to understand what tactics the lawyers were using. One item of evidence is very interesting: one of the main arguments by TMR in favour of the possibility

General Designer P. V. Balabuev says goodbye to the team of Antonov StC where he worked for 51 years, June 2005.

CHRONICLE OF ANTONOV AIRLINES: YEAR BY YEAR
Aiming at new heights (2006–2009)

Aiming at new heights

M ankind's advance to the 21st century was accompanied by a number of critical geopolitical changes, one of which was the new role of NATO. Established as a military political alliance with the sole purpose of protecting the participant nations' territories, this organisation transformed after disintegration of the Warsaw Pact into one of the counter-alliances aimed against new global threats. Accordingly, a new NATO strategy approved in 1999 envisioned abrupt activisation of Alliance activity outside of the countries which entered the organisation. In practice, it meant the necessity of a qualitative increase in the level of NATO troops' strategic mobility. A similar process of re-assessment of their own roles within the contemporary world commenced for the European states. A meeting of the leading European Union countries occurred in Helsinki in 1999 when they decided to create the joint military force of rapid deployment which could be deployed almost throughout the globe at any point where a threat to EU interests could arise.

Aviation transport is generally known as the most effective means to provide troops with strategic mobility. However, the aviation transport fleets of the European states and Canada have never fully complied with the new requirements and still remain non-compliant in both the type and the quantity. That has become one of the greatest problems

(2006–2009)

standing in the way of the new ambitious plans of the Europeans. A solution seemed to lie in the joint development and manufacture of the A400M new-generation military airlifter; however, as soon as this vehicle was not delivered for operation, another solution should have been found.

In 2000, the idea of long-term lease of transport aircraft from commercial airlines was put forward as a temporary solution by the European and North Atlantic administration of NATO. To make this idea effective, a special High Level Group was established in November 2002 at the Prague summit of NATO. This group was headed by the representative of the Federal Republic of Germany, the country declared as the Lead Nation in providing

the air transportation capacity for NATO. A year later Germany was entrusted with the same task by the European Union.

Having assumed this responsibility, the Germans started in-depth examination of all possible variants. They visited Antonov Airlines, Volga-Dnepr and Polyot operating the An-124-100, and Boeing manufacturing the C-17 Globemaster III. In addition, the European EADS company which proposed a tandem of the A-300-600ST Beluga and the A320 aircraft participated in the tender. During their conversations with the Ministries of Defence of the European countries, the High Level Group experts updated the demand for air transportation, and studied the conditions to be met. Soon, the Europeans, accustomed to working to set procedures, brought the aircraft and carrier selection process to the format of two projects: SALIS (Strategic Airlift Interim Solution as a temporary solution for strategic airlifting) and ECAP (European Capability Airlift Programme, the programme aimed at the implementation of airlift capabilities of EU countries). The first project initially involved 13 countries of NATO, the second project involved 10 countries of the European Union.

The volume of contracts which could have followed parameters of SALIS and ECAP seemed unprecedentedly immense, and for that reason, competition kicked off amongst the operators.

V. N. Kulbaka, Commercial Director of Antonov

V. N. Kulbaka, Antonov Airlines Commercial Director, addresses the NATO delegation. Gostomel, 18 May 2005.

An-124-100 participating in ILA-2004 Air Show.

German Minister of Defence Dr. Peter Struck inside the Ruslan fuselage listening to Deputy General Designer Aleksandr Kiva. Next to them are Yaroslav Skalko, Commander Ukraine Air Force, and Valery Kazakov, Deputy Minister of Industrial Policy of Ukraine. Berlin, 11 May 2004.

Airlines, recalls that *"the struggle was very harsh. During our long-time operation in the Western market we had accumulated enough experience and knew that not all the things in the much-praised West are perfect, transparent, and fair. Our participation in some tenders for a strategic transport aircraft of the Ministry of Defence of Great Britain, and later of the Ministry of Defence of Canada, made us think about political factors, lobbying and protectionism, however deeply hidden and much refined. Struggling with such monsters as EADS, which has a multi-billion turnover annually, is not simple. EADS played an intricate and exquisite but still very aggressive game, aiming to tame the An-124 operator, play the first violin in the project, assimilate the 'Ruslan' experience and use such experience in their development of the new A400M transport. The Boeing Company marched in step with EADS."*

Nevertheless, Antonov Airlines entered the struggle holding a number of trump cards from the very beginning. First, the An-124-100 Ruslan aircraft itself. Its maximum lifting capacity exceeded that of the C-17 by almost twice (120 tonnes versus 76.7

tonnes); the same could be said in respect of the cargo compartment volume and the flying range. The Ruslan had proved its capability in long self-contained operations far from its maintenance bases, and that was confirmed by its daily practical use; the aircraft was equipped with an onboard cargo handling system which was not available to the competitor. That system allows the aircraft to load and unload with no assistance from vehicles, including the direct loading from a truck via the rear cargo ramp.

Secondly, the financial aspect of the Antonov proposal turned out to be rather attractive from the budgetary point of view of the SALIS and ECAP member countries. The same money allowed them to lease three times more An-124-100 aircraft in comparison with the C-17. Taking into account the advantage of Antonov aircraft in their lifting capacity, the European states obtained an opportunity to deliver at the same cost six times more cargoes than when leasing Boeing aircraft.

Thirdly, Antonov Airlines suggested a system comprising the aircraft, crews, maintenance and air delivery management which by then had been in effective operation throughout the world market for 15 years. It was based on the high professional level of the airlines' flight and maintenance personnel through the experience of aircraft testing.

Another essential advantage of Antonov Airlines, as compared to other airlines that operated the An-124-100, was its direct contact with the design and certification services of Antonov StC, the Ruslan's designer and developer. All this allowed complicated problems to be settled promptly, such as the aircraft's service life/calendar operating time extension, making the required changes to its design, including those requested by the customer, the installation of onboard security systems and other special purpose equipment.

Finally, the reputation of Antonov Airlines was convincingly supported by its impeccable operation of the delivery of goods from the European states to Afghanistan and Iraq; that activity reached a peak of intensity just when the High Level Group procedures began.

Antonov Airlines' management actively informed the potential customers about all these advantage. Numerous meetings, discussions and presentations were held, and active correspondence continued. In addition to the Antonov Airlines personnel, leading experts of the entire Antonov StC started the fight to win SALIS and ECAP contracts. Having carefully studied all of the problems, they guaranteed that in six days following the date of receipt of an order, they would be capable of bringing the aircraft for the disposal of NATO and EU to any airport of the globe, and support their intensive flight operation for 60 days, minimum. For this purpose the airlines had

20 staffed flight crews, technical and maintenance personnel with huge experience of transportations, and a fully equipped base airport which could provide all categories of maintenance for the aircraft. Altogether, this allowed them to support at least 2,000 hours of annual operation for each aircraft that served SALIS and ECAP programmes.

Naturally, other proposals were presented to the High Level Group by other participants in the tender. The amount of information submitted to the High Level Group experts was such that no immediate choice seemed possible, so they decided to split the stages: identify the aircraft type first, then the carrier. Nonetheless, the initial victory was gained by the Ruslans. After a year of disagreement, on 12 June 2003, the summit of NATO countries in Brussels announced that the members of SALIS decided to lease five or six An-124 aircraft for a period of seven to nine years. Participants of ECAP did not arrive at any definitive conclusion at that time, and soon their project was terminated.

Seeking to consolidate the success, the Antonov team arranged a number of activities aimed at generating positive public opinion in the West about the potential cooperation. In particular, on 11 May 2004, at Berlin Schönefeld airport, a presentation was held by the Ukrainian Air Force Commander-in-Chief Lieutenant-General Yaroslav Skalko and the Antonov Airlines CEO Konstantin Lushakov to present the An-124-100 aircraft. Among the visitors was a delegation of the Ministry of Defence of Germany led by the Minister of Defence Dr. Peter Struck, and a delegation led by the State Secretary of the Federal Ministry of Transport, Construction

and Housing Mr. Thiel Braune. Both German chiefs highly appreciated the potential operation of the Ruslan, and expressed their hope that the transportation to be made by these aircraft for the NATO countries in future would be as effective as those they had made before.

Bright prospects to win the contract opened up for Antonov Airlines; however, almost immediately, one of the airline's Ruslans was arrested under a claim by TMR Energy Ltd. against the State Property Fund of Ukraine. Another Ruslan followed it after a couple of months. The project was thrown in jeopardy; during one of the meetings, NATO officials declared to the representatives of Antonov Airlines: *"We like working with 'Antonov Airlines', your Company renders high quality professional services, but ... if you fail to free the airplanes arrested in Canada and Belgium, you cannot participate in the project."*

That meant that the position of the Kyiv company was severely shattered. At the same time, SALIS decided that the contract would be concluded by NAMSA, the NATO Maintenance and Supply Agency. By the end of 2003, this structure prepared the regulations about working conditions (in fact, tender requirements) and forwarded this paper to all bidders. Having carefully studied these requirements, and assessing the situation of the Ruslans' arrest in view of the law suits for the liberation of the aircraft, the Antonov Company managers decided to take an unexpected step: instead of strengthening of their efforts to compete against the biggest Russian operator of the An-124-100, Volga-Dnepr Airlines, they suggested they made an alliance and prepared a joint tender proposal.

V. Y. Mosin, test pilot first class.

Official SALIS project opening ceremony. Representatives of the project participating countries are standing near the Ruslan SALIS GmbH aircraft. Leipzig, 23 March 2006.

SALIS programme transportations were performed with exceptional exactitude.

the aircraft, repairs and modifications, the number would be less. The only way out was consolidation of efforts with 'Volga-Dnepr'. Under a mutual arrangement, we decided to act on the tender with a joint proposal from two companies which together provided six aircraft: three from each company. Naturally, the same idea emerged in the heads of our EADS competitors. In this connection, both of us were invited to discuss the matter: the Volga-Dnepr Sales Manager V. A. Gabriel and me. Several meetings passed, and the essence of the EADS proposals was reduced to the following: our companies would take the role of contractors, while EADS would be the project leader. In such a proposal, the lion's share of profit would remain with EADS. Naturally, that did not suit us; we required participation only as full-fledged partners. Besides, the main reason for our negative impression of EADS was the eagernessof the European aircraft manufacturers to borrow our experience in the market in the delivery of unique and oversized cargoes, advancing their A400M project and squeezing out our An-124-100. One of their arguments at those negotiations was the proposal to submit an US$800 million bank guarantee, for example. Everyone knew that no first-class banks capable of providing such warranties were available at that time in Ukraine and Russia. While a monster like EADS with its multi-billion annual turnover looked at such a guarantee quite normally. Nevertheless, we decided to go along with the negotiating process with EADS as long as possible to prevent the initiation of new tender provisions or requirements which might be impracticable or awkward for us. Finally, we obtained what had been planned: one week prior to the tender closure we declared to EADS that we would proceed without them, as an incorporated team of Antonov Airlines and Volga-Dnepr."

The idea of consolidation turned out to be the determining factor, fitting the interests of both Russians and Ukrainians and, finally, those of NATO. The North Atlantic Treaty Organisation obtained a much more balanced transportation system, resistant to political risks, aiming at the fulfilment of the alliance's major functions. Access to long-term activity was gained by the Russians, while Antonov StC were saved from the necessity of sending almost all of their fleet to serve the NATO contract and thereby depressing the remaining market sectors. In addition, it was most important thing to counter the opponents' argument that the geography of flights of Antonov Airlines was limited because of the arrests of their aircraft. Such an argument lost any meaning: in case, if an aircraft could not fly from Kyiv to another country it was possible to send another aircraft from Ulyanovsk. Each and every NATO requirement could be met.

Below is V. N. Kulbaka's story about that dramatic moment in the struggle to win SALIS: "The requirement to provide six aircraft within 24 hours was one of the tender's unfeasible provisions. After all, we had only seven Ruslans in total, and if we consider the periodic scheduled maintenance of

Transportation of a concrete-laying machine from Lincoln, USA, to Tbilisi, Georgia. October 2006.

Dozens of meetings were held in 2004–05 with representatives of NAMSA, the High Level Group, other NATO structures, and the tender participants in order to discuss various provisions, terms and conditions of the future contract. *"A year of hard negotiations had passed before the definitive decision was taken,* writes V. N. Kulbaka. *"V. A. Gabriel and I met 12 times in Luxembourg and Germany with NAMSA people. Sometimes, the negotiations went dramatically. In the beginning the behaviour of the representatives of NAMSA was haughty and even cynical. For instance, they told us about the An-124-100:'You wish to sell us a bicycle at a Mercedes price'. So we had to explain to them intelligibly that they could find no other such bicycle in the world both in the past and in* the future, because that 'bicycle' was capable of carrying cargoes which no other aircraft of the world could transport, and that the availability of such an aircraft was good value for money. Each meeting was followed by extensive correspondence, and NAMSA requirement was always insistent: they needed our reply to any question within one or two days. This situation continued for more than half a year. NAMSA's non-constructive approach seemed unlimited. Despite it, we met all of their requests. Many of our colleagues lost faith in this project and told us that no success could be expected, because everything had been decided by the politicians, who would never allow East European cooperation with NATO. Nevertheless, our meetings, discussions and correspondence with NAMSA went on, and having

A Czech helicopter is being loaded for delivery to Iraq. 29 April 2006.

A German assault support helicopter is setting off for Afghanistan.

clenched our teeth, we continued to persuade NAMSA of the advantage of using our aircraft.

"However, everything comes to a conclusion, so having weighed all pros and cons, we decided to present a fitting rebuff. After one of the meetings in Germany I told them that once before the Western response had been demonstrated to us when we tendered for a strategic transport aircraft in Great Britain and Canada where we outbid the C-17 in all parameters, both technically and commercially, but the political solution prevailed. If the purpose of NAMSA negotiations was the same, I suggested we separate and meet in the market. My colleague V. A. Gabriel immediately added, that he felt as though we were at the project's funeral ceremony. We declared that since we were not a fire-fighting crew, thenceforth we would give NAMSA no more

answers within inconceivable time limits, but only when we would consider it necessary. That declaration was a cold shower for the representatives of NAMSA and the Bundeswehr. However, it was followed by constructive and fruitful activity which finally resulted in the Volga-Dnepr project which connected two opponent teams into a single group of associates."

As a result, NAMSA agreed to the participation of two operators in the project, although put forward a provision that the contract would not be made with each airline individually, but with a joint structure to be registered in one of SALIS countries, Germany preferably. According to NATO, the new business should work under Western law, and all of its contractual and financial terms comply with Western standards. On these conditions, and as

SALIS Closed Gap in NATO and EC Capabilities

Sweden has become the sixteenth country to join SALIS during the programme solemn presentation in Leipzig. In the presence of Alessandro Rizzo, NATO Deputy Secretary General, Dr. Franz Josef Jung, Minister of Defence of Germany, and other high-ranking visitors including ministers, state secretaries and gen-

erals, the representatives of Sweden standing right next to the parked An-124 aircraft, have signed the Adhesion Agreement approved by the signatures representing other fifteen member countries of the programme. Presently, the number of states who signed this agreement includes Canada, Great Britain,

Germany, France, Portugal, Denmark, Luxembourg, the Netherlands, Hungary, Norway, Finland, Czech Republic, Slovakia, Slovenia, Poland, and Sweden. Spain and Italy are considered as potential candidates.

Dr. Franz Josef Jung, Minister of Defence of Germany played as host, for the reason

A regular working meeting between managers of the Ruslan International programme partner companies: Antonov StC and Volga-Dnepr Group. Kyiv, 27 April 2009.

agreed by the parties, Volga-Dnepr set up in October 2004 a German company Ruslan SALIS GmbH, which united its efforts with Antonov Airlines and Volga-Dnepr within the SALIS project. Thereafter, Antonov Airlines and Volga-Dnepr signed contracts under 'Ruslan SALIS GmbH' to lease the An-124-100 aircraft, using the principle of equal participation in the activities requested by NAMSA.

A corresponding joint bid was forwarded to NAMSA and won in February 2005. This was followed by the painstaking efforts for finalisation of contractual terms and conditions, which proceeded until October. At the end of 2005, the contract passed the approval procedure in NATO legal structures, followed by its ratification by the member countries and, finally, it was ratified in the Bundestag. The work was finished by the signing

of the contract between NAMSA and Ruslan SALIS GmbH which came into force on 23 January 2006. According to the document, two An-124-100 aircraft, one Ukrainian and one Russian, had to be based permanently at the airport of Leipzig, Germany, and kept on air alert, taking off at a moment's notice. When requested, the partners had to provide four more aircraft.

We were required to provide in Leipzig the proper conditions for line maintenance of the aircraft with a time-frame of several months allotted for the task. However, NAMSA proposed not to wait until the Leipzig base was made ready, but to start operating earlier. Consequently, two Ruslans (one in Kyiv, and one in Ulyanovsk) went on watch as early as 28 February. On 23 March, both those An-124-100s flew over to Leipzig, where an official SALIS project

Manfred Sadlowski,
"Wehr Technik" magazine, No.1, 2006

that the Prague summit of NATO passed to Germany all administrative functions under the Strategic Airlift programme. The Brigadier General of Air Force Headquarters and Chairman of SALIS Management and Partnership Committee Mr. Jochen Bott informed that NATO together with EU had succeeded in

prompt preparation and implementation of the project.

Ruslan SALIS GmbH and NAMSA (NATO Maintenance and Supply Agency represented in Leipzig by Major General Karl Heinz Müntzer) became the project partners. Two An-124-100 airplanes each of 120 tons

load-carrying capacity are presently based at Leipzig airport and kept air alert to be used by any SALIS member country within 72 hours. Four more An-124-100 airplanes can be made available within 6 to 9 days.

Dr. Jung emphasized economic significance of the location selected as the home

The first days of the SALIS programme operations turned out to be very strenuous: during the period of time up to 10 April, the Antonov Airlines' An-124-100s made nine flights between France, UK, Germany, Norway, Iceland, Afghanistan and Lithuania. By the end of the year, the Antonov team also had to visit Gabon, Cape Verde, Cyprus, Congo, Pakistan, Tajikistan and RSA. They transported helicopters, ground vehicles, tents, supplies, potable water and provisions. All partners were acting in unison, strictly abiding by their commitments. Such a beginning caused understandable satisfaction for the customers. *"The first results of operations within the framework of SALIS initiative were on the whole positive. The principal 'endurance test' was the relocation of the German military contingent to the Democratic Republic of Congo. In my assessment, the test has been successfully passed. Our partners from France and Poland are of the same opinion. It has been a flying start and we intend to proceed with the project implementation with even greater confidence,"* remarked Lieutenant-General Klaus-Peter Stieglitz, Inspector (Commander) German Air Force in his interview to the German *WehrTechnik* magazine published in issue No. 4, 2006. In 2006, the flying time accumulated in the SALIS programme by Antonov Airlines alone was 1,193 hr 25 min. In addition to the actual flights, both Volga-Dnepr and Antonov Airlines were heavily involved in the work of outfitting the Leipzig aircraft maintenance base!

The official base opening ceremony took place on 17 January 2007. The presentation held on the occasion attracted over 130 official representatives of the NATO member countries, Ukraine and Russia, and of the State of Saxony where Leipzig airport is situated. The distinguished guests inspected the base facilities and equipment, which made it possible to perform all principal An-124-100 aircraft maintenance checks. K. F. Lushakov, Antonov Airlines Executive Director, and G. A. Pivovarov, Volga-Dnepr General Director, who made the presentation, outlined that henceforth the Ruslans would not need to return from time to time to their principal bases in Kyiv or Ulyanovsk, and this would result in the additional improvement of the cost-effectiveness of transport operations.

Commercial directors of Antonov Airlines, V. N. Kulbaka, and Volga-Dnepr, V. A. Gabriel.

Loading gas-processing equipment to be delivered to Libreville, Gabon. Calgary, Canada. August 2007.

opening ceremony took place. The ceremony was attended by NATO officials, representatives of the Ukrainian and Russian Embassies, Antonov Airlines, Volga-Dnepr, Ruslan SALIS GmbH, and ministries of the programme participating countries: United Kingdom, Hungary, Germany, Denmark, Canada, Luxemburg, the Netherlands, Norway, Poland, Portugal, Slovakia, Slovenia, Finland, France, Czech Republic and Sweden.

SALIS Closed Gap in NATO and EC Capabilities

base for the airplanes in Leipzig, Saxony. Besides the above-mentioned from the German side, the celebration was also attended by Dr. Peter Eikenboom, Secretary of State; General Wolfgang Schneiderhan, Inspectors General, and Lieutenant General Klaus-Peter Stieglitz, Inspector of Air Forces. Dr.Franz

Joseph Jung welcomed the representatives of partner countries – Russia and Ukraine: General Designer of ANTONOV Company Dr. D. Kiva, and President of Volga-Dnepr Group of Companies Aleksey Isaykin. Mr. Valery Gabriel, Managing Director of Ruslan SALIS and Commercial Director of Vol-

ga-Dnepr Group, made for the participants an unforgettable presentation of his firm. Among those present were two more guests from Kyiv: Konstantin Lushakov, Managing Director of ANTONOV Company and Valery Kulbaka, Commercial Director of ANTONOV Company.

After the presentation, its participants discussed further utilisation of the combined fleet of the An-124-100 aircraft for transportation of cargoes in the interests of the NATO nations. Summarizing the results of the discussion, Lieutenant-General Heinz Marzi, Deputy Commander in Chief of the German Air Force, said: *"We should continue our cooperation. Ukraine and Russia are working just fine. The German side is fully satisfied with the work. We see quite clearly that neither today, nor in the foreseeable future, transportation of large quantities of cargoes within short time frame is or will be possible without utilizing the An-124-100 aircraft."*

All further SALIS programme work proceeded in the same positive vein. Seeing the evident success of the programme, another two European countries – Belgium and Greece – joined it. In addition, several flights were made in the interests of the ministries of defence of Spain, Japan, Australia and Singapore. The aviators' work intensity grew accordingly. Now, up to three Antonov Airlines aircraft took part simultaneously in SALIS operations. The operating time of the Kyiv aircraft in 2007 was 1,421 hr 27 min, while in 2008 it grew to 2,075 hr 14 min. On the whole, in the first three years after the contract was awarded, Antonov Airlines aircraft transported

28,388 tonnes of various cargoes, and their flying time was 4,691 hours. Thus, two civilian carriers operating the Ruslans and working in unison finally managed to achieve the long-time ambition of all generals – assuring the true air mobility of troops – and practically demonstrated their ability to relocate considerable troops and stores to any point on the globe.

Especially worthy of mention here is the fact that

Loading the fuselage of the British Nimrod anti-submarine aircraft. Waddington Royal Air Force base, 19 December 2007.

Start of hydraulic turbine loading. Gostomel, 14 June 2008.

The An-124-100 airplane won the competition with the US Boeing C-17. And since the Airbus A400M was going to appear in 2010 at the earliest, and would not be operationally available until 2012, the Antonov became its timely replacement for NATO and EU. When talking to a magazine corre- spondent, Director of Leipzig airport Erik Malitzke said that his aerodrome met all requirements and was ready at any time for implementation of all necessary additional measures for the aircraft utilization.

Cargo tie-down operations in progress inside the Ruslan cabin.

N. Yu. Vasiliev, one of the key specialists of the commercial department.

Evolution of the Antonov Airlines empty aircraft flights ratio.

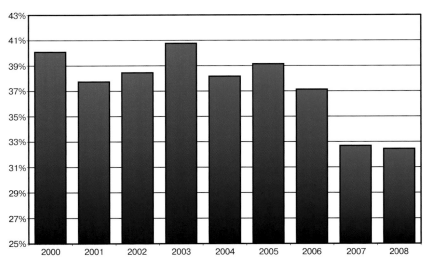

in the course of these activities excellent business and personal relations became established not only between the Ukrainian and Russian aviators, but also between them and their European customers. Being true professionals, these people continuously helped each other, striving to achieve the best results in their common cause. Such an attitude naturally evoked a mutual sense of appreciation. By way of an example, I would like to cite an excerpt from the letter of Francois-Xavier Herbert, NAMSA SALIS Office Chief, to Valery Gabriel and Aleksandr Gritsenko who managed the SALIS operations on the Antonov Airlines' side. The letter was written on 30 April 2009 – on the day when Mr. Herbert left his above-mentioned position for a new post: "I would like to avail myself of this opportunity to express my profound appreciation to you and the whole of the Ruslan SALIS personnel for helping us make this initially shadowy project really successful and transform it into a flagship NATO programme ... I am going to remember the years of our fruitful co-operation and will cherish the memory of the professionals always focused on attaining the best decisions for meeting the needs of the customer

nations. Besides this professional aspect, I will hold in remembrance the beautiful relations, especially the informal ones, that we had and which I am going to miss. I will try and meet and greet you again during one of your future visits to NAMSA. Three cheers to SALIS and Ruslan SALIS! With the warmest regards, Xavier Herbert." One should think that shaping such relations between the citizens of different nations is one of our first real successes on the arduous road to European integration that Ukraine is trying to follow today.

It should be noted here that successful transport operations performed on the orders of 18 countries were the best boost possible to the image of the Ruslan itself. During this period, the aircraft became an indispensable component not only of industrial logistics systems but also of the global security system. As A. N. Gritsenko remarked in 2008, "The results of our two companies' work under this contract during the three-year period clearly demonstrate that no alternative exists in the world today to the An-124-100 aircraft. This is also openly acknowledged by the NAMSA managers. They say that even if they had had illusions about the gradual replacement of the An-124-100 by -17 or 400 , they have none today. The new supervisor of our programme with NAMSA Mr. John Foster remarked during one of our conversations that he was considering utilisation of our aircraft at least as long as until 2015."

However, as the entire history of Antonov Airlines demonstrates, the good things of life need to be earned by hard work. Antonov had to fight hard for each contract and for each opportunity to earn the money needed so much by the company. Thus, as early as 2008, the company started discussions about the prolongation of co-operation in the framework of the SALIS project. In December, Antonov managed to sign a supplementary agreement to the contract to this effect and the contractual relations with NAMSA were extended until 31 December 2010. Later, Antonov Airlines and Volga-Dnepr faced an even more difficult problem – the aim to extend the mutually beneficial partnership with the European countries over the period of time when the A400Ms began entering service.

The successful start of cooperation on the SALIS project and the very efficient alliance with the former competitor – the Russian Volga-Dnepr Airlines – had quite an important effect on all the ensuing activities of the airlines. The collaboration with Air Foyle that had begun at the outset of Antonov Airlines and had done so much good to both sides, became a thing of the past in the middle of 2006 ... The split was quite civilized – as it should be between old partners. In the resulting situation, the parties agreed to terminate the effective Cooperation Contract upon expiry of its five-year period from

V. N. Korol, General Director, Antonov StC, negotiating with managers of Maximus Air Cargo of the UAE, which operates one An-124-100. Abu Dhabi, February 2009.

1 July 2006. The document determined the exact procedure of the joint operation's termination and reciprocal payments ...

In the second half of 2006, everything demonstrated the expediency of deepening the cooperation with Volga-Dnepr Airlines. By that time, both companies, having accumulated considerable experience in worldwide transport operations, came to understand that further improvements in the efficiency of air transport operations was possible only with deeper coordination of their activities. The time came to get rid of the dual nature of relations between Antonov Airlines and Volga-Dnepr, i.e. being competitors in the air transportation market, so that they could remain consistent partners in many respects connected with improvement of the Ruslans and the renewal of the aircraft's serial production, which was a matter of serious consideration at the time. When the joint contest of 2004 and 2005 for the SALIS contract ended with a splendid joint victory, formation of a strategic alliance between the Ukrainian and Russian carriers became practically inevitable.

To formalize the new alliance, Volga-Dnepr, as a more structurally market-oriented company (while Antonov Airlines remained just a structural division of the Antonov state-controlled company), registered the Ruslan International Ltd. (RI) company with a mission to conduct coordinated commercial and technical policy and improve the quality of services rendered by both partners. In practice it was organised so that the RI principal office, located at Stansted near London, accumulated the orders for air carriage from all agents of both Antonov Airlines and Volga-Dnepr. The office personnel, that

included Ukrainian, Russian and British specialists, compared the demand with the capabilities of the combined fleet of both carriers available at any given moment of time and planned the utilisation of the aircraft in such a way as to minimize empty flights. Undoubtedly, this was more easily done with double the number of aircraft available. It is interesting to note that that whenever RI managers signed a transportation contract they did not know exactly whose aircraft would be used for the mission. The job was given to whoever was free and closest to the cargo loading point. The principle of work distribution in proportion to the fleet of available aircraft and general commercial expediency was strictly followed. Another important principle of the joint activities was the mutual transparency of

Loading industrial equipment to be delivered to South Korea for an order by Samsung Electronics. Hahn, Germany, March 2008.

Aircraft of Antonov Airlines and Volga-Dnepr keeping watch at Leipzig airport.

Helicopters of the UN peacekeeping forces are delivered to their destination. April 2009.

market operations. A solution seemed to have been found that fully met the Antonov Airlines objectives as well as those of Antonov StC in general. However, as V. N. Kulbaka, who was put at the head of the Ruslan International Ltd. operations on the Ukrainian side, explained, "*This solution provoked serious resistance. Numerous*

complaints had been sent to different agencies. The situation inside the company was unsettled. Incessant revisions and audits – often blatantly biased – went on for three years. Of course, it was very hard working under such unsettling conditions, but, as they say, the dogs bark, but the caravan goes on. During the first three years of

The Ruslan is getting ready to be loaded at Warsaw airport. January 2009.

operations, the effectiveness of charter flights more than doubled! It may safely be said that no other airline in the world had attained similar results. Even in the conditions of economic slump our operational results improved considerably. There is no denying the fact that maintaining good relations with our new partners was not an easy job at all. It was by no means a surprise, since we had been in stiff competition for 15 years while operating in the cargo air transportation market. Nevertheless, we were managing to overcome all these obstacles – they all were but minor problems, just barnacles hindering a ship's progress."

It is important to note here that 2006, the year when all these changes were taking place, was one of the most testing years both for the Antonov Airlines and for Antonov StC in general. The point is that during the larger part of the year, three out of seven An-124-100s were practically withdrawn from active service (one for testing the new navigation equipment suite in the framework of the An-124-100 -150 programme and another two were undergoing the service life extension activities performed upon accumulation of 12,000 flying hours). Quite naturally, the operating time accumulated in Antonov Airlines' commercial flights in 2006 was at the level of 6,223 hours, which was only 250 hours more than the previous year. However, during the next year, the airline's performance again demonstrated appreciable growth. Compared to 2006, the number of flights increased by 15.8% and 33,977 tonnes of cargo

were transported, showing a 13.4% increase. Also interesting was the transportation geography of 2007. As before, principal scope of carriage was in the Eastern Asia region – over 36%, as well as in the Southern and Central Africa – about 20%. The customers in America and East Europe received almost equal shares of cargo – 7 to 8% each, while 14% of freight was transported to West Europe. In total, aircraft operated by Antonov Airlines landed during that year in 768 airports of 163 countries of the world. Was it not a convincing proof of the truly global nature of the Antonov Airlines operations?

With such an intensive work schedule, when literally tens of thousand tonnes of cargo had to be handled, specific memories of the individual transport operations are lost. The Antonov Airlines employees say that they saw a continuous chain of varying cargoes making it impossible to remember all of them. Still, some of the flights cling to memory. One of such memorable operations was the transportation in May 2006 of 72 high-priced cars (each costing in excess of US$100,000) to take part in the Gumball 3000 rally between Belgrade (Serbia) and Phuket (Thailand) then between Bangkok (Thailand) and Salt Lake City (USA). Another was the delivery in April 2007 of huge Rolls-Royce Trent 1000 engines for the Boeing 787s from East Midlands (UK) to Nashville (USA). The next month, Kyiv Ruslans made six flights to deliver four diesel engines each weighing 102 tonnes and four generators for a new electric power station in Antananarivo (Madagascar). Also memorable was the transportation in December 2007 of the British Nimrod antisubmarine aircraft from Waddington Royal Air Force base to the British Aerospace aerodrome in Woodford, where the Nimrod was later retrofitted and upgraded. As the runway in Woodford was comparatively short, landing at the aerodrome required high professional skill from the pilots.

In 2008, the number of remarkable flights grew even more. In March, several cargo items were carried from Germany to South Korea for an order from Samsung Electronics, which required the utilisation of dedicated loading ramps. In September, a 90-tonne excavator was moved on board a Kyiv Ruslan from Toronto in Canada to Brisbane, Australia, an 89-tonne generator from Delhi (India) to Kabul (Afghanistan), and a 72-tonne generator from Helsinki (Finland) to Baku (Azerbaijan). Overall, during 2008, the aircraft of Antonov Airlines made 782 flights (an increase of 29.5% on the figure for 2007) and transported 42,227 tonnes of cargo (up 24.3%), having spent 9,157 hours in the air above all the continents. About a third of all operations were of a unique nature, i.e. no other vehicle could have undertaken such transportations. As we can see, in spite of the global financial crisis, the primary business indexes of Antonov Airlines continued to improve. This gave grounds for the conclusion that the major problems of the transition period had been left behind, that the basic structures established jointly with the Russians between 2004 and 2006 had started operating properly, and that Antonov Airlines was rushing forward toward new achievements.

Antonov Airlines' aircraft provided the most prestigious rally in the world

CHRONICLE OF ANTONOV AIRLINES: YEAR BY YEAR
New role (2009–2013)

New role

The period 2009–13 in Antonov Airlines' history turned out to be special. At that time, some of its services and employees started providing scheduled passenger flights on regional routes in Ukraine, as well as on international air routes, alongside its traditional intercontinental cargo transportation business. This activity was so unusual for Antonov Airlines that it is difficult to find the right words to describe it.

The problem is that Antonov Airlines itself in the strict legal sense was not performing passenger flights; these services were rendered by the parent structure – Antonov StC. Antonov Airlines was only a participant in this, as it was a structural subdivision of the 'big Antonov' but had the resources needed for such activity, such as certified flight and technical personnel, as well as facilities and resources for aircraft maintenance and repair. However, first things first ...

By the middle of the 2000s, Antonov StC already experienced the commissioning of An-140 turboprop passenger aircraft. This experience turned out to be ambiguous. Many problems during the initial period of the aircraft's operation on the routes which perfectly naturally had been solved efficiently with the help of powerful state support during the Soviet period, turned into colossal problems under new economic conditions. There was not a single agency in modern Ukraine that could take on the problems connected with making the airliner compliant with the high market standards. Therefore, Antonov StC was forced to take on itself a large amount of this works and expense, as well as the thankless task of finding any element of public resources for launching the regular flights of An-140. Although this is a normal practice for aircraft manufacturers, Antonov StC at that time was only making its first steps towards the market economy, like all of Ukraine.

In principle, when the An-148 new-generation regional jet passenger airliner was created with wide international cooperation (14 countries participated), it was quite obvious that the highest priority should be given to the initial period of its operation. Just for the record: it was Antonov Airlines activity that provided the lion's share of the funds for the An-148 development and certification, but that's another story. By 2009, the airliner had passed all the tests, received its airworthiness certificate, entered serial production at the plants in Kyiv and Voronezh and received the first firm orders.

By that time, several airlines from Ukraine, Russia, Kazakhstan and other countries had expressed their

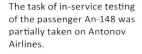

The task of in-service testing of the passenger An-148 was partially taken on Antonov Airlines.

(2009–2013)

desire to become the first operators of the new aircraft. But all of them had rightful fears about the difficulties that the pioneers always experienced as the process was about aircraft in-service testing rather than regular operation of the aircraft. During tests there are always some unforeseen schedule overruns, increase of expenses and other unpleasant 'surprises'. At the same time, the state was not in a hurry to cover all those risks. The situation became more challenging because of the extremely small number of aircraft that could be put into operation. At first it was one aircraft only; by the end of 2009 there were two of them, and later three.

In this situation, the management of Antonov StC once again showed admirable creative thinking and an exemplary concern for the future operators of its new product, but of course this had to be within the limits of the available capabilities. These capabilities included, first of all, the availability of facilities and resources for An-148 aircraft flight support, as well as of experienced crews who had performed a full cycle of flight and certification tests of the new aircraft, knew it like the back of their hand and were therefore suited perfectly for the initial period of operation. The idea emerged that since the aircraft were still small in number, and their market prospects were far from obvious, there was no point in burdening the airlines which were to become the launch operators with training their own crews and creating their own maintenance base. Instead, we could use Antonov StC's facilities that were already available, while the partner airline would be responsible for the route network development, ticket sales, passenger service, advertising, etc. In fact, it was a model of joint operation of the An-148. In such a relationship model, the risks associated in starting regular operation of a new airliner were not only the responsibility of the operator but also the aircraft designer.

It is worth noting that passenger transportation was not something completely unfamiliar to Antonov StC. Its crews have been performing charter passenger flights throughout the entire history of Antonov Airlines and continue to perform them from time to time today. For this purpose, Antonov StC's fleet has a special variant of the An-74T aircraft, which is actually a corporate aircraft of Antonov StC and is used mainly for business needs. From time to time, it is used by various delegations, working groups of specialists, sports teams etc.

When the first (and at the time only) An-148 entered passenger service, the 'seventy-four' became a swap plane, ready to save the situation in case of serious malfunctions of the main airliner.

The model of cooperation to bring the An-148 to the market proposed by Antonovans turned out to be quite attractive, and at the beginning of 2009 negotiations began with the main Ukrainian air carriers operating the regional routes. These included AeroSvit Airlines, Ukraine International Airlines (UIA), Dnepravia and others, but at the end of the day the contracts were concluded only with those three airlines. On behalf of Antonov StC the negotiations were conducted by the General Director V. N. Korol, Vice-President for Economics Yu. G. Andriienko, and the Head of Department A. D. Gridasov. Considering that inside Antonov StC the idea of joint operation of the An-148 was understood not only as a necessary support for carriers but also as a commercial venture capable of bringing money, it wasn't a surprise that at the end of the day Antonov Airlines was selected to make it a reality. K. F. Lushakov, E. A. Golovnev, already known to us from earlier in this book, and other employees of Antonov Airlines joined the negotiation process. The Ukrainian state leasing company Leasingtechtrans (later renamed as Antonov-Finance), which was the owner of the first batch of the An-148, acted as the third party

The delegation of Lithuania headed by President Valdus Adamkus (in a bullet-proof vest at the front) flew with the An-74T to Afghanistan on one of its charter passenger flights. Kabul, 5 May 2011.

Inside the passenger cabin of the An-148.

An-148 at Boryspil airport when it was flying under the flag of AeroSvit Airlines.

An-148 had been settled, and the aircraft could start flying.

The first regular flight of the An-148 took place on 2 June 2009. It was executed under the flag of AeroSvit. The flight was made by An-148-100B No. 01-01 (tail number UR-NTA), the first prototype aircraft, modified in accordance with the type design of a serial aircraft. The aircraft cabin had a two-class layout and was designed to carry 68 passengers (8 in the business class, 60 in the economy class). At first, the airliner with a group of journalists on board departed from Kyiv Boryspil airport to Kharkiv. Before the flight, a short briefing took place, at which the Minister of Transport and Communications of Ukraine Yosyp Vinskii emphasised that: *"This day is a landmark for Ukrainian civil aviation."* The airliner left Kharkiv with its first commercial passengers and landed in Kyiv 40 minutes later.

The aircraft was piloted by a crew headed by test pilot Sergei Troshyn. *"Strangely enough, for me it was a completely ordinary flight,"* he told Sergei Mikhailovich later. *"There were hundreds of such flights, if not thousands. Nevertheless, for me, as a test pilot and pilot specialising in charter cargo flights, working with passengers was something new. Passenger flights have their own unique features – you need to follow some specific procedures, which are not needed for cargo charter flights usually. I had to go through all these procedures, to study all*

in this process.

The outcome of the negotiations was the coordination of the cooperation scheme under which Antonov Airlines was responsible for the provision of aircraft (which Antonov StC received from Leasingtechtrans under a leasing agreement), aircraft insurance, flight crews and technical specialists, as well as the performance of heavy maintenance checks and the repair of aircraft at its base in Gostomel when necessary. Thus, by the early summer of 2009, the main organisational issues of joint operation of the

the new requirements carefully. One such feature was, for example, communication with passengers. Everyone knows that the pilot-in-command of an aircraft during the flight often addresses the passengers – to welcome them, talk about the flight, about the current altitude, speed, weather, etc. From my point of view, this practice is not quite right. The pilot must be completely engaged in controlling the aircraft and not be distracted by such things. But an order is an order, and all this had to be done. I was the first pilot of Antonov Airlines, which started performing passenger flights, so it was my duty not only to properly perform all the necessary actions, but also to teach others how to do them."

An official red-carpet welcome was waiting for the An-148 at Boryspil. Representatives of the mass media and officials came to the airport, among them General Director of AeroSvit Konstantin Botev, President of Antonov StC Dmitrii Kiva and the Head of the State Aviation Administration of Ukraine Alexander Davydov. After a short rally, the memorandum on further cooperation between Antonov StC and Aerosvit was signed with applause from those who gathered there.

In the following week An-148 No. 01-01 under the flag of AeroSvit performed 13 more flights, including flights to Odessa and Simferopol, having carried 792 passengers in total. After that, this aircraft participated in the Paris Air Show, and returned to performing passenger flights only in the

second half of the month. Thus, only 37 hours of regular flights were made in June; however, from July the total passenger flight time began to increase each subsequent month. By the end of 2009 this number reached 535 flight hours, 544 flights were performed within this period, and the number of passengers carried was 24,649 people, which is not bad for a solitary new aircraft. As the Antonov Airlines employees remember, it was a period of learning the business of passenger air transportation and gaining experience, as well as correction of errors, the number of which diminished progressively.

From the beginning of 2010, the rate of growth of An-148 passenger flights increased. Step by step, An-148-100B aircraft No. 01-09 (tail number UR-NTC) and No. 01-10 (tail number UR-NTD) joined the transportations, as well as Dniproavia and UIA Airlines, relations with whom were based on the same principles as with AeroSvit. The network of routes was expanding constantly. For example, in Ukraine, the An-148 flew to Dnepropetrovsk, Donetsk, Ivano-Frankivsk, Lviv, Mariupol, Odessa, Simferopol, Kharkiv and Uzhgorod. Outside the country, the routes of 'one hundred and forty-eighths' travelled to Aktau, Athens, Baku, Batumi, Belgrade, Budapest, Bucharest, Warsaw, Vilnius, Yerevan, Geneva, Kaliningrad, Copenhagen, Milan, Minsk, Moscow, Nizhnevartovsk, Riga, Rostov-on-Don, Thessaloniki, St. Petersburg, Sofia, Surgut, Istanbul, Stockholm, Tel-Aviv, Tbilisi, Helsinki and Zurich.

"Step by step, many pilots joined passenger flights," S. M. Troshyn continues. *"Among those who became pilots-in-command, I would name V. V. Goncharov, A. A. Gorin, V. I. Mosin, A. V. Spasibo, E. S. Riabinin. At first, we flew to all the major cities of Ukraine, then went abroad: Russia – Moscow, St. Petersburg – then the Baltic States,*

Ye.A. Galunenko and S. M. Troshin – pilots-in-command of the An-148 during regular passenger flights.

Briefing before the first commercial flight of the An-148 is presented by the Minister of Transport of Ukraine Yosyp Vinskyii. Boryspil, 2 June 2009.

The first passengers boarding the An-148.

Vadym Vyshnevskii from Kharkiv enjoying the privilege of becoming the first passenger of the new airliner.

Scandinavia ... Speaking about the unique features of passenger flights, it should be noted that the main source of this uniqueness are the passengers themselves. They can be different. Among the tens of thousands of people there always happened to be someone who was not all there, drunk, impetuous,

etc. So I want to thank our flight attendants. They solved all such cases in a very professional way, so that there were no threats of flight cancellation or

any other problems. By the way, at first we flew with our Antonov flight attendants only, but later the employees of AeroSvit and UIA began to be added to our teams. The reason was simple – the

passengers considered them to be, so to speak, the representatives of the corporate style and service of these carriers."

Yes, passengers are different. They can behave in different ways. They have different perceptions of flight, and the level of service offered by a carrier and, finally, the aircraft itself. Let me remind you – the An-148 was just entering operation and undergoing in-service testing. Accordingly, its first passengers were to some extent his test operators. Some of them liked it, others did not. Some felt pride that they were flying in the sky in their own Ukrainian aircraft, while others, on the contrary, complained about this. *"In 2013 I was flying with UIA in the An-148 on the Kyiv-Berlin route,"* recalls Nina Rahimberdina, one of the An-148 passengers. *"80% of the aircraft passenger capacity was used in that flight. Most of the passengers were surprised to learn that this was a new Antonov aircraft but some of them were indignant. One respectable young man from business class was complaining to flight attendants that he was not given a Boeing, but some creation of Ukrainian designers. He did not want to trust his life with them. He complained that the airline had not warned that there would be a Ukrainian aircraft.*

"I did not notice any particular happiness before the takeoff among other passengers either, but I, for example, was very pleased with the flight. A very pleasant first impression – the aircraft was new, fresh. Accurate, simple and clean design, beautiful interior, pleasant colours, comfortable chairs. I flew in the second row of the economy class by the window. Takeoff and landing was comfortable, like the whole flight actually. There were some shortcomings that irritated – some obsessive whistling, which was heard throughout the flight, and the air in the cabin was too cold and made my legs freezing. The rest was nice, comfortable and without complaint. At the end of flight, there were no more complains from the passengers."

Operation of the An-148 had a highly seasonal nature. The greatest number of flights was, of course, in the summer period and to the resort areas. From June to August, the flight time of each aircraft per month reached 200 flight hours or more. In other months, the intensity subsided, but even then some routes were loaded more than others. In the off-season the most popular flight was Kyiv-Donetsk. This route had two flights a day, and nearly always there were no spare seats in the aircraft. Most of the passengers on those routes were businessmen. In the period of 2009–13, Ukraine's economy was growing significantly and in tandem air transport passenger traffic was growing also. The intensity of An-148 flights grew accordingly. For example, just in the first half of 2011 the total flight time per month of these airliners increased 1.5 times. The

An-148 of UIA is ready to receive its passengers.

maximum number of passengers carried in Ukraine by these aircraft was reached in June 2013, when the An-148 was used by 13,775 people.

As one should expect, despite the long-term flight and certification tests, the so-called 'teething problems' of the new aircraft began to reveal themselves during the initial period of An-148 operation, which resulted in a noticeable number of various malfunctions and failures. In addition to this, the airlines began to receive punch list items regarding individual interior elements of the passenger compartment, furnishing equipment and proposals on how to improve interaction with various airfield services. Sterling work to eliminate all the identified shortcomings and to perform all forms of technical maintenance of the aircraft in regular operation was done by the then President of Antonov Airlines V. D. Inkov. Specialists from Antonov StC's Engineering Aviation Centre headed by L. P. Pustovoi were directly involved in this activity.

It is interesting to note that only heavy maintenance checks were performed in Gostomel, and line maintenance checks were carried out directly in Boryspil, the base airport of AeroSvit Airlines and UIA where a line maintenance base was organised. Technical staff certified by the State Aviation Administration of Ukraine was there all the time, as well as the necessary tools and equipment, pools of spare parts and consumables. Since the An-148 was a new type of aircraft, there was nothing similar to this support at the other airports to which it performed its flights. But there was a need to provide aircraft support in service, at least at a basic level. Therefore, each flight had two

technicians on board who performed all necessary procedures at the destination airport. At the initial stage of development of any aircraft this is quite normal practice and this practice is also cheaper than training personnel at every airport to which an aircraft is just starting to fly.

As already stated, by the summer of 2013 the intensity of An-148 flights under the flag of UIA, with Antonov Airlines pilots, reached its maximum for the whole period under review. Joint business operations successfully overcame all the difficulties typical of the initial phase of development. Of course, the relationships of the partners were not always ideal, but this, however, rarely happens in the business environment. Various tensions, mutual claims, delays in payments, and other difficult moments repeatedly happened during the course of work but the most important achievements were that the business continued to develop, the passengers were delivered to the destinations, and the An-148 became more and more consistent with the concept of what a high-performance passenger aircraft should be.

At that moment, the Ukrainian state, which was the owner of the first batch of An-148s, decided to transfer the aircraft to a state enterprise, SAE Ukraine, which specialised in providing air transportation services to top state officials. On 26 June 2013, the Order of the Cabinet of Ministers of Ukraine No. 612-r 'On the transfer of An-148 aircraft by the Antonov-Finance SE' was issued. Following this, all the contracts for financial leasing under which passenger transportations were carried out became invalid. On 27 August 2013 the President of UIA I. V. Miroshnikov sent a letter to Antonov StC, in which he informed them that from 11 October 2013 all three An-148s would cease performing regular flights by the company headed by him. That was the end of an unusual chapter in Antonov Airlines' history, when the air freight leader was undertaking passenger flights.

The achievements of this period were truly impressive: for 53 months, the crews of Antonov Airlines performed 7,791 flights on 38 routes and carried 37,8291 passengers in the An-148. The new aircraft spent 11,322 hours in flight performing commercial transportation. Therefore, we have good reason to say that Antonov Airlines successfully completed the in-service testing of the newest passenger airliner, which was quite an extraordinary task for a charter cargo airline. But, from the very beginning of this book, we have seen that Antonov Airlines is an extraordinary company, and that it is capable of fulfilling the most extraordinary tasks.

Predictably, actual operation encouraged the market's interest in the new Antonov passenger airliners. Since 2010, the An-148 has been actively operated by St. Petersburg's Rossiya Airlines, as well as other carriers. Even the government of Ukraine had a certain interest in the aircraft. In particular, Vice Prime Minister B.V. Kolesnikov decided to clamp down on supervising the preparation of a

consolidated order for these aircraft from Ukrainian airlines. In June 2011 a group of representatives of several domestic airlines worked with AviaSvit and Antonov Airlines to study the first experience of these aircraft operation. The outcome of this study was a package of preliminary orders for 22 An-148 and 28 An-158.

By the end of the first half of 2018, at the time of writing, 41 of the An-148 and An-158 aircraft are already in operation by 11 organisations in four countries. These aircraft have flown more than 180,000 hours on around 100,000 flights, and transported more than 6 million passengers. The flight time per month of each aircraft is now almost 300 hours, and in some cases it reaches a record level of 400 hours per aircraft. This exceeds the typical figures for regional aircraft and is more in line with long-haul airliners. That means that the great efforts of Antonov Airlines in the creation of a passenger Antonov aircraft proved not to be in vain.

Upon completion of in-service testing, An-148 aircraft were transferred to the Ukraina state-owned airline.

CHRONICLE OF ANTONOV AIRLINES: YEAR BY YEAR
Place in the sun (2012–2015)

Place in the sun

The second decade of the new century began well for Antonov Airlines. It was the start of a period of general business stability. The alliance with the Russians allowed some 70–80% of the world market of super-heavy and outsized cargo transportations to be controlled. It even allowed, to an extent, the carrier to dictate requirements to the customer. In that period, the aircraft of Antonov Airlines landed in over 800 airports of 178 countries of the world. The average flight time of each Ruslan accumulated during a year reached 1,100 hours, and the annual average cargo transported by one aircraft reached 36,700 tonnes. It meant that the time had come to reap the fruits of those mammoth efforts spent during the previous 20 years to gain that world market. Today, it is abundantly clear that from the commercial point of view this was one of the most successful periods in the airline's entire history.

It should be recalled that in 2006 the Antonov Airlines' strategic partner was changed to the Volga-Dnepr Russian Group of Companies. At that time, it already had a powerful international commercial structure with numerous branches in countries in Europe and the Middle East, but was still tied to the core vertical structure of the Russian authorities. As we have mentioned before, the co-operation with the Russians developed in two main directions. One was joint air deliveries for the benefit of the national structures of the NATO countries, in the framework of Ruslan SALIS GmbH (RS), a company established specifically for this purpose and registered at the request of the main customer in Germany. Another was the operation in the world market of

The joint fleet of Antonov Airlines and Volga-Dnepr Ruslans totalled 17 aircraft.

(2012–2015)

commercial traffic through Ruslan International Ltd. (RI), a company based in the United Kingdom.

"The RI registration location was not chosen at random," explains Andriy V. Blagovisnii, Vice President of *Ruslan International Ltd* for Sales in 2014–16. "Registration in England allowed us to be closer to the main customers, both to the brokers, and the forwarding companies, and to the cargo owners:

• *establishing an uninterruptible and transparent financial system for the payment of the direct operating cost of the executed flights;*

• *reaching an international level of trust among the companies, since in the case of disputes RI fell under the well-tried-and-true legal system of England;*

• *preserving the available professional personnel of Air Foyle HeavyLift Ltd that had an experience*

Andrii Blagovisnii, Vice President Sales Ruslan International, 2014–2016.

of previous work with Antonov Airlines, and also involving the personnel of Volga-Dnepr UK Ltd (the Volga-Dnepr affiliated structure)."

From the very start, the parties determined some main principles to follow in making their future partnership. Primarily, those principles related to work sharing in the management of their common business, and were somewhat different for the military and civil transportation markets. Thus, all incoming RS orders had to be divided between the partners 50:50. At the same time, inside RI, such division had to be made proportionally with regard to the accessible fleet of aircraft, in other words, taking into consideration the aircraft not involved in the performance of other contracts and ready to take off immediately. In addition, the partners agreed to arrange the allocation of contracts so that the location of aircraft was taken into consideration, and empty flights minimised, thus aiming to raise the efficiency of the common fleet which comprised at that moment 17 Ruslans and one Mriya. Finally, the parties agreed on the principle of cross transparency in their actions in the market, and, no less importantly, on the preservation of the individual and independent brand names of Antonov Airlines and Volga-Dnepr in their joint activity, external relations and PR campaigns.

In view of the above principles, Volga-Dnepr, as a more marketable structure and the sole founder of both new companies, suggested that Antonov StC controlled 50% of RS shares and 49% of RI stock. Yet a question emerged about the most consistent way of making this comply this with the law of Ukraine which in effect determined the corporate rights of state-owned enterprises. Such structures not only possessed the assets of other companies, but at the same time were controlled by the Fund of State Property of Ukraine. In general, there was a serious legal problem in obtaining the shares.

The Russians proposed an unusual solution: issuance of the appropriate holding of shares as a gift to Antonov StC. This solution had been meticulously analysed by the Antonov lawyers who came to the conclusion that this did not contradict the effective law. (Though it would be more correct to say that the Ukrainian law contained nothing about such an approach. Since this was not forbidden, it became permitted.) To lay aside any doubts, the Company appealed to the court of Kyiv to confirm the right to obtain shares as a gift, and received a positive legal

Michael Goodisman,
Business Development
Director of Ruslan
International.

decision in June 2006. Finally, the transfer of shares was registered according to the laws of Ukraine, Germany and Britain.

We have already mentioned that the Ukrainian and Russian teamwork was co-ordinated from two offices: RS in Leipzig and RI in Stansted. Both the Antonov Airlines and the Volga-Dnepr specialists remained there throughout. In unison, they solved all the practical problems, starting from the allocation of specific flights and ending with the analysis of each incoming invoice, and managing the timely receipt of money.

In the framework of RS, for instance, the technology of standard flights included the following. The Ministry of Defence of a SALIS participant country forwarded its application to the dedicated NATO agency to perform this or that flight, containing a preferred date, describing the cargo, naming the airports of departure and destination. The above-mentioned agency checked with RS about the feasibility of the flight, and asked for an approximate schedule. The RS Leipzig office experts processed the received data, and compiled the flight schedule, suggesting the flight route with the locations for landing, refuelling and the crew's rest, if necessary. Everything had to be agreed with the customer country Ministry of Defence, and the corresponding contract was signed. It was followed by the stage of making applications for flight clearance over the territories crossed by the route. After obtaining all permissions, the aircraft

departed. Upon termination of the mission, all papers confirming its accomplishment were signed.

The Senior Representative of Antonov Airlines with RS in 2011, A. N. Gritsenko, emphasised: "The most important thing is the economic component of the project. All SALIS member countries declare that the programme is economically effective, and what is important, it allows the organisation of the express delivery of freights, including the humanitarian aid, without contracting any additional tenders." In the author's opinion, the economic efficiency of the Ukrainian-Russian joint efforts under the SALIS programme was the reason NATO prolonged the contract until 2012. Then, a new tender for cargo transportation was announced to the participants of the project, and again was won on 9 July 2012 by the joint proposal of Antonov Airlines and Volga-Dnepr, and the programme continued. The tender committee letter read, in particular: "Ruslan SALIS is the only company which meets our requirements in full."

A maximum of three Antonov Airlines' aircraft could be used concurrently to fulfil NATO requests within the time period under consideration, 2006–15. One, An-124-100 aircraft from the Antonov Airlines fleet was held permanently in standby mode at the Ruslan SALIS GmbH base in Leipzig. Overall, this time period resulted in 1,901 flights of the Ruslans and 26 flights of Mriya, 115,466 tonnes of cargo were transported under the NATO contract, and the aircraft spent 17,218 hours in the air. And

Only the Ruslans can carry such oversize cargoes.

Contemporary industrial equipment is being placed into the containers dedicated for transportation inside the Ruslan cargo cabin.

that enormous, titanic activity was conducted at the highest level of reliability, professionalism and skill.

"As to RI," says Andriy Blagovisnii, "the company dealt first with the sales of An-124 charter flights in the world market, marketing promotion of services, technical assessment of various cargo loading potential, development of their loading/unloading procedures in coordination with technical specialists from Antonov Airlines and Volga-Dnepr, planning the relocation of necessary loading equipment in coordination with flight schedules, construction of routes, itinerary development, obtaining clearances for landing and crossing en route countries, 24/7 flight support. It is important to mention that the co-operation involved joint marketing and charter sale of the An-124-100 Ruslan aircraft only, while the air transportation business remained exclusive for each company for operation of other types of aircraft: the An-225 and An-22 for the Antonov Company, and the Il-76, B747, B737 for Volga-Dnepr.

"The An-124-100 aircraft fleets' amalgamation and the two companies' wealth of experience seemed beneficial for all parties. The customers obtained the opportunity to rely on the newly increased fleet of 13–15 aircraft, gaining the optimum price with an allowance for minimisations of empty flights since the nearest available aircraft would be sent to the location of cargo loading; a wider selection of loading equipment, standard procedures of operation and preparation of freight for delivery could also be proposed now. The

carriers could drastically increase their operating efficiency as well.

"Throughout its history, RI proved to be a responsible partner for all, both in executing the orders of many well-known companies, such as Airbus, Boeing, Bombardier, Spirit Aerospace, Thales Alenia, Shell, General Electric, Rolls-Royce, Siemens, Alstom, etc., and in rendering services to governments of the world leading countries: USA, Canada, Germany, United Kingdom, France, Spain, the Netherlands, Australia, Singapore, Japan, and others."

It should be mentioned that while staying in the EU legal framework, the partners paid much attention to the correct and legitimate management of their activities, including all financial transactions. From the very beginning of their teamwork, both RS and RI were audited regularly by in-house auditing services, and annually by Ernst and Young, one of the seven top auditing companies of the world.

All bookkeeping documentation and the companies' balances as of the end of each year were subject to a scrupulous analysis. Audit reports about RS and RI financial activities were annually forwarded to tax inspectorates in Great Britain and Germany.

The partners' diligence was highly appreciated. In 2010 RI entered the so-called 'Category One' of the United Kingdom of Great Britain & Northern Ireland companies' rating, which is determined by D&B, an internationally recognized leader in the

Paul Furlonger, Manager of the RI commercial department.

field of business information. By that time, D&B had collected and traced the credit, debit and marketing data of 240 countries covering a 166-year period of history; they could immediately supply their clients with information which allowed them to avoid major commercial risks. When RI was included in the 'Category One' list, Mr. Gareth Jones, D&B UK&Ireland Managing Director, named it *"a fantastic triumph of attaining such a result during one of the most severe declines of economy. Only 15% of the British companies were included in this category."* For that occasion, RI received a corresponding certificate.

To summarize my description of the positive aspects of the alliance with Volga-Dnepr, it may be mentioned that co-operation with the Russians enabled Antonov Airlines significantly to improve the operating efficiency of the entire fleet of aircraft. Thus, in the period of 2005 through to 2013, the ACMI rate value which represented the An-124-100

services in the market, increased almost thrice, and the volume of annual foreign currency earnings to Antonov StC from air transportation grew nearly four times. The Antonov Airlines profitability attained 15% while the majority of international air carriers normally show some 4–5%.

Such progress in business is very rare. Books are written about such achievements, and about the business people who manage to achieve such goals. However, any phenomenon in life has many sides. It never happens that one only enjoys benefits. If you look attentively, you will find a minus for each plus, and see the reverse side of each coin. Meanwhile, the co-operation with the Russians revealed a number of reverse sides.

First and foremost, we should not speak so much about the Russians but about Ukraine. The contemporary state machine of Ukraine is designed so that the government is not so interested in the national companies that work inefficiently and

Aerobatic aircraft housed inside the An-225 cargo compartment convert Mriya into a real aerocarrier.

2000 words on Ruslan International

Following the events of 9 September 2011, the subsequent military activity in Afghanistan and the impact of the TMR scandal on the business of Antonov Airlines and Air Foyle Heavylift in 2003/2004, it became clear to both Volga Dnepr and Antonov that demand for the An-124 was increasing significantly. NATO and individual governments competed amongst themselves for availability and Volga Dnepr struggled to supply the civil commercial market and fulfil the US military

requirements to support operations in Iraq. This competition and delays in the development of the A400 military transport aircraft culminated in NATO issuing a tender for the long-term provision of airlift support for NATO nations, pending the delivery of the A400. The tender was written in such a way that it was effectively not possible for any single operator to make a compliant bid. Consequently, Volga Dnepr and Antonov agreed to make a joint submission. This bid was successful and led to the formation of

a joint venture company based in Germany called Ruslan SALIS GmbH.

Volga Dnepr now had two significant military support contracts and was losing ground in the civil market, to both Antonov and Polet. In order to arrest that decline and to retain as much control of the supply of aircraft as possible, Volga Dnepr proposed that, alongside the Ruslan Salis joint venture, a further joint venture be established with Antonov, called Ruslan International. This company would combine

Loading operations never stop, despite rain or fog.

are heading towards bankruptcy. Such factories, as a rule, flounder helplessly in the stormy seas of the market, and have to get out of their economic predicament by themselves. However, should a state enterprise succeed in business and earn a little hard currency (or, maybe more than a little) such a company immediately becomes the subject of the most ardent governmental interest. The nature of such interest is, so to say, very peculiar. One may think that each interested party is trying to find its own way to take a small portion (sometimes it grows immensely) of this success. That was what we obtained: a 'wild capitalism' model.

The most favourite format of the said interest was inspection. Those inspections were numerous, versatile, long-term, scheduled, unscheduled, deep and careful. We had the inspections to verify 'some

negative facts' declared in some letters from certain 'experts in the field of aeronautical engineering'. Almost everything had to be checked. In 2006–14, the most usual was 'inspection of operating efficiency of Antonov StC in the frames of RS and RI joint ventures'. Inspections of the profitable operation of Antonov Airlines may seem absurd; nonetheless such inspections were conducted, too. Also, the income utilisation efficiency was analysed.

Generally, it was difficult to explain the reason for all those inspections, being an obvious, strictly forbidden by the law, intrusion into economic activity of Antonov StC. However, at the highest level (interdepartmental groups and commissions commissioned by the Prime Minister and the Cabinet of Ministers of Ukraine, the State Office of Public Prosecutor, the Fund of State property of Ukraine, the

Paul Furlonger

the expertise of the two companies' staff in the UK, pool the two fleets of aircraft and thereby increase the efficiency of the total operation, reducing the amount of empty flying undertaken by each partner. Consequently, the life of each airframe would be preserved better and the economic operating efficiency significantly improved.

Sadly, from the outset of the joint venture, active participation in the management of the joint venture was rather

one sided. Volga Dnepr sought to control all aspects of the RI business. It required ADB to use its costing and communication systems. It agreed to RI planning and programming RI flights, but in practice it retained complete, not just operational, control over all flights which operated on its aircraft. It continued to sell An-124 flights from Volga Dnepr offices under the Volga Dnepr banner irrespective of whether these flights should have operated under the RI banner or not. RI's GSA in the USA sold its

services as Volga Dnepr not as RI. Antonov's participation was sadly, although possibly understandably, much more passive. At the start of the joint venture Volga Dnepr was a privately owned airline pure and simple. Antonov Airlines was and still is a small but important part of a large state-owned organisation whose principal business remains design and construction. Inevitably, Antonov was focussed more on navigating

Continued on next page

Chris Fairchild, Ruslan International Operations Manager.

Inspection and Revision Administration of Ukraine, the Ministry of Taxes and Revenue of Ukraine) at least 12 inspections were arranged in the above-mentioned period of time. The inspections did not just follow each other: often a new inspection started while the previous remained unfinished.

An amazing fact is that none of the competent commissions discovered any violation in the bookkeeping and taxation, economic accounting, efficiency of income utilisation and completeness of the fulfilled obligations under each running contract of Antonov Airlines! None of the certificates and records made after those inspections contain any mention of any such violations. It was striking that the inspections proceeded in spite of all the results, with the persistence worthy of a better purpose.

Exhausted by these events, on 12 May 2014, the Antonov administration sent to the then Prime

Minister of Ukraine Arsenii Yatseniuk a letter signed by Dmitrii Kiva who headed the Company at that time, and attached thereto an extensive explanatory note in 33 pages describing the Operator's activity. The letter, in particular, said: *"Please be assured that in our economic activity, the Antonov Company strictly adheres to the requirements of Law. Please give your instructions to terminate the above-mentioned inspections of Antonov Company initiated by the letters of incompetent 'experts in the field of aeronautical engineering.'"* Only after this letter had passed all instances, and the government officials attended corresponding briefings, did the situation with the inspections show a gradual tendency to abate.

Another – and the principal – source of the negative side of the situation was, quite naturally, the Russians themselves. The essence of the

Massive industrial equipment is a substantial part of the cargoes carried by Antonov Airlines.

2000 words on Ruslan International

its way through the stormy seas of Ukrainian political instability and on simply using the revenue from Antonov Airlines to support the other work of the Antonov Design Bureau, rather than concentrating its efforts on development of the airline at the expense of its other activities. Regrettably, this meant that while Antonov marketed in accordance with the terms of the joint venture agreement, Volga Dnepr continued to market under both the Ruslan International brand and the Volga Dnepr

brand, meaning that the Antonov Airlines name was effectively lost from the market place.

Even in respect of the An-225, Volga Dnepr staff told prospective customers they could provide this aircraft 'through' Antonov. In other words, they promoted the idea amongst customers that Volga Dnepr also controlled this aircraft.

The RI business grew steadily in terms of the number of hours flown and revenue generated. The percentage of empty flying

dropped from around 45% to as little as 25% and the enormous demand generated largely by the conflicts in Afghanistan and subsequently Iraq resulted in the price being more than doubled within a couple of years. In these terms it was highly successful.

Volga Dnepr used the opportunity and the additional revenue to significantly expand its own business, employing significant numbers of additional staff and opening additional offices. Neither Ruslan International nor Antonov did the same.

Loading Augusta Westland helicopter. UK, autumn of 2014.

negative manifestation of this is clearly described in the text written specially for this book, and presented here as an insert, by Paul Furlonger, who has been fruitfully and for a long time working both with Antonov Airlines and Volga-Dnepr, and before that with Air Foyle and Air Foyle Heavylift, extending back to 1990. We shall just note that the negative goings-on observed by Paul had become apparent as soon as the alliance of the carriers took shape and had been combining in a striking way with the good things in the relationship between the Ukrainians and Russians.

As early as 2012, Mr. Furlonger wrote to express his *"... concern as to the future of Ruslan International and of Antonov Airlines ... Ultimately, their aim is to acquire total control of the commercial An-124 business. They care about Antonov only in so far as it is necessary to allow them to continue the operation of the aircraft. If they can they will remove that obstacle also. They believe they have the necessary facilities and expertise in Russia and in the factory in Ulyanovsk that they can do without Antonov completely ... I believe most strongly that the current situation is more dangerous for Antonov than it has ever been. I believe that this future is under even greater threat ... from the continued actions of Volga Dnepr."*

As relations progressed, the negative tendencies were aggravated and gradually began to prevail. They became so pronounced that even caused concern for the Ukrainian government. A dedicated interdepartmental working group was established,

Consequently, by sheer weight of numbers of people, Volga Dnepr became the predominant player in the market.

The history of Ruslan International became a microcosm and a reflection of the geo-political history of tri-partite relations between the West, Russia and Ukraine. The terms of the agreement which set Ruslan International up in the first place were repeatedly ignored or broken. The partners regularly disputed the allocation of flights and the balance of work. As the level of involvement of the US and their allies in Afghanistan and Iraq diminished so demand for An-124 flights fell and the partners in Ruslan International found themselves increasingly at odds as to the benefits of the joint venture to their individual businesses. The accounting for RI, the purchasing of third party services, the marketing and advertising, the storage of data, all were controlled by VDA. Another significant bone of contention between the partners was the life extension and development programme for the An-124 aircraft. As a country Russia declared that it should not be dependent on foreign powers for the certification of Russian-operated aircraft.

The annexation of Crimea spelled the beginning of the end as political pressure on both partners mounted and restrictions on trade took their toll on relationships.

By 2016 most European defence forces will have their A400 aircraft. The

Continued on next page

Graham Witton, the Ruslan International Managing Director.

on the instructions of the Prime Minister, for the audit of the Antonov Airlines operational performance under contracts with Volga-Dnepr. In its findings, the group stated that even the documents of entitlement and the instruments of incorporation of the RS and RI companies, which had been as we remember established by Volga-Dnepr, had laid the foundations of discrimination against the Ukrainian partner. In particular, these documents reserved for Volga-Dnepr the casting vote in all matters of joint operations, while Antonov Airlines did not even have a blocking vote, despite the fact that 49% of the RI stocks and 50% of the RS stocks were transferred to Antonov's full control.

No doubt, the partners maintained a civil attitude and strict compliance with all officially declared principles these legal technicalities would not have had any significant effect. But the fact was that the Russians' tactics had from the very outset begun to deviate from the generally accepted ideas

of equal rights and increasingly resembled the approach of 'Big Brother', which is so characteristic of the Russian mentality. Mr. Furlonger's text shows how it was implemented in practice. The principal manifestation of this tendency was the desire to redistribute the orders received by the joint office in favour of Volga-Dnepr with a subsequent shift in the share of the profit.

Thus, within Ruslan International, this tendency resulted in Volga-Dnepr's aircraft making 173 flights between September and December 2013, while those of Antonov Airlines made just 71, that is 2.44 times less. It was a gross violation of the principle of parity of flight distribution in proportion to the size of the available aircraft fleets, despite the fact that the Russians had more aircraft available. Let us make a small calculation. Volga-Dnepr had 10 Ruslans and Antonov Airlines had seven. One aircraft of each of the carriers was permanently on stand-by and making flights in the framework of the SALIS

Unique equipment is required for operations with unique cargoes.

2000 words on Ruslan International

multinational C-17 operation based in Hungary was fully operational. Russian airspace was closed to Ukrainian aircraft. The war, for want of a better word, in Eastern Ukraine had escalated to the point where Russia and Ukraine accused each other of shooting down the Malaysian Airlines flight MH17. The availability of spare parts and support for the An-124 and indeed all aircraft which had been designed, developed and built in the Soviet era and or periods when Russia and Ukraine enjoyed friendly relations

became increasingly difficult.

Ultimately, in late September 2016 Volga Dnepr announced that they would withdraw from the joint venture with effect from the end of that year. Such a rapid closure of the joint venture presented no difficulty for Volga Dnepr but created an enormous difficulty for Antonov. Nevertheless, against all odds, Antonov was able to obtain the assistance of some of the staff from Ruslan International and very rapidly set up new structures to ensure the continued survival

of the Antonov Airlines business and to return the name of Antonov Airlines to a prominent position in the market place. By the middle of 2018 Antonov Airlines was again competing successfully with and operating completely independently from Volga Dnepr. Hopefully despite increasing international regulation and the continuing difficulties faced individually and collectively by both Antonov and the Ukraine, Antonov Airlines can build on this solid new foundation and continue in successful

Heavy helicopter loaded into the Ruslan directly from a hangar after maintenance.

programme. Each of the partners each had, as a rule, one aircraft in heavy maintenance. Altogether, the ratio of available aircraft was 8:5, meaning that the Kyiv people could render only 1.6 less aircraft to the joint fleet than the Russians. Even if you take into account the fact that during some months one of the Kyiv aircraft was involved in tests under the aircraft avionics upgrading programme the ratio should have been 8:4, that is theoretically the quantitative dominance of the Russians could have been double, but it should not have made 2.44!

"Volga-Dnepr," explained Mr. Furlonger, *"have a large staff and a high overhead, they have financed a lot of acquisitions both of aircraft and for expansion of their business. Consequently they need a strong cash flow to service that debt. If the cash flow stops they will have great difficulty. The majority of the cash flow comes from the An-124 business. This why they are so keen to control it and to buy all the long term project business – it protects the cash flow. If they were truly interested in maximising the benefit of RI they would work with Antonov to allow the RI management to lead the development of the business and manage it more efficiently. Instead, they ignore almost every agreement they make. They are not always truthful with the staff and do whatever they think is appropriate for Volga Dnepr first and for themselves as individuals second."*

Not just Mr. Furlonger, but numerous other people directly involved in these events regarded the situation as a threat of loss of control over the Ruslan International operations on the part of

operation for many many years to come.

If Antonov believes that its manufacturing and design business can sustain it profitably in the future without Antonov Airlines and the An-124s that will be wonderful, because the whole point of Antonov Airlines was to help secure the future of Antonov as the organisation developed by Mr. Antonov himself. Antonov Airlines will have served its purpose and Antonov Company will be in the process of returning to its rightful place as the best

designer of transport aircraft in the world. However, the fear remains at the moment, that the political situation in which Antonov exists is such that the future of the Antonov design and manufacturing business without Antonov Airlines cannot yet be guaranteed or even confidently predicted.

Russia appeared to be working to return to state control much of the industries which they regarded as strategically important. In the oil and gas industry even the biggest foreign oil companies are being

forced and or bought out of their Russian investments by Rosneftgas and Gazprom etc. Instead of backing the An-148/158 family and the An-70 whole-heartedly, the Russians have taken their unsuccessful aircraft design and manufacturing organisations, restructured them into the United Aircraft Corporation and launched the Superjet 100 – a direct competitor to the An-148/158 family.

Continued on next page

Night-time loading at one of the US airports.

Antonov Airlines with subsequent eviction of the Ukrainian carrier from the market. Even more so, as the situation was continually developing from bad to worse, and not only in terms of sharing flights. At the turn of 2013–14, the Russian side made an attempt to close Ruslan International Ltd out altogether and create in its stead the Ruslan International GmbH as a subsidiary of Ruslan SALIS GmbH, thus actually transferring the office controlling the joint fleet from UK to Germany. This move was aimed at the further strengthening of control over the fleet of Ruslans on the part of Volga-Dnepr. The mechanism to attain this purpose was based on the fact that the staff of the British RI basically consisted of the people who had started their careers with Christopher Foyle and who were, therefore, emotionally connected with Antonov, and moving the office to Leipzig would in practice inevitably result in them quitting their

jobs. In Leipzig, where the Russians' positions were especially strong since they had an aircraft maintenance centre there, it was planned to hire new people for the office who would not be tied by traditions that had taken shape during two decades of joint work with Antonov and who would be more compliant to the Russians' plans.

No doubt, the proposal for the RI transfer to Germany was presented by the Russians under the pretext of striving for improved efficiency of joint operations, reduced office maintenance costs, a more favourable tax situation, etc. However, the true motives for this operation were no secret for anybody. Therefore, a fierce struggle began between the competing partners, and for Antonov it was either win or die. Several meetings between top managers failed to settle the dispute. Volga-Dnepr continued to insist on moving to Germany so

2000 words on Ruslan International

Russia, not entirely unreasonably, wished to retain control of both design and manufacturing facilities. Similarly and less reasonably, they appeared to wish not to see a strong independent Ukraine. Having spent 20 years deciding whether or not to commit to the An-70, either they or the Europeans and Americans, or all three, effectively prevented Antonov from selling the An-70 and the An-124 in the west. This is certainly true irrespective of the arguments

or propaganda put forward to explain the decisions not to buy such aircraft direct from Antonov.

The collapse of the Ruslan International joint venture might have been expected to trigger a price war and that the revenue earned by ADB from Antonov Airlines would have been reduced in the short term. However, whilst competition was and remains fierce, the price has been relatively stable. In the medium to long term the

interests of Antonov will be much better protected by the current arrangements than was the case during the period of the joint venture. The ONLY advantage to ADB of RI was the increase in the ACMI rate for the aircraft. A large part of that increase would most probably have occurred anyway because of the level of demand for the aircraft over the life of the joint venture.

On the other hand, the renewal of separate operation has allowed Antonov

Loading the Royal Air Force Tornado interceptor, November 2014.

Antonov resorted to an extreme step: in December 2013: the company notified the Russian side about its intention to terminate the 2006 Charter Agreement – the principal document governing its relations with Volga-Dnepr. The threat of the loss of a joint business which was bringing in considerable revenue sobered the Russians. A special joint working group was convened to resolve the situation. After several rounds of rather difficult negotiations Volga-Dnepr was forced to abandon the idea of the move and return to the partner principles on sharing flights.

However, the improvement in relations was short-lived. During that time, the Revolution of Dignity had already started in Ukraine. The leaders of Russia took a pronounced antagonistic stand with respect to Ukraine and this included cooperation in the field of aviation. Several months later the Crimea

was annexed and Volga-Dnepr's aircraft began flying to the peninsula taking part in the delivery of supplies for the Russian troops. This deplorable fact left no doubt about the future of Ukrainian-Russian cooperation in the super-heavy and oversize freight transportation. In 2014 it shrunk to a nullity and was formally terminated in 2016.

Description of the twists and turns of politics is not worth time here, however, no matter how large a part they played in the fate of Antonov Airlines. In the long run, for the majority of the Antonov Airlines employees the problem of relations with government authorities in Ukraine or with Russian partners were, though important, somewhat distanced since they had no contact with these problems in their routine work. Pilots and technicians, flight managers and office staff – all of them were doing their everyday work. And

to retain complete control of its assets, its brand and its destiny.

The current situation in Ukraine is more dangerous for Antonov than it has ever been. However, in this last 28 years the world has come to rely heavily on the quality, reliability and capability of Antonov aircraft and Antonov Airlines, the products, the people who work at Antonov and who have struggled to ensure its continued success, in the face of great uncertainty, great difficulty

and great political and economic change. Antonov Airlines has ensured economic success for countless projects and saved countless lives by creating and maintaining a whole new sector of the air freight market and giving industry the opportunity to do things not previously considered possible. All those involved may be justifiably proud of their efforts and safe in the knowledge that Mr. Antonov himself would as proud of them as of the aircraft and the airline

which bears his name. So long as the aircraft can be maintained in operational condition and funds generated to continue their development the future for Antonov Airlines is bright.

The Ruslan setting off for another commercial flight. Winter 2015.

did it as usual – conscientiously, professionally and with inspiration.

So, that seems to bring us to the conclusion of this book. Everything has been covered about the main spheres of Antonov Airlines' life and work up to the year 2015. Of course, the story is not complete, not all flights have been described, not all people mentioned, not all innovations given their due. Nevertheless, this particular fragment of the Antonov Airlines' history can be considered complete.

One may ask, why I chose to describe this particular period of time. Why not finish the book with a story of the latest events of 2018? The reason for such a strange (on the face of it) decision is that June 2015 became, in a certain sense, a crucial point in the history of Antonov StC in general and, quite naturally, of Antonov Airlines as well. At that time, on the initiative of state authorities (and let me remind that Antonov is a state-controlled company), D. S. Kiva was dismissed from his CEO position, and the new man on this post was appointed personally by President Petro Poroshenko. As to be expected, practically all of the managing personnel of the company were changed during the next few months, including the managerial staff of Antonov Airlines. At the time, K. F. Lushakov, who had held the post for a quarter of a century since 1991, also left his position as the Antonov Airlines Executive Director.

In short, 2015 marked the end of an entire era in Antonov Airlines history, the period connected with the people who are the heroes of this book. A lot of new people came in 2015 and thus, a new historic period began. It is difficult to characterize

this new period as yet. Suffice it to say that although just three years have passed, four presidents have already followed each other at Antonov during this short time span. (For comparison: Oleg Antonov had been running the company for 38 years.) The company has also seen several changes of the second- and third-level managers. It is important to understand here that the priorities, approaches and areas of current activity are also changing with the people. Yes, Antonov Airlines continues to operate,

perspective, if we summarize everything said in this book, these 26 years can be described in just a few sentences. But let us see some statistics first. During this time, Antonov Airlines made 14,029 freight flights and carried 757,156 tonnes of cargoes with the total accumulated fleet time making 160,262 hours. These figures are not just impressive, they arouse an involuntary urge to take one's hat off to such achievement, although the author does not wear one! Consider: this flying time is equal to more than 18 years spent in continuous non-stop flight! And having tried several times to imagine all those three quarters of a million tonnes of various cargoes one understands that the human imagination is powerless to do it.

But this is not what is most important. Above all is the fact that during all these years Antonov Airlines have been faultlessly performing their intended function, for which the carrier had been established within the Antonov StC structure almost 30 years back. The primary aim was the financing of the operations of the renowned aircraft manufacturing facility under the conditions of a complete lack of government support – both in terms of funds and in terms of orders. The money earned by air transportation was used to purchase a multitude of machine tools, computers, software products, laboratory equipment and a many other things required for the development of modern competitive aircraft. The accumulated funds were spent on scientific research, design and development activities. In fact, those very funds make it possible for Antonov StC to retain its position as the leading aeronautical company of Ukraine, thus creating

the Ruslans are still flying worldwide, cooperation with new partners is developing, and much needed funds for the current Antonov StC programmes are coming in. But it is still too early to describe these processes. They are too unclear and discrepant. Therefore, the author suggests that a chapter about today's Antonov Airlines be reserved for a future edition of this book.

The story of the period between 1989 and 2015 is, on the contrary, quite clear. From a wide

Mriya lands at its home aerodrome in Gostomel. Summer, 2014.

True professionals and patriots are working with Antonov Airlines.
Left to right: N. A. Dokukin, R. I. Tkachuk, V. N. Dernovoi, Y. A. Mindar, A. V. Pimenov, D. V. Antonov, S. N. Tsivak, V. V. Yepanchintsev, G. Y. Antipov, Y. I. Koshtskii, B. O. Ivanov.

jobs for about another 40 companies in the country.

It is also important to note that the Antonov Airlines operations served as an invaluable aid to the generation of a new system of support for the operations and continued airworthiness of the Antonov aircraft types. Many principles of this system have been tested on the Ruslans of the Company's own air transportation division. Finally, let us not forget that after the disintegration of the USSR, Antonov Airlines played a decisive part in retaining the An-124 as an aircraft type and keeping it at a state-of-the-art engineering level. Without commercial application (and Antonov StC was a pioneer in this field), in other words as a purely military airlifter, the Ruslan would barely have survived to today. It was its commercial application that made it possible to retain this truly unique aircraft in service and gave it prospects for future development.

How shall I finish my story of the Antonov Airlines activities? The title of an article comes to mind that was posted on one of the French web sites and told the story of how the participants of Paris–Dakar rally had managed to avoid a terrorist threat owing to the Antonov Airlines aircraft which had airlifted them with their cars over dangerous areas. 'Saint Antonov' – that was the article's title. A good title and no mistake. And it is suitable for

the end of my story about the path traversed by Antonov Airlines. Yes, it is a bit vainglorious, but what can one do if some people see the airline's work as comparable to the Acts of the Apostles?

Yet for us, who have been brought up irreligious, the airline's activities are connected more with the notion of progress in the wide sense of the word. The modern world is developing as, first of all, an economic system, and this development is constantly accelerating. New industries are being created and their accelerated deployment makes it possible to start gaining profit sooner, even in spite of the high cost of air transportation. More and more industrialists come to understand it, and the number of orders for air transportation is growing continuously. The average rate of growth of demand in this sector is double the respective figure for general cargo. And this means that the world needs Antonov Airlines. And Antonov Airlines is sure to deliver. This is evidenced by the airline's entire history which has earned it a place in the sun and allows it to advance into the future ...

The An-124 aircraft is as much the key hero of this book as Antonov Airlines, not only because it is the main transport of Antonov Airlines: the aircraft is so remarkable *per se* that it may remain for a long time a source of inspiration for many journalists, writers and film directors. It is unique in almost in all respects. Constructed 35 years ago, this strategic airlifter had been called the Kremlin's long arm to threaten the West; however, it soon entered perfectly into the world system of peaceful operation, becoming an irreplaceable link in the construction of large-scale industrial systems and the implementation of international projects in the field of aeronautical engineering and space research. This aircraft rescued refugees and victims during various natural disasters, delivered tanks, Christmas trees, elite horses, cruising yachts, concert equipment, reconnaissance aircraft, banknotes and pure gold. The list of its freight is endless; in this sense it could possibly be named the most versatile aircraft in the history of aviation. Finally, it just looks beautiful, as a real piece of art ...

ANTONOV AIRLINES AIRCRAFT
An-124-100 and An-124-100M-150 Ruslan

An-124-100 and

this, the effort to employ as much as possible the available design reserve of the An-22 aircraft for the new project seemed relatively moderate.

Namely, there was a proposition to equip the elongated fuselage of the Antaeus with a new wing (a straight wing, according to one version, or a swept one according to the other), a T-shaped tail and four or even six turboprop engines. However, this proposal was declined despite the fact that it promised the new aircraft construction within the shortest time limits. The reason for the decision lay in the fact that in case of such an approach, the new aircraft staying within the bounds of the average 1960s indices of its performance standards, i.e., load ratio, lift-to-drag ratio, fuel efficiency, could never become a worthy competitor to the C-5A Galaxy.

Actively continuing their research, the Kyiv bureau in 1968 designed the An-126 aircraft with 140-tonne capacity. It was already based on more advanced developments in aeronautical engineering, and though staying below the C-5's noise and emission characteristics, still promised to be much superior in its basic performance, sighting capability and defence system. The An-126 was planned to be fitted with six bypass turbojet engines mounted on pylons under the wing, and a cargo compartment of 37.5 m x 6.4 m x 4.4 m overall dimensions which admitted the arrangement of airborne equipment in two rows, and the simultaneous handling of cargoes not only via the rear ramp but using the forward ramp, too. This project seemed to be a Soviet reply to the Galaxy; the USSR aviation production and other allied industries' worked intensively and reported that all critical design development was completed. So, the technical risk in the construction of the An-126 was minimised.

During the same year, 1968, the An-126 design was approved by the Military and Industrial Committee of Presidium of the USSR, and preparation for a Decision of the CPSU Central Committee and Council of Ministers for the full scale aircraft construction and manufacturing began. In spite of the fact that the USSR Minister of Defence Air Marshal A. A. Grechko almost immediately signed the Decision, the Soviet bureaucratic

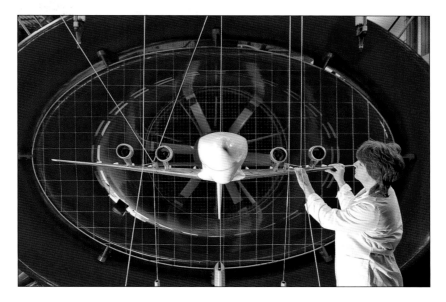

The Ruslan model in the wind tunnel.

procedures postponed its implementation for a period which exceeded one year. Throughout this period, Oleg K. Antonov and his close colleagues, as well as the scientists of TsAGI and other Soviet institutions, were not wasting their time. The design development, which in fact was a voluntary initiative, involved a number of well-known Soviet experts. One of those enthusiasts, G. S. Biushgens, one of the most eminent specialists in the field of aerodynamics in the second half of the 20th century, conducted the TsAGI research aimed at the improvement of heavy transport aircraft lift-to-drag ratio. During one of the discussions held at the end of 1970 he declared that he knew the way to surpass the American aircraft in the integrated parameters of aerodynamic quality. The results of these efforts were such that in the beginning of 1971 the Antonov Bureau had the opportunity of improving the designed power-weight ratio to such an extent that the future aircraft required only four instead of six engines.

"To be true, this transformation was supported, first of all, by the designer's gift of Oleg Antonov, his scientific foresight and personal courage," says Oleg. K. Bogdanov, the ADB leading specialist in aerodynamics for the An-124 project. *"In fact,*

An-124-100 and An-124-100M-150 main performance data					
	An-124-100	An-124-100M-150		An-124-100	An-124-100M-150
– length x wing span x height, m:	69.1 x 77.3 x 77.3		– with 120 t cargo:	4,650	5,200
– wing area, m²:	628		– with 40 t cargo:	11,350	1,1900
Cargo compartment dimensions, m			– without cargo:	14,200	14,400
– floor length (with ramps):	36.5 (43.7)		Flight speed, km/h:	800	850
– width (across floor):	6.4		Flight altitude, m:	9,000	11,600
– height:	4.4		Engines:		
Cargo compartment volume, m³:	1160		– type:	D-18T series 3 bypass turbojet engines	
Takeoff weight, tonnes	392	402			
Max payload. tonnes	120	150	– number x power, kN:	4 x 229	
Flight range, km:			Airfield length. m:	2,800	3,000
– with 150 t cargo:		3,200	Crew:	6	4

Construction of the An-124 prototype No. 1 in the shop of Kyiv Aircraft Manufacturing Association (KIAPO). Kyiv, 1982.

Oleg Antonov breaks a traditional bottle of champagne during the first An-124 rollout ceremony.

only some basic means of achieving the desirable technological level were outlined by the beginning of the 1970s, no concluding, comprehensively grounded results were available either in aerodynamics, or for the aircraft equipment and other components. But Antonov stepped up, and declared confidently: we can make an aircraft better than the C-5. That design, coded later An-124 or 'product 200', had been accepted by everyone with enthusiasm."

Having studied the new design scrupulously, the Military Industrial Commission of the USSR Council of Ministers Presidium approved the proposal of the aircraft industry ministries and defence for the An-124 construction on 2 February 1972. The Antonov Design Bureau was assigned with the task: to release in the nearest future the preliminary design for the construction of a new giant aircraft in a full-scale mockup. The objective seemed complicated: to surpass by twice the transport capabilities of the previous An-22 aircraft, to obtain significant maintenance reduction, improve self-sufficiency in operation, and ameliorate most of the important aircraft parameters. In 1973, the aircraft's appearance was determined, and its 1:1 wooden model soon built in Kyiv. Two 'mockup commissions' took place the same year: the so-called 'ministerial' or departmental level, i.e., the preliminary level, in June, and the governmental, 'high-level' commission, which was the customer, in October.

Both those commissions, basically, approved the selected design and layout solutions, including the wing aerodynamic configuration consisting of then standard structures. However, owing to the huge leap which the designers were facing in aircraft dimensions and technological level, to make it successful some revolutionary techniques were required. Piotr V. Balabuev, then First Deputy General Designer, formulated the problem as follows: *"Designing aircraft of an extra carrying capacity means that you have to look for the most progressive technological trends and ideas which often may not be current in manufacturing."* Therefore, the efforts to improve the aircraft design after its approval continued, and proceeded even at the stage of production drawing.

Use of a wing based on supercritical aerofoil was another key problem which caused discussions for the next four years. This was the first time it had been suggested in the USSR aircraft manufacturing history, and was accompanied by fierce exchange of opinions. *"Normally, we had to design thin swept wings. Use of a supercritical wing gave us a chance to make it thick, of a considerable reference height, while the wing aerodynamic drag was not increased,"* explained Viktor I. Tolmachov, the An-124 leading designer, about the benefit of the new wing. *"With other things being equal, the weight of such a wing is lower and the structure more manufacturable compared to the thin wing. The obtained inner space allows us to keep a substantial fuel reserve."* (The above quotation is interesting because at that time Viktor Tolmachov was an opponent of the new wing.) Simultaneously, the 'supercritical' approach concealed a high technical risk and put forward more new demands on the aircraft systems. Time was required to evaluate all the factors and make a correct decision.

However, no time remained. The Galaxy was adopted by the military forces, while its Soviet counterpart still remained on the drawing board. The Ministry of Aviation Industry and personally the minister P. V. Dementyev, a manager of strong will and high professionalism, categorically demanded the work was expedited. In April 1976 following ministerial discussions, Oleg Antonov had to grudgingly authorise the start of a standard wing

212

design. However – such was his scientific foresight and the administrator's talent – he continued the new wing design research with TsAGI scientists. On 29 June 1976, supported by the latest results, Oleg Antonov used the right of General Designer to declare his personal decision to give up all previous design work on the standard airfoil, and to initiate the supercritical airfoil project. At the same time, in view of the An-124's design importance, he headed the project management himself.

In spite of the fact that Antonov's decision promised to extend the aircraft construction period, the prospects of its high performance resulted in the consent of Dementyev and other high-ranking administrators from Moscow. In January 1977, the CPSU and USSR CM Central Committee's Enactment No. 79-23 was issued. It asserted the General Designer's findings and defined the new requirements of the An-124 aircraft (now under the code 'Item 400'). Devoting his vast experience to this aircraft would become his life's final effort, Antonov worked with the same inspiration and magnitude as back in the 1930–40s. Not only making decisions on any key problem (with no exceptions) in the creation of Item 400, Antonov used to frequently 'put his hand to the plough' in drawing numerous aircraft components, improving their shapes, and achieving the balance that would later become the feature of the Ruslan's appearance and structural integrity. The time proved the absolute correctness of Antonov's decisions including his selection of the new wing.

However, the An-124 was never the brainchild of just Antonov's talent. Thousands of people worked on this aircraft throughout the entire Soviet Union. To provide a proper technological level for Item 400, several Integrated Target Programme (ITP) packages were pioneered in the USSR to provide significant improvement in each aircraft component effectiveness, aerodynamic characteristics, structural strength and service life parameters, weight enhancement, power plant specific performance, functionality of systems and equipment, labour input to the aircraft maintenance and repair, etc. Adoption of ITP not only had a decisive role in the Ruslan design history, but gave a powerful stimulus to development of the entire aircraft industry. New tasks were determined for the engine manufacturers, avionic designers, metallurgists, developers of machine tools and production equipment, and, certainly, for aerodynamic experts and scientists of TsAGI and other industry institutions. The colossal potential of the USSR aeronautical industry was involved in the Item 400 activities. To find the best combination of parameters, computing centres analysed 540 possible versions of the aircraft aerodynamic configuration, 185 various models were blown

in wind tunnels, 36 wing versions tested. A great leap was made in the field of production engineering: the unique 28-m-long pressed wing panels, oversized fuselage panels, new specifically improved structural materials, including polymer composites, extended-life fixtures. As a result of such measures, the aircraft cruise lift-to-drag ratio increased by 20%, the load ratio grew by 10%, the engines reduced specific fuel consumption by 10%, the navigation accuracy increased four-fold, and the labour input in various maintenance procedures reduced two to five times in comparison with the An-22 and Ilushin-76 aircraft!

"Dozens of factories and institutions belonging to various ministries and departments participated in ITP," commented Oleg Ya. Shmatko, Deputy Chief Designer. *"To control this most sophisticated cooperation, the Central coordination board split into dedicated sections, and the Council of Chief Designers was formed; their sessions dealt not only with the topical issues of the An-124 construction, but with specific technological problems. As a whole, the management at both the interdepartmental, and the corporate level was grounded on the principle of responsibility for the final result."*

In spite of the entire country's efforts (no exaggeration) to create the An-124, the most difficult and critical decisions were taken by the Design Bureau. *"The giant aircraft is a government programme: a lot of departments, scientific institutes and factories are responsible for it. But the leading company should be a head thereto incurring the utmost responsibility itself,"* emphasised Nikolai P. Smirnov, Deputy Chief Designer for the aircraft systems.

Another specific feature of the An-124 was its longitudinal arrangement with small reserve of static stability. To provide normal flying on the Ruslan, it had to be equipped with a fly-by-wire (FBW) control

Fuselage of An-124 S/N.01-02 prepared for ground strength testing.

P. V. Balabuev, O. K. Antonov and V. I. Tolmachov greeting the test pilots. Gostomel, 24 December 1982.

The Ruslan's flight crew after the first flight. Gostomel, 24 December 1982.

Besides, the weight of such systems was inadmissibly excessive. At the same time, use of an FBW system allowed the aircraft to have a 3.7-tonne decreased wing and empennage loads and, and it lost three tonnes more due to the eliminated mass balancing of control surfaces. Moreover, they managed organically to integrate a new automatic system for the improvement of aircraft stability which prevented undesirable peculiarities of flight control at high angles of attack, and installed a stall warning and barrier system.

The An-124 design parameters were selected very carefully. When defining the cargo compartment dimensions a huge number of loading versions were studied for both military and commercial cargoes. Finally, the optimum arrangement two-row loading version was approved, with the compartment floor width reaching 6,250 mm. However, Oleg Antonov could not rely upon sheer theoretical assumptions or even scrupulous calculations in this very important issue. Under his initiative, for the first time in the company's history, a cargo compartment bench was constructed. Experimenters used it to roll through all possible combinations of equipment and vehicles of motorized infantry divisions and other major cargoes. This was followed by the General Designer's resolution to increase the floor width to 6,400 mm. Nowadays, when the Ruslan

system along with a number of analogue computing devices: that was quite new for a non-aerobatic aircraft. Another reason to use FBW system was the aircraft's extra size and, accordingly, the severe deformations of its airframe under the influence of external loads or resulting from thermal expansion. Application of conventional flight control systems, when command forces are conveyed to actuators by means of cables or stiff rods, seemed very problematic with such levels of deformation.

is generally used for commercial transportation of bulky cargoes, those additional 150 mm are sometimes of extreme importance.

The aircraft's features which finally determined its success include two cargo openings which allow the passage of wheeled vehicles and reduce drastically the time of loading/unloading. This complicated procedure is aided by a multicycle landing gear with kneeling capacity, reducing the nose ramp entrance angle. It was designed to reduce loads on the airfield surface and to expand thereby the network of base airfields. Special attention was paid to the landing gear dynamic and stiffness characteristics to avoid the shimmy phenomenon. Thirteen landing gear versions had been analysed in detail. The twin-deck fuselage arrangement with separated pressurisation of decks was unusual for ADB practice. However, this arrangement allowed the reduction in aircraft weight, increases service life, and improves the

flight crews' and attendants' safety in case of an emergency landing. The major part of the aircraft's avionics was arranged in the upper deck, dedicated compartments providing convenient access to them. This made possible the immediate elimination of any faults of the equipment both on the ground and in flight, thus contributing to the aircraft's maintainability in general.

A proper level of maintainability was a key issue in Item 400's development. An important component was the immediate diagnostics of the operating status of numerous systems and units critical to the flight safety within a limited period of time. With that purpose in mind, the aircraft was equipped with the airborne automated monitoring system (abbreviated to 'BASK' in Russian) which continuously monitored the operating parameters of the engines, the de-icing system, electrical power, pressure control and air conditioning, hydraulics, the aircraft landing gear units, etc. Another

The Ruslan's first take off. Kyiv, 24 December 1982.

An-124 Ruslan during one of its test flights.

General Designer Piotr Balabuev presents the An-124 to the Soviet press before its participation in the Paris Air Show. Kyiv, May 1985.

respects, not least in its transportation capacity, surpassing the *Galaxy* by 25%.

To make the dream come true ...

The design of a good aircraft is half the work; its successful construction is the other half. In view of the scale of the task and the tremendous loss in case of any error, construction of the An-124 was begun with an extensive programme of experimental trialling of the key design and layout solutions using numerous benches and prototypes. The efforts of the industry involved many factories in the creation of new materials and production technologies embodied in approximately 3,500 structure samples that had to be tested comprehensively. They constructed an experimental wing torsion box, two cockpit canopy versions, a large compartment of the fuselage middle section to try out the cargo floor design first and to conduct hydro fatigue tests later. The airborne systems were tested on 44 full-scale and experimental benches and testbeds including the landing gear, power plant system and auxiliary power unit, anti-icing system, hydraulic system, full-scale control simulator connected to the bench of wing high-lift devices and engineering flight simulator. The latter was used to complete testing of the most important flight conditions, including approach and touchdown, simulating almost 75% of failures. It allowed the industry to find the correct solutions beforehand, while still on the ground, and increased the safety of the future flights. In addition to the ground-based benches, the necessary experiments were conducted in

important function of BASK was monitoring the flight crew actions, in particular their compliance with the appropriate instructions of the Aircraft Flight Manual at takeoff and landing. Additionally, BASK was used to execute a number of absolutely new tasks, such as tracking of the weight and balance data in-flight variation, generation of data on failures for the emergency flight data recorder, and the communication system, determination of the maximum allowable take-off weight on the basis of airfield conditions, etc.

All this, and many other things that are impossible to be mentioned in one chapter of this book made the An-124 the new generation aircraft in many

Sometimes the An-74 was used as an escort aircraft for the An-124 test flights.

four flying laboratories. In total, the time of bench testing reached some 135,000 working hours. This time was intended to minimise the technical risk inevitably connected with the implementation of such an advanced design. Comparing the results, the leading designer for the An-124 experimental work Yuriy M. Kirzhner reiterated: *"Scrupulous bench trials allowed us to shorten the An-124 flight test programme by at least a hundred flights."*

The An-124 prototypes, including one aircraft dedicated for static testing, were constructed by the combined efforts of Antonov StC and the Kyiv Aircraft Manufacturing Association (KIAPO, nowadays a branch of Antonov StC). Preparation for the activities had begun long before the aircraft's final technical appearance was determined. In 1973, the Kyiv Aircraft Manufacturing Branch started the erection of huge engineering buildings with 100-m wide aisles, and since 1977 the progress of the construction had been under the vigilant eye of the Central Committee of Communist Party of Ukraine. The first package of the An-124 design documentation (Serial No. 01-01) arrived 1979, and manufacturing of production tooling began immediately. The aircraft manufacturing cooperation was very wide: the landing gear was manufactured in Kuibyshev, Russia, the engines in Zaporizhzha, Ukraine, the auxiliary power plant in Stupino (near Moscow) and hydraulic components in Moscow and Kharkiv. Altogether, over 100 factories were involved. However, the main partner of the two Kyiv factories was the Chkalov Tashkent Aviation Production Association (TAPOiCH), manufacturing the outer wing, the wing centre section and the bulky transverse structural members of fuselage. The completed components were transported on top of the An-22 aircraft from Tashkent, Uzbekistan to Kyiv, Ukraine.

In the early 1980s, construction of the first An-124 was at the peak of activity, and the highest personnel resources mobilized. Oleg Antonov named the project the *'main axis of advance'*. As soon the final assembly connected separate units, and the aircraft grew in size, it continued to excite the imagination more and more. Through the dense curtain of assembly toolings, electric cables and air routes the aircraft's enormous dimensions were not easily visible; however, they might be discerned. Hundreds of workers surrounded it, working simultaneously. The huge shop was always filled with the noise of riveting hammers and pneumatic drilling machines ... This picture gained by the author when he was still a very young worker can be never forgotten.

Strange enough, when the aircraft was almost finished, one could not say the same about its engine. The D-18T first bench test was commenced only three months prior to the An-124 takeoff. There

General Designer Oleg Antonov is making a presentation of the An-124 to the leaders of the USSR Air Forces. Gostomel, summer 1983.

were several causes for this delay, and the former chief of *Antonov* power plant department Viktor G. Anisenko explains one of them: *"The engine development had been entrusted to the 'Progress' Zaporizhzha design office headed by Designer General V. A. Lotarev. The US General Electric TF-39 engine of 18,200 kg thrust, installed on the C-5A was used as the prototype for the first D-18 design. However, soon it was found to be a solely military low-life engine. However, the management of the Soviet ministry of aircraft industry wished to have a unified large-scale engine suitable for application in commercial aviation as well, for instance, to power the Ilyushin-86 aircraft. From this point of view, the Rolls-Royce RB.211-22 was recognised as a more suitable counterpart. To purchase this engine, a delegation led by the Aviaprom's deputy minister for engine manufacturing Dondukov departed for Great Britain in 1976. I was a member of that delegation. We had a mission to make a copy of the RB.211-22 for which purpose we had US$12 million aiming to buy at least eight engines. However, the British immediately figured us out. They put forward the proposition of selling to us the number of engines sufficient to equip 100 aircraft, minimum. As a result, we failed to gain a full-scale demonstrator engine, and the D-18T engine construction started its unbeaten track based on the experience of development of the D-36 engine powering Yak-42 and An-74 aircraft."*

The important stage of any aircraft construction is its prototype strength testing. In case of the An-124 aircraft, a full system of static and fatigue tests was conducted on the same airframe for the first time in the world, a practice which allowed the avoidance of the construction of an extra airframe, saving an amount equivalent to US$40 million. The total time of static tests reached 60,000 hours.

Inside the nose flight
compartment of the Ruslan.

These unique activities were conducted in the new strength test laboratory of Antonov StC under the guidance of Yelizaveta A. Shakhatuni, Head of Strength Department. The strength of each critical component of the aircraft, except for the landing gear assessed for fatigue in Novosibirsk, was tested in Kyiv.

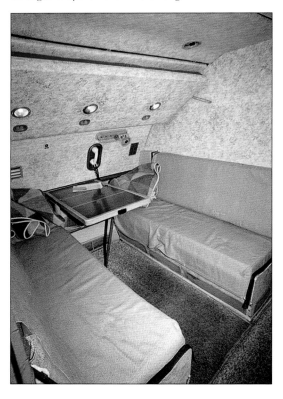

Flight crew's restroom and
aircraft galley.

Getting the feel of the sky

At noon on 24 December 1982, the An-124 taxied out to the factory aerodrome runway in Svyatoshin. Having done several rapid runs, the aircraft remained on the ground for some two hours. But, as soon as the lead clouds of the winter sky broke, and the sun looked out for a couple of minutes, the Ruslan started its first takeoff. It was controlled by test pilots V. I. Terskii and A. V. Galunenko, navigator A. P. Poddubny, flight engineers V. M. Vorotnikov and A. M. Shuleshchenko, and radio engineer M. A. Tupchienko. *"The aircraft climbed, light as a feather"*, Terskii recalled. *"Within one hour we accomplished the programme for the finalisation of stability and controllability characteristics and started to descend for landing in Gostomel. But having just touched the ground, we felt inside the cockpit such a severe vibration that we thought the entire structure would immediately collapse. Later we found out that it had been the main landing gear shimmy. However, we managed to abate the speed, taxied into the parking area, and got out cautiously. Despite only one landing gear door and a few connecting rods destroyed, Oleg Antonov, who arrived with compliments for us, looked very frustrated."*

Nevertheless, the Company rejoiced over the triumph. The flight was a success in general, so fifteen years of persistent work had not gone to waste. The common mood was expressed by Yuriy M. Kirzhner who composed a verse on the occasion of the event and presented it to Antonov that day:

It's for your wings and mighty shape,
And most fantastic features,
You have deserved the Ruslan's name,
The name of super creature.

So fly wherever men can send,
Unbounding all frontiers.
Serve us, and glorify your land,
Descendant of Antaeus.

The An-124 cargo compartment.

However, the holiday finished soon, and to continue the tests, the landing gear struts were temporarily equipped with the hydraulic shimmy dampers. (Consequently, those dampers were removed, but both the nose and the main landing gear units were considerably stiffened instead. In addition, the turnable main units obtained almost twice the reduced wheel axle offset.) The next flight of the Ruslan was made in a month's time. It began the first stage of the flight and structural tests that lasted in Gostomel until September 1983 and required 141 flights with a total flying time of 251 hours. At this stage of tests another Ruslan problem was revealed, which later become its main problem for many years: the low gas-dynamic stability of the D-18 engine, especially at takeoff. No later than during the eighth takeoff one of the engines failed as a result of surge. Since the Gostomel runway was then not as long as now, and no reverse thrust was available in the aircraft, a decision was made to land in Uzin. After landing it was discovered that the engine surge had resulted in the turbine wheel destruction, and the blades had damaged the engine nacelle skin. In other words, the engine failure was serious, and the pilots decided to fly back on three engines. The training included several ground runs with one and two engines inoperative, then the

Ruslan is a perfect means of military equipment transportation.

Fuselage nose cone up.

aircraft flew to Gostomel, from there to Svyatoshin and had the damaged D-18 engine replaced.

The following stage of flight tests proceeded till December 1984. Within that season, 157 flights were conducted with a total of 304 flight hours, including 18 at high angles of attack. Those difficult flights were made by a combined crew commanded by Terskii and colonel Belsky, test pilot of the USSR Air Force Scientific Research Institute. At the end of 1984, the tests included another An-124 (No.01-03) which was used for the assessment of safety in simulation of various failures. Following this programme, the aircraft had flown 289 hours, having accomplished 163 flights until 5 October 1985.

In May 1985, the Ruslan, already quite steady in the sky, was demonstrated for the first time to the Soviet press, and in a couple of weeks the aircraft debuted at the XXVI Paris Air Show (Le Bourget). The western journalists immediately christened it as "Russian miracle", "Superstar", etc., although almost every publication contained a sting in the tail. After that Paris visit, Pyotr V. Balabuev, who succeeded O. K. Antonov after his death in 1984 as the company leader, told: *"First the attacks seemed funny, caused bewilderment, but later became irritating. For example, the Lockheed chiefs admired our aircraft, but their conceited motto 'If you want to see the biggest aircraft in the world, come to Lockheed' was present everywhere. As a result, our staff when meeting visitors in the spacious cargo cabin of the Ruslan, were unable to speak about its performance without passion, but they were engaged in the argument unwillingly."*

To prove the An-124's superiority to the entire world, straight after the Air Show, the Soviet Aviaprom authorities made a decision to demonstrate some record flights. On 26 July Terskii's crew piloting the aircraft No.01-01 set 21 world records during the same flight. They included the absolute achievement in the lifting of a 171.219-tonne cargo to an altitude of 10,750 m, having obviously superseded the C-5A's result (111.461 tonnes to 2,000 m altitude). In May 1987 the An-124 No. 01-08 combined (including military personnel) crew commanded by Terskii fulfilled a non-stop 20,151-km flight along the boundary line of the Soviet Union. It lasted for 25 hr 30 min (the aircraft takeoff weight attained a record figure of 455 tonnes). Another world record for the flight range along a closed route was established, exceeding the achievement of the American strategic bomber B-52H (18,245.5 km).

In November 1983, the An-124 official joint tests started. The flight crews of aircraft Nos. 01-01, 01-03 and 01-07 included personnel of the Air Force scientific research institute and ADB pilots. The aerodrome situated in Chkalovskaya near Moscow was used to fulfil 189 flights having a total duration of 751 hours. At the same time, the Il-76 flying laboratory tested the D-18 engine in 414 flights (1,288 hours), while the An-22 No. 02-03 assessed the flight and navigation integrated system of the Ruslan (86 flights, 313 hours). In December 1986 the Official Test Report of the An-124 heavy long-range airlifter was signed stating the aircraft was compliant with the specified requirements.

In the following three years, An-124 special tests were conducted to determine its performance under the conditions of natural icing: in the spring of 1988, Terskii's crew on the Ruslan prototype No.1 made 37 flights in search of the icing regions over the Barents Sea area, from Novaya Zemlya to Medvezhii Island. Having found a cumulus cloud, the pilots penetrated it and collected some 90 mm of ice over the wing and tail, left the cloud and tested the aircraft's stability and controllability in the open sky. In those days, the An-124 was often convoyed by NATO aircraft approaching to the distance of 500 m to take a better photo of the 'Russian miracle'. The first landing of the Ruslan on an ice airfield located in the vicinity of Graham-Bell on Franz Josef Land was also made then. Concurrently, the Kurlin flight crew performed 10 flights of the An-124 prototype No.2 in the wake of another Ruslan in order to determine the capability of flight in dense battle formations. In 1989, the An-124 (No. 01-08) was re-equipped for air delivery operations: a series of dummy paradrops, air delivery of military equipment mockups, including cargo items weighing up to 25 tonnes, were conducted.

A special page in the story of the An-124 was the period of development and certification of the An-124-100 civil version carried out under the guidance of D. S. Kiva, who occupied then the position of the First Deputy General Designer. For almost three years, from January 1990 until December 1992, aircraft Nos. 01-01, 01-03, 05-07 and 02-08 were tried in a series of certification tests for their compliance with the NLGS-3 Civil Airworthiness Regulations of the USSR. The tests consisted of the assessment of flight performance, including high-temperature conditions of operation, determination of the best landing configuration, the procedure of reduced warm-up of engines at line-up, flight safety assessment with simulated failures of aircraft systems, detection of the noise level, etc. This work required 266 flights of 732 hours in total. During one such flight, on 13 October 1992, the An-124 No. 01-03 flown by the crew of S. A. Gorbik crashed. It was carrying out a task for the definition of controllability characteristics at maximum dynamic pressure. The tragic concurrence of a number of negative factors including a bird-strike resulted in the destruction of the aircraft radio transparent nose fairing at the moment of the highest aerodynamic load, and the entire fuselage nose was destroyed. The structural fragments damaged both right engines, which shut down. Those extraordinary conditions allowed no way out for the crew who could not reach the nearest airfield, and the aircraft crashed in a forest near Kyiv. Eight test crew members perished. It was a heavy loss for the Antonov team.

By then, however, the tests were practically over, and the An-124-100 Type Certification Basis which determined the technical configuration of the Ruslan civil version was prepared. The aircraft passed all tests and checks envisioned by the Airworthiness Standards, and the crash could not diminish its merits. On 30 December 1992 the Ruslan as a civil transport aircraft obtained the Airworthiness Certificate of the Aviation Register of C.I.S. Intergovernmental Aviation Committee.

Series production

Series manufacture of the An-124 aircraft was originally planned to be located in Kyiv; however, in the early 1980s, the government made a decision to involve the newly opened Ulyanovsk Aviation Industrial Complex (UAPK). To study the new aircraft production process, many specialists and workers from Ulyanovsk arrived in Kyiv. The Kyiv personnel shared their experience generously, assisting to arrange the new aircraft production on the Volga as soon as was possible. The second Ruslan, No. 01-03 (also known as the first of the series production), took off from Kyiv in December 1984 (Captain Y. V. Kurlin), while the first to fly in Ulyanovsk in October 1985 was A/C No. 01-07 (Captain A. V. Galunenko). Only 18 serial aircraft were manufactured on the banks of the Dnipro river (the last, No. 03-03, was constructed in 2003), and 36 aircraft manufactured on the Volga banks (the last, No. 08-02 A/C, in June 2004). With the prototype No.1 and the static test aircraft, 56 Ruslans were manufactured altogether.

Nose landing gear unit.

Further Development

The An-124 was planned as a baseline aircraft for a number of later modifications, including a tanker and a cargo/passenger aircraft. In optimistic forecasts envisaging the intensive growth of passenger transportation in the USSR, the latter version was transformed into a purely passenger modification of the Ruslan which could carry over 800 passengers over a distance of 10,000 km (similar to the A380, but 20 years earlier!). |Making such an aircraft required serious modifications to the fuselage; there was no difficulty in its implementation but the absence of a genuine demand for a giant passenger liner was the reason this design was put off.

Until today, the An-124-100, the Ruslan's civilian

Nose landing gear in the process of 'kneeling'.

Upgrading of An-124-100 S/N 01-06 to the An-124-100M-150 version completed. Kyiv, August 2004.

version (the ex-serviceman, so to say), remains the most common modification of the aircraft. The need for such aircraft became evident when the military An-124 was swept into the world's commercial traffic market, although without a formal right to this role due to absence of a Certificate of Airworthiness. Essentially, engineers stripped the aircraft of its military equipment, which had become unnecessary as well as some avionics and air delivery system equipment units, and changed the composition of the oxygen equipment. They also installed the equipment required for flying along international air routes – radios with the civilian frequency spectrum, flight and navigation instruments with scales graduated in feet, air traffic collision avoidance systems, etc. Since the expected service life in commercial operations is 1.7 to 2.2 times higher than in the Air Force, a new system of individual aircraft service life extensions was developed for the An-124-100 to ensure flight

safety even during high-frequency flight operations. Other important modifications were also made: the interiors of the living quarter compartments were improved, lavatories were installed, signs were made in English, etc. Manufacturing of the Ruslan's civilian version began in 1990–91 and, in March 1993, after completion of the aircraft certification tests, the Intergovernmental Ukrainian-Russian Resolution No. 490–93 was made in respect of the An-124-100. All in all, five civilian Ruslans (serial numbers: 03-03, 07-10, 08-01, 08-02 and 08-03) were manufactured up to mid-2004 in Kyiv and Ulyanovsk. At least 28 more baseline An-124s were reconfigured to the An-124-100. They were all launched into commercial service.

However, all these important and necessary activities barely affected the primary problem of both military and civilian Ruslans: the low gas-dynamic stability of the earlier-series D-18T engines. The teams of ZMKB Progress Design Bureau and

The An-124-100 used to support flights of Russia President Boris Yeltsin.

Motor-Sich PJSC were doing their utmost during the first half of the 1990s to procure funds for the engine upgrading. It was not before 1997 that they managed to start production of the series 3 engines, which benefited from the experience of the D-18T in service and implemented a full package of measures aimed at their improved reliability, cost effectiveness and endurance. The engines' time between overhauls reached 6,000 hours, and their declared service life was brought up to 24,000 hours. Unfortunately, the price of the new D-18T series 3 was about US$4 million, which was too expensive for the majority of Ruslan owners. Therefore, operators preferred to upgrade their available series 0 or series 1 engines during scheduled overhauls to bring them up to the series 3 level (and obtaining the so-called 'N-profile engines', with the N standing for 'reliable' in Russian) rather than purchase the new series 3 engines.

The requirements imposed by ICAO on the aircraft flying along international air routes are becoming stricter as time goes by. To assure compliance with these requirements, the equipment of civilian Ruslans is being continually improved. Thus, in the process of construction or refurbishment, the An-124-100s were equipped with engine nacelles with noise absorbing components to meet the aircraft noise standards of Chapter 3 ICAO Annex 16. They were retrofitted with 3MGPS satellite navigation system. The required modifications were also made on the An-124-100 to account for the vertical separation minima reduction to 300 m and a supplement to the Type Certificate was obtained. In addition, the US Honeywell TCAS-2000 traffic collision avoidance system and Russian SPPZ-3 ground proximity warning system were installed. Benefitting from experience in-service, changes were made to some elements of the wing and fuselage structures, the forward ramp and cargo floor structure was modified and corrosion protection of some vulnerable areas improved, etc.

Implementation of all these measures made it possible to consider a new significant extension of the aircraft service life. Such an extension was discussed in July 2008 at the conference held at Antonov StC between the An-124 Ruslan design authorities, operators, component suppliers and manufacturers of the aircraft. It was attended by representatives of Antonov Airlines, Volga-Dnepr and Polyot Airlines, Russian Air Forces, and also by Ukrainian and Russian industrial enterprises: Aviastar-SP, Aviapribor-Holding, Techpribor, Nauka, Teploobmennik, Elektroprivod, Voskhod, Spektr, Gidromash, Kotlin-Novator, KhAKB and others. Having thoroughly discussed the practical issues of service life extension and further improvements in the existing fleet of the Ruslans,

Ruslan next to its counterpart – Lockheed C-5B Galaxy. Oshkosh, USA, 1989.

An-124-100M-150 in certification testing at Flesland airport. Bergen, Norway, April 2007.

the conference participants signed a 'Decision ...', which later served as basis for the elaboration of measures for the extension of the designed service life of the in-service An-124-100s and their modifications to 45,000 flying hours, 10,000 flights and 40 years in operation.

Today, based on the results of additional fatigue testing of the aircraft components, analyses and calculations, records of the service life of each individual aircraft and the analysis of their in-service experience, the Ruslans are assigned a service life of 50,000 flying hours, 10,000s flights and 45 years. These figures exceed the service life of the upgraded Lockheed C-5M and of another US

airlifter, the Boeing C-17, whose service lives are 30,000–40,000 flying hours.

It is interesting to note that, in the course of the An-124-100 refinement that has been going on for 25 years now, the need for a more radical upgrading of the aircraft was becoming more and more evident. Therefore, in August 2004, Antonov StC finished the reconfiguration of one of the An-124-100s owned by Antonov Airlines into the new An-124-100M-150 version. The aircraft modified was the aircraft with serial number 01-06 – the first Ruslan that had served 12,000 hours in operation. This aircraft had its maximum payload increased to 150 tonnes and its maximum takeoff weight brought

Supplement to Type Certificate for the An-124-100M-150 has been issued. Paris Air Show, June 2007.

Ruslan S/N 08-03 is still the only aircraft initially built in the An-124-100M-150 version. Ulyanovsk (RF), May 2004.

up from 392 tonnes to 402 tonnes; its flight range was also increased, including the range with 120 tonnes of cargo, from 4,750 km to 5,300 km, and provisions were made to allow loading/unloading of single cargo items weighing up to 40 tonnes by means of the on-board cargo handling equipment. An important feature of the An-124-100M-150 was the easier and quicker loading procedure for single cargo items weighing up to 150 tonnes – it is for this purpose that the forward cargo door structure had been reinforced. Since the aircraft's weight had increased, it became necessary to improve the braking system and use heavier-duty wheel tyres. In accordance with current and anticipated Eurocontrol requirements, the P-RNAV precision area navigation requirements in particular, the new Ruslan was equipped with advanced navigation equipment. This also made it possible to reduce the flying crew complement from six to four crew members. The aircraft was also equipped with advanced lightning protection, thrust reverser control and engine vibration monitoring systems.

Certification tests of the An-124-100M-150 performed by Antonov StC crews with the participation of experts from certification centres of Russia – GosNIIGA and GosNII Aeronavigatsia – were completed in 2007. There were several test stages. The first, preliminary stage, was aimed at testing the functionality of the new equipment and studying the possibility of reducing the flying crew strength to four members. It was followed by the longest and most important stage of the optimisation work. During 2005 and 2006, the aircraft was flying around the globe carrying various cargoes on board. Thus, the equipment and new systems, as well as the reduced crew procedures, were tested

under real-life service conditions and the required modifications were introduced in response to feedback received during operations. The purpose of the final test stage was to validate compliance of the aircraft flight and navigation equipment suite with the B-RNAV and P-RNAV basic and precision area navigation requirements during terminal area departure and arrival procedures on the European aerodromes where such procedures are certified for application of the area navigation method. Under the actual operating conditions of congested air traffic it was necessary to confirm that the equipment suite performed all functions required for flying in the P-RNAV environment with specified navigation precision characteristics. Therefore, between 14 and 19 April 2007, the An-124-100M-150 was performing manoeuvres using standard instrument departure and arrival procedures in Vantaa airport (Helsinki, Finland) and Flesland airport (Bergen, Norway). According

First military Ruslans. Seshcha, late 1980s.

An-124 of the 566th Military Airlift Regiment of Russia.

Seshcha air base, summer of 1990.

Babiychuk, Deputy Chairman of the SAAU.

The second Ruslan reconfigured to the An-124-100M-150 version was the aircraft S/N 08-03 owned by Volga-Dnepr Airlines that had been built in Ulyanovsk in May 2004 and already contained a lot of the M-version features. Later on, other aircraft owned by Antonov Airlines and Volga-Dnepr were also modified.

Volga-Dnepr is also associated with the latest stage in the An-124 upgrading made jointly by the Ukrainian and Russian specialists. In the course of MAKS-2011 International Air Show in Zhukovskii in the outskirts of Moscow, Requirements Specifications for Research and Development of the *"An-124-111 Aircraft. Upgraded Version of the An-124-100-150 (An-124-100) of the Fleet of the Volga-Dnepr Airlines Ltd. powered with D-18T series 3M Engines"* were signed and the upgrading flow chart was elaborated and approved. The documents were signed not only by D. S. Kiva, Antonov President-General Designer, and A. I. Isaikin, President of the Volga-Dnepr Group, but also by General Designer of the Ivchenko-Progress I. F. Kravchenko and by V. A. Boguslayev, Chairman of the Board of the Motor-Sich JSC.

The An-124-111 concept was based on the latest developements in aeronautical thinking of that time. The aircraft was planned to be equipped with the 'glass cockpit', other new-generation on-board equipment, a fully-digital flight control system and a renovated power plant with full-authority digital engine control. It would have made it possible to considerably improve the aircraft's fuel efficiency and reliability, and reduce the noise levels and operating costs. The Ruslan would have become capable of performing the ICAO category IIIA landing.

It is interesting that the expected upgrading was actually regarded as an important practical step towards joint renewal of the Ruslan's production. Many important engineering aspects of the future production aircraft were planned to be resolved in the course of the upgrading and new customers, both military and civilian, were expected to be found. In particular, A. I. Isaikin claimed at the time that Volga-Dnepr was ready to order forty new Ruslans. Unfortunately, due to reasons well known, this exceptionally promising work was never completed.

In 2012, the An-124-100 was granted a next Supplement to Type Certificate attesting its capability to carry 135 tonnes of cargo (its earlier cargo-carrying capacity had been just 120 tonnes). This resolution was adopted on the basis of the analysis of the years of An-124-100 operational experience and results of structural tests that had been carried out continuously in Kyiv. Moreover, the permitted number of flights with pressurisation of the cargo cabin was increased and, consequently, the Ruslan's capabilities were expanded in terms of transportation of cargoes requiring the maintenance

to the Eurocontrol requirements for air navigation precision, the aircraft should not deviate from the desired flight path by more than one nautical mile (1.85 km). The new Ruslan demonstrated its ability to maintain its flight path with deviation of less than 0.3 nautical miles. Thus, it demonstrated full compliance with Eurocontrol's RNP-1 navigation precision requirements. It should be noted that it was the first time the tests for compliance with P-RNAV requirements were performed on Ukrainian aircraft.

The appropriate Supplement to Type Certificate for the new Ruslan modification was issued to Antonov in June 2007 during the Paris International Airshow. Handing the document over to General Designer D. S. Kiva, V. V. Bespalov, Chairman of the CIS Interstate Aviation Committee Aviation Register, noted, in particular: *"This document proves that the An-124 will meet international requirements for years to come. It gives us confidence in the Ruslan's great future."* Later, a renewed An-124-100 Type Certificate issued by the State Aviation Administration of Ukraine was presented by D. G.

Ruslan crew that made the round-the-world flight via both poles. Australia, 1990.

of specified pressure and temperature.

Today, the Ukrainian team is responsible for further An-124 improvement on its own, without the participation of the Russian Federation companies. Understandably, the scale of the activities has dwindled considerably, and plans of renewed serial production have had to be given up. Nevertheless, the most pressing requirements are still being implemented. Thus, in 2017, the radar that had been installed in Soviet times was replaced by modern US equipment with lower weight, overall dimensions and power consumption. As a result, the aircraft received a new radome without the characteristic 'beard' of the earlier version and having smoother contours.

Starting from 2019, provided that it is re-equipped with new D-18 series 3M engines, the Ruslan will meet the aircraft noise requirements of Chapter 4 of the ICAO Annex 16. The key element in this case is not the noise-absorbing engine nacelle, but the engine itself, the noise of which will be 10 dB lower. In combination with other current improvements, this will allow the aircraft to remain within the level required by ICAO until 2023 or 2025. But even after this time, the An-124-100s, as well as other Ruslan modifications, are not going to lose their competitive edge. New ways are sure to be found to support their compliance with all requirements that will appear in the sphere of commercial aviation. The retirement age will not be reached by the majority of the Ruslans before the second half of the 2040s, or even the middle of the following decade. It means that today the aircraft is at the height of its capabilities.

At the turn of the century, the An-124's future was associated not only with transportation but also with participation in a number of space programmes as a launch platform for the air launch of carrier rockets. Calculations demonstrated that, when launched from an aircraft, the weight of the payload placed into orbit by a rocket was 20 to 25% higher, allowing the launch cost to be reduced and making the project more attractive commercially. To enable participation in such activities, the An-124-100 had to be equipped with systems enabling the loading of the transport and launch pod with the rocket into the aircraft cargo compartment, its ejection in the launch area, rocket guidance and control systems, and the transmission of telemetry data to the Launch Control Centre.

By late 2008, joint efforts of the scientists of Russia and Ukraine led to development of several

One of the military An-124s used for transportation of military equipment in the course of troop withdrawal from Germany, April 1994.

Ruslan owned by the Antonov air transportation division. Malta, September 1990.

aerospace projects based on the Ruslan. However, none of these projects reached a practical implementation stage. Most regrettably, the current state of Ukrainian-Russian relations leaves no hope for these projects to be put into effect. Yet, Russia is not the only country anxious to reduce the cost of placing payloads into circumterrestrial orbit. This

An-124-100 of '224th flying squadron' at final approach. Early 2010-s

task is important for the entirety of humanity. The Ruslan is the most suitable aircraft for the purpose, and will remain so for future decades. So, it is quite probable that we shall still see the An-124 used as a flying space launch facility.

In military service

An-124-100 of Titan Airlines is taking off. Hannover, 2000.

After the end of the Official Tests, the An-124s began to be adopted by the Military Airlift Aviation

units in active service. The new heavy strategic airlifter played an important role in the Military Airlift's doctrine envisaging its use as a carrier of over-size military vehicles, cargoes and personnel to areas of hostilities or military exercises. For the first time ever, the aircraft made possible carrying by air virtually 100% of the vehicles and weapons in service with the Army, Air Forces, Air Defence and Strategic Missile Forces.

The An-124 was first adopted by the 12th Mga Military Airlift Division, which comprises three regiments of the An-22s (the 566th stationed in Seshcha, Briansk region, the 81st in Ivanovo, and the 8th in Tver, all of them in Russia). According to the decision of Marshal A. N. Yefimov, Commander in Chief of the USSR Air Forces, the air base in Seshcha was selected to become the first base location for the new gigantic aircraft. It was there that the first An-124 (S/N 01-04) landed 10 February 1987 flown by the crew commanded by Lieutenant-Colonel V. V. Nikolayev. This aircraft was built in Kyiv. Four days later the first aircraft manufactured in Ulyanovsk, An-124 (S/N 01-07), arrived. During the next two years eight more aircraft were delivered to the unit from both manufacturers. The Ruslan that came to replace the Antaeus turned out to be much more complex than its predecessor, and its assimilation required immense efforts. A large team of industry representatives was sent to Seshcha for prompt solution of any emerging problems. The initial stage of the Ruslan's service saw many problems related to engine propulsion, frequent avionics failures, insufficient fuselage sealing, and also a lack of the required quantities of ground servicing equipment. All the necessary steps were made to eliminate the detected deficiencies; in particular, the D-18T main duct cowls were reinforced and other elements of the engine structure were modified.

Gradually, the Ruslan crews were changing from training flights to performing their basic functions, although their first flights were connected with the transportation of cargoes for the victims of the devastating earthquake in Armenia in December 1988, rather than with military missions. During this relief operation, nine military Ruslans made 28 flights and transported 2,058 tonnes of food supplies, medications and rescue equipment to Zvartnots airport, having accumulated 377 flight hours. The flights continued during the next year, when the regiment transported to Armenia another 7,645 tonnes of cargoes and equipment. In the meantime, deliveries of the Ruslans to the 566th Regiment continued, and their fleet numbered 28 aircraft in 1989. In consideration of the growing number of aircraft in the regiment, the USSR MoD Directive dated 25 January 1989 raised the 235th Military Airlift Regiment, allotted to the 12th Military Airlift Division and also based at Seshcha.

On 28 March 1991, M. S. Gorbachov, Supreme Commander in Chief, issued the order for the An-124 adoption by the armed forces.

Two years earlier, the USSR government officially approved utilisation of the Ruslans for civilian air transportations on domestic and international air lines and both regiments began performing worldwide commercial flight on requests from companies. The money earned in commercial operations was used to purchase spares for aircraft, improve flying crew training, pay for housing construction and solve other issues. From December 1990, military Ruslans began to be used for the carriage of humanitarian aid to the USSR from abroad, and later the aircraft performed transportation missions in the interests of the Russian economy. For instance, on 5 June 1995 the crew of Colonel N. Podrez of the 235th Regiment carried two bearings for an ore-dressing plant mill, each weighing 40 tonnes, from Vostochnii aerodrome to Polyarny settlement. In March-April 1996, flight crews of the 566th Military Airlift Regiment performed, under general guidance of Colonel General V. V. Yefanov, a unique transport operation: they carried 602 tonnes of nonferrous metal ores and rare-earth ores from Tenkeli aerodrome in Yakutia to Novosibirsk in six flights

and brought back 462 tonnes of food supplies and consumer goods. It was the first time in service that the Ruslan had made landings on natural-surfaced airfields covered with compacted snow and breakstone, while the temperature dropped as low as minus 40 degrees.

During this period of time, the Ruslan crews also performed military operations on special missions from the Russian government and MoD both domestically and abroad (Australia, Morocco, Vietnam, Germany, Denmark, Switzerland, Malaysia, etc.). For example, armaments and a

An-124-100 of Polyot Airlines landing. The Netherlands, 2004.

Ruslans of Volga-Dnepr Airlines at their home base in Shannon, Ireland.

An-124-100 of Antonov Airlines on the runway of Macao airport.

aeronautical equipment from Transcaucasia to Russia on the Vaziani-Mozdok and Gyandja-Ulyanovsk routes. Between 14 December 1994 and 13 January 1995, the aircraft of the same regiment made 35 flights carrying cargoes, materiel and personnel to the North Caucasus, to the area of hostilities in Chechnya (Mozdok airport). The aircraft accumulated 1,274 flying hours, and 1,833 servicemen and 2,247 tonnes of military cargoes were relocated.

Starting from April 1994, the An-124s were used for scheduled flights in support of the Russian troops' withdrawal from East Germany, and the aircraft carried not only the military equipment, but also personnel and families with their belongings. On 22 June, the MoD of the Russian Federation, with a view to improving efficiency of the An-124 fleet utilisation, ordered relocation of the 235th Military Airlift Regiment to Ulyanovsk and 26 Ruslans set up their base at the factory aerodrome next to the manufacturer's workshops.

The disintegration of the USSR seriously upset the plans for further An-124 operation by the military airlift forces. This was due, primarily, to the drastic reduction in MoD and RF government funding. All activities such as the required modification, reconditioning and repairs, which had earlier been performed on the aircraft of both regiments by the manufacturer's repair teams, were now practically discontinued. Therefore, the aircraft of both regiments came to the brink of losing their flightworthiness. After 1996, the An-124s of both regiments faced a new problem connected with the expiry of calendar service life (10 years for aircraft manufactured in 1986). Extensive investigations carried out by specialists of Antonov, TsAGI and NIIERAT made it possible to find a solution. The concept of 'overhaul-free An-124 operation', put forward by P. V. Balabuev, was approved and the Ruslan became the first of the Antonov aircraft to be maintained in condition. In accordance with the An-124 Aircraft Operational Status Investigation Programme, all aircraft, as soon as such activities were paid for, were thoroughly inspected by a joint inspection team and received recommendations regarding measures to be taken for release to further service.

However, not all problems could be overcome. In numerous cases, a reasonable solution was to re-equip the aircraft with series 3 engines. However, the military very often could not afford to do this because of their high price. Such a situation resulted in the notorious crash of the Ruslan of the 566th Regiment in Irkutsk on 6 December 1997. After the tragedy, the government and MoD of the Russian Federation prohibited utilisation of the military Ruslans which had no civilian certificate of airworthiness for commercial flying. Consequently, during half of 1998 both regiments stood idle and

variety of equipment for production development was delivered to Vietnam. Flights to other countries were made occasionally, in particular for rendering assistance to flood victims, delivering vehicles for joint military exercises or equipment for extinguishing oil field fires, etc. The crews of both regiments also transported military vehicles, equipment and other products of the Russian industry for participation in international air shows and demonstrations.

Military pilots picked up the baton of setting records on the Ruslans. Thus, on 1 December 1990, the An-124 S/N 05-07 started its round-the-world flight from Australia (Melbourne) to the South Pole then to North Pole and then back to Australia with intermediate stops in Brazil (Rio de Janeiro), Morocco (Casablanca) and the USSR (Vozdvizhenka). The crew commanded by Head of the Air Force *GNIKI* Lieutenant-General L. V. Kozlov included pilots and specialists of the 235th Military Airlift Regiment. The An-124's round-the-world route was away from international airways with more than 90% of the route running above unmarked water areas of four oceans and above the empty snow-covered Antarctic. Thus, there was practically no ground radar and navigation support. *"The round-the-world mission offered a unique opportunity,"* said L. V. Kozlov *"to rigorously test operability of all components, units and systems of the Ruslan in different geographic latitudes of the global ocean, under rapidly changing meteorological and geophysical conditions."* The 50,005-km long flight was accomplished within 72 hr 16 min, average flight speed being 680 km/h. During this round-the-world flight the crew managed to set seven world flight speed records.

During 1992–94, the Ruslans began serving their main intended purpose: transportation of military vehicles, equipment and cargoes. During these years, the crews of the 235th Military Airlift Regiment participated in the transportation of

were mostly involved in the preventive measures recommended by the accident investigation board. Finally, as a result of a number of consultations between all interested parties, operation of the An-124s by the 566th Military Airlift Regiment was resumed. The resumption was preceded by tests accomplished by crews of the M. M. Gromov Flight Test Centre on the aircraft whose engines had been modified for improved margins of gas dynamic stability. Similar modifications were done at the time on selected Ruslans – money was lacking for the rest.

In 1998, Military Airlift of the Russian Federation was reorganised into the 61th Air Army; up to 40% of its structural units were reduced in force, including the 235th Military Airlift Regiment which was disbanded. Flightworthy Ruslans of the regiment returned to Seshcha again. The reorganisation however did not discontinue the above-mentioned negative processes: in 2001, the 566th Regiment had only 11 aircraft in flyable condition, which were used occasionally for training flights within the Briansk region. Other An-124s were facing retirement. Thus, in the global military-political situation of the end of the 20th century, the An-124 remained unclaimed as a strategic airlifter. It is most convincingly demonstrated by the figures of annual flying time of the military Ruslans, which were six to seven times lower than that of their commercial brethren.

That was, probably, why the Russian military were anchoring their hopes on commercial structures that could have helped restore the Ruslans' airworthiness in full and start their intensive operation. In 2000, the Russian Polyot Airlines JSC leased, through the Roskomimushchestvo Agency, four military An-124s for upgrading to the An-124-100 version and utilisation in the Air Launch space programme. Active flying operations of the aircraft soon began; however, these were exclusively for commercial purposes and no longer had any connection with space projects. Later the 61st Air Army Command ordered the aircraft to be returned and disputes, and even court actions, ensued. As a result, operations of all leased aircraft were discontinued. Two of the aircraft upgraded to type An-124-100 (S/N 01-09 and S/N 05-03) were at the point of being returned to the military in the winter of 2008–09, although they were already not airworthy. The other two (S/N 02-05 and S/N 02-07), still non-modified but also not airworthy, have still remained since 2001 on the manufacturer's aerodrome in Ulyanovsk, practically ownerless. Another attempt at the improvement of combat capabilities with the help of commercial structures was made in 2003, when the government of Moscow and the RF Air Force Command signed a General Agreement on co-operation stipulating transfer of another six An-124s allotted to the 61st Air Army to Atlant-Soyuz Airlines. It remained a paper agreement due to a number of reasons, so the optimistic expectations that the people in uniform pinned on the 'kind and generous' businessmen never came true.

With the coming new century the Russian military made an attempt to revive their Ruslans, of which they had 26 as of early 2018. The best-preserved aircraft were entered in the Register of Civilian Aircraft of the Russian Federation in the early 2000s, thus forming the so-called '224th flying squadron'. The squadron strength varied in time and included a maximum of nine An-124s in flightworthy condition. All these aircraft (serial numbers 01-09, 05-02, 05-03, 050-4, 05-09, 06-01, 06-02, 06-03 and 06-04) were upgraded to the An-124-100 version. All of them in fact remained military property and were based at Seshcha and flown by military crews, and overall responsibility for flight safety was with the Military Airlift. There is practically no hard data about the 224th squadron's activities; however, it looks as if they were not very successful commercially. At the end of 2017 the

An-124-100 owned by Volga-Dnepr Airlines landing. Kabul, Afghanistan, September 2003.

squadron was disbanded and there were rumours of bankruptcy.

The remaining 17 aircraft are still in the military airlift fleet of the Russian Federation. They remain based at Seshcha and partially in the Ulyanovsk-Vostochny airport. Only four of these aircraft have been modified to type An-124-100 (the so-called military airlift version, i.e., not fully up to the production aircraft level – these are S/N 02-09, 05-06, 06-05, and 01-10). Thirteen more are in prolonged storage; that is, they have been grounded for 20 years and more, serving as a source of spare parts for the flying aircraft.

Thus, as of early 2018, practically all flying Ruslans of the Russian military are modified to the standards of the An-124-100 civilian version type certificate. Nevertheless, after the war with Ukraine began and relations with Antonov StC were severed, none of these aircraft possesses airworthiness in terms recognized by ICAO. All of them only have releases for flight issued by the Russian aviation authorities. Therefore, the areas of their operations are limited to the territory of the Russian Federation itself and such countries as Armenia, Belarus, Indonesia, Iran, Kazakhstan, Syria, Turkey, Uzbekistan and a few others.

A sideline that took the lead

As soon as it appeared, the An-124 became for the West a new symbol of the Soviet threat, since it offered a qualitatively new level of strategic mobility for the Soviet troops. The world's interest in the aircraft was keen, the 'cold war' was becoming a thing of the past and ideas of peaceful utilisation of the aircraft were in the air. The aircraft was first demonstrated to the West at the Paris Airshow of 1985, where it attracted the immediate attention of the representatives of world's leading freight airlines. It was gradually becoming clear that the Ruslan was an aircraft of unique transportation capabilities and which had potential to earn money. The more so since funding of Antonov StC activities from the state budget was beginning to fail. The company's management succeeded in making a good assessment of the situation and changed its approach towards self-financing and set up an in-house transportation division, which is actually the subject of this book.

The Russian Volga-Dnepr Airlines joint stock company, created on the basis of the Ulyanovsk Aviastar industrial facility with the participation of Antonov StC, Zaporizhzha Motor-Sich JSC, Kyiv Aviant facility (now part of Antonov) and several banking structures, has done a lot to strengthen the Ruslan's reputation. Today, Volga-Dnepr owns 12 Ruslans, while its first An-124 (nationality mark USSR-82042) was obtained in 1990. In 1991, Volga-Dnepr formed a joint venture company with the British HeavyLift Airlines and a second Ruslan-operating commercial carrier appeared in the world market. Over the years, Volga-Dnepr as a classical aircraft operator has traversed a long path similar on the whole to that of Antonov Airlines. It has performed a number of unique transportation operations. Thus, in 1990, it carried 60,000 live chickens in a single flight from Forli (Italy) to Tripoli in Libya. In May 1992 it transported 52 tonnes of gold worth 230 million pounds sterling from UAE to Switzerland. An entire botanical garden was brought from Congo to Riga. In 1995, Volga-Dnepr aircraft flew from Rio de Janeiro to Singapore carrying equipment for the petroleum industry and bringing back electronic equipment to Manaus in Brazil. In 1997, they transported cars, which participated in the Master Rally'97 race, bringing up to 54 on board in one flight. One of the company's An-124-100s took part in the *Star Wars* film epic shooting when they carried filming equipment and a spaceship mock-up weighing over 100 tonnes from London to Toza in Tunisia. In the same year, super-heavy Komatsu-510E trucks (each weighing 103 tonnes) were carried from Chicago to Polyarny for the Almazy Rossii-Saha diamond mining company. In one of the return flights, the fuselage of the Global Express business jet prototype was brought from the Japanese Kansai to Toronto. On Christmas Eve of 1998, a huge fir tree weighing 40 tonnes was carried from Canada to New York. Volga-Dnepr also has to its credit the transportations of the US satellites to the Baikonur spacecraft launching site, Sukhoi Su-27 fighters to Vietnam and China and Sukhoi Su-30s to India. In the new century, the range of the unique Volga-Dnepr's missions has become even more varied.

Having acquired considerable experience in the world market, Volga-Dnepr broke up with HeavyLift and began operating on its own, increasingly preferring dialogue with Antonov Airlines rather than competing with it. For the period of 2006–16 the company actually became a strategic partner of the Kyiv operator, yet later it changed sides again. This area of business is too politically minded and partnership issues are very often resolved without consideration of economic expediency ...

In the wake of Antonov Airlines and Volga-Dnepr the An-124s appeared in the fleets of Rossia state air carrier, Antonov AirTrack, Ajaks, Polyot, Transcharter and Titan airlines. However, all these companies, with the exception of Polyot, either lost their aircraft very soon or even ceased to exist themselves. Polyot, on the contrary, expanded its business using the Ruslans leased from the Military Airlift Forces of Russia. Polyot's business also came to an end in 2014 and the carrier had to return its leased An-124s to their owners. In fact, by the end

Libyan An-124-100. Kyiv, 2002.

of 2017, just the above-mentioned 224th Flying Squadron remained in the market.

Thus, the An-124 acquired a sideline – the civil freighter aircraft profession. This change proved to be momentous for the aircraft, helping it not only to remain flying, but also to become one of the most successful commercial aircraft. It was in this role that the Ruslan became known to the world. It has become firmly anchored in the list of aircraft that not only showed themselves to advantage in the transportation market, but also created a new sector of the market for themselves. In the first five years following its launch in commercial service, the mean annual growth of global unique-freight air traffic volume reached 26%. The number of companies commanding the services of the An-124-100 just in the United States doubled every four years. At present, the market growth persists, although at a slower rate. In these conditions the aircraft naturally enjoys even wider popularity. This is evidenced by the emergence of new Ruslan operators: the Libyan International Transport and Public Works Company operating two An-124s, Maximus Air Cargo of the United Arab Emirates owning one aircraft, and Azerbaijani Silk Way airlines with two Ruslans.

What's in store?

It seems evident that all Ruslans involved in commercial transportation (and there are 33 of them as of early 2018) are not going to stay out of work for decades to come. And the An-124 as an aircraft type is also in its prime – the middle of its life cycle. According to experts, the aircraft may well remain operable for 30 or even 40 more years. It will undergo new upgrading allowing the Ruslan to remain up to date and commercially efficient.

At the same time, the small but continuous growth of demand for oversize cargo transportation in the global market is insistently calling for the expansion of the aircraft fleet or for the appearance of new counterparts with similar transportation capabilities.

This possibility of the new counterparts is probably the saddest section of this book. The source of sadness is the fact that Ukraine and Russia have most probably lost their historic chance of resuming serial production of the aircraft, which is very much in demand for the world economy. This happened because the production renewal project was a joint effort and could not be otherwise. Ukraine on its own does not possess the economic potential sufficient for independent production of such an aircraft. Maybe Russia could have built an aircraft of similar dimensions by itself, but that would be quite a different aircraft, as all the design solutions for the new An-124 versions, all the 'know-how', the quintessence of thirty years of Ruslan operations – everything – is centred in Ukraine. Russia would have to start from scratch ... Naturally, any new Russian aircraft will cost a different level of money, and this fact makes the prospects of its appearance rather hazy.

Furthermore, so much had already been done for the renewal of An-124 production! A decision had been signed at the inter-governmental level regarding immediate measures for the renewal of serial manufacturing and the staged upgrading of the An-124-100 aircraft at the manufacturing facilities of the Russian Federation and Ukraine. In 2005, the joint Russian-Ukrainian meeting held at the Federal Agency for Industry reviewed and approved the business plan, in accordance with which final aircraft assembly was to be set up at Aviastar-SP JSC (Ulyanovsk, Russia). The An-124 Aircraft Family

Serial Production Renewal Project was included in the Russian Aircraft Industry Development Strategy and the Federal Task Programme of Aeronautic Equipment Development in 2002–06 and during the Period of Time until 2015. In 2006, discussions were held between enterprises in Russia and Ukraine concerning the Ruslan production renewal programme and a resulting Agreement was signed setting forth the procedure for upgrading and construction of the An-124 Ruslan aircraft family. *"This is a workable solution ... Technologically, we are ready to resume serial production of the An-124 jumbo aircraft family,"* said V. V. Savotchenko, Executive Director of Aviastar-SP.

In 2006, the Volga-Dnepr Group and Motor-Sich JSC, as two joint stock companies, set up a joint venture designated Cargo Air Craft JSC for management of the Ruslan production renewal project. The following August, Antonov StC agreed to join the new structure as a shareholder and signed an appropriate agreement. Moreover, the document declared the intent of the signing parties to place a launch order for seventeen new Ruslans. *"Today our agreement with Motor-Sich was joined by a new, key participant – the Antonov Company that created this unique aircraft. Cargo Air Craft JSC will consolidate the efforts made by companies in Russia and Ukraine to implement the project,"* said A. I. Isaikin, Volga-Dnepr Group President, commenting on the event.

In a nutshell, the An-124 serial production renewal project was based on the following principles: a market-commercial approach with governmental support from both countries; active attraction of foreign investment; the revival of high-end production technologies; creating new jobs; retention and development of the Russian-Ukrainian monopoly in the ramp-equipped cargo aircraft in the world market; integration with Western manufacturers of components; preservation of strategic aviation for use of the interests of the two states. Flow charts were prepared for production renewal in parallel with aircraft manufacturing. And the duration of the full production cycle renewal

was estimated at 33 months with the first aircraft to be built 36 months after the funding start. The initial production rate was set at two to three aircraft annually. Similar organisational activities were under way at 173 enterprises supplying materials for manufacturing the Ruslans and at 186 component item supplier facilities. A new D-18T series 4 engine was also being developed. In 2008, the Russian United Aircraft Corporation and Ernst &Young, the world leader in the field of consulting and audit, completed the analysis of the Ruslan production renewal project business plan. According to this document, over seventy new aircraft of the An-124 family were planned to be delivered to air carriers by 2030.

Antonov was preparing a new, radically upgraded Ruslan version (with improved cargo-carrying capacity and transportation efficiency, longer flight range, new flight and navigation equipment suite, and engines modified to comply with the latest ICAO standards) for the prospective new stage of serial production. However, no concrete aircraft versions for production had been identified. It could have been the An-124-300, designed to deliver heavy cargoes over two times longer distances than the previous Ruslan version. Yet a less radical modification could also have been approved for serial production. In any case, renewed production could have opened new opportunities for significant improvement of the aircraft performance at a comparatively low cost. It would have considerably increased the aircraft's commercial appeal in the world market and would not have left many opportunities to its rivals for decades to come ...

But alas ... this is all in the past today, with little likelihood of a return. The present-day condition of the Ukrainian-Russian relations spells the death of industrial co-operation in the foreseeable future. The more so since it concerns such an area as strategic aviation transport. The Antonov StC management, if it ever returns to the idea of renewing the manufacture of the Ruslan, will need to give serious thought to finding new partners.

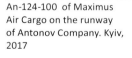

An-124-100 of Maximus Air Cargo on the runway of Antonov Company. Kyiv, 2017

In the first hundred years that followed the Wright Brothers' historical flight, the growth in aircraft takeoff weight has remained one of the principal trends in progress. Recalling the history, one could speak about the brilliant talents of Igor Sikorsky, Claude Dornier, Andrei Tupolev and Howard Hughes, picture a majestic panorama of the efforts of a number of companies, such as Bristol, Convair, Boeing and Lockheed, aimed at the construction of the then biggest aircraft. Each of those aircraft was a visible symbol of technical progress and consequently not only served the personal ambitions of the designers, but was was a serious source of national pride. In the last 30 years, however, the position of the leader of this contest belongs to only one aircraft, the Antonov 225 Mriya. Its takeoff weight has attained a fantastic total of 640 tonnes, exceeding by 65 tonnes the parameters of its closest competitor, the Airbus A380. Any non-standard aircraft has had a non-standard history. The Antonov 225's biography confirms this fact. The project was born behind the impermeable curtain of privacy of Soviet space programmes, but became a world sensation before it took-off. In one and a half years, Mriya flew around the globe, shining as the brightest star at most prestigious air shows, decorating the covers of all aeronautical magazines without any exception, but then it was soon left inactive, abandoned at a suburb on its home aerodrome and transformed into a source of spare parts for the commercial flights of the Ruslan. For seven long years it remained a sad monument to the aircraft industry of the instantly extinct land of the Soviets. But a miracle happened. Mriya took off into the sky again. As 30 years before, the aircraft claimed the attention of the aeronautical community. It revived, and started a new life in the virgin territory of commercial operations carrying super-heavy and oversized cargoes.

ANTONOV AIRLINES AIRCRAFT
An-225 Mriya

An-225

Space is calling

The mid-1970s were marked by significant success in outer space exploration. By then, the USSR and the USA satellite groups had transformed into the integral ingredients of military and economic infrastructure, long-term piloted stations were housed in the earth's orbit and initial steps away from confrontation to international cooperation in this domain were made. It looked then as if the tempo of space development would grow briskly, which meant a demand for new, reusable facilities for taking payloads into orbit. Such facilities, being used frequently, had to

An-225 Mriya, the world's biggest aircraft, with the highest lifting capacity.

exceed the conventional one-shot mother missiles in their economic efficiency.

Under this banner, the United States deployed intensive efforts in the creation of the reusable space transport system – the Space Shuttle; very soon the USSR, also in the spirit of that time, made a decision to develop their own system with similar characteristics. On 17 February 1976, the CPSU Central Committee together with the USSR Council of Ministers issued a confidential Decision, No.132–51, about the construction of the Buran (blizzard) and the Rassvet (dawn) space systems – the latter was subsequently renamed the Energia (energy). The space vehicles of unprecedented size and

Mriya

weight had to be assembled directly at the space-launch complex at Baikonur from separate units manufactured by factories in the USSR's central regions. Therefore, delivery of the carrier rocket units and of the assembled orbiting spacecraft over a distance of some 1,500–2,500 km was required. An additional problem was that the design length of some components reached 60 m and were 8 m in diameter. Furthermore, depending on the task to be carried out in orbit, the Buran would need to make landings on numerous airfields located throughout Soviet Union territory, from Ukraine to the Far East. It would be necessary therefore, to bring it back to Baikonur again, the place of its next start.

All this was a tremendous technical and economic problem. It could not be solved by automobile, railway or water transport because of the lack of roads, and it was impractical to build new or upgrade existing highways, modify bridges, widen many tunnels, bring higher electric power lines, etc. The only realistic means of delivery was transportation by air. Being well aware of this fact, the top officials from the Ministry of the USSR Aircraft Industry approached Oleg Konstantinovich Antonov with a request to develop an aicraft design specifically intended for the transportation of space system components. Roughly at the same time, at the end of 1980/beginning of 1981, Gleb E. Lozino-Lozinskii, General Designer of the NPO Molniya scientific and manufacturing association which was designing the Buran, shared his new ideas with Oleg Antonov at several working meetings. His understanding of the task was even wider: the development of a reusable space transport system that avoided the usual vertical launching and employed a horizontal start of the system with an aircraft as the first stage, and a small space shuttle with its own fuel tank as stage two. For this, the aircraft had to be transformed from a relatively simple carrier into a real flying space launching site that could piggyback a shuttle with a tank – a load of 170 tonnes in total – and support its placement in orbit.

Oleg Antonov had not been approached at random: his Design Bureau was busy designing the An-124, an aircraft with a highest lifting capability at that time. The future Ruslan could be used well as the basis for both a space cargo carrier, and a flying cosmodrome: its maximum allowable payload, not exceeding the airframe structural limitations, was exactly the requested 170 tonnes. (One can compare this with the An-124 load-carrying world record established later: 171,219 tonnes.) The only problem was that the Ruslan was coming into being later. First, its prototype had to be constructed and tested, which would take years. Also, it is worth mentioning that the baseline Ruslan version did not fit the concept of 'launching from the spacecraft top', principally as its vertical tail would collide with the jet streams of the shuttle engines. Antonov could not agree to any tail modification because the design had been approved by all of the customer institutes and had passed the commission. For these reasons, the

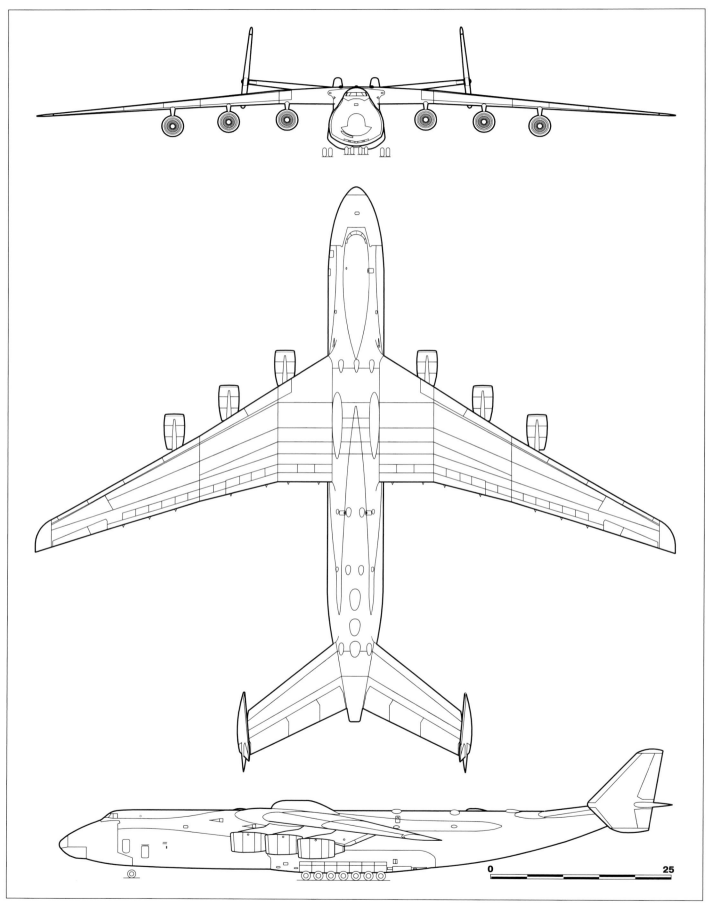

0   25

Kyiv designers decided to attempt to adapt the well-known An-22 Antaeus in a carrier role. The modification required for this task seemed realistic, and feasible, in two options: the accommodation of cargoes either on the fuselage top or inside it. The latter solution would require the heavy 'inflation' of the fuselage tail portion, the diameter of which had to reach 8.3 metres. The first solution appeared unpromising due to complex problems with the aircraft's directional stability and controllability caused by such an extra-large external load; the second solution failed because of the structural strength and layout problems. In toto, neither modification could be regarded even as an interim measure.

The situation required the space system creators to direct their eyes towards the VM-T design this was a modification of the 3M strategic bomber constructed under the guidance of V. M. Myasishchev back in the mid-1950s. It could settle the issue at least for the period of time required for the construction of the first Energia-Buran system. The modification included the improvement of the serial aircraft structural strength, fitting it with the external store attachments and a twin-stabilizer vertical tail, which would allow it to carry long cargoes on top of the aircraft. The modified aircraft turned to be extremely stressed in many strength and aerodynamic parameters, and the cargo space dimensions were too big. For instance, the Energia carrier's central unit diameter exceeded the VM-T fuselage diameter by 2.5 times. As a result, some flights (in total, both VM-T aircraft constructed throughout the period from 1982 to 1988 made 150 flights for delivery of the Energia-Buran system components from manufacturers to the space launch facility) were connected with risks, and ended safely only due to the flight crew members' personal courage and professionalism. Moreover, the VM-T's transportations failed to cover the entire range of cargoes. In particular, the Buran could be lifted only with its vertical tail and all airborne equipment removed; therefore, for it air launch in the way the B747 launched the American Shuttle was unachievable. And finally, the age of the aircraft manufactured a quarter of the century before the events in question, required a substitute

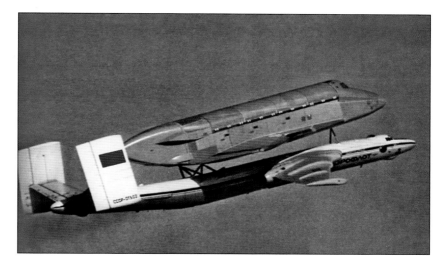

to be urgently found.

In view of all these circumstances, the attention of the space industry became focused on the O. K. Antonov Design Bureau again, especially as the

VM-T aircraft could transport the Buran only disassembled.

Ruslan flight tests had been planned for the end of 1982. Its potential transportation capabilities promised that it could carry the Energia-Buran system parts assembled, and the Energia core unit even adjoined, i.e. with the hydrogen and oxygen tanks as a single piece. Nonetheless, the single-

The An-225 wing manufactured in Tashkent was carried to Kyiv in parts on top of the An-22 aircraft.

An-225 main performance data			
Aircraft overall external dimensions, m		**Max payload, tons**	250
– length x wing span x height	84 x 88.4 x 18.1	**Cruising speed, km/h**	750-800
Cargo compartment dimensions, m		**Cruising altitude, m**	9,000-12,000
– length x width x height	43.3 x 6.4 x 4.4	**Practical range with 200-ton cargo, km**	4,000
Floor area, m²	280	**Max range, km**	14,000
Volume, m³	1,300	**Airfield length, m**	3,000-3,500
Engines:		**Crew number**	6
– type:	D-18T series 3 bypass turbojet		
– number x power, kN:	6 x 229		

An-225 rolled out from the Antonov assembly shop, 30 November 1988.

Mriya's first flight on 21 December 1988.

After the successful first flight. Left to right: A. M. Shuleshchenko, S. F. Nechayev, V. A. Gusar, M. G. Kharchenko, A. G. Bulanenko, P. V. Balabuev and A. V. Galunenko.

stabilizer vertical tail of the Ruslan prevented the transportation of very long cargoes. However, the NPO Molniya designers had obtained by then the latest results of their studies aimed at a reusable horizontal launch transportation system and came

to a conclusion that the weight of the load to be launched from the aircraft should be considerably higher than 170 tonnes: some 220, even 270 tonnes. Eventually, it became absolutely clear that the An-124 aircraft could be used neither as the first stage of the system, nor as a carrier of the Buran and

Energia components. It was necessary to design another, more capable and versatile load-lifting carrier aircraft.

The problem struck the imagination. Not only because of its grandiosity in the sense of technology, but from the financial point of view: such a sum of money seemed impossible to obtain. However, genuine fame awaited: without joking, the world's biggest aircraft had to be made! Designs for the future giant were immediately submitted from several institutions: regrettably some of them, as the experts reported, were too vague in their imagined ways to implement this project. The task required considerable designer experience, knowledge of specifically designing large aircraft and uncommon technological capabilities. However, no criticism of those designs is intended here. The main result was that all of them envisioned the making of an absolutely new aircraft, to be emphasised a giant aircraft, with all economic after-effects secondary. And the national economy of the 'advanced socialism' country was already encountering significant problems, and a programme on such a scale (in addition to other numerous burdens) would probably be unsuccessful.

No alternative with lots of choice

Alas, the ADB project which envisioned construction of an aircraft based on the maximum use of the existing An-124 components was not possible but a new project was born in the Department of Advanced Designs supervised by O. K. Bogdanov. Initial sketches of the new aircraft appeared on the drawing boards of the General Views Team (headed by O. Ya. Shmatko) in the second half of 1983, and the future aircraft was conceptualized prior to the beginning of summer next year. Emphasis was made on the use of the Ruslan outer wing original panels, exactly as manufactured by the Tashkent aviation production association. The new wing obtained considerably larger dimensions at the expense of a new wing centre section having an increased span, and equipped with two supplementary D-18T engines used by the An-124. The fuselage was extended due to additional inserts in the constant cross section part ahead of and behind the wing centre section, while its upper surface was equipped with attachment fittings for external cargoes. As soon as the loads on the fuselage tail section increased drastically, it was suggested to remove the cargo door therefrom. The nose landing gear had to be reinforced, the number of main landing gear units rose to seven at each side, their four rear rows being castored. Obviously, the tail unit was transformed into a twin-finned structure. The aircraft was equipped with a pressurisation and thermal control system to monitor external cargoes and maintain interior pressure. Thus, it was an aircraft design which could not only safely carry the Buran and Energia units but also serve as a first stage in an advanced reusable aerospace system, and additionally be used for delivery of various cargoes used in the national economy.

The future An-225 concept obtained its final configuration under the guidance of P. V. Balabuev who had headed Antonov StC since 1984. He managed wide-scale activities for the coordination of numerous issues with airspace companies, established manufacturing cooperation within the industry framework and guaranteed mutual understanding with the new aerospace system customers. They approved the design performance characteristics for the versatile airlifter project on 16 October 1986, and the Decision of the Central Committee of the CPSU and the Council of Ministers of the USSR No. 587-132 was issued on 20 May in the following year, enforcing the An-225 programme in law.

Full scale development of the new aircraft took three and a half years. As a rule, such a period of any aircraft's construction is characterised by significant changes in the preliminary design, especially if at the beginning the designer intended to use any unaltered units from other aircraft. Normally, the stage of detail designing ruthlessly ruins many illusions; however – again, as a rule – nobody minds this, for the order is already in the bag. It should be emphasised that during the period in question the initial design concept mentioned underwent almost no changes due to the high level of its performance. As a result, the An-225 detail design and construction phase went, in general, very smoothly: the company was assisted by its huge experience of building numerous air transport families; in addition, the personnel was at the top of its game. Nevertheless, it was not a slack period at all, quite the contrary: Antonov StC and hundreds of subcontractors worked hard to put the design into life. The cooperation pattern used for the aircraft's construction followed in general the procedure that had worked faultlessly in building the Ruslan prototypes. The outer wings and the new wing centre section were manufactured by Tashkent, and arrived in Kyiv on top of the Antaeus. The landing gear was made in Kuibyshev, the hydraulic system components in Kharkiv and Moscow, the Kyiv Aircraft Manufacturing Association (nowadays a branch of Antonov StC) took an active part in the construction of many components and units. In total, over 100 manufacturers were involved in the project.

The Dream came true

November, 30th, 1988 was the An-225's birthday. The aircraft saw the light –literally – on a gloomy

day when a dank autumn was transformed into a snowy winter; the aircraft was solemnly rolled out from the assembly shop under the open sky. Thousands of designers and workers participating

Presenting the An-225 at a press conference. 30 November 1988.

in the meeting on this occasion noticed for the first time the name Mriya on the fuselage, approved the previous night. Some short speeches were made, and the numerous creators of the newborn giant returned to the shops and work stations to celebrate its birth with whatever was at hand. The aircraft was towed off to the factory aerodrome and handed into the arms of its test team, and its General Designer gave a series of long interviews answering the questions of journalists. In addition to other issues, P. V. Balabuev commented on the aircraft's name: *"The Dream means the infinity of human thoughts and desires. The Dream brings us forward and never disappears, as long as human beings stay alive on the planet. And as soon the aircraft was born in the Ukrainian land, let it bear on its side the name*

Demonstration of the An-225 to the highest authorities in the USSR. P. V. Balabuev and M. S. Gorbachov. Boryspil, February 1989.

An-225 in one of its initial test flights.

which is 'Mriya' in our native language."

The good 'inheritance' that the new aircraft received from the An-124 had a positive impact on the length of time of the ground tryout of the An-225 airborne systems. Very quickly, on 3 and 4 December, the aircraft made its first independent promenade at the factory aerodrome in Sviatoshyn: a variety of taxying, turns and runs attaining a speed of 200 km/h, raising its nose gear off the ground. The aircraft behaviour seemed to comply absolutely with the predictions, so the maiden flight was appointed for a date soon therafter, 20 December. However,

Report of General Designer P. V. Balabuev presented significant applications for An-225.

on that day the weather conditions prevented the An-225 from taking off into the sky. The cold day which followed was not promising at all again: low cloud base, crosswind and headwind with squalls of snow. But nevertheless, the aircraft was brought to the runway. Having run some 950 metres, Mriya easily lifted off and entered the overcast winter sky. The aircraft was piloted by the following crew: first pilot A. V. Galunenko, second pilot S. A. Gorbik, senior flight engineer A. M. Shuleshchenko, flight engineer V. A. Gusar, navigator S. F. Nechayev, radio engineer V. K. Belousov and leading flight test engineer M. G. Kharchenko.

During the first flight, that lasted 1 hour 14 minutes, the new aircraft's stability and controllability were assessed in the usual manner and the operation of airborne systems and equipment verified. The flight revealed the full conformity of the actual An-225 parameters to the calculated ones, and the conformity of the aircraft's actual behaviour with the bench-simulated performance. Everything had been so successful that the emeritus test pilot of the USSR A. V. Galunenko mentioned to journalists after the flight: *"Believe me, absolutely no complaints at all. Everything is right as nails. The designers fit us, and we fit them: if you go on producing such aircraft, no service of test pilots is required any more."*

Undoubtedly, in his response Alexander Vasilyevich Galunenko simplified the situation somewhat; however the later aircraft tests proceeded without any serious problems. It was extra proof that the idea of designing the An-225 on the basis of the Ruslan was correct as it passed all the necessary checks. The structural commonality of many assemblies and components, and the common identity of many parts in airborne systems and equipment of these two aircraft helped to reduce the number of the An-225's experimental flights greatly. On 28 December Mriya accomplished its second flight, and on 1 February 1989 it was demonstrated to Soviet and foreign journalists at Kyiv Boryspil airport. March, 22nd became one of the most significant days in the An-225's history: it fulfilled a flight aimed at breaking a world record. Following the careful weighing of the cargo, which reached 156.3 tonnes, and sealing the single-point fuelling system fillers, Mriya took to the air. The tally of its record achievements started immediately after lift-off. Challenging the American Boeing 747-400, which then held the record maximum takeoff weight (404.8 tonnes), the An-225 immediately overtook this achievement by 104 tonnes. During that remarkable flight, Mriya set in fact 110 world records, not 106 as had been supposed before! The records included a breakthrough in the speed of flight over a 2,000-km-long looped route with a 155-tonne payload (815.09 km/h) and the flying altitude record with the same payload (12,430 m). Having flown for 3 hr and 45 min, Mriya landed.

As a matter of fact, the An-225 had not been designed to establish new records and soon afterwards the aircraft started its direct mission. On 3 May 1989 Mriya took off from Baikonur aerodrome, piggybacking its cargo number one: the Buran aerospace vehicle weighing over 60 tonnes. In the 10 days that followed, the crew headed by Galunenko accomplished a number of experimental flights to assess the controllability of this cluster of aircraft and cargo, and to measure flying speeds and fuel consumption. On 13 May the unique transportation system executed its 2,700-km-long non-stop flight

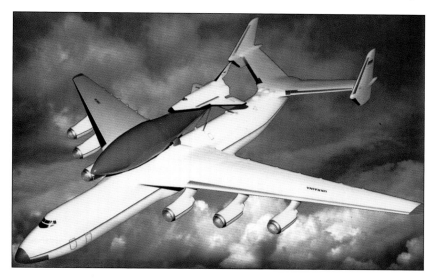

from Baikonur to Kyiv. The flight took 4 hr 25 min; the takeoff weight reached 560 tonnes.

An period of triumph for the aircraft and its designers started. During a short parking time in Kyiv, thousands came to see that striking cluster of two huge flight vehicles. Numerous photographs made during the flight, were published in USSR

Artist's view of the MAKS (top) and Svityaz Reusable Aerospace Systems.

Mriya visited many corners of the Soviet Union during flight tests. Yelizovo airport, Kamchatka, 1990.

Buran being installed on top the An-225. Baikonur aerodrome, May 1989.

Howeve, Paris was only the beginning of the unprecedented triumph. In August 1989, the aircraft departed for another air show in Vancouver, Canada. Having seen the An-225 in flight, the Canadian Prime Minister Martin Brian Mulroney said that *"the Soviet pilots who had arrived to Canada in their airplanes arranged a holiday for us."* In September Mriya visited Prague and was demonstrated at the Exhibition of the Council for Mutual Economic Assistance, CMEA. Next year the aircraft participated in the Farnborough Air Show, Great Britain, and attended two U.S. air shows, in Oklahoma City and in Seattle. The biggest aircraft in the world attracted the attention of a mammoth number of American citizens. The participants of the flights recall that probably the longest queue in the United States could be seen those days near the An-225, such was the number of people eager to enter its interior. *"We manufacture the biggest passenger airplanes of the world,"* noticed Rick Hawkinson, a representative of the Boeing company. *But we make a bow to the Antonov-225."* In 1991 the aircraft attended Shannon, Ireland, in 1992 visited Montreal, Canada, Columbus and Las Vegas, USA. In August 1993, the An-225 was met by the visitors of MosAirShow at Zhukovsky near Moscow, and in December it flew to the Dubai exhibition in United Arab Emirates. In 1994 the giant from Kyiv was applauded by Singapore and Sharjah. It is worth mentioning that the An-225 flew to all those shows and displays not empty but carrying various examples of Ukrainian products.

newspapers and magazines. When Mriya bearing the Buran arrived in France, to take part in the 38th International Air Show at Le Bourget, they were met by the admiring gazes of hundreds of thousands of visitors that came there from all corners of the planet. The An-225 aircraft instantly became the world sensation. *"A miracle of technology, challenging anything imaginable in our impetuous time!"*, *"I am gazing at this fantastic craft, and my heart is filling with pride for the power of the human mind"*, *"The aircraft as huge as your Soviet country"*, *"Thank you ..."* all these enthusiastic impressions were to be found in the weighty multi-language visitors' book placed inside the An-225 during the Air Show.

At that time, the aircraft performed its first commercial flights, too. In May 1990 the An-225 piloted by S. A. Gorbik and I. I. Bachurin carried from Chelyabinsk to Yakutia the T-800 tractor, the weight of which exceeded 110 tonnes. That expedition to a Far Polar area was of great experimental value, in addition to pure economics, since some new important data was collected to study the transport capabilities of the aircraft, and its operation, in the conditions of the Far North. Flights to the USA and Canada followed, and hundreds of tonnes of humanitarian aid therefrom were delivered to Ukraine. Nonetheless, the global glory obtained by the aircraft so quickly was only one side of the coin. At the time when enthusiastic speeches were growing louder abroad, the practicable prospects of the An-225 were becoming increasingly vague. For a number of different reasons, the progress of the Energia-Buran Programme initially shifted into low gear and subsequently was brought to complete rest. There were also difficulties with the funding of the An-225 Official Tests. Ambiguity in the Russian-Ukrainian relations first appeared and, after disintegration of the Soviet Union, developed into a major tangle on the intergovernmental level, due to the lack of proper agreements. In short, when this

Wing high-lift devices on the trailing edge.

time of turbulent change came to 'one-sixth of the earth' it overshadowed everything else, including the fortunes of the world's largest aircraft.

All the fall-out, plus the aircraft's diversion for modification and participation in international shows, led to delays in the Joint Official Tests, which began on 15 May 1989. By the time of the USSR's disintegration, a total of just 113 valid test flights had been made with an overall duration of 253 hr 6 min, including 14 flights with the Buran shuttle orbiter (28 hr 27 min). These test flights had been made from aerodromes located in different climatic zones of the USSR: in Gostomel, Akhtubinsk, Baikonur, Boryspil, Vnukovo, Yelizovo, Ramenskoye, Chkalovskaya, and Khabarovsk. After the separation of Ukraine and Russia became a reality and people had time to think of other things, testing of the An-225 was resumed, however in a considerably reduced scope. This was not only due to scanty governmental financing: initially, the primary mission of the first An-225 had seen testing for its suitability for transportation of the Energia-Buran components, but this project was practically closed by that time. Therefore, a considerable part of the test programme, which called for flights with 10 different types of 'space' cargoes (in addition to the Buran itself) on external stores, was not even performed. The main focus was on testing for an aerodynamically 'clean' aircraft.

By the time the aircraft was laid up in April 1994, Mriya accomplished a total of 339 flights (including commercial transportation flights and participation in air shows) with an overall duration of 671 hours. Findings on the Results of Official Tests of An-225 No. 01-01, which validated the practical conformance of the demonstrated aircraft performance figures with the intended characteristics, were signed on 5 January 1996. It should be noted that simultaneously with the Official Tests the aircraft was involved in the civil aircraft certification process; many of the flights performed were deemed valid in the civil

certification programme, yet a considerable number were special-purpose certification test flights. Actively involved in the certification activities were the staff of Aviation Registers of the CIS Interstate

D-18T engine nacelles.

Main landing gear.

Aviation Committee and Ukraine, specialists of certification centres of Russia and Ukraine, and numerous independent experts. The activities were

Mriya with Buran in the first joint flight, May 1989.

T-800 tractor loaded aboard during preparation for Mriya's first commercial flight. Chelyabinsk, May 1990.

barely sufficed for the small fleet of Ruslans. The giant's future seemed rather hazy, and they gradually began to strip it of its engines and some avionics units, to install them on the Ruslans which had become Antonov StC's principal bread-winners. Luckily, these costly items were suitable for both aircraft types – another positive effect of the decision to design the An-225 on the basis of the An-124.

However, even in these conditions the creators of the wonder aircraft did not lose heart and pursued their work on versions of the aircraft for different types of operations. This work began even before the Soviet Union's disintegration. Thus, on 21 June 1991 an international aerospace system intended for the exploration of space near Earth, consisting of the An-225 and the 250-tonne Interim HOTOL space shuttlecraft developed by British Aerospace of the UK, was presented at the European Space Agency headquarters in Paris. The two aircraft fitted almost perfectly as the An-225 had been designed from the outset for the air launch of this type of spacecraft. Implementation of this project promised an almost fourfold reduction in the cost of launching the payload into orbit compared to the vertical launch alternative. Among other things, the HOTOL could have been more efficient than other spacecraft in the delivery of crews to orbiting space stations and their evacuation in emergencies. However, the project very soon demonstrated a most serious drawback – the complete lack of governmental funding both on the Ukrainian and on the British sides. And it turned out that private investors preferred to invest only in those business spheres that offered quick return. Whenever the period of profit taking is prolonged, finding an investor becomes practically impossible. This copy-book maxim became fatal for Mriya-HOTOL project.

Regrettably, about a dozen other An-225-related projects suffered the same fate. By the mid-1990s, NPO Molniya finalized the concept of the MAKS Reusable Aerospace System designed to deliver 8.5 to 10 tonnes of payload into orbit in the manned version and 18 to 19 tonnes in the unmanned version. It is interesting that in spite of the very slow progress of the programme activities, MAKS has not yet become obsolescent and still remains one of the most advanced aerospace systems. The Svityaz aerospace system was designed on the basis of the An-225 and several components of the Zenith-2 launcher to allow injection into low orbits of up to 8 tonnes of payload. This system, however, was no luckier than the others: its development was included in the Draft Space Programme of Ukraine for the period of 2002–06, but was never completed.

It should be noted that the search for a worthy use of the aircraft was not limited to space applications.

discontinued when no more than 15 to 20 test flights remained to be made. However, this unfortunate fact was of minor importance: the chances that the aircraft could be used for commercial transportation at the time where close to zero.

Troublesome times

The pendulum of the An-225's fate that had soared to the height of glory swung downwards as sharply, and, it seemed, froze at its dead point for good and all. The aircraft itself was stuck for years on the outskirts of the aerodrome in Gostomel in the suburbs of Kyiv. The principal missions that Mriya had been designed to perform vanished with the closure of the Buran programme, and there were no chances at that time for the aircraft's commercial success in the transportation of standard cargoes – the abrupt changeover in world fuel prices resulted in plummeting demand in the CIS countries for air transportation, including unique transport operations. And abroad, the transportation jobs

There was, in particular, a project for the An-225's refurbishment into a super-airliner for the transportation of 328 passengers in the conditions of extra comfort on air routes up to 9,700 km long, for example, London–Abu Dhabi–Singapore–Sydney. The three-decker fuselage was planned to accommodate sleeping compartments, standard passenger seat compartments, a shop, a restaurant and a casino. In this configuration the aircraft was planned to be equipped with Western manufactured engines and equipment but the Western aircraft manufacturers started talking about a comparable level of comfort only after Airbus started developing their A380 jumbo passenger airliner. The prospect of a new international aero/maritime rescue system with Mriya delivering 'piggyback' the Orlionok airfoil boat developed by R. E. Alekseyev NPO of Nizhny Novgorod to vessels in distress could have

Mriya – Buran duo.

Pilots of the *Mriya* visually demonstrate the tremendous dimensions of the aircraft standing on its top

Pilots's stations (top), Flight engineer's station (middle), Navigator's and radio operator's stations (bottom)

been very opportune. As with the spacecraft, the Orlionok would be launched from the An-225, land on water and take the people in distress on board

to deliver them by sea to the nearest port under its own power. Owing to its high cruising speed, such rescue system guaranteed much shorter rescue times for seamen.

Unfortunately, none of these projects was ever realised. Nevertheless, the unique aircraft's developers believed that the peerless An-225 would find a worthy application and serve the cause of engineering and social progress for many years. Gradually, the search tapered off, since none brought an actual result, yet the main idea crystallized: should the An-225 be destined to show itself to the world again, it would appear as nothing exotic, but as a plain and ordinary commercial aircraft, yet capable of transporting exceptionally heavy and over-size cargoes, beyond the capabilities of other aircraft. The impressive capabilities of the An-225 could have been demonstrated as early as 1993, when the need arose to deliver huge petroleum refining tubing from Volgograd to Kola Peninsula in north-west Russia. The traditional land route was by rivers to the Arctic Ocean and then by sea. Since the route could not be traversed within one navigation season, the transport operation was scheduled to take two years. Using the An-225 for the transportation would have made it possible to bring the transit time down to two weeks. However, even this absolutely zero-risk (as it seemed) enterprise was never implemented ...

Tomorrow is another day ...

However, despite all of this, reasonable proposals for the delivery of some unique cargoes using the An-225 started appearing more and more often. Inquiries were coming from abroad: *What's happening with the aircraft? Why is there no news of it? Could an order for transportation be placed?* In 1995, when the market began clearly demonstrating a demand for transportation of cargoes more heavy than those within the Ruslan's capabilities, the first plans were made for renewal of the An-225 airworthiness. Antonov's General Designer signed the required in-house documents, including those required for completion of the aircraft's certification tests. But the disastrous accident with the An-70, followed by mobilisation of the company's resources for construction of its second flying prototype and later for development of the An-140, postponed implementation of the plan by several years.

During all this time the Antonov Airlines air transport division of Antonov StC was receiving requests for commercial utilisation of the An-225. Thus, Siemens requested transportation of a 196-tonne electric generator, General Electric was interested in aerial delivery of a steam turbine weighing more than 200 tonnes, Airbus Industrie requested transportation of structural components of the A380 airliners and the new A340 aircraft versions. Investigation was also made into transportation of the Boeing aircraft fuselages on external stores from manufacturing facilities in Europe to the assembly line in Seattle (USA). According to K. F. Lushakov, the Antonov Airlines Executive Director, by the late 1990s a considerable potential demand for the services of such unique means of transportation as the An-225 took shape.

As a result of thorough analysis of the current situation, Antonov CEO P. V. Balabuev made a decision about renewal of the An-225's airworthiness after its prolonged downtime and the aircraft's upgrading in accordance with the present-day requirements for commercial aircraft flying along international air routes. In summer 2000, practically as soon as the An-140 certification testing programme was completed, work began on the An-225. The company started the activities at its own expense jointly with Motor-Sich JSC, which delivered the engines at its own cost and undertook to provide their maintenance support. The share of the Zaporizhzha company in the aircraft reconditioning costs, and consequently in the future profits, amounted to 30%. Furthermore, a large number of other companies were involved in the work on the contractual basis to supply the An-225 with new or used and reconditioned equipment units, aircraft systems components, and individual structural elements. An especially large list of equipment was taken on the by Ulyanovsk Aircraft Manufacturing Complex that manufactured the Ruslans. *"We have not taken a single kopeck of the Ukrainian taxpayers' money,"* that was the answer of P. V. Balabuev to numerous questions from the press about the cost of the activities.

By mid-November, diagnostics of the airframe and aircraft systems condition were completed, the majority of the required parts and equipment components were manufactured, repaired or purchased, and installation of the engines began. At the same time, the An-225 was being modified into a fully-fledged commercial aircraft capable of flying worldwide without limitations. (It will be recalled that initially Mriya had been intended only for flying within the territory of the USSR.) The aircraft was equipped with air traffic collision avoidance systems, equipment supporting reduced vertical separation minima, and also with new radios to meet current ICAO requirements. Moreover, in view of the expected transportation inside the fuselage of single-piece cargo items weighing about 220 tonnes, the cargo floor and forward ramp were reinforced. In February 2001, installation of the engines was completed, in March operability of numerous systems was finally restored and on 9 April the finished aircraft was rolled out of the shop and handed over to the test team.

The day of 7 May 2001 was memorable in the history of the aircraft, as well as in the history of Ukraine and the air transportation business in general. It was the day of the giant's 'second first flight' – its second birth, if effect. After thorough ground testing, having made a dozen taxiway and runway runs on the Gostomel airfield, Mriya, with the registration UR-82060, took wing after a seven-year time-out. It was flown by the crew headed by A.V. Galunenko and made a 15-minute flight.

Aircraft galley.

Flight crew rest compartment.

In the seven years of downtime, the An-225 was stripped of its engines and part of the equipment.

Gostomel, spring 2001. Airworthiness renewal work under way in the new hangar of the Antonov StC Flight Test and Development Base.

And once again, just as 12 years earlier, it was widely discussed on television, aviation magazines published picture spreads of the flight, and almost all newspapers made reports.

Thereafter, the aircraft made several test flights required for the completion of the certification testing programme. On 26 May, during a public demonstration at the new runway opening ceremony at Kyiv Boryspil Airport, Chairperson of

the CIS Interstate Aviation Committee T. G. Anodina handed over the aircraft type certificate to its developers. After that, Mriya flew to France where it was demonstrated at the 44th Paris International Air Show at Le Bourget. The An-225's graceful flight in the Parisian sky was highly appreciated by experts and commanded the admiration of the public. Not that that was new for the Antonov aircraft, and the times when this was the sole purpose of going

to Paris were long gone. The purpose of bringing Mriya to the world's most prestigious air show was to find customers. But while the professionals held discussions, the air show guests felt it their duty to personally visit the largest aircraft in the world. Out of 300,000 people that visited the air show, about 200,000 walked around the An-225's cargo compartment, making about 2,000 entries in the visitor's book. Here is what Anatoly Vovnianko, Deputy Chief Designer, said about the event: *"It seemed that during the air show, the An-225 was visited by more people than all other aircraft taken together. From morning till the evening there was a solid stream of people waiting in line, five abreast, to see Mriya, when one to two persons were entering other aircraft. Besides us, the visitors' keen interest was aroused by the Boeing C-17 and Airbus Beluga. There were lines of about 20 people waiting to get inside –five visitors were allowed to enter every five minutes."*

"In Paris Mriya produced the effect we had been aiming for and attracted interest in exactly the area we had been targeting," emphasised V. P. Kazakov, Deputy Chairman of the State Committee for Industrial Policy, at the press conference dedicated to the air show results. *"The An-225 appeared at a very good time: there are now over-size cargoes in the market that cannot be delivered using the An-124-100."* A similar point of view was held by the influential *Financial Times,* which published an article on the six-engine giant, the dream of Antonov that came true. The newspaper wrote that Mriya, having lost its prestigious role of the Soviet 'shuttle' carrier platform, had finally acquired a new sphere of application and, in spite of the difficulties, was entering the air transportation market that autumn.

However, in order to effectively enter this market, the second part of he work had to be done – the aircraft had to be prepared for efficient commercial operation. In particular, to assure better suitability for the infrastructure of modern airports, the An-225 had to be fitted with a built-in tow-bar. A dedicated loading trestle bridge was designed for loading cargo items with a weight of up to 200 tonnes. To allow for transportation of these kinds of cargoes, a number of the hydraulic system components and the aircraft landing gear were slightly modernized. And finally, acceptable work and rest conditions were created for the maintenance team which made part of the aircraft crew, and for cargo attendants. These activities that were completed in spring of 2002, could have taken less time if the aircraft had not been involved in several events during this period. For example, in August 2001, Mriya took part in MAKS-2001 Moscow Aerospace Show, where it successfully represented the aeronautical industry of Ukraine

together with other aircraft – the An-70, An-140 and An-74-300. Owing to its impressive characteristics, the An-225 very soon won wide acclaim and became one of the symbols of the young Ukrainian state. Therefore the aircraft was simply destined to take part in numerous demonstration flights and in

Mriya back in the air. 7 May 2001.

The *Mriya* is equipped with theengines designed and constructed in Zaporizhzhia (Ukraine)

the air parade dedicated to the 10th anniversary of Ukrainian independence.

Another occurrence that took place during this period of time also became momentous in the aircraft's life. On 11 September an attempt was made by the An-225 to set a large number of national and world records in two categories of land turbojet aircraft: C-1 and C-1t (with takeoff weight exceeding

The new runway opening ceremony at Boryspil Airport. 7 May 2001.

300 tonnes). During one flight, the crew, with A. V. Galunenko in command, set the following absolute records: a payload weighing 253.820 tonnes was lifted to the altitude of 2000 m; 763 km/h speed was attained in the closed-course 1,000-km long flight with 250 tonnes of cargo aboard; and 250 tonnes of cargo were lifted to the altitude of 10,570 m.

Previously, the world weight-lift record in the C-1 category was held by the An-124, which had lifted 171,219 tonnes (in 1985). The An-225 was the record breaker in the C-1t category lifting 156.3 tonnes (in 1989). The same aircraft also held the previous altitude-with-payload records: in 1985,

the Ruslan lifted 170 tonnes to 10,750 m, and in 1989, Mriya took 155 tonnes to 12,430 m. As for the flight speed, the preceding record in the C-1 category was set by the Il-86 in 1981 – the aircraft carrying 80 tonnes demonstrated the speed of 962 km/h in the closed-course 1,000-km flight, while in the C-1t category no such records had yet been set. In February 2002, diplomas were received from the Fédération Aéronautique Internationale certifying the records set by the An-225. Considering that, according to the Federation regulations, record achievements are established at 5-tonne payload increments, Galunenko's crew set a total of 124

Five tanks were used as payload for setting the absolute world payload record on Mriya. Gostomel, 11 September 2001.

world records on the 11 September flight. And since those were simultaneously the first achievements registered as national records of Ukraine the total was even larger – 214 all in all!

Here is what Aleksandr Galunenko said about the record flight: *"From the point of view of the test pilot it was just a regular test flight. Although the type certificate for the aircraft had already been received and such a flight was not required for the certification process, it was important for us to understand the aircraft's capabilities. We did not take much fuel, based on the flight mission calculation, so the takeoff weight was comparatively low – just 590 tonnes, whereas nowadays we are allowed to fly with 640 tonnes! We took tanks by way of payload – they are sufficiently heavy and very convenient in terms of loading and unloading. Imagine if the payload were of iron ingots – that would have been a lot of extra trouble! Five tanks plus the test equipment still remaining on board made up the total of the record payload.*

"The flight itself consisted of two stages. The first was to set a speed record, for which purpose we followed the route forth and back between Gostomel and the Zmiyiny Island in the Black Sea so as to remain within the national boundaries of Ukraine. The second stage was for lifting the payload to altitude and this was done in the test flight zone in the Gostomel aerodrome terminal area. We climbed smoothly to a little above 10,000 metres, then accomplished a slight dynamic manoeuvre and, owing to the loss of dynamic energy, additionally climbed to some 400 m. And we never exceeded the allowable angle of attack in the manoeuvre. As a matter of fact, the entire flight was performed within the operational envelope of speeds and angles of attack, strictly within the limitations of the An-225 Aircraft Flight Manual. No doubt, had we exceeded the limitations we could have easily attained higher results, but why go off the deep end? In any case, these records are not going to be topped for a long time."

The An-225 landed triumphantly. The Antonov StC management and employees, representatives of Kyiv municipal authorities and foreign diplomatic representations came to meet the aircraft at the aerodrome. Smiling crew, laden with flowers, descended the air stairs and Aleksandr Galunenko made a report to the Head of Antonov Flight Test Base A. G. Bulanenko about the accomplished flight mission. An improvised press conference was held on the spot, under the mighty aircraft's wing, with the pilots and designers the men of the day.

The An-225 made its first commercial flights as part of Antonov Airlines at the turn of 2001 and 2002. These flights convincingly demonstrated that the aircraft was capable of efficient commercial operations not only in unique transportation missions

for delivery of over-sized and super-heavy cargoes, but also when carrying 'general cargo'. It is only

Two flying giants: the An-225 and Boeing 747.

important that the cargo weight be 150 tonnes and higher – and the aircraft will be unsurpassed in terms of operating cost effectiveness. And the fact that this outstanding aircraft remains one-of-a-kind is no problem at all. It successfully copes with the scope of unique transportation work available in the world

Nose cone lifting system and kneeling system of Mriya are similar to those used on the Ruslan.

Mriya at Le Bourget, June 2001.

The staff of Antonov Airlines is proud of opportunity to operate the world biggest aircraft.

In 2009, having undergone a full package of required rework and testing, Mriya re-commences route flying.

today. Yet, the scope of such work is steadfastly growing and it is quite possible that Antonov will have to complete construction of the second prototype, which is stored today (in the form of individual components – fuselage, outer wing panels, tail unit ...) in one of the company's workshops.

And the first Mriya, having occupied its merited place in the fleet of Antonov Airlines, has now entered maybe the most important stage in its biography. In recent years it has added to its credit numerous breathtaking transport operations, new records and commercial achievements, and is looking forward to future glory.

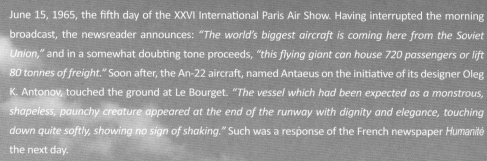

June 15, 1965, the fifth day of the XXVI International Paris Air Show. Having interrupted the morning broadcast, the newsreader announces: *"The world's biggest aircraft is coming here from the Soviet Union,"* and in a somewhat doubting tone proceeds, *"this flying giant can house 720 passengers or lift 80 tonnes of freight."* Soon after, the An-22 aircraft, named Antaeus on the initiative of its designer Oleg K. Antonov, touched the ground at Le Bourget. *"The vessel which had been expected as a monstrous, shapeless, paunchy creature appeared at the end of the runway with dignity and elegance, touching down quite softly, showing no sign of shaking."* Such was a response of the French newspaper *Humanité* the next day.

In fact, as far as the aircraft payload and cargo compartment dimensions (32.7 x 4.4 x 4.4) were concerned, the An-22 surpassed at that time any aircraft in the world. Before its construction, the American Lockheed C-141 Starlifter carrying 32.6 tonnes was considered to be the leader among air transport aircraft. Despite the fact that the An-22's supremacy did not last for long – the Lockheed C-5A *Galaxy* made its first flight in June 1968 – without doubt, it had started a new era of global aeronautical engineering. *"By making this aircraft,"* commented O. K. Antonov, *"we have broken a psychological barrier based on the fear of a very 'thick' fuselage ... A new generation of large aircraft called 'widebody' came into the life."*

ANTONOV AIRLINES AIRCRAFT
An-22 Antaeus

An-22

Birth of Antaeus

In the early 1960s, the Ministry of Defence of the USSR committed to the aircraft industry the task of designing an air delivery system for intercontinental ballistic missiles (IBM) in order to establish a base for the Soviet Union nuclear potential. According to the plan, aircraft had to deliver special-purpose stores (rockets, launching equipment, etc.) to the nearest aerodrome from the launching site, and thereafter helicopters brought them directly to the underground silo. It was found that the VT-22 airlifter project which had been recently started by the Antonov Design Bureau (ADB) and which was intended for transportation of heavy military vehicles of ground forces including T-54 tanks complied with the required task in many respects. The army counted on the further development of this project with the purpose of obtaining a full-grown strategic military cargo transport capable of carrying not only IBMs or tanks but the entire range of military and engineering products transported normally by rail. In addition, the national economy required an aircraft for delivery of bulky cargoes, including to the distant regions of Siberia, the Far North and Soviet Far East where no other means of transportation was feasible.

The task of construction of such an aircraft appeared to be hyper-sophisticated (with no exaggeration); in addition, it had to be implemented for the first time within international practice. To realise it, the ADB designers had to use in a large number of daring design solutions in the An-22. For example, in view of the oversized cutout in the fuselage for the future cargo door, it was necessary to replace the single-fin tail unit used previously on Antonov aircraft with a new original two-fin empennage featuring extended forward offset of vertical tips.

For the first time in the practice of ADB, all connections of the aircraft manual flight control system were supplied with irreversible hydraulic actuators. For emergency procedures, transition to manual control by means of servo tabs was envisioned. The requirement to ensure operation of such heavy aircraft from/into various airfields, including soil sites with a low surface strength (below 6 kg/sq. cm) determined the use of a multi-wheel landing gear with protruded-section tyres of low pressure. The wheel-to-shock absorber levered suspension allowed the provision of a long stroke of shock absorbers with rather short struts, thus lowering the cargo compartment floor height over the aerodrome surface as much as possible.

The An-22 allowed not only synchronized but also individual retraction and extension of the main

Antaeus

landing gear, which contributed to the aircraft's safety during operation.

For the first time, the An-22 structure extensively employed single-piece sections – 15-metre-long pressed panels and large-sized extrusions of up to 5 metres in length: this solution decreased the airframe weight by approximately 5 tonnes. The new aircraft was equipped with four NK-12MA turboprop engines arranged on the wing so that 45% of its area was intensively blown by the propellers. As a result, the maximum lift coefficient of the wing increased by almost 30% (the same effect, but on a much larger scale, was used for the An-70 aircraft later).

On 18 August 1964, on the USSR Air Fleet Day,

The An-22 is one of the genuine masterpieces of aeronautical engineering.

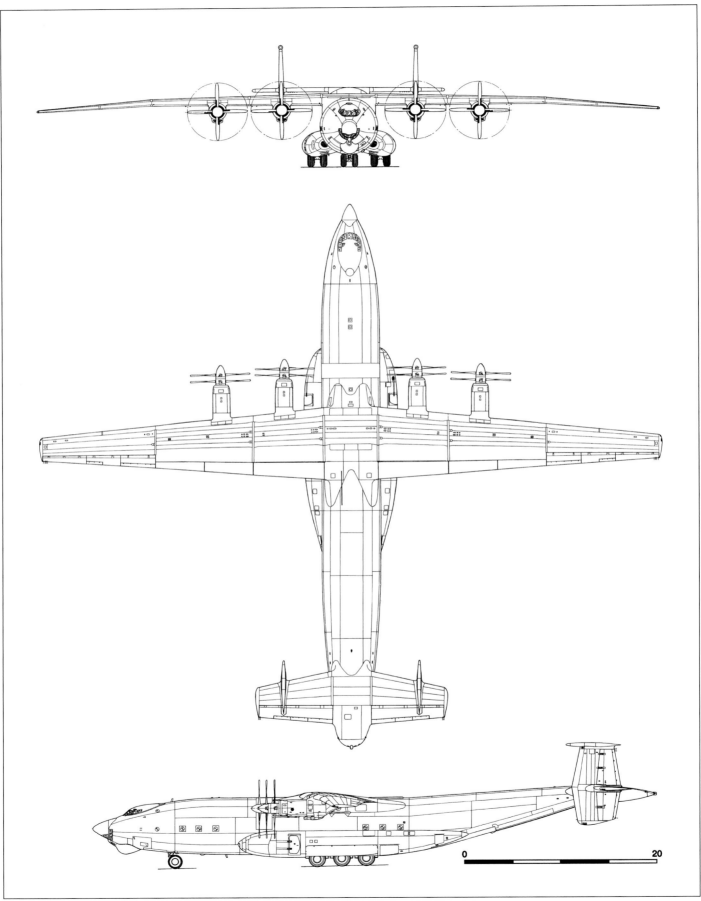

following an inauguration ceremony, the first An-22 prototype No. 01-01 (USSR-46191) was delivered for flight testing. One month later, another static test prototype was installed in the ADB laboratory. The strength of the airframe main structures and components had been tested for several months until December 1966.

Way to formation

The initial taxyings and runs were made by the An-22 in August, though its ground tests advanced, generally speaking, too slowly. The aircraft was several times rolled back into the shop for various modifications, in particular improvement of the landing gear. However, having passed all necessary tests and checks, the An-22 aircraft accomplished its maiden flight on 27 February 1965. The crew consisted of Y. V. Kurlin (pilot-in-command), V. I. Terskii (co-pilot), P. V. Koshkin (navigator), V. M. Vorotnikov (flight engineer), N. F. Drobyshev (radio engineer), M. P. Rachenko (electrical engineer), and

V. N. Shatalov (leading engineer for flight tests). The maiden flight was followed by others, though their rate of increase could not be called high: before the break in tests caused by the Paris Air Show, the An-22 had accumulated only six flights.

The pace accelerated when more aircraft constructed at the Tashkent aircraft factory, where its serial production was deployed, were involved in the Antaeus flight programme. Following definition of the aircraft's basic flight performance, another substantial part of the test programme was devoted to studying the An-22's behaviour in airdrop procedures aimed at personnel and cargo delivery. The technique of paradropping mono-cargo items with 20 tonnes maximum weight was mastered step-by-step and put in practice.

October, 27th, 1966 opened the list of the Antaeus world records. The crew of test pilot I. E. Davydov lifted a 88.103-tonne cargo to the height of 6,600 m, having set 12 records during the same flight. The previous world record reached in 1958 by J. M. Thompson, USA, on the Douglas C-133

An-22 full-scale wooden mockup, 1961.

An-22 main performance data				
Aircraft overall external dimensions, m		**Cruising speed, km/h**		600
– length x wing span x height	58,1 x 64,4 x 12,5	**Cruising altitude, m**		10500
Cargo compartment dimensions, m		**Practical range with 60-ton cargo, km**		3100
– length x width x height	33,4 x 4,4 x 4,4	**Max range, km**		8500
Engines		**Airfield length, m**		2500
– type	NK-12MA	**Crew number**		7
– number x power, e.h.p.	4 x 15000			
Max payload, tons	60*	** 80 tons for restricted number of flights*		

The An-22 prototype rollout. Kiev. 18 August 1964.

Maiden flight of An-22 No. 01-01. Kyiv, 27 February 1965.

(53.5-tonne cargo to 2,000-metre altitude) was broken by an extra 34.6 tonnes. Then on 17 October 1967 Davydov's crew surprised the world once again: freight weighing over one hundred tonnes (100,444.6 kg) was lifted to the altitude of 7,848 m. As of today, the absolute records of lifting capacity established by the An-22 have been broken by the An-225 aircraft, but the number of Antaeus world records still totals 41.

According to the programme of State official tests, the Antaeus performed 40 flights to test stalling modes. For safety reasons, the aircraft was

equipped with an anti-spin parachute, the 100 m long static line of which could counteract a 50-tonne force. Flights were conducted over desert terrain near Tashkent, Uzbekistan, by the reduced crew, including Yu. V. Kurlin (pilot-in-command), Yu. N. Ketov (co-pilot) and V. Vorotnikov (flight engineer, who combined the functions of navigator and radio engineer). As a result of these tests it was established that with correct and well-timed pilot actions, the An-22 recovers from a stall with no delay, therefore its has little likelihood of going into a spin.

The Antaeus No.1 flight crew before the departure for Paris. Left to right: V. I. Terskii, N. F. Drobyshev, P. V. Koshkin, A. P. Eskin, V. N. Shatalov, Yu.V Kurlin, V. M. Vorotnikov and P. M. Radchenko.

An-22 Antaeus at Paris Air Show, 1965.

The An-22 proved effective in operation from/into dry and swampy areas, as well as from snow-covered ground.

For their achievements, the An-22 test pilots Yu. V. Kurlin and I. E. Davydov were decorated with the Gold Stars of Heroes of Soviet Union in 1966 and 1971 correspondingly. In April 1974, the Antonov Design Bureau was decorated with the Order of Red Banner of Labour for construction of the An-22 aircraft and two Deputy Chief Designers, P. V. Balabuev and A. Y. Belolipetskii, and turning lathe operator V. V.

Naumenko, were awarded the title of Hero of Socialist Labour (the highest civilian award of the former USSR).

In early 1970s, the Antaeus underwent multifarious renovation that led to some reduction of the aircraft weight, an increase in its in-service reliability and a lowering of maintenance costs. From 1972, the upgraded version was launched in serial production under the An-22A designation. The next year, the Air Force Scientific Research Institute for Aircraft Maintenance and Repair (NIIERAT) together with ADB prepared a programme of An-22 lead aircraft testing which provided operational monitoring of the aircraft with an advanced accumulation of service time in hours and landings. These efforts, as well as extensive studies of the Antaeus fatigue resistance conducted by Antonov StC's strength test laboratory, allowed at the beginning of the second millennium the assigned service life of the aircraft to be raised to 10,000 flight hours or 40 years of operation. Nowadays, these efforts which proceed at Antonov StC continuously have resulted in the An-22 having a service life of 20,000 hours, 4,000 flights, and 50 years.

In the land of Uzbekistan

Start of the batch production of the outsize transport raised many non-standard problems for the personnel of Tashkent Chkalov Aircraft factory (since 1973 known as TAPOiCH, the Russian abbreviation for 'Tashkent Aircraft Manufacturing Association', plus the name of a prominent pilot Valery Chkalov) which had to be solved for the first time in Soviet aircraft manufacturing practice. The factory floor spaces had to be fundamentally increased and all manufacturing processes modernized. Due to the activities of the parent ADB representative office, plenty of innovations that had been developed and approved in Kyiv were introduced into series production quite effectively.

The broad panelling of the An-22 structure allowed implementation of an advanced method of airframe assembly using coordinate spot dimples which allowed a 15% reduction of labour coefficient, a shorter assembly cycle, improved the stock identification and simplified the fixtures used. Automatic control units for argon-arc welding of aluminium and magnesium alloy parts were introduced. From 1971, manned air-tight compartments filled with extremely pure argon were used for the welding of titanium parts. The factory immediately mastered the innovative technology of adhesive/welded connections for load-bearing panels of the fuselage and empennage. As a result of all these and other innovations, the labour-output ratio of the An-22 batch production was reduced seven times! The production output of the Antaeus accelerated. In 1969 only five aircraft were constructed; their number increased to 11 in 1975. In total, from January 1966 until January 1976, TAPOiCH jigs released 68 An-22 aircraft, including 28 in the An-22A version.

Winged soldier and worker

Field tests and operation of the Antaeus in military aviation transport divisions started in January 1969. As early as June 1969, three An-22s participated in the 'East' manoeuvres, delivering military

Tests for the airdrop of single-piece cargo from the An-22 No.01-06 aircraft.

An-22 assembly shop at TAPOiCH (Tashkent Chkalov Aircraft Factory). Early 1970s.

Loading military equipment, vehicles and personnel in the An-22 Antaeus. 1970s.

Its huge belly opened, and paratroopers rushed down. One could not believe that all of them came out of the same aircraft ... The new 'Antaeus' aircraft generation has radically changed our military aviation transport, turning it into a powerful tool in the hands of General Headquarters," wrote the Red Star newspaper dated 12 March 1970 about the An-22's participation in the Dvina manoeuvres.

Even earlier, at the stage of prototype factory testing, the An-22 aircraft began its service in the USSR national economy. One of previous chapters of this book devoted to the experience of freight transportation for the national economy by ADB aircraft within the period preceding establishment of Antonov Airlines, describes in detail how in 1969–70 the crews of V. I. Terskii, Y. N. Ketov, Y. V. Kurlin and I. E. Davydov flew the An-22 aircraft to Siberia and to the Soviet Far North, making an invaluable contribution to the development of these remote regions. Soon the baton of their relay race was picked up by military pilots: in January-March 1973 eight military Antaeus aircraft conducted over 100 flights in the Siberian Tyumen region for transportation of industrial cargoes and vehicles. Within 27 flight days, they delivered to customers 4,010 tonnes of various cargoes. In December 1975 the Antonov-22 transported a further 1,920 tonnes to Samotlor region, and the list could be continued. Operation in severe northern conditions proved the high reliability of the Antaeus.

In December 1988 when Armenia was shocked by a destructive earthquake, military An-22s stood vigil round the clock delivering the emergency and first-aid freights (food, medicines, warm clothes, vehicles to remove blockage, etc.) to devastated areas. The high intensity of flights required the maintenance personnel to perform their procedural activities at night, in continuous shifts, in order to ensure the serviceability of the fleet. That December, the An-22 aircraft made 647 flights in total, transported 5,600 tonnes of cargo, 1,636 persons and 161 cranes, presenting a powerful contribution to the amelioration of the consequences of the disaster.

Perfectly controlled by flying and maintenance crews, the Antaeus very soon turned to be a 'fly-by-wire tool of the Kremlin' which could be immediately and effectively used to influence the course of events at any point of the globe. For example, in July 1970 five An-22s accomplished 60 flights to deliver humanitarian aid to the people of Peru after a severe earthquake. Later that year, in December, four An-22 aircraft brought vital freight to several Indian areas suffering from flood. In the spring and in the autumn of 1972, nine Antaeus aircraft delivered military equipment and wheeled vehicles to the United Arab Republic, and brought back three Israeli Centurion tanks captured by the Egyptian troops. One of few instances of passenger

equipment, cargoes, and personnel. "Before the An-12 turbine rumble had time to fade away, the famous 'Antaeus' appeared over the battle field ...

transportation by the Antaeus occurred in Egypt as well. In the autumn of 1972, during evacuation of the Soviet personnel from Egypt, one An-22 aircraft took aboard 700 persons – in fact, as many as Oleg Antonov promised at the Paris Air Show back in 1965.

In October 1973, during the next Arab-Israeli conflict, nine aircraft delivered military equipment and freight to the Middle East. In November 1975, 17 aircraft delivered 1,089 tonnes of cargo to the National Army of Angola. During the time of the Mongolia/China tense relations, in March 1977, 32 An-22 Antaeus aircraft performed 68 flights, having delivered to the border of Mongolia 1,250 tonnes of freights and military vehicles. In November-December of the same year, the An-22 made 18 flights to Ethiopia, having transported 455 tonnes of cargo, including 37 combat vehicles ... The list could be continued extensively, as flights of this kind proceeded up to the beginning of 1990s.

Fulfilment of all these government tasks demanded that An-22 crews acquired a high professionalism and assumed special responsibilities. However, in some cases even more was demanded: the absolute guarantee of accomplishing the task. This occurred when the Antaeus crews were responsible for Leonid Brezhnev's visits to the USA, India, Cuba and Mongolia in 1973–76. Or in 1977, when one of the Soviet nuclear-powered satellites could have fallen in an unknown area. The entire regiment of

the An-22 was kept in operational readiness for the transportation of special equipment intended to counteract possible ground contamination. Fortunately, the special operation did not need to take place. According to TASS information, the satellite burnt out completely in the upper atmosphere layers.

An-22 aircraft of Russian MTA. Early 2000s.

Paratroopers occupying their seats in the An-22 cargo compartment mockup.

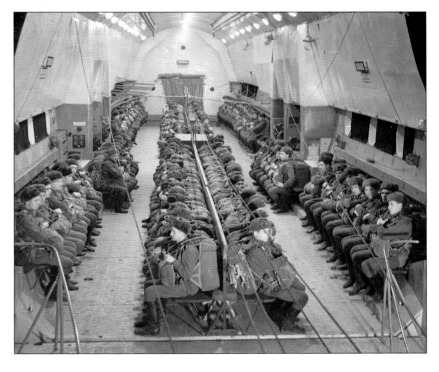

As with other Soviet aircraft, Afghanistan became a special chapter in the Antaeus biography. The An-22 flights to that area began prior to the entry of Soviet troops: on 20 March 1979 in Bagram Airfield five Antaeus aircraft first touched down. During the night of 26–27 December, 52 An-22s in battle formation of groups of five and six aircraft flew to Kabul. Landing and takeoff in the airport of the capital of Afghanistan were performed in difficult conditions. The strip was shaded, no aircraft lights were allowed; at the runway end were just two motor vehicles marking its beginning with their lights. At the landing run, during actuation of reversers a certain delay occurred because of the negative thrust in the air with reduced density. Unloading of personnel and vehicles was conducted with the engines running. Later, the Antaeus made many shuttle voyages, transporting to Afghanistan military equipment of all sorts, including Mi-24 helicopters, various freights, army personnel, and brought back numerous wounded and sick persons.

As with other aircraft, the Antaeus crews had to acquire the experience of takeoff and landing with high gradients. As with the lighter aircraft, the An-22 climbed and descended following an abrupt spiral track, at high angles of roll and pitch, never exceeding the limits of the aerodrome protected zone. However, this piloting demanded a high level of sensitivity and skills from each crew member, the maximum use of the aircraft's stability and controllability reserve, in combination with an absolute reliability of flight and navigation equipment. The Antaeus' mighty body withstood the increased loadings, and none of its flights to Afghanistan ended with substantial damage, the crews returning safe to the bases.

Another milestone in the Antaeus biography, which brought to light its striking transport capabilities, was its application for delivery of the externally attached wing centre section and outer wing for the An-124 Ruslan and An-225 Mriya aircraft; the huge parts were transported from Tashkent, Uzbekistan, to Kyiv, Ukraine, and later on to Ulyanovsk, Russia. Practical implementation of this project was preceded by a massive programme of computation and research activities for comparative analysis of possible ways of transportation by land, water and air. The optimum

This photograph was taken according to a sketch drawn personally by Oleg Antonov in 1966, to show the potential growth of Kyiv aircraft manufacturing capacities.

An-22 Antaeus carrying An-26 and Tu-144 fuselages.

results showed air transportation provided a high degree of manufacturing practicality for delivering the wing components, ensuring their safety and regular delivery. Having started in summer of 1980, these flights proceeded until autumn 1994. Altogether, in 14 years of operation two specially converted An-22 aircraft made over 100 flights, having proved the genuine multifunctionality of the Antaeus.

The chaotic 1990s could not deprive the Antaeus of busy operation. As earlier, the aircraft were involved in the transportation of personnel, combat equipment and material to hot points and trouble spots; however, now not so much out of, but within, the borders of the former USSR. Thus, in 1990, 15 aircraft made 96 flights to Nagorny Karabakh, Chechen region, delivering 821 tonnes of special

cargoes and 915 military personnel. In August 1992 transportation of the contingent of peace-keeping forces to Abkhazia, and evacuation of civilians from there took place. At that time, 2,068 tonnes of freights and 1,390 persons were transported. At the very beginning of the first Chechen conflict, on 11 December 1994, 11 Antaeus aircraft delivered to Mozdok, Beslan and Vladikavkaz 594 tonnes of military cargoes during 36 flights. In the period from 12 January to 31 January 1996, when the Russian Federation performed a operation for the transportation to Bosnia of the Russian peace-makers, the An-22 performed 23 flights.

During the following years, the An-22 accomplished successfully a number of commercial missions. Not only Antonov Airlines, but the aviation

The Ruslan outer wing loaded on the An-22 Antaeus. Tashkent, 1984.

The An-22's first transportation of the An-124 wing center section from Tashkent to Kyiv, 1980.

transport of Russia was involved in the process. For instance, in March-May 1995 they delivered the Su-27 fighters bought by Vietnam to the customer in this country, and in 1997 delivered to Algeria the batch of T-72 tanks which was had been offered to the Algerian army. One Antaeus owned by Antonov StC in 1992 was leased by the Bulgarian Air Sofia airline, and performed flights to many countries under the flag of Bulgaria. In 1997, the An-22 was used to supply the An-140 prototype construction in Kyiv: in February it delivered the prototype wing from Kharkiv, and in September the engines from Zaporizhzha. Later, the Antaeus aircraft which belonged to Antonov StC were extensively employed in the An-140 and An-148 aircraft programmes: They transported some already assembled components for these passenger aircraft from Kharkiv and Voronezh, and from also Kyiv to Iran where they were used to finally produce first aircraft of manufactured locally.

Legally, Antonov Airlines always has been and still remains the sole commercial operator of the An-22 Antaeus. Through the airline the aircraft undergoes permanent upgrades and improvements, and receives new equipment. In particular, in 2006, the aircraft wing panels were reinforced to allow it to keep its lifting capacity at the level of 60 tonnes. The following years the Kyiv-based Antaeus was equipped with new collision avoidance systems, flight data recorders, etc. Today the aircraft complies with the ICAO requirements for long-haul commercial aircraft. In March 2016 the State Aviation Administration of Ukraine issued the An-22 aircraft with Limited Type Certificate No. TL0072.

Other than the Kyiv-based Antaeus, as of the end of 2017, eight more aircraft of this type still remain in operation; all of them are in the Russian military aviation transport. However, only two or three aircraft are kept airworthy. As far as their equipment is concerned, they are well behind the Antonov Airlines' aircraft as they are principally flying in Russia. However, during 2015–2017 several Russian An-22s were repeatedly seen at some Syrian air bases, in particular Khmeimim, where they made flights to support groups of Russian Aerospace Forces in the country. Technically, the An-22s can remain in service until 2024; however their future depends entirely on the will of the Russian Joint Command, and its desire to support them in a proper operating status. Perhaps the biggest problem of these aircraft today is still their propellers' service life. If the problem persists, the flying career of the Antaeus could be terminated prematurely.

Yury Kurlin, the Hero of Soviet Union, and the USSR Test Pilot Emeritus who accumulated over 3,000 hours flying the Antaeus, called it a *"big barge floating in the ocean of the air. It has low speed, high lifting capacity, simplicity of control, off-the-road flying capabilities, being very unpretentious in operation – these are the main features of this aircraft worker."* Fifty years of the An-22 in-service experience have validated the conceptual solutions established in its design. The aircraft is familiar with the aerodromes of more than 100 countries on five continents worldwide. No doubt, this outstanding aircraft will be recorded in the history books as a genuine masterpiece of engineering.

One of the Antaeus aircraft is still operated by Antonov Airlines.

The An-12 belongs to the category of remarkable aircraft. Constructed at the right time, at a good technological level and manufactured *largo manum*, this user-friendly and unpretentious aircraft which is easy to maintain put not only Antonov StC name on the map and made it popular throughout the world, but, together with A. I. Mikoyan's fighters and A. N. Tupolev's passenger airliners, made famous the entire Soviet aircraft industry famous. Most probably, since the mid-1960s, no important event in the history of the USSR and even of all mankind could occur without the An-12's participation. From the development of uninhabited regions and rendering assistance after natural disasters to direct involvement in various military confrontations and revolutions, such was the range of the An-12 operation that it remained along with the Lockheed C-130 the main transport aircraft of the planet for years.

ANTONOV AIRLINES AIRCRAFT
An-12

An-12

Conversation about economy

In the summer of 1955, Nikita Sergeyevich Khrushchev, First secretary of CPSU Central Committee, attended the Antonov Design Bureau *"to make the acquaintance of its workers and engineers"*. Then, the factory was being upgraded: the work for the An-8 aircraft was going successfully; the group of young designers was growing and gaining experience; Oleg Konstantinovich Antonov was full of creative plans. Khrushchev familiarized himself with the An-8 construction in detail. However, his interest was attracted by the aircraft passenger version presented as a wooden full-scale mockup. Its wings, tail, twin-engine power plant and the landing gear looked like typical components of a standard transport, but the fuselage was unusual: circular in the cross-section, pressurized, optimised for transportation of passengers. The honoured guest was curious about the foreign competitors of the project, and the experts mentioned that any similar aircraft of such class had four engines, which meant the tendency to provide higher level of safety for passenger transportation. Nikita Khrushchev agreed that the Soviet aircraft should be powered by four engines too. Probably the idea which brought into life the An-12 aircraft was expressed by Oleg Antonov at that moment.

A four-engine passenger aircraft, as Antonov said, had to be designed so that its baseline platform could be used easily to produce an air transport version. In fact, only one project was needed for two versions differing just in the fuselage tail portion and the airborne equipment. Such an approach allowed the cost and time of design to be drastically reduced, expedited preproduction and the series manufacturing of the aircraft, facilitated training of pilots and maintenance personnel, and simplified operation. In addition, passenger aircraft equipped with the landing gear of the airlifter could be operated within an expanded network of aerodromes, including unprepared

An-12 is working hard for more than sixty years

and unequipped airfields, mixing the security of the centre of operations with circumferential air routes. And finally, in case of the war, they could be immediately converted into military cargo aircraft by replacing the civil tail unit with a military one.

Khrushchev never remained indifferent to an idea that promised so many advantages. Recalling his meeting with Antonov, he stressed: *"This designer spoke to me about economy."* Such a conversation seemed to be an extraordinary event in those years, therefore it impressed the First Secretary greatly. Soon after, pursuant to the Decree of the USSR Council of Ministers dated 30 November 1955, the creation of the An-10 and An-12 aircraft twins was started. The above-mentioned document included more tasks: chief designers N. D. Kuznetsov and A. G. Ivchenko had to design the NK-4 and AI-20 turboprop engines, while S. V.Ilyushin had to equip his new Il-18 passenger aircraft with those engines. Actually, it was the first time in USSR post-war history when a competition for the best passenger aircraft design

had been announced. Each contestant held his own 'ace': in the case of the Ilushin-18, profitability in the operation of long-haul airlines, in the case of the An-10, a broad network of aerodromes and the military cargo aircraft version.

Appearance of the twins

Oleg Antonov commenced designing the An-10/12 enthusiastically. Apart of his purely professional interest in such a non-standard aircraft concept, he wished to break the monopoly of Tupolev and Ilyushin for passenger aircraft, making his own trademark name known to millions of future air travellers. No doubt, moving away from their main trend of concern towards passenger transport specialisation was met with little enthusiasm among his closest colleagues, however Antonov's creative energy and excitmennt carried along the entire Design Bureau team after a while.

By then the company already numbered 1,500

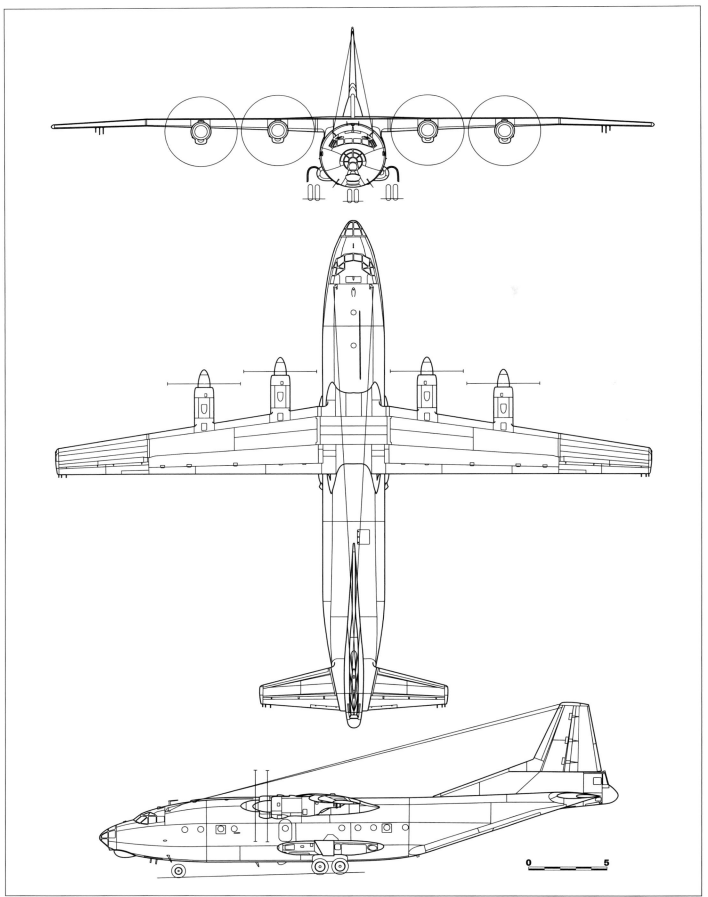

0 _____ 5

employees, including some 250 designers, mainly recent graduates from universities. In order to assist them in assimilating the complex science of aeronautical engineering, special groups had been formed which were forwarded to the aircraft factories of Kazan and Moscow (Factory No. 30). Under Tupolev and Ilyushin's kind permission, the young specialists made their acquaintance with the engineering specifications of the Tu-16 and Il-28 aircraft, and adopted the best and the most rational design solutions. For their studies, several volumes of structure analysis and strength calculations for these aircraft were received. That is why many of the future An-8 and An-10/12 aircraft parts were so similar to their counterparts designed by the Moscow design bureaus, and in the end a single school of the USSR aircraft design was established.

N. S. Trunchenkov was nominated the An-10 leading designer; the same position for the An-12 project was held by V. N. Gelprin. The General View Team was headed by N. A. Nechayev, the Fuselage Team by S. D.Yelmesiev, the Wing Team by A. A. Batumov and the Landing Gear Team by N. P. Smirnov. Hydraulics was the domain of A. N. Kondratyev, electrical power systems designed by M. S. Galperin, radio systems by V. A. Danilchenko. All the equipment/furnishings, including the seats had to be designed by the Design Bureau as well, and for this purpose a special team under the supervision of N. A. Pogorelov was nominated. Oleg Antonov personally took part in both solving the main problems of the aircraft general layout, and in designing many units. Having a well-developed sensitivity to arts, Antonov paid much attention to the passenger cabin interior designs where he widely used some Ukrainian national motifs.

Residence of the Design Bureau in the territory of Ukraine had another consequence, much more important for the fate of the An-10/12 aircraft. The company's geographical position played an active role in the choice of engines. The options included the N -4 advanced engine of 4,000 ehp, with high specific performance characteristics, and the AI-20, the engine of the same power, which was probably not so refined although designed on the basis of a well-tested design approach. Due to Ivchenko's reasonable conservatism, his AI-20 exceeded the Kuznetsov's product in both reliability and operating

safety. The Antonov team was split between the supporters and opponents of each engine. Being not sure which to choose, Oleg Konstantinovich Antonov made the following decision: to equip the An-10 prototype with the N -4 engine, and the An-12 prototype with the I-20 engine. Strangely, but the problem was finally solved by the Central Committee of Communist Party of Ukraine. They had a simple judgement: as soon as the aircraft was built in

The An-10 and An-12 aircraft-twins in Kyiv-Zhuliany airport

Ukraine, its engine should be also of Ukrainian origin. That was why the AI-20 engine was given a start in its long and glorious life.

Apart from the engine choice issue, no other serious problems arose during the aircraft design. The common configuration, same structural layout and airborne utility equipment of the 'twins' had been thoroughly tried on the An-8. Recent photographs of the C-130 aircraft, which had appeared in the newspapers, justified the solutions adopted. The An-10 prototype (bearing the factory index 'U', i.e. 'Ukraine') constructed in Kyiv made its first flight on 7 March 1957. The An-12T (Transport

An-12 assembly line at Irkutsk aircraft factory, 1957.

An-12BK main performance data			
Aircraft overall external dimensions, m		**Max payload, tons**	20
– length x wing span x height	33.1 x 38.0 x 10.5	**Cruising speed, km/h**	600
Cargo compartment dimensions,m		**Cruising altitude, m**	10,500
– length x width x height	13.5 x 3.12 x 2.5	**Practical range with 20-ton cargo, km**	300
Engines:		**Max range, km**	6,300
– type	AI-20	**Airfield length, m**	1,200
– number x power, e.h.p.	4 x 4,000	**Crew**	5

Second An-12 prototype under test.

An-12 ready for testing with ski landing gear with an An-10 in the background.

version) detail design was finished in 11 months; its construction at the Irkutsk aircraft factory No. 90 took one and a half years. Thanks to its similarity to the 'tenth model', the An-12 had no prototype at all: the aircraft No. 1 initiated its serial production.

Construction of the An-12 resulted in the award of the Lenin Prize of USSR to O. K. Antonov and the leading designers: A. J. Belolipetskii, V. N. Gelprin, E. K. Senchuk and E. A. Shakhatuni.

Unity and conflict of opposites

Despite the passenger version priority, the An-10/12 general arrangement, overall dimensions, fuselage cross section, parameters of the wing, tail, and landing gear were determined on the basis of the aircraft's military functions. The aircraft design presupposed manufacturability of both versions on the same production line (thanks to wide unification of parts

and assemblies) and conversion of one version to other was originally planned whenever necessary (due to the available production breaks). For the airframe main assemblies the first serial aircraft commonality factor reached 86%, and 100% for the power plant.

However, advancing to such, generally speaking, laudable standards caused obvious absurdities in some cases. For instance, the An-12 early series aircraft had their middle fuselage of pressurized design (as in the An-10) and the non-pressurized tails. In its turn, the An-10, due to the same (as in the cargo version) arrangement of its floor, had a redundant passenger compartment volume and an apparent deficiency of space for baggage. All this could have easily been ignored if such an approach did not result in the aircraft weight increasing, especially in case of the An-10. Deterioration of its load-to-takeoff weight ratio in comparison with the Il-18 was notable, and Ilyushin mentioned it repeatedly considering the entire An-10/12 concept as erroneous and fallacious.

Nonetheless, Antonov quite consciously accepted some weight default, considering it as a acceptable pay-off for the above mentioned benefits. From the present-day point of view such a standpoint would be out of the question, however in those days the country had plenty of aviation fuel in stock, and the only driver for any project was to accelerate progress, therefore the An-10/12 concept looked rather attractive and even reasonable economically. After all, it allowed a powerful military airlifting potential to be built up by making passenger aircraft!

However, often the practical implementation of attractive ideas looks very different to the theoretical reasoning. The different dedicated equipment of the two aircraft, the gradual updating of their versions and the use of different manufacturers resulted in the fact that in the course of batch production, the An-10 and the An-12 were becoming more and more dissimilar structurally. Thus, after production of approximately 100 aircraft, the An-12 middle fuselage section became non-pressurized. Then, the wing panels reinforcement followed, flap hinge-fitting systems were changed, and so on. These distinctions between the aircraft increased and varied, and soon special proof was required to confirm the practical implementation of the initial idea of the An-10's transformation into the An-12. To demonstrate that it was still possible, the Voronezh aircraft factory converted at least one aircraft quite successfully. However by this time, the Antonov-Tweve had already transformed into an individual aircraft type, and developed completely independently, in line with its main purpose.

Road to the sky

On 16 December 1957, at half past two, in the presence of personnel of the Irkutsk factory No. 90, the An-12 flight crew including the Hero of Soviet

Union Y. I. Vernikov (pilot-in-command, LII test pilot), G. I. Lysenko (co-pilot, transferred to the Design Bureau from the GVF Scientific Research Institute of Civil Aviation), P. I. Uvarov (navigator), I. M. Morozov (flight engineer), M. G. Yurov (radio engineer) and V .G. Zhilkin (gunner) lifted the aircraft S/N 7900101 into the sky for the first time. The aircraft lifted off a little bit earlier than planned. Following retraction of flaps and reduction of engine power to the rated value the aircraft started climbing. The landing gear was not retracted. Suddenly, the pilots felt the vibration of the fuselage nose, and Vernikov made a decision to abort the flight. Having stayed in the air for 9 minutes, and having attained the altitude of 880 metres and the speed of 340 km/h, the An-12 wheels successfully touched the ground.

Soon, the experts discovered that the aircraft nose vibration had been caused by the non-closed nosewheel door. That shaking was of no hazard, but Vernikov, who had been nominated for the pilot-in-command position just a few days before the flight and had no time to study the aircraft in detail, had shown

An-12 prepared for flight to Antarctica. (In the foreground: Oleg Antonov, in a light coat).

Adoption of the An-12 brought the Military Airlift capabilities to a qualitatively new and higher level.

275

In early 1960s An-12 deliveries to civil aviation began.

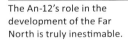

The An-12's role in the development of the Far North is truly inestimable.

control levers positioned to Flight Idle. Following throttle transfer to Ground Idle, the resultant negative thrust forced the aircraft to descend too fast. Therefore, piloting at landing was difficult, followed by a rough touchdown. During the sixth flight, the abrupt altering of the throttles at the stage of flareout caused one throttle to jam. The Twelfth dipped its wing so severely that it touched the ground, then the aircraft rolled to the opposite side and overran the runway. The test was interrupted while a new landing technique was prepared (the inboard engine controls in the Ground Idle position, the outboard engine set at the Flight Idle).

Furthermore, those tests revealed the unfavourable combination of the aircraft's lateral and longitudinal stability degrees, the improvement of which required a change in the dihedral and the replacement of the outboard wing. During the first flight, when the cargo door was opened, fuselage deformation occurred due to air loads and the door panels could not be locked. The aircraft landed with the cargo door open. Later, the fuselage cut-out zone was reinforced.

sensible care. So, to avoid repetition of this kind of trouble, the door mount was seriously reinforced. Starting with flight number two, G. I. Lysenko was appointed the leading pilot for the factory tests.

The An-12's strong and weak features were discovered during the initial flights. Pilots noted its unusually high power-to-weight peculiarity and lift-to-drag ratio which then seemed enormous. Because of its sharp takeoff, the unloaded test aircraft often failed to attain the desired angle of takeoff in time, therefore liftoffs occurred at an increased speed. In view of the powerful torque reaction of four counter-rotating propellers, the right landing gear strut was loaded more than the left one, and the aircraft taking-off showed a tendency to turn to the right. It was not possible to counteract this effect with the brakes because of the narrow wheel track. The defect was corrected only through the installation of the pedal-controlled nose landing gear steering mechanism on the aircraft that followed.

The An-12 manifested rigidity on landing as well, being reluctant to touch down with the throttle

In eight months, the An-12 had completed the programme of factory tests (more than a year had been required for equivalent testing of the An-8 aircraft, and even two years for the An-10), accomplished flights with the maximum drag and demonstrated landing with one and two engines inoperative. Already three prototype aircraft were flying by the end of trials in August, 1958. In parallel, flight crews were retrained to control the new aircraft. On one occasion, the factory pilot Yeliferov, trying to keep the aircraft's straight motion at takeoff on the ground run abruptly braked the left landing gear wheels. The aircraft was wrapped in smoke, two pops sounded, and numerous pieces of rubber flew all over the place. Nonetheless, the An-12 took off. At landing, the pilot braked again, and two more shots sounded. All four wheels were

An-12 tested on a sodden airfield.

torn off. The leaning aircraft roared over the runway pavement on its wheel hubs.

Another funny situation occurred when the aircraft was commanded by the pilot Petrov. Having retracted the landing gear with the left hydraulic system, he forgot to position the valve in neutral. Yeliferov who was co-pilot, at approach set the valve of the right hydraulic system for the undercarriage extension, but also forgot to return it into the neutral position. A fight of two hydraulic systems started: bypass and relief valves shot, pipelines vibrated, landing gear struts convulsed. The right-side system won, and the landing gear extended. However, as soon as the aircraft touched the ground, the left system started retraction. Fortunately, this was the time when both pilots were paying attention to the position of the valves, and they succeeded in correcting the error. The An-12 stopped with its legs semibent.

At the end of August 1958, the first An-12 was ferried to the Tretyakovov aerodrome near Moscow. Although the flight from Irkutsk was performed at the altitude of 9–10,000 metres, all airport chiefs along the route knew that the new aircraft was in the air. Manifesting excessive curiosity, they distracted the crew on the radio, and Lysenko had to repel their approaches politely but resolutely. Moreover, somewhere near Gorky, the An-12 was surrounded by a group of fighters.

Soon the An-12 arrived at the Frunze Central aerodrome in the middle of Moscow, for the demonstration to the top brass. When landing, due to the uncoordinated actions of a mixed crew (G. I. Lysenko was the pilot-in-command, and the right seat was occupied by one of the Irkutsk factory pilots), the aircraft bounced roughly, turned 90 degrees, touched the ground with the right engine propellers and came to stop. The right landing gear was destroyed.

To continue testing, another An-12 (serial No. 8900102) was delivered from Irkutsk to Moscow/ Ramenskoye. For the first time a heavy aircraft was used to research stalled performance, and it was proved that there was a time gap between the beginning of the stall to the involuntary entry

An-12 Cyclone weather reconnaissance aircraft.

'Tanker' flying water-spraying laboratory.

into spin, and this time may be used by the crew (and must be used) to take adequate measures to prevent crashing. Today such a test is mandatory for all aircraft.

At the end of 1958, the An-12 arrived for State Tests at the Moscow Air Force Scientific Research Institute (NII VVS), but the programme was still part-conducted in Kyiv. Starting in October 1959 and until April 1960, personnel and cargo air delivery procedures were tried and worked out. Except for Lysenko, the aircraft flight crews were headed by Y. V. Kurlin and I. E. Davidov.

Production and modifications

In the USSR, the An-12 was serially produced at three aircraft factories in:

- Irkutsk – 155 aircraft built during 1957–1962;
- Voronezh – 258 aircraft built during 1960–1965;
- Tashkent – 830 aircraft built during 1962–1972.

Flying laboratory – ejection seats test bench.

Of the total aircraft built, 183 were directly supplied from the USSR to 14 countries: India, Bulgaria, Indonesia, Iraq, Poland, Czechoslovakia, Egypt, Yugoslavia, Algeria, Guinea, Ghana, Cuba, China and Yemen. At least 11 other countries purchased the An-12s second-hand and third-hand.

In the course of production and operation, the aircraft went through a series of modifications featuring these differences from the baseline model:

An-12A (1961): AI-20A engines (4,000 ehp) installed, as well as four additional flexible fuel tanks in the wing in the vicinity of the engines (with the total tank capacity brought up to 16,600 litres). Cargo capacity increased to 20.

An-12B (1963): Integral fuel tanks made in the outer wings (with the total tank capacity brought up to 19,500 litres). TG-16 turbogenerator installed in the left landing gear fairing to provide for in-flight engine restart and supply of power to the aircraft system up to 1,000 m altitude. A flight engineer station added. Loading/unloading equipment upgraded.

MiG-19 fighter re-fuelling from the An-12BKT tanker aircraft.

An-12P/AP/BP (1963–89): Fuel tanks with a total capacity of 9,830 litres installed under the cargo cabin floor.

An-12BK (1967): AI-20M (4,250 ehp) engine installed, equipment suite upgraded. Cargo door opening increased to 105 mm at sill. TG-16 turbogenerator replaced with the TG-16M enabling engine restart up to 3,000 m altitude. Remote-controlled GL-1500DP winches, beam cranes with lifting capacity of 2,300 kg and cargo loading bridges/seats installed.

Furthermore, regardless of the production version, the An-12's flight/navigation, radio communication and special-purpose equipment was continually improved.

It emerged in the course of service, that the An-12 was suited to a much wider range of missions than initially expected. In view of this, in addition to the above-mentioned main versions, the An-12 was re-equipped into at least 27 more special-purpose modifications, including:

An-12UD/UD-3 (1960): extended-range An-12 version with two/three additional fuel tanks (4,000 litres each) in the cargo cabin.

An-12PL (1961): polar An-12 with non-retractable ski landing gear with air heating of frozen skis to move the aircraft off from rest. Two aircraft were built.

An-12T (1961): tanker aircraft, intended to carry aircraft and motor fuels, rocket propellants and oxidizing compounds in reservoirs installed in the cargo cabin.

An-12BM (1962): An-12B version for investigation of the long-range radio communication via the Molniya-1 satellite. Four radio equipment operators were accommodated in the cargo attendants' compartment. One aircraft was re-equipped into this configuration.

An-12BK (1963): search and rescue An-12BK version equipped with Istok-Golub direction-finding equipment for location of working UHF radio stations.

An-12B-I (1964): a version of the An-12B equipped with Fasol individual radio counter-measures station. Seven aircraft built.

Search-and-rescue An-12BK escorted by a Norwegian F-104G.

Soviet An-12PP jammer
aircraft in the livery of Syrian
Air Forces.

An-12BP (1968–69): radioactive atmosphere contamination reconnaissance aircraft.

An-12BKV (1969): bomber and minelayer aircraft equipped with a fixed conveyor for release of 12-tonne bombs.

An-12B Cubrik (1969): aircraft equipped with a set of equipment for investigation of infrared radiation of overwater, ground and air targets and for the testing of infrared equipment units.

An-12PS (1969): aeronautical marine search and rescue system based on the An-12B. Intended for search and evacuation of astronauts after ditching and for rescue of seamen in distress. The aircraft carries and delivers the Type 03473 rescue boat with a crew of three to the rescue water area.

An-12BSh and **An-12BKSh** (1970): navigator training versions of the An-12B and An-12BK for group training (10 stations in the cargo compartment) of trainee navigators for the Military Airlift Forces.

An-12BL (1970): experimental aircraft based on the An-12B and equipped with X-28 anti-radar missile system to reduce losses when penetrating hostile air defence.

An-12BK-IS (1970): An-12BK equipped as a version of the An-12B with the *Fasol* and *Siren* individual radio counter-measures facilities accommodated in four pods on external stores. Forty-five aircraft re-equipped.

An-12PP (1970): An-12B/12BK group defence jammer version. Equipped with automatic spot and barrage jammers for active and passive jamming of enemy missile guidance radars. Equipped with special radiation-absorbing means of biological shielding for crew protection against ionizing radiation. 27 aircraft built.

An-12BK-PPS (1971): group defence jammer version of the An-12PP. Differs from the An-12PP in the *Siren* repeater jammer additionally installed in external pods. 19 aircraft built.

An-12BK-PPS (1974): improved effectiveness group defence jammer version of the An-12BK. Differs from the An-12BK-PPS (1971) in the improved mission equipment (including automatic infrared jammer). The jammer aircraft make it possible to mask the direction of flight, composition and formation of the military airlift squadrons; jam the operating radars of air defence missile systems, fighter aircraft, missile target seekers (infrared inclusive), radio and radio link communication networks of the enemy.

An-12BK-IS (1974): the An-12BK equipped with Barrier and Siren individual radar protection facilities and automatic IR jammer. 105 aircraft re-equipped.

An-12M (1972): AI-20DM engine (5,180 ehp) with AV-68DM (4.7 m) propeller installed. Flight performance improved. One aircraft re-equipped.

An-12 version for MCA (Ministry of Civil Aviation) (1959–1972): Civil aircraft without

Y-8A – a Chinese replica of the An-12.

Air bombs on the An-12BKV bomber conveyor.

weapons (sometimes with a tail cabin) and air delivery system equipment. RBP-3 radar replaced with PO3-1 ground mapping radar. On some of the aircraft, the gunner cabin was replaced with a compartment with 16 extra storage batteries.

An-12BKT (1972): refueller for the front-line aviation aircraft. Volume of fuel that can be transferred: 19,500 l. Two fighters can be simultaneously refuelled on the ground.

An-12B (1972): laboratory for metrological calibration of regimental test and measurement equipment.

An-12B (1972): laboratory for flight accident investigation activities; the aircraft has a laboratory compartment and additional furnishings. One aircraft re-equipped.

An-12BSM (1973): civilian (MCA) version for transportation of containers. Equipped with two crane beams with a total lifting capacity of 5,000 kg, roller tracks and guides. Special flooring is installed between frames 34 and 43 for floor levelling. The aircraft carries eight type PA-2.5 pallets, or eight UAK-2.5 containers, or four PA-5.6 pallets, or four UAK-5A containers.

An-12BKK Capsula (1975): Military Airlift Aviation commander's lounge version. Equipped with pressurized cabin (capsule). One aircraft re-equipped.

An-12BKTs Cyclone (1979): laboratory based on the An-12BK for investigation of meteorological processes. Equipped with measurement and computing facilities and means for treatment of clouds. Two aircraft re-equipped.

In addition, the An-12s were widely used as flying laboratories in a wide range of scientific and research missions. At least 10 such laboratories were built, including the aircraft for:
• testing the AI-24 engine with AV-72 propellers for the An-24 (1959);
• development and final adjustment of the landing system for descent vehicles of spacecraft (1960);
• development and final adjustment of the Polyot-1 air navigation system and Kupol cargo delivery system for the An-22 and Il-76 aircraft (1961);
• investigations of aero photographic cameras and optoelectronic aerial reconnaissance systems (1965);
• testing of the Prostor thermal imager for generation thermal maps of terrain and fire maps (1968–71);
• investigation of missile launch detectors, laser illumination detectors and signal intelligence facilities (1971);
• testing of the new ejection seats, including those installed in the prototype tail cabin and allowing ejection at any angle relative to the horizon using various means, jet propulsion inclusive (in the 1970s);

Mockup of the An-40 designed as further development of the An-12. 1964.

• generation of artificial icing (Tanker, 1981);
• testing of the new facilities for location of submarines (in 1980s).

It was this operational flexibility that made the An-12 popular and one of the most successful of the Soviet aircraft.

A version of the An-12 designated Y-8 was also manufactured in China by Shaanxi Aircraft Company. This aircraft was created by copying the An-12BK, which had been purchased by the Chinese earlier, without any consultation with the Soviet side. The

Y-8 made its first flight on 25 December 1974. It was produced in several modifications: civil transport version, military airlifter, maritime patrol, unmanned air vehicle carrier, airborne early-warning station versions, versions for transportation of helicopters and animals, a version with pressurized fuselage, etc. A total of about 170 aircraft were constructed. Recently, the Y-8 has undergone a period of intensive upgrading, the Chinese specialists involving the participation of the world's leading manufacturers of transport aircraft – Lockheed Martin (Y-8-100 and Y-8F-200 versions) and also Antonov and Pratt &Whitney Canada (Y-8F-600 version).

Adopted by the armed forces

The An-12s started entering service in 1959. They were first adopted by two regiments of the 12th Tula Military Airlift Division of the Guards, which was charged with the performance of army testing and development of the approach to new aircraft employment. Colonels N. G. Tarasov and A. E. Yeremenko, commanders of these units, working in close contact with representatives of the Design Bureau, handled the mission brilliantly. Under their command, large formations of the An-12s were ferried from their home bases in Novgorod and Seshcha to regions with varying climatic conditions (Moldavia, Central Asia, Far North, Far East), landing on minimally-prepared unpaved airfields, and were used to optimize aerial and airlanded delivery procedures.

As and when the 'Twelves' were mastered by their flying crews, they began to be operated in the interests of the army and the economy. Thus,

Aerial delivery mission.

in order to alleviate the negative after-effects of Penkovky's treason, a squadron of 35 Antonov aircraft commanded by M. M. Gamaris flew for several months in areas beyond the Arctic Circle on troop redeployment missions. When the need arose for express delivery of the eight-tonne building compressors from Krasnoyarsk to Norilsk, the An-12 was used for the mission. The aircraft payload at the time was limited to 12 tonnes; however, the squadron commander Lieutenant-Colonel Sharafutdinov took the initiative and ordered two compressors to be loaded aboard. The flight went on well, and the An-12's permissible load was increased to 16 tonnes.

This occurrence demonstrated that the An-12 gained the confidence of crews from the outset of its service. Reliability, the ability to operate in adverse climatic conditions and maintenance simplicity became, for years to come, the aircraft's 'stock-in-trade'. Its popularity grew, as well as the rate of serial production. Simultaneously with the Tula Division, the An-12s were adopted by the 3rd Vitebsk Military Airlift Division of the Guards, and later by other military units.

The An-12 became the aircraft that made the air-transported troops of the USSR a powerful tool of the country's geopolitical influence. The Soviet Union also acquired the ability to promptly respond to events happening around the planet: helping the victims of natural calamities, supporting national liberation movements, etc. Expressing his gratitude to the Antonov team, army general V. F. Margelov, Commander, petitioned in 1977 for the team to be awarded the honorary title of the 'Communist Labour Collective'.

Assault capabilities of the Air-Transported Troops grew considerably after the troops mastered, in addition to air-drop delivery of personnel (up to 60 paratroopers from one An-12), the paradropping of armoured self-propelled vehicles, which, for reasons of safety, were dropped on parachute platforms separately from the crew. General Margelov, who considered the parachute reliability to be sufficient and was literally in love with the An-12, was not at all happy with the latter fact. Striving to prove the feasibility of paradropping people inside combat vehicles in principle, he decided to take the jump personally. However, Minister of Defence Malinovskii flatly denied the general permission to jump. Then the jump was accomplished by his son, A. V. Margelov, who later became an ATT colonel. The experiment was a total success.

The initial period of service uncovered not only the An-12's merits, but also a number of 'childhood diseases'. Working on their elimination and trying to meet customer requirements, the Antonov specialists were developing new versions of the aircraft. The principal areas of this work involved extension of the flight range, improving operating

self-sufficiency, and development of a number of special-purpose modifications. A lot of attention was paid to improving the aircraft's reliability. In time, the number of flight accidents related to deficiencies in design and manufacturing decreased to 10–12%.

Yet, even when the equipment failed, pilots often managed to complete the flight safely. In 1961, a crew commanded by Gamaris was flight testing an An-12 intended for delivery to India. In the course of approach, a warning of failure to extend the right landing gear was received. It was night-time. The pilot in command flew the aircraft over the control tower. The light of a floodlight from the ground enabled the crew to see that the landing gear strut was jammed in semi-extended position. Having climbed to 3,000 m and flying in circles the crew proceeded to the recommended emergency procedures. The ground personnel also stayed alert: within an hour they woke up the entire engineering support service, and found V. V. Filippov, Military Airlift Chief Engineer, in a theatre. Filippov contacted Oleg Antonov, and they

Armoured personnel carrier loaded into the An-12

The An-12 aircraft in Kabul airport, 1980

In 1966, the An-12s opened Aeroflot's first international cargo air line between Moscow and Paris

An-12 cargo cabin.

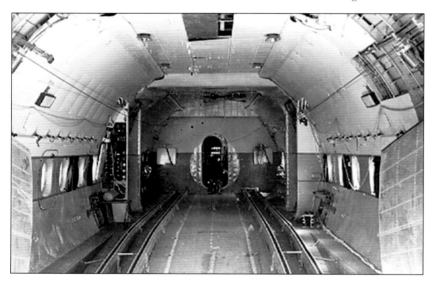

An-12BK loaded from truck body

made a joint decision: if the strut failed to extend the aircraft should land on a unpaved surface with the landing gear up. However, the crew wanted to save the aircraft intended for export, therefore, they used a crash-axe and crowbar to cut through the floor in the area of the landing gear compartment. The flight engineer, with rope tied around the waist, crawled through the cut-out area and attached an air delivery system cable to the strut. The other end of the cable was tied to a winch, and thus the stut was forced to the extended position. The young officer was decorated with the 'Red Star' order for this deed, and having a crowbar aboard became a good tradition among the An-12 crews.

Wide-scale aircraft operations also brought about instance when people made mistakes while the aircraft demonstrated its best qualities. In November 1988, an completely uncontrolled military An-12 had been flying at the altitude of 8,000 m for an hour and a half in the airspace between Chelyabinsk and Ufa. Six crew members of the aircraft were unconscious due to oxygen deficiency caused by an improperly closed emergency exit door. The aircraft was veering and changing flight levels at random, yet all of the three civil aviation ATC control centres and three anti-aircraft defence posts in whose radar field the aircraft was flying ignored the situation. These services only responded when the radio transmitted the co-pilot's desperate cry: *"Where are we?!"*

The military airlift units that had adopted and mastered the An-12 were occasionally used by the Soviet government to deliver humanitarian aid and other cargoes to different parts of the globe. In such cases, the aircraft, as a rule, had civilian registration marks and the crews wore civvies. When a disastrous earthquake struck in Peru in 1970, the aircraft of the 3rd Division of the Guards were urgently repainted in Aeroflot colours, even though this delicate operation had to be performed in the rain and night-time. A group of 35 aircraft headed by divisional commander Major General N. F. Zaitsev flew from Moscow to Lima (with landings in Iceland, Canada, Cuba and Columbia) loaded with medicines and food supplies. However, it was an open secret that the aircraft belonged to the military. One of the local newspapers published a photograph of Zaitsev in uniform. Because of burn scars on his face and the low print quality the picture looked scary. And the caption read: *"The most ferocious general arriving in Peru from Russia"*.

The An-12 became a true 'workhorse' for Soviet military specialists many long years. At the same time, it remained a sufficiently up-to-date and competitive aircraft. In 1991–92, i.e. 30 years after the An-12's first flight, Russian military pilots of the Air Force Research Institute (NII VVS) set 39 world records of flight speed and altitude on the aircraft.

Half a century in combat

Because its merits, and also the USSR policy of rendering assistance to numerous friendly regimes, the An-12 found itself in the front line of the 'fight

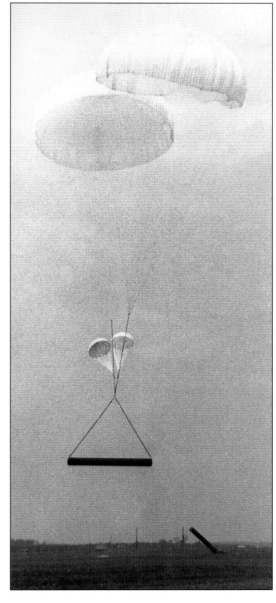

Experimental airdropping of large-diameter pipes from high altitude, 1966

for the better future' and took part in a multitude of conflicts and wars. Probably the An-12's first combat experience was in India. In October 1962, during armed conflict over disputed territories near the Chinese-Indian border in the Himalayas, Chinese troops surrounded several Indian high-mountain base stations. Military transport aircraft, including the An-12, were used to deliver ammunition and supplies to these stations. A considerable part of the delivered stores was paradropped, with the losses of the freight amounting to 5% only (and this was in the mountains!). The rest was delivered to the nearby air bases and then carried by light aircraft to the mountain air strips. There was no counteraction on the part of Chinese air forces and no An-12 losses were reported.

During December 1965–January 1966, in the course of conflict with Pakistan in Kashmir, the Indian An-12s were involved in the transportation of troops and cargoes to the combat area and evacuation of casualties. It was as early as 1971 during the war with Pakistan that the Indians considerably 'diversified' the aircraft's combat employment. Thus, on 12 January the An-12s, together with the -119, dropped an assault party in the vicinity of Dacca in Eastern Pakistan (later the capital of Bangladesh) of a battalion that cut the routes of supply of the city's garrison. At the same time, the An-12s were used as night bombers. Several night-time raids of targets in Western Pakistan were been reported, during which up to 16 (!) tonnes of air bombs were taken aboard. One of the An-12s was intercepted by a Mirage, but managed to escape. None of the An-12s was destroyed by the enemy.

The combat history of the Indian 'Twelves' continued to the turn of 1980s and 90s, when the country was involved in the war against the forces

Experimental airdropping
of pipes from low altitude,
1966

An-12s assaulted on the ground. In the October war of 1973 the Egyptian An-12s performed only transportation missions, also carrying weapons from the USSR. The UN troops were also transported to the region by Egyptian Antonovs, while Polish contingent was brought in by their own An-12.

The Iraqi An-12s did a lot of different jobs: transportation in the course of incessant fights with the Kurds in 1960–70s, fetching weapons from other countries during the war against Iran in 1980–1988, maritime reconnaissance and refuelling missions. The An-12s, having detected enemy ships in the Persian Gulf, guided the F.1 Mirages and MiG-23BNs equipped for in-flight refuelling to their locations. Thus, on 12 August 1986, several Mirages, having refuelled their tanks from the An-12s, dealt a strike against oil facilities on the Tirri Island and three Iranian ships. No flights of Iraqi An-12s have been recorded during the 'Desert Storm' operation. None of these aircraft were flown to Iran either. Nevertheless, two of them were destroyed on the ground by laser-guided bombs during the assault of British Buccaneers on 27 February 1992.

The An-12 performed a considerable number of combat missions on the African continent. In Sudan, the government air forces used the aircraft in the civil war in the south of the country during the 1970s. In Algeria, in the mid-1980s the An-12s took part in the conflict between government forces and detachments of the Polisario Front. During the period between 1975 through to the end of the 1980s, Cuban and Soviet An-12s delivered military cargoes to Angola. During the critical days of autumn 1975, a couple of An-12s brought in ammunition and instructors from Cuba that made it possible to frustrate the South African offensive on Luanda. While carrying cargoes inside the country, the An-12 often came under fire from the Unita forces, but there were no aircraft losses. The An-12s of Ethiopian air forces were used to repel the Somali aggression in 1977, as well as being deployed against the separatists of Eritrea (which was at the time an Ethiopian province), and in a number of interior provinces of the country. On 18 January 1984 one An-12 was destroyed on the ground during shelling of the government aerodrome by Eritreans.

Unfortunately, armed conflicts in Africa continued in the 21st century, resulting in the continued employment of the An-12 on the continent. Thus, during the war in Congo in early 2000s, these aircraft, belonging for the most part to Ukrainian commercial carriers, were transporting weapons, ammunition and other cargoes in the interests of the fighting parties and carrying groups of militants.

For a long time the An-12s were the basis of the fleet of military transport aircraft of the Warsaw Treaty countries. The aircraft played an important part in a number of large-scale joint military exercises of

of the 'Liberation Tigers of Tamil Eelam' in the northern part of Sri Lanka. The An-12s were used for transportation and, due to the poor air defence of the 'Tigers', suffered no losses. The Sri Lankan Air Forces also had two Y-8s that were used for patrolling the Palk Strait where the 'Tigers' were ferrying weapons, ammunition and people. Detecting trespassers, the crews called up border patrol boats.

During the period of 1962–67, Egyptian troops took part in the civil war in Yemen. Supplies were delivered to the troops by the An-12s – both Egyptian and Soviet. In the course of the 'Six-Day War' with Israel, on 6 June 1967, Egyptians lost at least eight

the Pact countries. During the 'Dvina' maneuvers, for example, about 200 An-12s dropped 8,000 paratroopers with combat vehicles in just 22 minutes.

The combat biography of the Soviet An-12s started with the delivery of military aid to numerous 'friends of the USSR', and this was often delivered directly to the area of hostilities. Thus, after the 'Six-Day War' ended, during the summer and autumn of 1967, the Soviet An-12s and An-22s delivered combat MiG-17s, MiG-21s and Su-7s to Syria and Egypt (up to 150 aircraft all in all, according to some sources). During the 1973 war, under the conditions of threat from Israeli fighters, the An-12s again took part in the air bridge operation carrying aircraft and tanks to the Middle East. A squadron of An-12PPs based at Siauliai (Lithuania) bearing Arab markings covered the air raid of Syrian assault aircraft against the Israeli 'Hawk' anti-aircraft missile systems. During the civil war in Nigeria in 1967–70, the country's government also purchased combat aircraft from the USSR. In 86 flights the Soviet An-12s delivered to that country 41 MiG-17s, four MiG-15UTI with required spares.

The An-12s played an important part in the Warsaw Pact invasion of Czechoslovakia in August 1968 to put down the 'Prague Spring'. The first aircraft with paratroopers landed in Prague Ruzyne airport and, after having captured the airport with lightning speed, the troops flooded the capital. The entire advance guard of the Soviet troops, including combat and transport vehicles, was delivered to Prague aboard the An-12s. The Czechoslovak army put up no resistance, and there were no aircraft losses.

Perhaps it was in Afghanistan that the An-12s were used on the widest scale. Both Soviet and Afghan pilots flew the aircraft. The principal missions were the deliveries of people and cargoes from the USSR and back and transportations inside the country. The notorious 'Black Tulip' – the aircraft that ferried the fallen troops from Afghanistan – was also an An-12. The An-12s proved indispensable in the Afghan conditions: unlike the Il-76 they could land on unpaved high-elevation airfields. Survivability was another important quality that proved itself in Afghanistan. The press often described occurrences when the An-12s with hundreds of bullet holes caused by enemy fire on airfields and with damaged systems and wounded crew members took off successfully and reached their destinations.

Losses of the An-12s in that war were connected with the use of Stinger portable air defence systems. The Stingers helped Mojahedins to shoot down several An-12s: on 30 September 1980 (45 people killed), 25 April 1983, 11 November 1984, and, it is believed, on 2 September 1987 (6 people killed). After the Soviet troops were withdrawn, in mid-1989, the government of Najibullah used the An-12s to deliver supplies to troops surrounded in

Jalalabad. The aircraft were also used here as bombers. Flying at altitudes out of reach of the Stingers, they performed carpet bombing missions. After 1992, the fleet of Afghan An-12s was split between the political forces that came to power. An

The An-12 has earned a reputation as a true workhorse both in military and civil aviation.

aircraft owned by one such force on 10 February 1993 landed, due to adverse weather conditions, at Termez, Uzbekistan. The aircraft crashed on landing, yet none of its eight crew members or 111 armed passengers suffered any serious injury.

The An-12s took part in the civil war in Yugoslavia, having played an important role in the evacuation of the federal army from Bosnia, Slovenia and Croatia. The Russian contingent of the UN forces in the region also used the An-12.

Air Forces of almost all countries that emerged from the territory of the former USSR had An-12s. In particular, it is known that these aircraft were used during the conflict between Georgia and Abkhazia. In October 1993, two Ukrainian An-12s delivered humanitarian aid to Georgian refugees and evacuated many of them from the combat zone (while being repeatedly fired at). Most widely, the An-12s were used when Russian troops entered Chechnya in December 1994.

Emergency landing in December 1990 in the environs of Kyiv. All 17 of the aircraft occupants survived.

About 9% of all flights of Antonov Airlines are performed by the An-12.

Peaceful professions

It should be noted that the An-12's career in civil aviation started hurriedly – from flights to the Arctic and the Antarctic that were much-talked-of at the time. On 5 April 1960, regular flights of the An-12s to the North Pole started with the delivery of cargoes to the NP-8 station. On 15 December 1961, an Il-18 and an An-12 departed for the Antarctic. The 26,423-km-long route crossed four continents and two oceans. The An-12 covered the distance in 48 hr 7 min. Along the way to Mirny station, the aircraft refuelled at Tashkent, Delhi (India), Rangoon (Burma), Jakarta (Indonesia), Darwin and Sydney (Australia), Christchurch (New Zealand) and the US McMurdo Antarctic station. The aircraft was flown by experienced polar pilots: B. Osipov (captain), P. Rogov (co-pilot), V. Steshkin (navigator), I. Naikin and V. Sergeyev (flight engineers) and N. Starkov (radio operator). At Mirny, the An-12's wheels were replaced with skis that had been brought along. Then the aircraft, with scientists aboard, made a series of flights over unexplored areas of the Antarctic, landing on strips selected during flight. The aircraft returned to Moscow on 2 February 1962.

As and when the Air Force demand was satisfied, the An-12s were delivered to Aeroflot, where they received a high rating. Fourteen civil aviation administrations of the USSR were successfully using the aircraft for transportation of various cargoes: construction equipment, cattle, food supplies, valuables, and humanitarian aid. Container traffic also started in the country with the An-12 (in October 1977). The traffic handling cost was a record-breaking low – 10 kopecks per tonne/km. In June 1965, the An-12 along with the An-22 was demonstrated at the XXVI International Air Show at Le Bourget, France. On 3 February 1966, the An-12s opened Aeroflot's first international freight route, Moscow–Riga–Paris and covered the route in 5 hr 30 min flight time. In July 1969, the second route, Vladivostok–Amsterdam was opened.

The An-12s played an important role in the economic development of the northern regions of the USSR during the 1960s and 1970s. Truly boundless spaces reachable only by aircraft, due to the absence of railways and roads, were celebrated in a popular song, but this was a rough fact of life rather than a poetic metaphor. The problem was becoming especially acute when you not only had to reach some point on the map, but also had to deliver a heavy oversize cargo, such as, for instance, for the petroleum industry or power equipment. In such cases, the An-12 and the Antaeus came to the rescue.

Thus, it was the An-12 that delivered huge numbers of large-diameter pipes for oil and gas pipelines. As a rule, the aircraft unloaded the pipes at the nearest landing strip, whereupon they had to be brought to their destination by rivers and impassable roads. It was then that the idea cropped up to deliver the pipes directly to the designated pipeline location by either paradropping, or a free-fall drop from low, grass-cutting, altitudes. Experimental drops of pipes measuring 1.44 m in diameter and 12 m in length and weighing between 3.5 and 4.3 tonnes were performed at the new Antonov flight test base at Gostomel in the environs of Kyiv during March–April 1966. The low-altitude drops were performed from 5 to 10 m height using one 4.5 sq.m extractor parachute. The drops from the altitude of 300 m were performed using two parachutes, each with an area of 550 m2. In spite of all these efforts, none of the tested methods was adopted by oil industry. This was due to the fact that the pipes, however dropped, slightly deformed when they struck the ground, and the deformation created difficulties for subsequent pipeline welding.

As well as the Soviet Ministry of Defence and Ministry of Civil Aviation, the An-12 was also operated by companies of the USSR aircraft industry, including Antonov StC. And it was one of the company's aircraft that suffered probably the best-known flight accident of the An-12s, which was later called 'the tangerine flight'. In December 1990, the aircraft carried 12 tonnes of tangerines from Batumi to Kyiv. During descent, the aircraft entered clouds and the co-pilot, instead of turning on the anti-icing system, shut off all fuel cut-out switches. The engines shut down. The aircraft hit the ground and 'broke up' completely. The tangerines scattered over the area. It was only through the captain's (A. Slobodianiuk) skills, the An-12's ruggedness and sheer good luck that all 17 aircraft occupants survived and came out unhurt.

The An-12 became known abroad not only for to its feats of arms. When in early 1980s a severe drought hit Ethiopia, a group of 12 aircraft owned by Aeroflot was delivering food supplies to the affected regions and transporting government troops, starting from 1984. Some of the An-12s of this group later remained in Africa after the disintegration of the USSR. In Angola, for instance, they were flying under Russian colours. The flights were made under the UN aegis. Despite the agreement reached with Unita about termination of hostilities, the aircraft often came under fire from the militants. Thus, on 26 April 1993, one of the An-12s was shot down, with one crewmember killed and six wounded. The aircraft made an emergency landing and was never restored thereafter. Another An-12 was fired at when flying in Angola on 19 July 1994; the flight engineer was slightly wounded.

Life goes on

Today, at the end of the second decade of the 21st century, veteran An-12s still remain in service and continue flying worldwide. Even though their fleet has dwindled considerably during the recent decade, they are still playing an important part both in military aviation (basically in Russia, where about 80 are operated) and in commercial cargo transportation. It is primarily this kind of traffic that is served by the An-12 today.

After disintegration of the USSR, many An-12s showed up in the air forces of almost all countries that emerged in its territory. A considerable number of these aircraft, still with a significant part of their assigned service life unexpired, were withdrawn from military service in the 1990s and were handed over to new large and small airlines. The latter, owing to the low purchase price of the aircraft, made a good profit operating them. However, because of the limited air transportation

market in the CIS countries, owners of the An-12s were looking and still continue to look for revenue in the countries of Africa, Asia, and in problem regions of the world, including those with armed conflicts – in Angola, Congo, Sri Lanka. Almost all transportations in such places are unscheduled and characterised by insufficient managerial oversight, aircraft overload, unsatisfactory meteorological support, incomplete scope of maintenance checks, sometimes insufficient skill of the flying crews, bad condition of landing strips, etc. Yet, even in such conditions, the An-12 demonstrates its best qualities – high reliability, the ability to use unimproved airfields, and low-cost transportation.

The Antonov StC, for its part, was never indifferent to the situation. The company capitalized on every chance it had to influence the course of An-12 operations by sending its specialists to airlines and aviation administrations of numerous countries, appealing to ICAO and other agencies intended to supervise safety of air transportation. It was a difficult job, since at the turn of the new century the An-12s were operated in Angola, Armenia, Afghanistan, Belarus, Bulgaria, Georgia, Guinea, Egypt, Zimbabwe, India, Iran, Yemen, Kazakhstan, Kirgizstan, China, Congo, Moldova, UAE, Russia, Sudan, Uzbekistan, Ukraine, Ethiopia and Equatorial Guinea. Moreover, the An-12s made one-time flights to about twice as many more countries. Figuratively speaking, the An-12s started migrating around the world, changing

About 200 An-12s are still flying worldwide at the turn of the second decade of the 21st century.

hands now and again. In the majority of cases, the owner, operator and aircraft registration holder were different persons, and this made it difficult to supervise their continued airworthiness. However, *Antonov* was doing its best to maintain the required An-12 maintenance and overhaul standards.

The latter is in every way a key issue for a veteran aircraft. For its successful operation, Antonov, with the participation of leading research institutions of the USSR military and civil aviation, developed a system of aircraft overhauls. The first An-12 overhaul in the air force system was started in 1963 by the 123rd Aircraft Repair Facility in Staraya Russa, Novgorod region. In 1968, the An-12 major overhaul procedure was assimilated by the 325th Aircraft Repair Facility in Taganrog, Rostov region, where the An-12s undergo overhauls to this day. In the civil sector, the An-12 overhauls were initiated in 1964 by Civil Aviation Facility No. 412 in Rostov-on-Don. Major overhaul and service life extension work is also done in India – in Chandigarh , Punjab state. Resident Antonov StC representatives worked at all the overhaul facilities. During the 1990s, the network of overhaul agencies was supplemented by several periodic maintenance bases, in particular ones located in Sharjah, UAE and Bulawayo, Zimbabwe.

Nowadays, such bases, established with some of the major An-12 operators, serve to maintain airworthiness of the majority of these aircraft. The required modifications of aircraft structure prescribed by service bulletins or ICAO requirements are also done here. For example, the aircraft are re-equipped with a new type of flight data recorder, oxygen equipment and crew seat harnesses, and other items of items are replaced. The aircraft are also equipped with new navigation aids, radio communication facilities, collision avoidance systems, etc. Demand for such services remains, as the number of

commercial An-12 operators is still rather large. Among such major operators of the aircraft are the Ukrainian airlines Ukraine-Aeroalliance and CaVok Air (operating seven aircraft each), AeroWiz of Ukraine and RubyStar and Grodno of Belarus (each having five aircraft).

It is evident today that in terms of consumer requirements the An-12 can be expected to meet the demands of numerous air carriers for years to come. As of the end of 2017, an imposing fleet of An-12s still remains in service and comprises about 200 aircraft both in military and commercial service. Consequently, service life extension is one of today's most pressing problems for this aircraft. To identify the feasibility and the conditions of the aircraft's service life extension, Antonov has for years been carrying out investigations of the aircraft's structural condition in the course of endurance tests that were only completed in 2011. After the tests, the residual strength of structural zones with fatigue cracks was determined, load-carrying structural members were fully inspected, the operational condition of long-life aircraft was investigated, and the aircraft fleet service experience analysed.

The results of these investigations were used to elaborate measures to be implemented for service life extension. The aircraft on which these measures have been implemented, as of late 2017, have a service life of 55,000 hours, 18,000 flights and 55 years of operation. This, however, is not the limit. Investigations demonstrate that the An-12's operating time can well be extended to 60 years. It means that several dozens of aircraft may well continue flying until the 2030s, and some probably longer. This allows one to believe that the An-12 may remain a means of transport as much in demand in the 21st century as it was in the past.

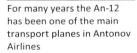
For many years the An-12 has been one of the main transport planes in Antonov Airlines

Paraphrasing the well-known maxim of military pilots, we can say that in order to succeed in the air one should be well trained on the ground. No matter how far the Antonov Airlines aircraft fly, regardless of which continents they may visit to do their heavy work, they finally come home, returning to Kyiv-Antonov airport, their main base, an important subdivision of Antonov StC.

ANTONOV AIRLINES BASE AIRPORT

Antonov Airlines

The aerodrome and the nearby military station were built before the World War II in the suburb of Gostomel settlement, 25 km north-west from Kyiv. It is known that during the War, the aerodrome was used as a base for German bombers, and, after the liberation of Kyiv, for the Soviet Il-2 assault aircraft. In the mid-fifties, the regiment was re-equipped with the MiG-15 aircraft; however its further existence was not too long and lasted until 1957. The Khrushchev Soviet Army Reform led to the liquidation of the regiment, and the aerodrome became empty, the military station accommodating an independent signal battalion. Many of the demobilised personnel of the aircraft regiment remained in the settlement or in the adjacent town. In 1959 they were recruited as the workers of OKB-473 (experimental design bureau), as they called Antonov StC in those days.

In 1956, the An-8 aircraft was constructed by the bureau, and in 1957 the An-10 aircraft. The Sviatoshyn airfield located in Kyiv close to Antonov StC was utilized then mainly by the Kyiv aircraft factory which manufactured the An-2 aircraft, and sometimes by Aeroflot crews. This airfield was not just congested, but too restricted for the new and rather large aircraft. In addition, in the spring and in the autumn the short soil runway of Sviatoshyn aerodrome became soft and unsuitable for flights. During these seasons, the new Antonov aircraft had to be either relocated to Kyiv Zhulyany airport equipped with a concrete runway but having insufficient number of parking places, or kept immobile waiting for good weather. Such a situation was unacceptable for Antonov as the serial An-12 aircraft from Irkutsk, and the An-10 from Voronezh were expected to arrive for testing. At the same time, the newest An-24 passenger aircraft was already under construction in the Antonov shops.

In 1958 O. K. Antonov addressed the Kyiv military district headquarters with a request to allow the Company to operate one of the empty military aerodromes near Kyiv. After a year of negotiations, in a directive of the Ministry of Defence of the USSR the Gostomel aerodrome was transferred for

Base Airport

the Company to use as a flight-test base. The first landing on the unpaved runway of this aerodrome was made by the An-8 prototype aircraft in the beginning of March 1959 and by the beginning of May the personnel occupied with testing of aircraft, moved to Gostomel. Several small wooden houses, similar to wagons with iron ovens inside, were constructed for the staff. A brick one-storey building inherited from the military detachment was dedicated for storage of parachutes. An unpaved 2,000 m-long runway had two stopways of 200 metres each paved with metal plates.

Step-by-step, the building of vital structures was started. Initially single-storey, and then two-storey, wooden panel board houses were erected. It should be noted, at that time no hard roads connected the settlement of Gostomel with the aerodrome, a paved road stopped suddenly at a half-kilometre distance from the aerodrome checkpoint. Both in the autumn and in the spring the trucks which carried employees from Kyiv failed to cover this half-kilometre distance, so the personnel had to

walk to the checkpoint knee deep in mud. Urgent communication with the main Antonov site in Kyiv was made by means of the An-2 aircraft.

In July 1959 the aerodrome was honoured with the visit of the First Secretary of the Central Committee of the CPSU Nikita Khrushchev. The aircraft already operating then, An-8, An-10, An-12 and An-14, were demonstrated, with flight commentary by O. K. Antonov. This visit served as a powerful impetus to further development of Gostomel flight test base.

In August 1958 the Hero of Soviet Union, test pilot Aleksei N. Gratsianskii from the Aviation Industry Ministry's Flight Service Administration, was employed by Antonov. He was appointed Deputy Chief Designer for Flight Tests and became the initiator and the organiser of the subdivision for conducting flight testing. The Desagn Bureau-473 order issued 11 November 1960 amalgamated numerous isolated teams into a unified structural division named the Flight Test and Development Base (FT&DB, in Russian abbreviated as LIiDB).

Deputy Chief designer
A. N. Gratsianskii is a founder of the Flight Test & Development Base.

Flight Test & Development Base panorama, 1968.

Personnel of the Flight Test Station. In the middle of the photo: FTS Chief A. A. Kruts; on the left: A. I. Samartsev; on the right: S. A. Gorbik, L. V. Zhebrovskii, V. I. Veresoka; sitting third to the right: V. N. Shatalov. Gostomel, 1970.

It was headed by engineer R. S. Korol assigned in 1961 as Deputy Chief Designer for Flight Tests following A. N. Gratsianskii's transfer to another position. In the years that followed, FT&DB was sequentially headed by: V. N. Shatalov from 1968, A. G. Bulanenko from 1981, N. I. Onopchenko from 2007, V. D. Inkov from 2008, A. N.Gritsenko from 2010 and Y. V. Pakhomov from 2015.

In the beginning, FT&DB consisted of three departments and several auxiliary units. Its structure included:

- Department 700, A department of flight tests which employed a number of test engineers specially trained for implementation of flight tests.
- Department 710. A department dedicated to the preparation of aircraft for flight experiments. It included several laboratories for inspection of onboard instruments, test and recording equipment, and a production bay for aircraft modification.

- Department 750 or FTS (Flight Test Station, in Russian abbreviated as LIS). This department included the flight service, and other services: aeronautical engineering service, airfield, medical, parachute, rescue, radio, and air traffic control.

In addition, the following was available: a garage with special-purpose vehicles, a warehouse for fuel and lubricants and a fire brigade. In 1960, a weather station was organised in Gostomel which was administratively subordinated to the Kyiv hydro-meteorological centre. For the 60 years period that has passed since then, almost each of these services grew into a large subdivision equipped with all necessary infrastructure to cope with their tasks at an advanced level. Some new subdivisions emerged

Soft-surface runway in Gostomel. 1960.

During the An-124 tests. Left to right: L. V.Zhebrovskii, V. M. Tkachuk and M. A. Kozlov.

due to the continuous sophistication of aircraft equipment, and of corresponding test methods.

The most extensive changes to the FT&DB structure and production capacities occurred during construction of the An-124 and An-225 aircraft, and in connection with the beginning of Antonov Airlines operation. Timely and improved maintenance of the above-mentioned large aircraft required construction of another huge hangar and a shed in order to conduct maintenance at any time and in any weather condition. In addition, aircraft parking areas for routine maintenance, the ramified infrastructure of power supply, facilities for water and compressed air supply were arranged. After 2008, significant repairs to and renovation of both hangars were made: the buildings obtained modern equipment, were winterized to economize energy resources and were given modern energy-saving lighting. So now both the buildings and working conditions inside completely comply with contemporary requirements. A new up-to-date fire brigade located in immediate proximity to the runway has recently been put in operation.

It should also be noted that in this 60-year period of FT&DB's history, this development of infrastructure (essential for effective maintenance and servicing of aircraft) has also resulted in the substantial growth of the number and qualification of the experts occupied with these important activities. During the initial era of the flight-test subdivision, competent assembly workers that gained experience in prototype construction usually became aircraft mechanics.

Later on, when the aircraft manufactured by serial factories started to arrive for testing, the aeronautical engineering service employed demobilised army

aircraft mechanics, civil aviation engineers and technicians, and graduates of aeronautical higher education institutes. Its administration played an important role in staffing the division and educating its skilled personnel, including A. A. Kruts, Y. M.

Near the An-14. Left: O. M. Papchenko; next to him: test pilot V. A. Kalinin.

Skoroded, A. I. Samartsev, L. V. Zhebrovskii, V. M. Tkachuk, V. A. Borisenko, V. I. Veresoka, A. D. Donets, A. A. Bogatov, L. P. Pustovoy, A. P. Petrichenko and many others.

Today the aeronautical engineering service employs over 450 persons, with more than half of the engineers and technicians directly involved in aircraft maintenance. The rest of the personnel deal with modifications and repairs, keeping documents, the inspection of various activities on the aircraft and maintaining the fleet in operating condition. Since the moment when the airlines started their business activities, the maintenance personnel are periodically, several months per year, occupied with corresponding procedures away from their aerodrome base, correcting discovered defects, replacing airborne equipment and repairing structural components. Each aircraft crew always comprises a technical team headed by one of the most qualified engineers. And each aircraft always has a reserve of the most important items without which, in case of failure, continuation of a flight would be impossible.

At the same time, the most labour-consuming categories of maintenance under service bulletins, modifications and upgrades of any type of Antonov aircraft are performed at the airlines home aerodrome in Gostomel.

The aerodrome itself, which in 1959 was just a field covered with waist-high grass, has now changed beyond all recognition. Half a century ago, its barbed-wire fencing was dilapidated and a wide pathway ran across the airfield. Dwellers in neighbouring villages used the pathway to pay visits to each other,

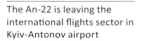

The An-22 is leaving the international flights sector in Kyiv-Antonov airport

and after flights the airfield served as a cow pasture. The local tradition of crossing the airfield and using it for cattle was only overcome in mid-1970s, when a concrete fence was built around the perimeter and the construction of a concrete runway began. Today, a video surveillance network covers the entire airfield territory. Tremendous work by the personnel of all the aerodrome services has transformed the neglected field into a modern aerodrome.

During the first years of operations, flights were only performed in the daytime, as the existing radar equipment did not allow flying in the dark. The flight operations manager was stationed in a military-style mobile control centre with just a single radio station available. The meteorological station equipment made it possible to determine only the immediate weather conditions.

Practical aerodrome modernisation began only when the Antonov Design Bureau started earning additional money by cargo transportation operations, which are described in the first chapter of this book. Before that time, the USSR Ministry of Aviation Industry had been allocating meagre funds for this purpose. The earnings were used to gradually purchase radio/radar equipment for the aerodrome and erect a five-storey building with a hangar and a flight control tower. In 1980s, when aviation fuel supply became a problem and the need for fuel grew because the An-124 testing was under way, a railway branch line to the aerodrome was built. Credit for this should be given to I. I. Yakubovich, the then Chief Engineer of the Flight Test and Development Base. Over the years, other Chief engineers and their Deputies, including G.

F. Dziuba, G. A. Cherniak, O. M. Papchenko, A. N. Borovkov, A. D. Donets, A. F. Lastovetskii, A. S. Makiyan and A. P. Tovstonogov, put in tremendous work, as well as their heart and soul, into the FT&DB development. Their contribution to the creation of a powerful multifunction aircraft base at Gostomel cannot be overestimated.

It is interesting to note that even after active operations of the Antonov Airlines began, the Gostomel aerodrome in the legal sense remained nothing more than a base for aeronautical equipment testing. It was impossible to depart on an international flight from Gostomel – in order to cross the USSR border you needed to make an intermediate flight stop at Kyiv Boryspil airport or at any of the Moscow airports having an international status and the appropriate airport services. This was a major inconvenience, since it necessitated the need to pay for airport takeoff and landing charges as well for other services, and additional landings also resulted in the accelerated expiry of the precious service life of the aircraft. After several years of inconvenience, the practice was adopted of inviting passport and customs control teams from Boryspil airport to Gostomel before each international flight or the return of an aircraft to base. But this was not an acceptable solution either, since it reduced the efficiency of short-cycle order operations. In short, the lack of passport and customs control stations at Gostomel was a major hindrance to the management of commercial flights.

A logical way out of the situation was to transform the flight test base into an international airport. O. M. Papchenko, FT&DB Chief Engineer,

and his deputy for aerodrome support Y. V. Baitsur were at the head of the team working on a solution to this major issue. The work was authorized by the decree of the Cabinet of Ministers of Ukraine dated 15 October 1992. A considerable number of problems were outlined and solved in the course of the work –an especially difficult one was to integrate the traffic of the new international airport terminal into the air space of the Kyiv air traffic hub. Another was the length of the concrete runway, which was 2,700 metres. In response to critical remarks by the Flight Safety Inspectorate, the runway was extended in 1997. At the same time, a separate sector for international flights was equipped with a system of warehousing facilities for handling and storage of cargoes, customs and biological inspections.

As a result of these strenuous efforts, on 16 September 1998 the airport was finally certified and officially opened for international air service. In September 2000, Antonov StC's administration addressed a request to the State Department for Air Transport of Ukraine to memorialize Oleg Antonov by renaming the Gostomel airport 'Kyiv-Antonov' airport. The appropriate registration certificate No. AP 09-07 was received on 16 October 2000. Today, it is a class 'B' international airport, included in the Jeppesen worldwide aeronautical information publication.

Nowadays, the airport has a 3,500 m-long and 56 m-wide runway and is capable of serving all existing aircraft – from ultralight craft to the gigantic An-225. Its radio/radar equipment and lights, air traffic control and meteorological support allow around-the-clock operation of the airport and

Yu.V. Pakhomov, Head of Flight Test & Development Base since 2015

It is not often that so many aircraft of Antonov Airlines can be seen together. Gostomel, October 2007.

A new FT&DB hangar allows concurrent maintenance of several aircraft.

All complex work on airplanes, including control surface rigging, is performed indoors.

serve international flights. The airport's instrument landing systems for adverse weather conditions are certified to ICAO category 2 for 149° heading and ICAO category 1 for 329° heading.

The structure of all the airport services ensures it functions to the standards of the world's freight airports. A dedicated Aerodrome Operation Department supports the functioning of all radio/radar facilities, lights and surfacing. There is also a Cargo Handling Department – a division essential for the support of the commercial operations of Antonov Airlines and other carriers using the Kyiv-Antonov airport. The weather station equipped with up-to-date measurement tools and facilities makes it possible to receive a weather bulletin for any part of the globe in a matter of minutes. The airport has its own medical service, a power supply department, fuel and lubricants provisioning service and a search and rescue service. Because of the wide range of its missions, a multifunction shipping department was organised at the airport. It is equipped with special-purpose aerodrome vehicles and other transportation, two railway locomotives and civil engineering equipment. In recent years, the shipping department has been additionally equipped with new vehicles including aerodrome towing tractors, air starter units and buses. All these divisions ensure the efficient and coordinated operation of the complex Kyiv-Antonov airport facility.

The flight operations service has also undergone considerable change compared to the time when Antonov Airlines was entering the market. Previously, commercial

Flights were performed by crews that were qualified as test pilots. No doubt they also held licences of civil pilots, navigators, flight engineers and radio operators, but still the principal jobs of the flying crews were connected with aeronautical equipment testing. As the aircraft fleet and the number of commercial flights grew, the flight

operations service began employing new specialists from military and civil aviation who were retrained for the Antonov aircraft. The veterans were replaced by young test pilots joining the ranks of commercial pilots. Today, flying crews of Antonov StC mainly consist of commercial pilots and flight engineers. The company's flying personnel, managed by pilot first class D. V. Antonov, is about 160-people strong. Of course, there still are the so-called 'pure' test pilots – a group of about 10 with Hero of Ukraine S. M. Troshin, Honoured Test Pilot, at the head.

The shed built in 2001 makes work on the aircraft comfortable both in the summer heat and in the rain.

If necessary, work in the shed never stops, even at night.

Yu. M. Zinchenko and A. G. Chernyshov keeping watch at the traffic control tower.

Pilots and other flying specialists have always been the pride of Antonov. They were not only doing their test pilots' or commercial pilots' jobs with honour, but also did it in such a way that managed to create their own original Ukrainian school of flight testing of all types of transport category aircraft. Beside the people mentioned above, the company division was managed by such outstanding personalities as Hero of the Soviet Union V. V. Migunov, A. F. Mitronin, A. A. Kruts, V.

N Shatalov, V. E. Chebotariov, I. D. Babenko, N. S. Vasiliev, and M. G. Kharchenko.

It can be said that today the Antonov Airlines' base aerodrome is a freight aviation facility capable of serving aircraft of all types and of handling all types of freight, as well as freight storage, customs and passport control services, and loading cargoes on motor vehicle and railway transport. More than twenty air carriers, both Ukrainian and foreign, have contracts with Kyiv-Antonov airport

Specialists of the maintenance department keep the Antonov Airlines aircraft in the highest working condition.

Kyiv-Antonov airport is equipped with up-to-date radio and lighting facilities.

for landing and servicing of aircraft. Before 2013, Gostomel periodically hosted the Aviasvit-XXI International Air Show that used to attract a large number of participants and visitors. Each such air show was a festive aviation event where the achievements of Ukrainian and foreign companies were demonstrated, scientific conferences were held, and top class flying and skydiver teams demonstrated their skills. However, all that has been said above does not mean that the Antonov Airlines' base aerodrome has attained perfect condition and cannot be developed further. On the contrary, the more it becomes involved in the global air transportation business, the more evident it becomes that a lot of problems still remain to be resolved.

The airport structure needs to be upgraded, made less complex and more flexible and efficient, better adapted to commercial missions. No doubt, there exist even more radical plans for

Today, Kyiv-Antonov airport is capable of serving the worlds' largest aircraft.

View of Kyiv-Antonov airport. 2015.

Kyiv-Antonov airport hosted several Aviasvit-XXI International Airshows.

turning the Gostomel facility into a freight air hub of at least a regional, if not a continental, significance. However, their implementation depends on a number of factors, which are beyond the control of the airport management or even the management of Antonov StC. The air cargo transportation business, as has been repeatedly emphasised in this book, is strongly dependent on the current condition of the world economy, and the successful functioning of a freight hub in Ukraine is also conditioned by the situation in the country. Nevertheless, we at Antonov remain optimistic. And we have firm belief in the bright future of Ukraine, making our best efforts to realise it.

Index
Names

Companies

Places